The Best from
Libby Hillman's Kitchen

Treasured Recipes from
50 Years of Cooking and Teaching

✴

Forword by Janet Greene

The Countryman Press
Woodstock, Vermont

Ma Chère Malinda,
Merci beaucoup
pour ton amité ...
tu es un rayon
de soleil dans
ma vie —
Bises —
Betty

Library of congress Cataloging-in-Publication Data

Hillman, Libby
    The best from Libby Hillman's kitchen: 50 years of cooking and teaching/ forword by Janet Greene.
       p. cm.
    Includes indexes.
    ISBN 0-88150-279-0
    1. Cookery. — I. Title
TX714.H554   1993   93-30026
641.5 — dc20   CIP

Cover and text design by Elizabeth Lewis
Cover photograph by Greg Bolosky / Perspectives Photography
Interior illustrations by Elizabeth Lewis © 1993 by The Countryman Press, Inc.
Typesetting by Leslie Carlson
Printed in the United States of America

Published by The Countryman Press, Inc.
P.O. Box 175
Woodstock, Vermont 05091

Contents

Foreword

"LIBBY'S THE ONE WHO STARTED IT ALL!" This banner headline ran across a page of the *Great Neck Record* (Long Island, New York) in 1976.

You will soon meet Libby Hillman as she discusses the way she cooks. And, being Libby, she is likely to forgo mentioning the achievements that have gone into her sparkling credentials for teaching people how to cook; she is also likely to neglect mentioning her four highly praised cookbooks. So I, being a perennial student of hers and a solid friend of some years' standing, offer a few details and their dates.

Libby Gerber was born in New York City in 1919, and by 1927 she had begun to study the piano. Two things became compelling forces in her life: her love of music and her desire to be a teacher. After high school Libby was steered to the Juilliard School of Music, from which she graduated in 1939 with a Bachelor of Science degree in Music Education. Even before she received her degree, Libby was teaching piano privately, and from 1936 to 1940 she worked as a music counselor at summer camps. At one such camp Libby met a young industrial chemist named Herbert Hillman. They were married in 1940, and Libby continued to teach music until the babies came—David in 1943, Donald in 1945, and Betty in 1949.

Reporters often ask Libby when she started to cook in earnest, perhaps expecting to hear of childhood triumphs in the kitchen. Instead, she says she became serious about cooking when she was 21 years old and making meals for Herb. Libby drew on her inherited sense of good food.

Not until 1947 did Libby get the urge to teach again; but this time it would be cooking, not music. Her inspiration was the CBS television series featuring Dione Lucas, a noted chef and author who had started her own cooking school in Manhattan. Always the teacher, Libby was especially drawn to the demonstration techniques Dione used in her lessons on the art of cuisine. That year Libby gave her own first lesson to help raise money for her sons' nursery school.

The cook at the school was a gifted pastry maker, but she shied away from demonstrating her specialty to an audience. She suggested that Libby might be willing to use the cook's recipes and do the program herself. Indeed she was. Danish and puff-pastry became Libby's mainstay program after the Hillmans moved from

New York City to New Hyde Park, Long Island, where she expanded her benefits for good causes.

Libby and her family lived in the Great Neck School District, which urged her to turn professional. She agreed to give ten lessons in a series called "Adventures in Cookery." The series was an immediate hit and grew year by year as Libby developed a complete program of cookery. Noted authors, teachers, and journalists—among them James Beard, Craig Claiborne, Pierre Franey, Florence Lin, Madeleine Kamman, and Grace Chu—accepted her invitations to participate in her guest series.

By 1969 the time had come for a change. At the urging of the director of the Great Neck Public School Adult Program, Libby became coordinator of the Great Neck Adult Cooking Program. Before long she was engaging other teachers and training talented students to step into her place, and she initiated a program to train future teachers to give cooking lessons. Libby began to devote more time to the cooking school she had begun at home, and she initiated her summer seminars in Vermont.

The Hillmans first came to Vermont in 1963 for the celebrated Marlboro Music Festival. They rented property in Dover, and by 1970 Libby's plans for a summertime live-in cooking school at nearby Mount Snow fell into place. For eleven years students flocked to the week-long seminars for demonstrations by Libby and her staff. For three years Georges Pouvel, a noted teacher of cuisine, traveled from France to join Libby at her Vermont school. Each day, Sunday night through Friday, the class developed individual projects for hands-on experience. Each student chose a recipe in advance to work on alone or in a group supervised by Libby. And always there was the music—the Marlboro Music Festival was close by.

Around the edges of her special projects and her increasingly popular series for Great Neck adult education, Libby somehow made time to write three successful cookbooks between 1963 and 1971: *Lessons in Gourmet Cooking, The Menu Cookbook for Entertaining,* and *New Lessons in Gourmet Cooking.* Her fourth book, *Fresh Garden Vegetables,* was written in 1981 for the Great American Cooking School series.

Meanwhile, Betty Hillman finished her studies at the French government's Lycée Technique Hotelier in Paris, and with her parents' blessing, opened her own restaurant in West Dover, Vermont, in 1975. Le Petit Chef did so well that Betty bought a larger location on Route 100 between Wilmington and West Dover.

After Herb's retirement in 1982, the Hillmans bought a mid-nineteenth-century farmhouse in Whitingham, Vermont. When they left Long Island for good, the New York State Assembly passed a resolution honoring Libby as "an extraordinary educator in the field of cooking" and praised her contribution to education in the State of New York.

Libby now prepares storybook meals in her marvelous kitchen with its hilltop view of Lake Sadawga and the mountains beyond it. Men and women call to reserve time for lessons; and Libby continues to do her favorite thing—teaching.

Janet Greene
Putting Food By

The Way I Cook

I grew up in a home where the kitchen was our social space; sights and smells of food were a large part of our lives. I observed my mother's swift hands kneading dough, stirring soups, or sautéing onions. And there was never a cookbook in sight.

Since my marriage in 1940, I have cooked with pleasure. I changed from a career in music education to a lifetime pursuit of cooking professionalism in 1953. I cooked first and gained practical experience; then bit by bit, like a gigantic jigsaw puzzle, I began to fashion a career and a lifestyle out of my growing knowledge of culinary techniques.

In the early years of my marriage, our small kitchen was equipped with wedding gifts—Wear-Ever aluminum, some cooking tools, and a few trays. Occasional visits to Macy's department store inspired new ideas. My purchases of new utensils and equipment reflected the recipes I was trying as I broadened my scope. My kitchen slowly grew.

My pantry was stocked with the usual cans of soup and tuna. Beans, grains, rice, and pasta were always a part of our diet, but my interest in cooking soon added many more items to those simple stocks. My selection of baking ingredients grew by leaps and bounds, and my shelves began to bulge with all kinds of supplies for American, French, Italian, Mexican, Greek, and Oriental cooking.

In today's world there is a proliferation of cookbooks, not to mention juicers, microwaves, and other fancy machines. The real scent of cooking has been lost in many homes, and yet I am optimistic. My many years of teaching have taught me that there are large numbers of men and women who cook for themselves and for their families.

People have asked me one question over and over: "What is your specialty?" My answer is always the same: My interests run the entire gamut of the meal, from appetizers and breads to main courses and desserts. I love to teach and inspire students, just as I have been inspired.

Of course, my cooking repertoire has grown through the years as a result of study and travel and from my associations with professional chefs, guest teachers, and friends. Many people have been part of my education—all of us share a deep and common interest in cuisine.

My office contains a good library of cookbooks, and I refer to them often to add to my cooking knowledge for both professional and daily activities. I also find improvisation a lot of fun. I keep my leftovers, favorite supplies, and tricks and treats in my cupboard, refrigerator, or freezer. Even half a cup of carrot purée can be thinned out with broth or water to become a very good soup for two. Very often I am faced with a small leftover chicken that is hardly enough for two but always enough for a Chinese-style stir-fry or Chicken Pot Pie.

Many of my cooking plans come from my tours through the market. If the green beans look very fresh, I buy enough to use hot and then cold in a salad. When I cook a Ratatouille, inevitably there is leftover, and I use it as a base for baked fish; other times I may add it to a fish or chicken stew. These are all spur-of-the-moment ideas. My husband often asks, "Do you think anyone else in the world is eating this same dish tonight?" It would be impossible to properly note the many combinations and mixtures of food that we feast on. Imagination combined with basic cooking knowledge adds much to the enjoyment of cooking and dining.

Everyone has his or her personal preferences. The contents of your cupboard won't exactly resemble mine—or anyone else's. You will learn to pick and choose as I have.

Most fresh vegetables and fruits are absolute essentials in the kitchen, but there are a few special items that every good cook requires. Lemons, limes, and oranges are flavor enhancers and sit on my counter within arm's reach. The tomato is perhaps America's greatest gift to cuisine (never refrigerate them!). Onions, garlic, shallots, and potatoes should be stored in their own bins, whereas salad greens, carrots, and celery must all be refrigerated. With these few staples on hand, you can add any other ingredients you like to your regular shopping list.

Our family of five grew up while I was developing my career and writing my first books. At the table, we talked food, food, and more food. They hardly ever cooked with me, because the kitchen was my domain, but they were my guinea pigs. Now I have the greatest fun kneading bread and making pizzas and cookies with my three grandchildren. The little ones, five and seven years old, can pipe out chocolate decorations on cookies. Katie, now 16, was able to twist Challah dough at the age of seven. She is currently our expert on guacamole. Of course, the best surprise of all is our daughter, Betty, owner of Le Petit Chef. She stepped right into my shoes and now commands an excellent kitchen in her own restaurant.

This book is only a sample of my everyday cooking. Night after night my husband and I sit down to dinner with a sense of anticipation, relaxation, and joy. We wish you the same!

Basic Ingredients

All of us like and dislike certain foods—perhaps in childhood we were forced to eat the foods we now refuse to touch. The first classes I taught professionally were called "Adventures in Cookery," and it truly *was* an adventure to expand my own palate as my students slowly expanded theirs.

There are certain basic ingredients that I use daily, and these are always on my shelves. I continually try (and occasionally add) new basics, and I suggest that you, too, substitute and expand this list as you wish. Use your imagination and cooking style to create your own list of basic ingredients.

Butter
Unsalted butter is best for baking. If you use lightly salted butter, use less salt or no salt at all.

Cheese
Gruyère and Parmigiano-Reggiano are two great cheeses used for cooking (and for eating). A small amount goes a long way for flavor.

Gruyère   *Parmesan*

Eggs
Cookbooks generally specify large eggs (about 2 ounces). I use extra-large brown eggs, and I find very little difference between the two. Brown eggs are no different from white except that the yolk is a deeper color.

Flour
My recipes specify the type of flour. If you prefer to stock one flour, buy unbleached all-purpose flour. When a recipe calls for cake flour, substitute 2 tablespoons cornstarch in each cup of all-purpose flour.

Herbs

Learn about herbs by using and tasting them. Although fresh herbs are preferable, they are not always available. Purchase small amounts of dried herbs in leaf form, and crush them between your fingertips before adding to food. Add only small amounts of strong herbs—you can always add more. Fresh dill and varieties of parsley are available year-round. Stock them as quick seasonings for both cold and hot dishes. A bouquet garni is frequently called for in recipes—tie together 2 sprigs parsley, 1 sprig thyme, and 1 small bay leaf.

Margarine

I never use margarine. The latest research shows that margarine is not a healthy substitute spread because it is hydrogenated.

Milk and Cream

Use whole milk, 2 percent, 1 percent, or skim milk as you please. Sauces can be made with lower fat milk—experiment! Recipes specify light, half-and-half, whipping, and heavy cream. Use milk as a substitute when necessary.

Oil

I use a simple, pure olive oil almost exclusively in cooking and salad dressings. I like corn oil for baking. Canola, peanut, safflower, and soy oils are all available for your personal choice.

Salt

Recipes generally specify kosher (coarse) salt for cooking and table salt for baking. Sea salt is excellent for cooking, but be sure to adjust the amounts specified to suit your taste. I use salt sparingly, but I place sea salt in a grinder on the table for guests.

Sugar

If you bake, stock confectioners' and brown sugar (light and dark) as well as granulated sugar. Light brown sugar is used more often than dark brown, which burns easily. Sugar amounts are flexible in many of the desserts.

Vegetables

I am never without onions, celery, carrots, and potatoes. With the addition of pasta, rice, or beans, we always have an easily cooked vegetarian meal. Add shallots, garlic, and mushrooms for flavor enhancers. In the summer our vegetable garden is our market, but otherwise we buy vegetables in season as often as possible.

Vinegar

White vinegar is basic—always have a supply. I steep sprigs of tarragon in cider vinegar for my salad dressings. In July I add a handful of raspberries to a good white wine vinegar. Balsamic, red wine, sherry, and champagne vinegar all appear at specialty stores.

Wines

Sherry, Madeira, and port are fortified wines (17 percent or more alcohol) and are staples in my kitchen. Even 1 tablespoon at the end of cooking adds a zip. Choose light, inexpensive wines to your taste for actual cooking. Dry vermouth may be substituted for white wine in some dishes. Refrigerate recorked white wines. Red wines can be recorked as well, but taste a drop before using to make sure the wine hasn't turned to vinegar.

Bread

B read is the everlasting treat of all home baking. The realization of that simple fact came to me only after many years of teaching adults. In the early years, I was entirely involved with teaching new techniques, opening minds to creative ideas in cookery. Since local shops provided freshly baked goods daily, bread baking rated low in the priorities of the home cook.

I discovered for myself how satisfying the homemade loaf could be. Imagine, only three magical ingredients—yeast, water, and flour—will bubble in minutes to prove that a loaf can easily be made. How simple and wonderful to plunge your hands into the risen dough and watch it rise again and again. Certainly you will read stories of both amateurs and professionals who use yeast cultures, wood-fired stoves, and special tiles. Remove the mystique of those requirements. Experiment with the recipes in the pages that follow. Discover how a few ingredients can make a superbly baked loaf of bread. The timing for beating, rising, and baking is flexible—it can fit into anybody's daily schedule.

Since I associate breads with yeast-risen doughs, I have omitted the quick breads (which are really borderline cakes). Scores of these recipes are constantly published, and you probably have your favorites. The one exception that I must include is the classic American Biscuit, a basic beauty.

Some Yeast Bread Basics

Equipment

Strong hands and arms can easily mix bread dough, but as a time saver I use an electric mixer on its own stand with work bowl, paddle, and dough hook. I most often use the paddle only. Then I knead by hand because I enjoy it. Use the dough hook, if you wish. It works very well, but two or three minutes of hand kneading will finish forming the dough into a smooth and elastic ball. You will actually feel the change with your hands as the dough goes from being a limp blob to having a firm texture.

I choose black metal pans for browning, although any oiled pans or Teflon-lined ones will do. Aluminum cookie sheets or jelly-roll sheets are suitable for round or free-formed loaves. Cornmeal sprinkled on the sheets helps the breads hold their shapes. Invest in three- or six-form divided pans for baking the characteristic long, skinny baguette shapes. Pans for Brioche or white bread styles are described in the individual recipes.

Flour

Gluten is the proteinlike substance found in flour that develops elasticity and strength, forming the walls that hold the air pockets in the dough. Kneading the dough by hand or with a dough hook in a sturdy mixer develops the gluten. Unless other flours are indicated in the recipes, use wheat flour labeled "unbleached all-purpose enriched flour." High-gluten flour, as indicated in some recipes, is being sold as "bread flour" in supermarkets and is also available in specialty shops. After a little experience you will probably enjoy using whole grain, rye, oat, and corn flour in small substitutions. Experiment with your own combinations for texture and flavor. When baking for someone with a wheat allergy, substitute rice flour.

Yeast

Always use one type of yeast and become familiar with the way it behaves. I use active dry yeast, bought either at the supermarket in 2½ teaspoon dated packets (Fleischmann's or Red Star) or at a specialty food store in bulk. To ensure quality, I keep all yeast refrigerated in an airtight container. My recipes usually call for 1 tablespoon active dry yeast, which is equal to 3 teaspoons, but the ½ teaspoon less in the packet does not make a significant difference. Because 1 tablespoon is a minimum amount compared with other recipes, and because the rising temperature

I recommend is 68° to 70°F rather than a very warm place, strong yeasty odors are rarely a problem.

Sprinkle yeast onto warm water (105° to 115°F), just comfortable to touch, in a work bowl. If the water is too hot, the yeast is killed; too cold and the reaction is slowed. Instructions often suggest the use of a little sugar in the warm water to help activate the yeast, but this is not necessary. Never use salt when dissolving yeast. Since flour feeds the yeast so well, I use a blanket of flour (see page 4 for yeast instructions).

Sourdough Starter
Instructions for making and using a sourdough starter can be found on page 7.

Oil and Butter
For the small amount of fat used to lubricate bowls and pans (and in cases where fat other than butter is called for in a recipe), I have always used corn oil. Olive oil is specified for Italian-style doughs. Where butter is a classic requirement, as in Brioche and some white breads, I do not substitute. If you prefer margarine or another oil, that option is yours. As in all my cooking, whenever butter is taboo in someone's diet, I choose a different bread in which butter is not a requisite.

Glazes and Toppings
There are various glazes for breads. The simplest is to spray water over the breads *in the hot oven* every few minutes during the first half of the baking time. This will not only produce crustiness, it will also add a shine. Some bakers like a dusting of flour over breads before baking for a rough "country" look, making spraying unnecessary. For glazes, referred to as "baker's wash," choose from the following and brush over loaves before baking:

- Lightly beaten whole egg or lightly beaten egg with 2 tablespoons water, milk, or cream for gloss
- Beaten egg yolk with a drop of water for a dark, shiny gloss
- Beaten egg whites for a brown crust but no gloss
- 2 tablespoons cornstarch mixed in 1 cup cold water and cooked until clear. Cool before brushing on loaves. (This glaze is used most often for rye and pumpernickel breads.)

General Procedure

Although individual recipes include special directions, study this sequence, which is used again and again in my yeast-risen bread recipes.

Starting the Yeast

Pour warm water into the work bowl. Sprinkle dry yeast on top and cover with 2 cups flour. DO NOT STIR. Let rest for at least 10 minutes while the yeast is "fed" and begins to "work." You will notice yeast bubbling around the sides of the bowl and through the flour.

Mixing, Beating, and Kneading

After the yeast rests, add the other ingredients (sugar, salt, oil, and so on) and about 1 more cup flour. Beat about 1 minute, and then gradually

Paddle

add flour while beating constantly. The dough will come away from the sides of the bowl. Change from the paddle to the kneading hook and knead for a few minutes. Transfer the dough to a floured surface, and knead by hand to feel the texture of the dough (A) Fold the dough over toward

Kneading hook

you (B), then push it down and away from you with the heel of your hand (or hands) (C). Turn it a quarter turn (D) and repeat (E). You will notice how the dough changes from a limp structure to an upright, firm ball that is smooth and elastic. I enjoy hand kneading the dough entirely rather than using the dough hook, but that takes me a few minutes longer.

A.   *B.*

C.   *D.*   *E.*

The Rise

Use the same work bowl or another large, deep bowl. Pour 1 teaspoon oil into the bowl. Turn the dough around in the oil to coat its surface. Cover the bowl tightly with plastic wrap, and let the dough rise at room temperature for at least 1½ hours (or up to 3 hours to accommodate your schedule). Do not try to rush this first rising; double or more in volume is your goal. Test by poking your finger into the dough. If the dent remains, the dough is ready for the next step. A short second rising develops flavor and an even texture but is not absolutely necessary if time is short.

✹ Suggestions

- The recipes for all basic French and sourdough breads make delicious rolls. Divide the dough into six lengths, then into five or six pieces each. Shape them as you wish (see page 17 for some suggestions), and bake at 400°F for 30 minutes.

- If there are children in the household, involve them in handling the dough. They will love to touch its springiness. They can form their own little breads from smaller pieces of dough. These breads can then be baked with the larger loaves.
- Experiment with substitutions of other flours—whole wheat, rye, oat bran, buckwheat, soy, and so on—but start with small amounts. I do this constantly, with excellent results. Make a friend of your neighborhood baker or bagel shop. They will be happy to supply you with special flours and other ingredients if you cannot find another source.
- I find that room temperature (68° to 70°F) is perfectly fine for rising doughs. After several baking sessions you will find the best place in the kitchen for rising doughs.
- Bread-baking enthusiasts can start breads early in the morning before a workday. Give the dough a quick rise before breakfast. Punch the dough down, cover it with plastic wrap, and refrigerate until evening. Continue the rise again before dinner and finish later in the evening.
- You can refrigerate risen doughs, punched down, in plastic bags for up to three days. Freeze dough the same way in loaf-sized portions for up to a month. Homemade breads keep well. Day-old breads can be freshened with a spray of water and heated in a 400°F oven for 5 minutes. Wrap breads in plastic wrap or aluminum foil for freezing. Breads can be defrosted at 350°F for 30 to 40 minutes in their aluminum-foil wrapping, or they can be unwrapped, sprayed with water, and baked for 15 minutes at 400°F. A great deal depends on the size of the bread; repetition will give you expected results.
- Leftover bread makes excellent melba toast and, of course, bread crumbs. Package other bits and ends for the freezer, to be always on hand for stuffings and puddings.

Recipes

French Bread
Makes 2 or 3 large loaves or 6 baguettes (long, thin loaves).

The basic French Bread can be the key recipe to many yeast-risen doughs. My method for dissolving the yeast in water and covering it with flour will be repeated again and again. It is foolproof. Omit the sugar, usually suggested in recipes, and never use salt at this point. I always ask students to memorize this recipe so they can bake bread even when they are away from home.

    2½ cups warm water (110°F)
    1 tablespoon active dry yeast
    6 to 7 cups unbleached flour (all-purpose or high-gluten)
    1 tablespoon salt
    1 tablespoon sugar
    1 tablespoon oil (for bowl and pans)

Pour warm water into the bowl of an electric mixer. Sprinkle yeast on top and cover with 2 cups flour. Do not mix! Set aside for 10 minutes. A few minutes more or less are not critical.

Add salt, sugar, and 2 additional cups flour. Beat well with the flat paddle of the mixer for 2 to 3 minutes. Gradually add 2 more cups flour, until the dough becomes elastic and starts to pull away from the sides of the bowl. If the machine has a kneading hook, knead for 3 minutes, adding a little more flour so the dough forms a ball around the hook. The absorption of flour varies. Sometimes more or less flour will be needed to form the dough into an elastic ball and pull it away from the sides of the bowl. Always reserve some flour if you are going to knead the dough by hand.

I enjoy kneading by hand, and I use a floured board. Use quick, rhythmic motions to prevent sticking. Kneading by hand takes 5 or 6 minutes.

Pour 1 teaspoon oil into the mixing bowl. Roll the dough in the oil to barely coat it. Cover the bowl with plastic wrap. Allow the dough to rise more than double in volume at room temperature. This first rising should be very slow, a minimum of 1½ hours; if necessary to suit your schedule, it may be extended to 2 or 3 hours.

Punch the dough to release air and flatten it. Roll it into a ball again and place it in the bowl. Cover the bowl with plastic wrap for a second rising. Allow the dough to rise again for 30 to 40 minutes at room temperature. This second rising may be shortened or omitted if time does not permit, but a second rising improves texture and flavor.

Oil two baking sheets or a vented six-form French bread pan. The dough will make two or three large, 14-inch loaves or six long (12- to 14-inch), thin loaves (baguettes).

Transfer the dough to a floured surface. Flatten it into a rectangle, about ¾ inch thick. Cut the dough into two, three, or six lengths for different sizes. Loosely twist each piece into corkscrew shapes, tapered at each end, and place into oiled pans. Allow to rise for 20 minutes.

In the meantime, preheat the oven to 450°F. Place a pan of hot water on the bottom rack of the oven to produce steam. Keep a spray bottle filled with water handy. Bake the breads for 40 minutes, misting them with the water every 5 minutes for the first 20 minutes. If the breads are baking and browning unevenly, reverse the pans in the oven. If they appear to darken too quickly, reduce the heat to 400°F. Always cool breads on racks immediately after removing them from the oven. If more crustiness is desired, place the breads on open racks in a hot oven or heat them before serving.

✳ *Suggestion*

For Italian breads, add ¼ cup olive oil (optional) to the mix. Sprinkle the tops with sesame seeds. In northern Italy, salt is omitted from the dough. Thick slices are served at the table to be dipped in extra-virgin olive oil and then sprinkled with salt.

Rye Sourdough Starter

I started using sourdough when I realized that my taste for rye or pumpernickel bread could only be satisfied with a sourdough starter. The mixture of flour and water plus yeast ferments overnight to a bubbly consistency, producing the winelike flavor characteristic of New York rye and pumpernickel.

1 tablespoon active dry yeast
3 cups warm water
3½ cups medium ground rye flour
1 onion, peeled whole and scored in three places with a sharp knife

Stir yeast and 2 cups water in a 2- or 3-quart glass, ceramic, or plastic container. Add 2 cups rye flour and stir until well mixed. Place the onion in the mixture. Cover loosely with a cloth. Let stand for at least 24 hours.

Remove the onion and discard. Beat in 1½ cups rye flour and 1 cup warm water. Cover with a cloth. Let stand at room temperature for another 24 hours. This period of fermentation will make the mixture smell sour and look tannish. This second step is called "feeding."

As this starter is used, it may always be replenished by feeding it 2 parts flour to 1 part water but always in small amounts. Refrigerate between baking times. Feed with flour and water; set aside at room temperature for at least 12 hours before using again.

✳ *Suggestions*

- I often feed the starter with unbleached all-purpose flour. If I have not used the starter or fed it at least once a week, I test it by feeding it with flour and water. If it bubbles in 20 minutes, it is active.
- Sourdough French Bread may be made by mixing a new starter with unbleached white flour (omit onion) or using the same starter as for rye. Substitute 1 cup water for 1 cup starter in the French Bread recipe. Do not hesitate to experiment.

Sourdough Rye Bread
Makes 2 or 3 large loaves or 6 baguettes.

1¼ cups warm water
1 tablespoon active dry yeast
2 cups unbleached all-purpose flour
2 cups Rye Sourdough Starter (page 7)
1 tablespoon salt
3 tablespoons caraway seeds
1 cup medium rye flour
1 to 2 cups high-gluten or unbleached all-purpose flour
Oil for baking sheets
Cornmeal for baking sheets
1 egg slightly beaten for egg wash

Pour warm water into the bowl of an electric mixer. Sprinkle yeast on top and cover with 2 cups all-purpose flour. Do not mix! Let stand for about 10 minutes.

Add sourdough starter, salt, caraway seeds, and rye flour. Beat for 1 to 2 minutes. Gradually add 1½ cups high-gluten or all-purpose flour. Beat until the mixture comes away from the sides of the bowl. Another small amount of flour may be added so the dough is not sticky. Work the dough with the kneading hook for 3 to 4 minutes, or follow the next direction for kneading by hand.

Use a plastic scraper to clean the dough from the sides of the bowl, and form the dough into the shape of a ball. Transfer to a surface sprinkled with rye flour. Knead the dough by hand for 4 to 5 minutes. Add rye or white flour, sparingly, to keep the dough from sticking. Stop kneading when the dough is well shaped and not limp. It should be smooth and elastic. Place the dough in a floured 5- or 6-quart bowl. Cover the bowl with plastic wrap, and let the dough rise for 1½ hours.

Punch the dough down to release the air. With a plastic scraper, scoop the dough out onto a floured surface. Cut the dough into two or more parts, depending on the size of the breads you are baking. Roll each piece of dough into a ball. Cover with plastic wrap to rest for 20 minutes.

Sprinkle cornmeal on one or two oiled baking sheets. Breads must be well separated to bake well. The French vented baking pans can be used to make long, narrow breads.

Flatten each piece of dough into an oval. Roll up as a jelly roll, pressing each enclosure. The shape should be tapered at the ends and higher in the center for the traditional bread. Sometimes I make a round ball shape or "party ryes"—long and narrow. Place the breads on the baking sheets. Cover with a towel, and let rise until almost doubled in bulk.

Preheat oven to 425°F. Set a pan of very hot water on the lowest shelf of the oven. Keep a water sprayer handy for misting the loaves during baking. Brush the loaves with egg wash, or use the cornstarch glaze (page 3). Slash the surface of the breads, using a razor blade or very sharp knife, making two or three evenly spaced diagonal lines.

Set the breads in the oven. Mist with water every 5 minutes for 20 minutes, opening and closing the oven door quickly. Turn the bread pans around if the breads are browning unevenly. Bake for another 20 minutes. Immediately remove the breads from the pans and cool on a rack.

✳ *Suggestion*

If your breads spread and flatten out during baking, try the following method. Press your dough into an oval. Fold it in half, then in thirds, and repeat until the dough resists the folding. Place it on an oiled baking sheet that has been sprinkled with cornmeal. The cornmeal will keep the dough from spreading out of shape. This method can be applied to other breads as well.

Black Pumpernickel
Makes 2 or 3 loaves or 6 baguettes.

There is no such thing as pumpernickel flour. The flour is rye flour colored with caramelized sugar, which can be made at home. Professionals buy this coloring and do not use cocoa or coffee.

½ cup sugar
¼ cup boiling water
2 cups warm water
2 tablespoons active dry yeast
2 cups unbleached all-purpose flour
2 cups Rye Sourdough Starter (page 7), at room temperature

1 tablespoon plus 2 teaspoons salt
1 cup medium rye flour
1 cup coarsely ground rye flour
Cornmeal for baking pans
1 to 2 cups additional all-purpose flour

Spread sugar on a 10-inch heavy aluminum or stainless steel skillet. Heat over medium-high heat, and stir until the sugar turns a deep brown, almost black. Just as it starts foaming and boiling, carefully add the boiling water, at arm's length because it will steam up. Stir to dissolve the sugar for a minute or two. Pour the liquid into a Pyrex measuring cup. It should measure ½ cup. If it measures more, cook the mixture again to reduce the amount. Cool.

Pour warm water into the bowl of an electric mixer. Sprinkle yeast on top and cover with 2 cups unbleached all-purpose flour. Do not mix! Let stand for about 10 minutes.

Add the ½ cup caramelized sugar, sourdough starter, salt, and medium rye flour. Beat for 2 to 3 minutes. Gradually add coarsely ground rye flour. If the dough is very sticky, add all-purpose flour until the dough comes away from the sides of the bowl. Pumpernickel dough tends to be stickier than regular rye dough, so add more rye and white flour as you knead to make a firm ball of dough. Proceed according to the instructions for Sourdough Rye Bread (page 8). If you prefer a shiny crust on pumpernickel, brush the tops with a cornstarch glaze (page 3).

Dough for Pizza
Makes enough for four 10-inch pizzas.

There is no doubt that the pizza has become an American favorite. It is basically nutritious as well as delicious. The toppings can range from tomato to the fanciest of wild mushrooms, sliced vegetables, seafood, salami, and imported cheeses. In other words, you can combine ingredients to suit your taste and budget. Although you can follow the basic French Bread recipe (page 5), I think the use of some whole wheat flour and oil adds crispy texture and good flavor.

2½ cups warm water
1 tablespoon active dry yeast
5 cups unbleached all-purpose flour
1 cup whole wheat flour
1 tablespoon salt
1 tablespoon sugar
2 tablespoons olive oil

Proceed to make the dough as described in the recipe for French Bread. Add 1 additional cup all-purpose flour, whole wheat flour, salt, sugar, and oil after yeast, water, and flour have rested for 10 minutes. Gradually add 2 more cups flour, until the dough becomes elastic and starts to pull away from the sides of the bowl. Work the dough with a kneading hook for 3 minutes or knead by hand. Form the dough into a ball and cover with plastic wrap. Allow the dough to rise for 1½ hours.

Use a plastic scraper to scoop dough out onto a floured surface. Divide the dough into four equal parts. Form each into a ball and enclose each ball in a floured plastic bag twice its size. The dough will be easier to roll into shape if you refrigerate it at this point for 45 minutes. The dough can be kept in the refrigerator for up to three days and frozen for up to a month.

When ready to make the pizza, preheat oven to 500°F. Oil an 11- or 12-inch pizza pan (preferably black). Flatten a ball of dough on a floured surface with a rolling pin; roll it into a circular shape. Place the dough on your fist and stretch the edges as you turn it. Be careful not to tear it (the very edge will form the rim). Place on the oiled pizza pan. If the dough contracts, let it rest for 10 to 15 minutes. You will then be able to press it out to meet the edges of the pan.

Spread on the sauce and toppings of your choice. Bake on the lowest rack in the oven for 7 to 8 minutes. If it is browning too fast, lower the heat to 400°F. Bake for 3 to 4 minutes more, until bubbly and crisp.

Generally, some form of tomato sauce is spread on the unbaked dough. Use ½ cup Tomato Sauce (page 88) or canned crushed tomatoes, just enough to coat the top. Add any desired garnishes.

Garnishes for Pizza

For cheeses, try Parmesan, mozzarella, Gruyère, fontina, or goat cheese (any one or a combination).

For spices and raw vegetables, try oregano, basil, mushrooms, garlic, olives, red and green bell peppers, or jalapeño peppers.

Also try topping the pizza with sautéed, steamed, or parboiled vegetables (zucchini, eggplant, summer squash) and meat or fish (salami, sausages, anchovies), your choice.

✳ Suggestions

- Bake pizza dough with just a brushing of olive oil for 5 minutes. Place freshly sliced tomatoes on top with cheese. Finish baking.

- Spread ¼ cup sour cream on pizza dough. Sprinkle the top with chopped chives and parsley. Bake for 10 minutes until crisp and brown. Before serving, place strips of smoked salmon (at room temperature) pointing into the center.
- Combine ¼ cup mayonnaise, 2 tablespoons chili sauce, ½ teaspoon Worcestershire sauce, and a few drops Tabasco sauce. Spread mixture on pizza dough. Bake for 5 to 7 minutes until lightly browned. Strew 1 cup leftover cooked fish or seafood on top. Sprinkle with Parmesan cheese. Bake for 3 minutes until hot.
- When making dough for pizza, reserve one piece of dough to make Savory Bread. The dough can be refrigerated for up to three days for this preparation. With a rolling pin, roll dough on a floured surface into an oval shape. Experiment with various fillings (olives, anchovies, herbs, cheese, scallions, ham, and so on), and roll up as you would a jelly roll. Score the top in four or five places. Allow to rest for 20 minutes, and then bake at 400°F for 30 minutes. Use as an appetizer bread or serve with a salad for a light meal.

Sesame Seed Cracker Bread
Makes eight 8-inch-round crackers.

Everyone enjoys breaking and munching these large, crisp crackers. Once you have mastered the pizza dough, you will certainly want to proceed to baking these delicious crackers for family snacking and cocktail parties.

1 recipe Dough for Pizza (page 10)
¾ cup sesame seeds
Flour for the rolling surface

Make the Dough for Pizza. Let it rise as directed. Punch it down and divide it into eight equal pieces. Form each piece into a ball, and place each ball in its own plastic bag. Allow room in the bag for the dough to expand when you seal it. Refrigerate for at least 1 hour or for up to a day.

When ready to bake, work with one piece at a time. Mound 1 tablespoon sesame seeds on a floured surface. Lightly press both sides of the dough on seeds. Repeat with remaining pieces. Cover with a cloth. Preheat oven to 375°F.

You will need several ungreased cookie sheets, depending on how large you make the round crackers. With a rolling pin, roll each ball into a large round, flat shape. (If the dough resists the rolling and pulls back, follow the Dough for Pizza recipe and stretch the dough over your fist.) If you make eight rounds, you will be able to fit two on a sheet. As the dough rests, it stretches more easily. I sometimes make rounds as large as 12 inches by stretching. Then I can fit just one on the average cookie sheet.

Bake the crackers 17 to 18 minutes until lightly browned and crisp. The browning will be uneven, so be careful not to burn them. It is usually wise to bake these while you are involved with other kitchen tasks, because the timing of rolling, resting, and baking may take more than an hour.

St. Joseph Scallion Pie (Barese)
Serves 12 to 18.

You would think that the following recipe is just another bread with a filling of scallions and anchovies, but to watch Marie Agresti demonstrate this so-called "pie" to my Vermont students was a real experience. From beginning to end, it was a labor of love and authenticity. Enjoy this hearty bread with a salad for a light supper. The bread is named for St. Joseph, the patron saint of Barese in Italy.

Dough
1 cup warm water
1 tablespoon active dry yeast
3 to 3½ cups unbleached all-purpose flour
4 tablespoons olive oil
1 teaspoon salt

Filling
8 bunches scallions
Four 2-ounce cans anchovies, washed and diced
½ pound black olives, diced
1¼ cups olive oil
Freshly ground pepper to taste

Pour warm water into the bowl of an electric mixer. Sprinkle yeast on top and cover with 2 cups flour. Do not mix! Set aside for about 10 minutes. Add 3 tablespoons olive oil and the salt. Gradually beat in 1 cup flour to form a soft dough.

Transfer to a floured surface and knead, using the remainder of the flour. Continue kneading for about 5 minutes or until the dough holds its shape. Use more flour, sparingly, if it is necessary. Pour the remaining oil into a large bowl. Roll the dough in the oil to coat it. Cover the bowl with plastic wrap and allow to rise for 1 hour.

Prepare the filling while the dough is rising. Trim the ends of the scallions. Wash and dry well, then cut into thirds. Sauté scallions in ½ cup olive oil until soft and limp. Mix scallions with anchovies and olives. Cool.

Punch the dough down to release the air. Use a plastic scraper to transfer the dough to a floured surface. Divide the dough in half. Cover with plastic wrap or a towel to rest for 10 minutes. Oil a rectangular baking pan (13" x 9" x 2"). With a rolling pin, roll both pieces of dough into rectangles, the approximate size of the pan.

Place one piece of dough parallel to you. Spread half the filling on top. Sprinkle with ¼ cup oil and freshly ground pepper. Cover the filling with the second piece of dough. Spread the remainder of the filling and ¼ cup oil on top (A).

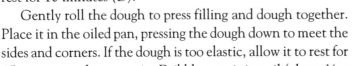

With your hands under the dough at either side, fold the dough toward the center. Do the same with the opposite side (B). Then fold the dough in half (C). The filling will be enclosed. Cover and let rest for 10 minutes (D).

Gently roll the dough to press filling and dough together. Place it in the oiled pan, pressing the dough down to meet the sides and corners. If the dough is too elastic, allow it to rest for 15 minutes and press again. Dribble remaining oil (about ¼ cup) on top and allow to rise for 30 minutes.

Preheat oven to 325°F. Bake for 1 hour. If the bread browns too quickly, cover lightly with aluminum foil after 30 minutes. Serve warm or at room temperature.

✳ *Suggestions*

- The dough can be preprepared and refrigerated for up to three days or frozen for up to a month. The filling can be prepared one or two days in advance.
- The filling is also an excellent topping for pizza.

American White Bread
Makes 2 loaves.

Although the American-style white bread has oftentimes come under comical criticism by purists, white bread is traditionally the favorite for morning toast and luncheon sandwiches. In small towns where bakeshops are few, country cooks have always relied on their own home ovens to produce some excellent white breads, quite different from the prepackaged types. How many of us know that the French bake a white bread as well and call it their sandwich bread?

1 cup warm water
1 tablespoon active dry yeast
5 to 6 cups unbleached all-purpose flour
2 teaspoons salt
1 cup warm milk

2 tablespoons honey or 1 tablespoon sugar
3 tablespoons oil or 2 tablespoons softened butter plus 1 tablespoon oil

Pour warm water into the bowl of an electric mixer. Sprinkle yeast on top and cover with 2 cups flour. Do not mix! Allow to stand for about 10 minutes.

Add 2 cups flour, salt, milk, honey (or sugar), and 2 tablespoons oil (or butter). Beat in the mixer for 2 minutes. Add more flour as needed, so that the dough forms an elastic ball and comes away from the sides of the bowl. Remember, the ability of flour to absorb liquid varies. Sometimes only 5 cups flour are sufficient. Always reserve some flour if you are going to knead by hand.

If the machine has a kneading hook, change to the hook and knead for 3 to 4 minutes. If you wish to knead by hand, knead the dough on a floured surface for 5 to 6 minutes.

Drop a teaspoon of oil into a large bowl. Roll the dough in the oil so that it is barely coated. Cover the bowl with plastic wrap and set aside for 1½ hours at room temperature. The dough should rise to twice its original volume. Punch the dough down and again roll it around into a ball and place in the bowl. Cover the bowl with plastic wrap, and allow the dough to rest for 15 minutes.

With the remaining oil, grease two bread loaf pans (8½" x 4½" x 2½"). Place the dough on a floured surface. Cut the dough into two equal pieces. Pat each piece into a loaf shape and place into the oiled pans. Allow to rise for 20 minutes. Preheat the oven to 400°F.

Bake the bread for 45 minutes. Remove from the oven to a cooling rack immediately. If more brownness is desired, the breads can be baked for an additional 5 to 6 minutes on a cookie sheet in an electric oven or on the open rack of a gas oven.

Pullman or French White Bread (Pain de Mie)
Makes 2 loaves.

In France the French sandwich bread called *pain de mie* (usually translated as "Pullman bread") is mainly used for open sandwiches, canapés, and specialty recipes. The bread is also called *pain Anglais* ("English bread"), which is used for delicate tea sandwiches. Until recently the French were not acquainted with the American style of sandwich making.

I believe that the translation of "Pullman" derives from the shape of the baking pan. The baking pan, as manufactured in France for this bread, is in the shape of a long rectangle with a cover—the shape of an old Pullman sleeping car on a train. The cover is used in baking so that when the bread rises in the pan, it reaches the top to make it flat on all sides. Directions for improvising with the American loaf pan will be given in the recipe. Although the ingredients are similar to American White Bread, they are greatly enriched with butter. The result is a delicious and tightly textured bread— a base to hold spreads and fillings.

    1 cup warm water
    1 tablespoon active dry yeast
    6 to 7 cups unbleached all-purpose flour
    2 cups milk, at room temperature
    1 tablespoon salt
    1 tablespoon sugar
    ¼ pound (8 tablespoons) butter

Pour warm water into the bowl of an electric mixer. Sprinkle yeast on top and cover with 2 cups flour. Do not mix! Set aside for 10 minutes.

Add 2 cups flour, milk, salt, sugar, and 7 tablespoons butter. (Reserve 1 tablespoon butter for greasing the bowl and baking pans.) Beat for 3 to 4 minutes, adding more flour gradually. Always reserve 1 or 2 cups flour for kneading and to flour the work surface. When the dough comes away from the sides of the bowl, change to a dough hook or knead by hand for a few minutes until the dough is smooth and holds its shape.

Grease a large bowl with a small amount of the remaining butter. Place the dough in the bowl and cover the bowl with plastic wrap. Set aside at room temperature for 1½ hours until the dough has risen to more than double its original volume. Punch the dough down and roll it by hand into a ball. Cover the bowl with plastic wrap again and let the dough rest for 20 minutes.

Use the remaining butter to grease two bread loaf pans (8½" x 4½" x 2½"). Grease two cookie sheets in the centers where they will cover the bread pans when turned upside down. Prepare weights to keep the covers down tight during baking. If you own French bread molds, grease their bottoms and sides and the inside of their sliding covers.

Place the dough on a floured surface. Cut the dough into two equal pieces. Pat each piece into a loaf shape. Place them in the pans—the dough should fill the pans no higher than halfway up the sides—and cover. If you are using the American loaf pan, cover with the greased cookie sheets and place the weights on top. Allow the dough to rise for 45 minutes. Preheat oven to 425°F.

Bake the breads for 25 minutes. Remove covers. The dough should have risen to the top of the pans and formed a crust. Bake for another 20 to 30 minutes until browned. Remove from the baking pans immediately and place on a cooling rack.

Easy Soft Rolls or Bread
Makes 2 breads or 24 rolls.

Breads that contain milk and eggs are rich in color and flavor. In fact , they are enriched enough to become cakes with just a few additional ingredients. Rolls and breads, even with eggs, should not be too sweet, however. The following recipe is a good base for rolls and morning cinnamon bread.

½ cup warm water
1 tablespoon active dry yeast
4 to 5 cups unbleached all-purpose flour
½ cup milk
2 teaspoons salt
⅓ cup sugar
2 eggs
6 tablespoons unsalted butter, cut into six pieces
1 tablespoon unsalted butter for greasing bowl and pans
1 egg stirred with 1 tablespoon water for egg wash

Pour warm water into the bowl of an electric mixer. Sprinkle yeast on top and cover with 2 cups flour. Do not mix! Let stand for about 10 minutes.

Add milk, salt, sugar, and eggs. Beat for 2 minutes. Continue to beat while gradually adding 2 more cups flour, alternating the flour with pieces of butter. Reserve some flour for kneading. When the dough comes away from the sides of the bowl, change to a kneading hook for 3 to 4 minutes or knead by hand on a floured surface for 5 to 6 minutes. Use additional flour, if necessary, so the dough holds its shape and is smooth and satiny when finished.

Place the dough in a greased bowl and cover the bowl with plastic wrap. Allow to rise at room temperature for 1½ hours or until the dough has risen to twice its original volume. Punch the dough down.

Transfer the dough to a floured surface. Punch the dough down flat. Cover with plastic wrap and allow to rest for 8 to 10 minutes.

For 24 rolls: Divide the dough in half. Cut each half into 12 pieces. On a floured surface, roll each piece into a 4- to 6-inch length (sausage shape). Twist each into a figure-eight shape, drawing the ends through the loops for a knot. Twist or make snail-like shapes. The pieces may be shaped into round balls as well. Place rolls on greased cookie sheets 1½ inches apart, and allow to rise for

Twist   *Spiral*   *Figure Eight*

45 minutes. Preheat oven to 375°F. Brush the rolls with the mixture of egg and water, and bake for 20 minutes.

For 2 breads: Press the dough down with your hands to an approximate 8- or 9-inch square. Cut the dough into six lengths. Using your hands, roll each length into a rope. Make a simple braid with three ropes. Place the braid into a greased bread pan. Repeat with the remaining three ropes to form another loaf. As an alternative, twisted loaves can be baked on greased cookie sheets. Allow to rise for 45 minutes or until almost double in size. Preheat oven to 375°F. Brush the breads with the mixture of egg and water. Bake for 45 minutes for browning.

✸ *Suggestions*

- When eggs and butter (or any fat) are added to yeast-risen dough, the rising will be much slower.
- For shiny finishes on rolls or breads, egg yolk alone will produce the shiniest and darkest crusts when brushed on before baking. Egg plus water is the usual baker's wash for a shiny finish. Egg white alone will produce a brown finish but little sheen. Milk or cream can be added to the egg instead of water for the wash.
- Try making sweet rolls. Roll each length of dough in sugar and cinnamon to make a sweet-flavored rope. It may be twisted or not.
- Roll out half the dough and experiment with fillings of sugar, cinnamon, and nuts for a simple yeast cake. Shape into a loaf or ring.
- Butter muffin pans. Sprinkle brown sugar in the bottom. Add raisins or nuts, if you wish. Place snail-shaped dough into each muffin space.

Challah (Rich Egg Loaf)
Makes 3 breads.

When I was a child, breads were purchased daily at a grocery or bakeshop, but Friday was the day when that special bread aroma wafted through the house. My mother baked the Sabbath bread, called Challah, every Friday. What I had taken for granted as a weekly home bread, I later discovered was closely related to one of the great basic French doughs, the classic Brioche (page 20). The only difference between Challah and Brioche is one ingredient. Oil is used for making Challah, whereas butter is used for making Brioche. Si Graf, a professional baker, shared his knowledge with me to perfect a foolproof home recipe. I have taught his six-braided loaf ever since, and it has become my preferred recipe for Challah. I have also adapted Si's rich yeast dough for the Brioche that follows.

1¼ cups warm water
2 tablespoons active dry yeast

5 cups high-gluten or unbleached all-purpose flour

¼ cup corn oil

6 or 7 egg yolks

1 egg

1 tablespoon salt

¼ cup sugar

1 egg, lightly beaten, for egg wash

Oil for greasing bowl and pans

Russian caraway seeds or poppy seeds (optional)

Braiding Challah

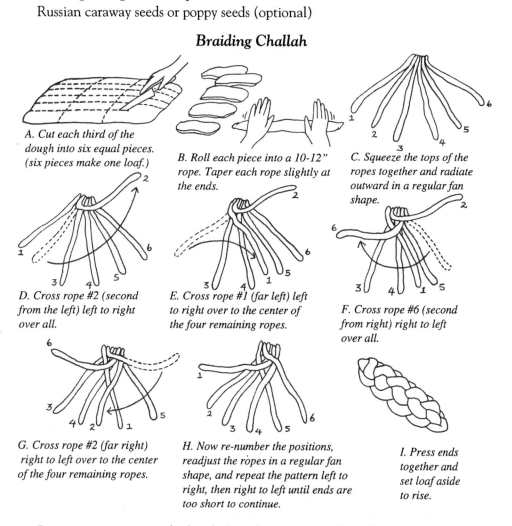

A. Cut each third of the dough into six equal pieces. (six pieces make one loaf.)

B. Roll each piece into a 10-12" rope. Taper each rope slightly at the ends.

C. Squeeze the tops of the ropes together and radiate outward in a regular fan shape.

D. Cross rope #2 (second from the left) left to right over all.

E. Cross rope #1 (far left) left to right over to the center of the four remaining ropes.

F. Cross rope #6 (second from right) right to left over all.

G. Cross rope #2 (far right) right to left over to the center of the four remaining ropes.

H. Now re-number the positions, readjust the ropes in a regular fan shape, and repeat the pattern left to right, then right to left until ends are too short to continue.

I. Press ends together and set loaf aside to rise.

Pour warm water into the bowl of an electric mixer. Sprinkle yeast on top and cover with 2 cups flour. Do not mix! Let stand for about 10 minutes.

Pour the ¼ cup corn oil into a 2-cup glass measuring cup. Swirl the oil around in the cup. Add the egg yolks and the whole egg to measure 1 total cup—a little more won't hurt. The eggs will come away clear if the cup is coated with oil. Pour eggs and oil, salt, and sugar into the bowl. Beat the mixture for 3 to 4 minutes. Gradually add 2 more cups flour as the beating continues. When the dough gathers around the beater and comes away from the sides of the bowl, you are ready for kneading. If you wish to knead by machine, change from the beater to the kneading hook. Use more flour, if necessary, and knead for 2 to 3 minutes.

If kneading by hand, as I do, transfer the dough to a floured surface and knead for 4 to 5 minutes. The dough should take shape, lose its limpness, and become smooth. Place the dough into an oiled 6- or 7-quart bowl, turning the dough to grease it all over. Cover the bowl with plastic wrap, and allow the dough to rise for 1½ to 2 hours or until it is more than double its original volume.

Turn the dough out onto a floured surface. Press it into a large, flat rectangle— about 12 inches by 9 inches. Cut into three equal pieces, and cut each of the three pieces into six pieces. Set aside the six pieces for each of the three breads. Cover all the pieces with plastic wrap, and allow the dough to rest for several minutes.

Roll one set of six pieces into six 10- or 12-inch lengths. Follow the diagram on page 19 to form a braid as shown. Place the bread on an oiled pan.

Repeat for the other breads. Set aside to rise for 30 minutes. Preheat the oven to 300°F.

Brush the breads with the egg wash. Sprinkle with the caraway or poppy seeds, if you wish. Bake for 10 minutes, then raise heat to 325°F and bake for 10 minutes more. Raise heat to 350°F . Continue to bake for 15 to 20 minutes. The breads may have to be reversed in the oven for even browning. Remove the breads from the oven, and immediately place them on racks to cool.

Brioche
Makes sixteen 3- to 4-inch Brioches.

  1 cup warm water
  2 tablespoons active dry yeast
  5 cups high-gluten or unbleached all-purpose flour
  ¼ cup sugar
  1 tablespoon salt
  ¼ cup warm milk
  3 eggs and 3 egg yolks to make about 1 cup
  ½ pound (2 sticks) unsalted butter, melted
  2 tablespoons melted butter for greasing pans
  1 egg, lightly beaten, for egg wash

Pour warm water into the bowl of an electric mixer. Sprinkle yeast on top and cover with 2 cups flour. Do not mix! Let stand for about 10 minutes.

Stir sugar and salt into the warm milk until dissolved. Add milk (with dissolved sugar and salt), eggs, and egg yolks to the yeast, water, and flour mixture. Beat in the mixer for 1 minute. Gradually add 3 cups flour, and beat at medium speed for 2 minutes.

Add melted butter slowly. When the butter is completely incorporated, beat the dough vigorously for at least 4 minutes, perhaps longer, until the dough comes away from the sides of the bowl. It will look shiny and slippery. Scrape the dough clean from the sides and bottom of the bowl into a smooth mass. Cover the bowl with plastic wrap, and let rise for 1½ to 2 hours.

Punch the dough down and gather again into a smooth mass. Cover with plastic wrap, and refrigerate for a minimum of 6 hours to overnight. If the dough rises in the refrigerator, punch it down again. The dough will sometimes taste yeasty (too much fermentation) if the air is not released by punching the dough down.

When ready to bake, brush the insides of sixteen 4-inch Brioche tins with melted butter. Place on two cookie sheets.

Remove the dough from the refrigerator. Flour a working surface. Use a plastic scraper to smoothly transfer the dough to the floured surface. Shape the dough into a 14-inch sausage shape. Cut off one-fourth of the dough and set aside.

Divide the larger piece of the dough in half and then into eight pieces each (A). Flour your hands well. Roll each piece into a ball (B) and place in the buttered tins. Press down as you do this (C). Flour your index finger and press a cavity into the center of each one (D).

Divide the smaller (one-fourth) piece of dough in half and then into eight pieces each (E). Roll each piece into a small ball, and then roll them into a pear shape, making a point at one end (F). With a cup of water close by, dip the point into the water (G) and place the dough point down into the cavity of each Brioche (H).

A.   B.   C.   D.

E.   F.   G.   H.

Use scissors to cut four snips, evenly separated, around the Brioche. Brush the tops with egg wash. Cover with a towel, and let rise for 1½ hours at room temperature. This is a slow rise.

Preheat oven to 375°F and bake for 25 to 30 minutes. Remove to a cooling rack immediately.

Multi-Grain Bread
Makes 2 loaves.

2½ cups warm water
2 tablespoons active dry yeast

2 cups high-gluten or unbleached all-purpose flour
1½ teaspoons salt
¼ cup honey
¼ cup molasses
¼ cup oil
1 cup rolled oats (old-fashioned, not instant)
½ cup cornmeal
1 cup coarsely ground rye flour
1 cup oat bran
½ cup soy flour
¼ cup sesame seeds
2 cups unbleached all-purpose flour
Oil for greasing bowl and pans

Pour warm water into the bowl of an electric mixer. Sprinkle yeast on top and cover with 2 cups high-gluten or all-purpose flour. Do not mix! Let stand for about 10 minutes.

Add salt, honey, molasses, oil, and oats. Beat for 3 to 4 minutes in the electric mixer. Gradually add other flours, sesame seeds, and most of the all-purpose flour, until the dough comes away from the sides of the bowl.

Remove the dough to a floured surface. Knead by machine or hand for 3 to 4 minutes, using more all-purpose flour, if necessary. The finished dough should be firm and round, not limp and sticky.

Place the dough in an oiled bowl about three times as large as the size of the dough. Cover the bowl with plastic wrap, and set aside for 2 hours to rise to double or more in volume.

Oil two 9-inch bread loaf pans or cookie sheets. Preheat oven to 350°F.

Punch the dough down. Use a plastic scraper to clean the dough from the sides and bottom of the bowl. Transfer the dough to a floured surface and cut it in half. Fold each piece of dough in half and seal the edge. Place seam-side down in oiled pans or on cookie sheets. If using bread loaf pans, press the dough into the corners.

Bake for 50 to 60 minutes. Remove from pans and cool on a rack.

✷ Suggestions

- For an herbal flavor, omit the sesame seeds. Instead, add ¼ cup mixed dried herbs—oregano, thyme, and savory—and 2 tablespoons freshly minced garlic.
- Shape these loaves into free forms, large ovals, or rounds. Place on oiled cookie sheets sprinkled with cornmeal. Bake for 35 minutes at 375°F.

Carrot and Currant Bread
Makes 2 loaves.

My enthusiasm for bread baking spurred me to experiment with variations on the theme of the old-fashioned potato bread. By adding 1 cup cooked mashed potato to the American White Bread recipe (page 14) and reducing the water to ½ cup, you have another very white, soft-textured sandwich bread. My imagination ran wild, and I decided to use leftover purées of carrot and butternut squash instead of potato. Obviously, any root vegetable can be used as an interesting addition for bulk, color, and flavor.

    1¾ cups warm water
    1 tablespoon active dry yeast
    5 cups unbleached all-purpose flour
    1½ cups cooked, puréed carrots
    ½ cup currants (or raisins)
    ½ cup oat bran
    2 teaspoons salt
    1 tablespoon brown sugar
    2 tablespoons maple syrup

Pour warm water into the bowl of an electric mixer. Sprinkle yeast on top and cover with 2 cups flour. Do not mix! Let stand for about 10 minutes.

Add 1 cup flour and all other ingredients. Beat for 2 to 3 minutes. Continue beating, adding remaining flour gradually. The dough will start hugging the beater and come away from the sides of the bowl. Use a plastic scraper to transfer the dough to a floured surface. Knead for a few minutes until the dough takes shape and is not limp. Transfer the dough to an oiled bowl, and cover the bowl with plastic wrap. Let rise for 1½ to 2 hours.

Punch the dough down to release air. Cover the bowl with plastic wrap again and let rise for 20 to 30 minutes. Oil two 8- or 9-inch bread pans. Place the dough on a floured surface and divide in half. Fold each piece in half and seal the edge. Place seam-side down in the oiled pans. Let rise for 20 minutes. Preheat oven to 400°F.

Bake breads for 40 to 50 minutes. Lower temperature if the breads brown too fast. Remove from baking pans immediately and allow to cool on racks.

Biscuits
Makes 12 drop biscuits, 16 two-inch rounds (cut out), 14 three-inch rounds, or 24 miniatures.

The baking-powder biscuit is a delicious and quick all-purpose bread. I once timed the preparation and it totaled 5 minutes. The ingredients are average pantry products, so there's no need to buy the expensive packaged combinations of flour, shortening, milk, and leavening. Memorize the proportions and, with some experience, you will be confident enough to make personal changes. Try butter for richness or buttermilk for flavor, a touch of sugar for shortcake or herbs and cheese for savory munchies.

> 2 cups unbleached all-purpose flour
> 2 teaspoons baking powder
> ¼ teaspoon baking soda
> ½ teaspoon salt
> ¼ cup shortening
> ¾ cup milk or buttermilk

Sift flour, baking powder, baking soda, and salt into a 3-quart bowl. Add shortening by cutting it and blending it into the flour with a six-wire pastry blender. This is an old-fashioned method, but it works. In less than a minute the mixture should look like coarse crumbs.

Gradually add milk or buttermilk to moisten the mixture. Use a fork or your hands to quickly form a ball. Handle the dough for no longer than 30 seconds—the less handling, the better.

Pull off a small piece of dough (about a rounded tablespoon). Roughly make a ball and place it on a Teflon-coated or lightly greased cookie sheet. Continue with the remainder of the mix, placing rough balls 1 inch apart on the cookie sheet. Bake at 450°F for about 15 minutes until lightly browned. Serve the biscuits piping hot under the cover of a napkin. Biscuits can be baked in advance and reheated before serving.

For roll-out biscuits: Transfer the dough to a floured surface. Tap the dough gently to even out the thickness. With a rolling pin, roll lightly from the middle outward and then toward you to a thickness of about ¾ inch. Use a 2-inch cookie cutter to make shapes. Place them directly on the cookie sheet. Bring leftover ends together to roll out the remainder of the dough. Handle gently and use extra flour, as needed. Bake as above.

✸ *Suggestions*

- After the milk is added to the dry ingredients, mix in 2 tablespoons herbs—chives, parsley, or marjoram, fresh or 1 tablespoon dry—for savory miniatures.
- Add ½ teaspoon each curry and chili powder for a spicy biscuit.
- Up to ½ cup grated cheese or bits of crisp bacon are good additions.
- Drop any one of these biscuit mixtures in tiny mounds (1 rounded teaspoon) onto a lightly greased cookie sheet. Bake at 450°F for about 10 minutes.
- Use the same recipe to make shortcake, but add 1 tablespoon sugar to the dry ingredients. Use half butter and half shortening to enhance the flavor. Preferably use the roll-out method with a 3-inch biscuit cutter or an 8-inch pie form.

2

Appetizers

I agree with many of my friends: Appetizers are so tempting that most people would opt for an entire meal of these varied tidbits. There are cocktail parties and certain occasions when buffet appetizers do become dinner. An appetizer before dinner should actually be a small teaser to whet the appetite but not satisfy it. On the other hand, there are more formal appetizers, served at the table, that become first courses.

My husband and I always have an appetizer as a relaxing prelude to dinner. Sometimes it is a leftover cut into tiny pieces and placed on points of toast. In the summertime it can be a beautiful opener, making use of our fresh garden vegetables. Year-round my shelf might offer a tin of anchovies, a jar of olives, or some toasted almonds. There are always the last spoonfuls of cottage cheese or yogurt, easily combined with herbs to make simple dips.

I always provide small dishes, napkins, and forks for guests. This is standard procedure in our home when we begin with appetizers in the living room.

Avocados

My husband and I are partial to avocados and always make sure we buy them a week in advance, leaving time enough to ripen. The small California avocados are our favorites. They sit on the counter next to lemons, limes, and oranges — staples in our kitchen. I always use a spoon to scoop out the flesh of an avocado, then I mash it with a fork. I never use a processor. I always keep a lemon close by for a quick squeeze of juice as I work with avocados.

Unfortunately, avocados discolor when peeled and sliced, even with the use of lemon juice. If possible, cut them about 30 minutes before serving. Cover cut or leftover avocado tightly with plastic wrap, the best method to keep it from discoloring.

- If the avocado is beautifully ripe (soft to a gentle touch through the skin), mash it with a fork and add lemon juice. Serve it as a butter with fresh bread.
- Arrange alternate slices of avocado with melon and grapefruit. Place strips of prosciutto over the melon.
- Serve slices of avocado with crabmeat or shrimp with a dressing of your choice on the side.
- Place a slice of avocado in a leaf of endive. Place the endive in rows or in a circle on a platter. Spoon a few drops of Chili Pepper Paste (page 27) on top or a decorative strip of sweet red pepper.
- Make your favorite guacamole recipe, and add 1 or 2 tablespoons Chili Pepper Paste or diced Italian black olives.

Tomatoes

When tomatoes are in season, and in our garden as well, we delight in using them day after day.

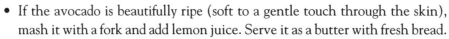

- Arrange a platter of freshly sliced tomatoes alternating with thinly sliced oranges and red onion. Sprinkle with minced fresh herbs and balsamic vinegar.
- Alternate slices of tomato with sliced Swiss Gruyère, fontina, or mozzarella cheese, and garnish with basil leaves, fresh cilantro, or Italian parsley.
- For a hot hors d'oeuvre, place shavings of cheese on sliced tomato. Broil until the cheese bubbles.
- Top each slice of tomato with two strips of smoked salmon or a few flakes of smoked trout.

- Scoop out cherry tomatoes and stuff each one with an anchovy and a leaf of Italian parsley. Another time use the Eggplant Caviar (page 31) as a stuffing.

Recipes for Cold Appetizers

Roasted Garlic
Makes about ½ cup.

If you have mastered the chapter on bread baking, you probably realize that there is nothing more delicious than freshly baked bread. Use Roasted Garlic, one of the best substitutes for butter, as a spread.

3 whole buds garlic (use less or more, as you wish)
2 to 3 tablespoons olive oil

Preheat oven to 375°F. Use a sheet of heavy aluminum foil, large enough to enclose the three buds. Pour 1 teaspoon of the oil in the center of the foil. Place the buds of garlic close together on the oil. Pour another teaspoon of oil on top of the garlic. Enclose the garlic in the foil. Bake for about 1 hour until the garlic feels soft to touch. Be careful, it will be very hot.

Allow to cool for 15 minutes. Cut garlic horizontally. Squeeze out pulp into a small bowl. Add the rest of the oil as you smooth the mixture with a fork.

✹ Suggestions

- Use as a spread on bread, crackers, or toast.
- Use as a seasoning in various vegetable, fish, and meat dishes.
- Refrigerate in a covered jar for up to one week.

Chili Pepper Paste
Makes ⅔ cup.

During a visit to Santa Fe, New Mexico, I purchased a large *ristra*—red chili peppers strung on a cord and hung to dry. I have continued to use the peppers with interesting results. Dried chili peppers are available in the vegetable departments of most supermarkets. Depending on the peppers (veins and seeds hold the hot spice), they can range from mildly hot to very, very hot. The color and the seasoning are spicy accents in combination with beans, avocados, vegetable stews, and chilis.

8 dried red chili peppers
½ cup liquid from soaking peppers in water
½ teaspoon salt
2 tablespoons olive oil

If you are allergic or react to a strong pepper aroma, wear latex gloves. Detach stems from chili peppers, and clean the insides, removing the seeds. Soak the chili peppers in hot water until soft. Purée them in a food processor with ½ cup of the soaking liquid to cover. Strain the mixture into a saucepan, add salt, and simmer for 10 minutes. Stir in olive oil. Use at once or refrigerate up to two weeks.

✳ *Suggestions*

- Use as a spread or dip or as a seasoning in Peppery Chick-Peas (this page).
- Use as a spread for canapés. Top with sliced black or green olives.
- Add 1 or 2 tablespoons to Tomato Sauce (page 88) or Brown Sauce (pages 86 and 87) for spiciness.
- Combine with mayonnaise or other salad dressings and dribble over greens, shredded cabbage, and carrots.
- Use in fillings for tortillas or pita bread.

Peppery Chick-Peas (Garbanzos)
Serves 6 to 8.

Chick-peas, also called garbanzos, are not only nutritious, they are versatile. As children, we ate chick-peas as we did peanuts, with a mere sprinkling of salt and pepper. Aside from appetizers, use cooked chick-peas as a nutritional and economical protein, combining them with soups, stews, and vegetables. Since chick-peas are bland, the Chili Pepper Paste in the preceding recipe adds interesting spice and color.

1 cup dried chick-peas or 1 can (19 ounces) chick-peas, drained and rinsed
6 cups water
1 teaspoon salt
1½ teaspoons freshly ground pepper
Bouquet garni
2 tablespoons wine vinegar (red wine or balsamic)
½ cup minced red onion
¼ cup Chili Pepper Paste (page 27)

As you would with any dried beans before cooking, soak dried chick-peas in 3 cups water overnight and discard water before cooking. (**Note:** A faster method of preparing chick-peas involves bringing them to a boil for 3 minutes, covered. Then turn off heat and allow to rest for 1 hour. Drain off water.) Combine chick-peas and 3 cups cold water in a 2- or 3-quart pot. Add salt, ½ teaspoon freshly ground pepper, and bouquet garni. Cover and simmer for 1 hour or until the chick-peas are tender but not soft. Drain liquid and reserve for other uses, like soups and stews.

If you are using canned chick-peas, rinse them in cold water and drain well.

Toss chick-peas with vinegar, red onion, and Chili Pepper Paste. Add salt and pepper, if necessary. Serve in a bowl with a scoop for pick-up. Refrigerate chick-peas in a covered jar if they are not used immediately.

✳ *Suggestions*

- Purée the mixture and serve it as a dip.
- Make an extra amount. Use as an extender for leftover turkey, chicken, and fish dishes.

Fresh Tomato Salsa
Makes 2 ½ cups.

3 pounds ripe tomatoes, skinned and seeded
4 scallions, minced
2 tablespoons each minced fresh basil and Italian parsley
2 tablespoons wine vinegar
Salt and freshly ground pepper to taste

Ripe tomatoes will skin easily when dipped into boiling water for 30 seconds and then refreshed in cold water. Cut them in half horizontally. Squeeze out the juice and seeds. Cut out and discard the core. Dice the tomato coarsely.

Mix tomatoes with all other ingredients. Season to taste. If too much liquid accumulates after the mixture sits, pour the liquid off or reserve it for Vegetable Stock (page 62) or stews.

✳ *Suggestions*

- Add 2 tablespoons each Chili Pepper Paste (page 27) and chopped fresh cilantro.
- Add minced cucumber, green pepper, and 2 tablespoons olive oil.
- Use the salsa with chips, sliced avocado, or wrapped in romaine lettuce.
- Any of these mixtures are bases for tortilla fillings as well as pita sandwiches.
- Room-temperature Tomato Salsa makes a light, delicious dressing for piping hot linguini or spaghetti.

Grated Black Radish
(Round Black Spanish Radish)
Serves 6 to 8.

This big, round black radish is easily found in markets during the fall months, but occasionally I hunt them out in the spring as well. The skin of the radish is black, but when peeled, the usable flesh is white. Traditionally, I use a dressing of rendered chicken fat and grated onion, but my neighbor (who was born in Switzerland) offered this Swiss version.

> 1 small onion
> 1 black radish (about ½ pound)
> 1 tablespoon lemon juice
> 2 tablespoons olive oil
> Salt and freshly ground pepper

Cut onion in quarters. Peel radish and cut into chunks. Use the grater attachment of a food processor to shred both. Transfer to a bowl. Stir in lemon juice, oil, and salt and pepper to taste. Set aside or refrigerate to allow the grated radish to absorb the seasoning and mellow. Prepare 1 hour ahead of time or refrigerate for up to three days. Use the recipe as an accompaniment to pâtés or as a side dish to poached or smoked fish.

Celery Root or Jicama in Mustard Dressing
Serves 6 to 8.

Celery root and jicama are prepared in the same way as Grated Black Radish (this page), but each has its own distinctive flavor. Black radish is the sharpest. Celery root, also called celeriac, is grown for the root portion, not the rib and leaf of celery. Jicama is the mildest and sweetest-tasting of the three. Although each of these root vegetables is different in taste, this dressing suits any one as an appetizer salad.

Celery Root

If you are cautious about using raw eggs for this homemade mayonnaise, simply substitute ½ cup mayonnaise for the egg and reduce olive oil to ¼ cup.

Jicama

1 egg
2 tablespoons lemon juice
4 teaspoons Dijon mustard
½ teaspoon salt
½ teaspoon freshly ground pepper
½ cup olive oil
1 or 2 celery roots or jicama (1 to 2 pounds), peeled and cut into thick slices
1 tablespoon each minced fresh chives and parsley

Place egg, lemon juice, mustard, salt, and pepper in the food processor. Use the metal blade and run the processor for 30 seconds. Add oil gradually; stop when the mixture emulsifies and thickens. Taste and adjust seasoning with more mustard, salt, and pepper to taste.

Remove the metal attachment and clean off the dressing clinging to the blade into the bowl. Change to the grating disk of the processor. Place slices of celery root or jicama in the feeder and in seconds the root will be shredded. Transfer to a bowl. Add chives and parsley. Stir well. Serve in a mound on leaves of curly greens or ruby lettuce.

✳ *Suggestions*

- Use the dressing as a filling for leaves of endive, radicchio, or sweet red pepper.
- Add chunks of poached chicken for a summer salad.

Eggplant Caviar (Potlijel)
Makes about 2 ½ cups.

I use eggplant year-round, whether it is grown locally or not. Eggplant Caviar and roasted peppers are staples in my refrigerator. Soon you will be wondering about the size of my refrigerator. It is just average, but I have kept a 40-year-old one in our garage for overflow.

1 eggplant
1 green pepper
2 or 3 sweet red peppers
1 small onion
⅛ teaspoon red pepper flakes
Salt and freshly ground pepper to taste
2 tablespoons wine vinegar or lemon juice
1 tablespoon olive oil (optional)

Puncture the skin of the eggplant in 4 or 5 places. Place a rack 4 or 5 inches below the broiler, and heat the broiling unit in the oven. Put the eggplant and peppers on a baking tin. Broil them for 15 or 20 minutes, turning them occasionally. The eggplant should be soft when pierced with a fork. If the peppers are charred before the eggplant is finished, transfer the peppers to a brown paper bag. Fold the top of the bag to enclose the peppers and allow to cool slowly. Do the same with the eggplant when it is soft. Remove the skin and seeds from the peppers. Cut the eggplant in half, vertically, and scrape the flesh from the skin (it will practically slide off).

Chop the onion in the food processor for 10 seconds until minced. Add the green pepper, half the amount of red pepper (reserve the remainder), the eggplant, and the red pepper flakes. Turn the machine on and off to chop ingredients roughly; do not purée them.

Transfer the mixture to a bowl. Season with salt and pepper. Vinegar or lemon juice and oil may be added at this time. Sometimes I omit them. Serve in a bowl as a spread. Cover and store in the refrigerator for up to one week.

Slice the reserved red pepper into strips. Place in a jar and cover with olive oil. Refrigerate for garnishes or make extra for the classic combination of red pepper and anchovy (see below).

✳ *Suggestions*

- For a spicy touch, char a tiny hot green pepper with the sweet ones. Add with the rest.
- Add a few tablespoons Tomato Salsa (page 29) to the Eggplant Caviar.
- Toss ½ cup Eggplant Caviar with a green salad. An oil dressing will be unnecessary for people counting calories.

Baked Peppers and Anchovies
Serves 8 to 10.

In a totally different interpretation of this well-known combination, Baked Peppers and Anchovies can be served as a spread or a dip. Use it as a filling for artichokes and mushrooms.

    1 can (2 ounces) anchovy fillets
    2 pounds green and/or red sweet peppers
    ½ cup olive oil
    4 cloves garlic, minced
    1 teaspoon freshly ground pepper

Cut anchovies into small pieces. Set aside and keep the oil. Wash peppers; remove seeds and veins. Cut the peppers into strips. Preheat oven to 300°F.

Use an 8- or 9-inch shallow baking dish. Mix the anchovies with their oil, peppers, olive oil, garlic, and freshly ground pepper in the baking dish. Toss to mix well and evenly coat the pepper strips.

Cover with aluminum foil and bake for 45 minutes, stirring once or twice. Uncover and cook for 30 minutes more. Serve at room temperature with plenty of crusty bread for spreading and dunking.

✳ Suggestion

If you are not an anchovy enthusiast, substitute 8 ounces peeled, sliced onions, two more cloves garlic, minced, and salt to taste. Of course, you will lose the special taste of the anchovies, but the substitution will give a delightful flavor all its own.

Danish Karse Dip

Makes 2 cups.

Fresh greens and herbs are the key to this aromatic combination with Danish blue cheese. In Denmark, *karse* is the word for cress, hence the name. The Danes enjoy this spread on rye bread and use it as a salad dressing, too. I like it as a dip or dribbled on freshly sliced tomatoes or a few leaves of greens. Store leftovers in the refrigerator and use it as a spread for canapés.

Karse

½ cup sour cream (or substitute yogurt or light sour cream)
¼ cup mayonnaise
1 tablespoon fresh lemon juice
1 clove garlic, minced
¼ cup each minced watercress, spinach, and parsley
1 tablespoon each minced fresh dill and tarragon
2 scallions, minced
¼ pound Danish blue cheese, crumbled

Spinach

In a bowl, mix sour cream, mayonnaise, lemon juice, and garlic until well blended. Add greens, herbs, and scallions, and, lastly, cheese. Cover the bowl and refrigerate for at least 1 hour for the flavors to combine. The mixture may be stored in the refrigerator for up to three days. Serve with raw or steamed vegetables, crackers, or chips.

Italian Parsley   *Curly Parsley*

Gravlax (Swedish Marinated Salmon)
Serves 12.

Many years ago we had our first taste of Gravlax at the splendid table of the Operakallaren Restaurant in Stockholm. Swedish friends provided the recipe, a household basic in Sweden.

    3 pounds center-cut fresh salmon, boned but not skinned
    1 large bunch fresh dill
    ¼ cup kosher (coarse) salt
    ¼ cup sugar
    2 tablespoons white peppercorns, coarsely
        cracked

Cut salmon in half lengthwise. Wipe salmon dry; be sure all bones are removed. Cut dill in two or three places. Crush salt, sugar, and peppercorns together.

Place one fillet of salmon in a glass, enamel, or china dish. Spread half the crushed seasoning on the fish. Lay dill on top. Spread the remaining crushed seasoning on top of the dill. Cover with the second fillet of salmon, flesh-side down. Place a board or plate on the fish. Weigh it down with bricks, stones, or heavy cans. Store in the refrigerator.

Turn fish every 12 hours, basting it each time with marinade that has accumulated in the bottom of the dish. Repeat this procedure for 2 days minimum (3 days maximum, if the fillets are thick). Scrape off seasoning and dill. Slice thinly and serve with fresh dill, black pepper, lemon, and Mustard Dill Sauce (below). Pass thinly sliced pumpernickel bread.

To keep Gravlax for long periods (up to two months), cut into four sections and freeze each section separately. Thaw each piece separately (in the refrigerator), as needed. When the fish is slightly thawed (stiff sherbet stage), slice as thinly as possible. Brush each slice with a flavorless vegetable oil and serve.

Mustard Dill Sauce

    4 tablespoons Dijon mustard
    1 teaspoon dry mustard
    3 tablespoons sugar
    2 tablespoons white vinegar

3 tablespoons freshly chopped dill
⅓ cup vegetable oil

Mix the mustards, sugar, vinegar, and dill together until thoroughly blended. Add oil and stir briskly. Serve on the side with Gravlax.

✸ *Suggestions*

- Sometimes I substitute honey for sugar in the dressing. Serve with cured meats and thinly sliced salami.
- Try adding a small amount of horseradish to the dressing, and serve with other varieties of smoked fish.
- Keep the sauce refrigerated. Add yogurt for a quick dip.

Purée of Cod (Brandade de Morue)
Serves 12.

This classic salt cod purée, native to the Mediterranean coast, has taken on great popularity. Salting was, and still is, used as a preservative for storing an overabundance of fish. Salt cod, the classic ingredient for this recipe, needs to be soaked according to the directions on the package. Here, I have substituted fresh cod or scrod so that soaking is not necessary, but try it both ways to test your preference.

2 medium potatoes, peeled and thinly sliced
¼ teaspoon kosher (coarse) salt
1 pound fillet cod or scrod
2 cloves garlic
½ cup warmed heavy cream
½ cup olive oil (or more for preferred consistency)
Salt to taste if fresh fish is used
Freshly ground pepper, preferably white

Place potatoes in a pot with water to cover. Add salt. Cook covered for 8 to 10 minutes or until potatoes begin to soften. Place fish on top of the potatoes. Cover the pot and simmer for another 10 minutes. The fish should flake easily and look opaque when finished. Place potatoes and fish in a strainer over a bowl. Reserve or freeze the strained broth for Fish Stock (page 61) or fish stew.

Mince garlic in the food processor. Add fish and potatoes, running the processor for just 30 seconds. Gradually add warmed cream and oil as you process the mixture until it is creamy. More or less oil can be used. A substitution of broth for oil is possible as well.

Transfer the mixture to a bowl and season with salt and freshly ground pepper. Serve on greens with toasted French bread. The purée can be kept in the refrigerator for up to three days.

✻ *Suggestions*

- Use as a dip with chips and crackers.
- Mound the purée on a bed of greens. Poke strips of red and green sweet peppers and leaves of endive in the mound for dipping.

Shrimp Remoulade
Serves 12 to 14.

A bowl of shrimp on a buffet table or passed around in a small group disappears before one can reach for seconds. The supply of shrimp can hardly keep up with demand, making shrimp a luxury food. Most of the shrimp available in stores has been frozen, so you should buy shrimp when you are ready to prepare them; do not refreeze.

You may recognize that this recipe is based on one of Craig Claiborne's articles in the *New York Times*. Since I always have Dijon mustard on hand, I use it instead of Creole mustard as suggested. Suit yourself with the other ingredients; a little more or less won't hurt. This recipe is a winner.

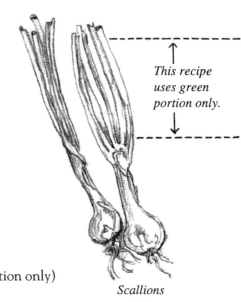

This recipe uses green portion only.

Scallions

4 quarts water
1 bay leaf
2 cloves garlic, smashed
2 teaspoons salt
8 peppercorns
1 lemon (juice and rind)
2 sprigs parsley
¼ cup Creole or Dijon mustard
¼ cup tarragon vinegar
½ teaspoon salt
1 teaspoon freshly ground pepper
1 tablespoon paprika
1 cup olive oil
2 tablespoons prepared horseradish
1 tablespoon finely minced garlic
1 bunch scallions, chopped (green portion only)
1 tablespoon minced Italian parsley
¼ teaspoon Tabasco sauce (you may use less to taste)
2 tablespoons ketchup

2 to 3 pounds cooked shrimp (12 to 16 shrimp to the pound), shelled and halved lengthwise

2 lemons, sliced, for garnish

To cook the shrimp: Boil water with bay leaf, garlic, salt, peppercorns, lemon, and parsley. When the water comes to a boil, add the shrimp. Bring to a boil again and boil for 1 minute. Drain in a colander, running cold water over the shrimp. Peel and devein.

When I use large shrimp, I split each cooked shrimp in half for better bite-sized portions.

Put mustard in a 2-quart bowl. Add vinegar, salt, pepper, and paprika. Beat with a wire whisk until well blended. Gradually add the oil with your other hand as you continue to beat. Stir in all other ingredients except the shrimp and lemon slices.

When the dressing is well mixed, add the shrimp, turning them over in the sauce. Refrigerate for several hours or, for even better flavor, prepare 1 day in advance to allow the seasoning to mellow. When ready to serve, place the shrimp carefully on a large serving platter, one overlapping the other. Garnish with sliced lemon wedges. Pass small plates and forks—this is not a pick-up appetizer.

✹ *Suggestions*

- Use the shrimp for a fancy canapé. Decorate with chopped chives.
- Alternate shrimp with avocado slices at a formal dinner as a first course.

Timbale of Smoked Salmon
Serves 8.

Smoked salmon is an elegant treat, simply served with capers and freshly ground pepper. When it is formed in a timbale with a smidgen of caviar, it is worthy of a celebration.

6 ounces smoked salmon, thinly sliced
1 teaspoon ketchup
1 teaspoon Worcestershire sauce
3 or 4 drops Tabasco sauce
1 cup heavy cream, whipped (light cream may be substituted)
2 ounces fresh salmon caviar
1 cucumber, unpeeled, sliced, and cut into half-round slices

Place a slice of salmon between two sheets of wax paper. Tap it gently to spread the salmon. Line eight 4-inch ramekins on the bottoms and sides with salmon, using as many slices as necessary. Reserve the remainder.

Mince the remaining salmon. Mash well with the ketchup, Worcestershire sauce, and Tabasco sauce. Fold in whipped cream first, then gently fold in 2 tablespoons caviar.

Fill the lined ramekins with the mixture, and refrigerate for a minimum of 2 hours or overnight.

When ready to serve, use a dull knife to loosen the salmon around the sides of the ramekins. Unmold onto individual salad plates. Surround with half-round slices of cucumber. Drop a speck of caviar onto the cucumber slices.

The timbales can be unmolded ahead of time and refrigerated for several hours in advance.

Roberta's Chevre Cheesecake
Serves 20.

Good cheese on a cracker is certainly the easiest appetizer to prepare. Many Americans have acquainted themselves with the great varieties of imported cheeses and frequently use them as hors d'oeuvres.

Here is one outstandingly rich party hors d'oeuvre that you might treasure for a special occasion. Roberta Hershon, Boston food consultant and writer, shared the recipe with me after I praised her Chevre Cheesecake.

Crust
1 tablespoon unsalted butter
3 tablespoons plain bread crumbs
⅛ cup ground walnuts or pecans
⅛ cup freshly grated Parmesan cheese

Filling
1½ pounds preservative-free (if possible) cream cheese at room temperature
8 ounces chevre (Montrachet or other goat cheese)
4 eggs
½ cup heavy cream

Preheat oven to 325°F. Butter a 9-inch springform pan with butter. Cover the entire outside of the pan with heavy aluminum foil to seal it.

Mix the remaining crust ingredients together. Sprinkle them into the pan, turning the pan to coat well. Refrigerate.

Prepare the filling in the bowl of a food processor fitted with the steel blade. Mix cream cheese and chevre until smooth. Add remaining ingredients and blend until well mixed. Pour the mixture into the crust-lined pan.

Set the springform pan in a pan large enough to hold it without the sides touching. Pour enough boiling water into the larger pan to come halfway up the sides of the springform pan. Bake for 1 hour, 20 minutes. After this time, turn the oven off and cool the cheesecake for about 1 hour with the oven door slightly ajar. Transfer the pan to a rack and cool to room temperature. Chill before unmolding, then transfer cheesecake to a serving dish.

You may refrigerate the cheesecake for up to two days. Serve with French bread, crackers, strawberries, grapes, and pear and apple slices.

Fried Wonton Skins
Makes 24 wontons; serves 4 to 6.

There are many luscious and savory fried appetizers, but fried wontons are the easiest and fastest to make. Wonton and egg-roll skins are now available in supermarkets. Take 10 minutes to fry a basketful of crisp pick-ups.

1 package wonton skins
1 quart corn or peanut oil

Make a stack of six or eight wonton skins. Cut them in half to form triangles. Make three cuts the length of the triangle, leaving the corner intact. These cuts form a fancy curl when the wontons are fried.

Heat corn or peanut oil to 375°F. (The heat is right when a cube of white bread toasts in 30 seconds.) If you own a wok, you may use it for frying the wontons, but any deep, heavyweight pot (4- to 5-quart) will do.

Lay out double sheets of paper toweling on the counter. Fry only five or six wonton triangles at a time. Remove to drain on the toweling when fried. Allow to cool. Serve fried wontons in a basket. It will empty fast!

✴ Suggestions

- Fry egg-roll skins in the same way as wontons. Devise different ways to cut the skins to make different shapes—noodles, squares, or larger chips.
- If you are not using the full package of skins within three days, divide into useful amounts. Wrap them in plastic wrap, then in aluminum foil, and freeze for up to two months.
- If you live near an Oriental food shop, look for shrimp chips. They come in different colors, puff up as they fry, and have a distinctive shrimp flavor.

Carpaccio
Serves 10 to 12.

Many years ago, my friend and successful restaurateur, Maria Brigida, took a busman's holiday to Venice, her birthplace. There she became privy to the original recipe for Carpaccio, which she shared with me.

1½ to 2 pounds fillet of beef, trimmed
2 tablespoons sesame oil
1 teaspoon coarsely ground black pepper
1 tablespoon lemon rind
2 teaspoons Worcestershire sauce

Ask your butcher for the center cut of the beef fillet, trimmed well. Heat a skillet and then add oil. Brown the fillet on both sides to sear the surface—just 2 or 3 minutes. Place on a sheet of wax paper and cool.

Rub the fillet with black pepper, lemon rind, and Worcestershire sauce. Wrap in plastic wrap and freeze.

It is easier to cut paper-thin slices when the meat has been frozen and then slightly defrosted. If you are freezing days or weeks before serving, defrost the beef in the refrigerator for 3 or 4 hours. It should still be firm to the touch.

Place sliced beef on individual serving plates or on a platter. Spoon the following sauce on the slices, then shave Parmesan cheese on top.

Sauce for Carpaccio

1 egg yolk, at room temperature
1 teaspoon Dijon mustard
1 teaspoon Worcestershire sauce
¼ teaspoon salt
¼ teaspoon pepper
2 tablespoons lemon juice
2 tablespoons white vinegar
¾ cup olive oil

Whisk the egg yolk with the mustard, Worcestershire sauce, salt, pepper, lemon juice, and vinegar. When the mixture is well combined, gradually mix in oil. If the sauce is being prepared in advance, refrigerate.

✷ *Suggestion*
If you prefer not to use egg yolk in the sauce, substitute ½ cup mayonnaise and reduce oil to ¼ cup.

Recipes for Hot Appetizers

Bagna Cauda
Serves 8 to 10.

Bagna Cauda literally translates to "warm bath." For our purposes it is actually a warm sauce with lots of garlic and a touch of anchovy. Whether it is served fondue style or merely in a heated bowl, it will keep warm while you dip crudités and crusty bread.

    1 cup olive oil
    1 cup whipping cream
    1 or 2 buds garlic (16 to 18 cloves), peeled and sliced
    One 2-ounce can anchovy fillets, rinsed and chopped
    Salt and freshly ground pepper
    Crudités—red and green bell pepper slices, endive leaves, celery ribs, carrot
       sticks
    Chunks of crusty, day-old bread

Cook the oil, ½ cup of the cream, and the garlic at a simmer for at least 30 minutes, stirring occasionally. When the garlic feels mushy when pressed, add anchovies and remaining cream. Continue to cook for about 10 minutes or until mixture is smooth and thickened. Taste, then add salt and freshly ground pepper as needed.

If you are serving fondue style, transfer the sauce to the fondue pot. Arrange crudités and a basket of bread. Heat the sauce in the fondue pot and place over a burner or a candle holder. Otherwise, arrange the crudités and bread in a large, round tray, leaving space in the center for the bowl of hot Bagna Cauda.

Salsa de Jitomate (Tomato Sauce)
Serves 8.

Tortillas, the basic bread of Mexico, make tasty hors d'oeuvres for parties. Our host at a Mexican home served tostaditas, quartered crisp tortillas, with this salsa as well as with cheese, as in Chili con Queso (page 42).

    2 tablespoons oil (corn, peanut, or olive)
    1 onion, minced
    1 clove garlic, minced

2 large tomatoes (about 1 pound), peeled, seeded, and chopped
¼ teaspoon sugar
2 or more fresh serrano chilis (tiny, green, and very hot)
Salt and freshly ground pepper to taste
2 tablespoons chopped fresh coriander leaves (cilantro)
6 tortillas, cut in quarters, fried in oil or broiled for 1 minute
4 ounces Monterey Jack cheese, sliced and divided into 24 pieces

Heat oil. Sauté onion and garlic until limp and not brown. Add tomatoes, sugar, chilis, salt, and pepper. Simmer for 10 to 12 minutes. Taste and adjust seasoning. Add coriander and simmer for another minute.

Place tostaditas on a baking pan. Place a spoonful of sauce on each one and top with a piece of cheese. Pop under the broiler until cheese bubbles. Serve immediately.

Chili con Queso (Chili with Cheese)
Serves 8 to 10.

2 tablespoons oil (corn, peanut, or olive)
1 large onion, minced
2 tomatoes (about 1 pound), peeled, seeded, and chopped
1 green chili, peeled and chopped with seeds (your preference of mild or hot)
Salt and pepper to taste
8 ounces cream cheese
¾ cup cream (either heavy or half-and-half)
¼ teaspoon cayenne pepper (optional)

Heat oil in a 2-quart saucepan. Sauté onion until limp. Add tomatoes and chili. Season with salt and pepper to taste. Cook uncovered for 10 to 15 minutes. Add cheese and stir. When the cheese begins to melt, add cream. Since the green chilis may be fairly mild, the cayenne pepper adds just enough spark. Use at your own discretion. Serve hot or cold as a dip for tostaditas (described in the preceding recipe). Packaged chips may be substituted.

✴ *Suggestions*

- Green Anaheim chilis are not very spicy. They grow in the Southwest and California and are sold in many supermarkets around the country. If you prefer more spice, add a jalapeño pepper. However, beware of the white membranes in the jalapeños—they are even sharper than the seeds.
- Wear gloves when handling hot peppers such as serranos and jalapeños. Be careful never to touch your face and eyes before taking off the gloves or washing your hands.

Crisp Potato Nest
Serves 4.

Crisp Potato Nest has become a signature hot appetizer at our daughter's restaurant. The special piece of equipment used to fry the potatoes is called a bird's-nest fryer, but you can easily improvise with a 4- or 5-inch steel strainer. Serve Crisp Potato Nest as a first course for a special formal dinner. Choose a filling like sautéed onions, leeks, mushrooms, ratatouille, or even the Seafood Maryland (this page).

    5 cups corn oil (or oil of your choice)
    4 all-purpose potatoes (about 1¼ pounds)

Heat oil slowly in a deep, heavyweight saucepan or a fryer. Wash and peel potatoes as the oil heats to 375°F. Use the julienne attachment to the electric food processor or cut the potatoes into fine strips by hand. Blot the potatoes on paper toweling. Line the bowl of a strainer compactly with the strips of potatoes, leaving a cavity in the center.

When the temperature is ready, lower the strainer into the oil. If you are using a single strainer, press the potato with a spoon. When the potato is golden, carefully release it onto the paper toweling. Start again with the next potato.

Make the potato nests hours in advance. They can be refrigerated, if necessary, for up to three days. Reheat in a 250°F oven for 10 minutes. The filling you choose should be piping hot when served in the potato nests. Serve on leaves of ruby or green curly lettuce, or for an especially attractive appetizer, serve the nest on a single leaf of radicchio.

Seafood Maryland
Serves 8.

Imagine, even canned tuna fish is a possible substitution for the elegant crabmeat in this recipe. The seasoning is a typical Baltimore dressing. You will want to use it for hot and cold seafood, as I do. Extend the portions for a superb main course.

    1 pound (about 2 cups) crabmeat or other seafood
    2 tablespoons minced celery
    2 tablespoons minced red or green bell pepper
    2 tablespoons lemon juice
    3 tablespoons mayonnaise
    1 teaspoon Worcestershire sauce

Few drops Tabasco sauce (to taste)
1 tablespoon sherry
Salt and pepper to taste
1 tablespoon minced parsley
2 tablespoons dry, plain bread crumbs

Mix all ingredients, except bread crumbs, in a bowl. Divide mixture into eight scallop shells or small ramekins. Spread bread crumbs on top.

Preheat oven to 400°F. Bake for 10 minutes. Serve at once.

✹ Suggestions

- Use seafood mixture as a filling for crêpes or large pasta shells.
- Add 1 cup Fish Stock (page 61) for a Seafood Pasta Sauce.
- Add 1 tablespoon Chili Pepper Paste (page 27) for a fiery addition.

Shrimp Toast
Serves 8.

Shrimp Toast stretches a small amount of shrimp to serve eight people with very satisfying results.

8 slices white sandwich bread, at least two days old
¾ pound shrimp, shelled and deveined
6 water chestnuts, minced
½ teaspoon salt
¼ teaspoon sugar
1 tablespoon sherry
1 tablespoon cornstarch
1 egg, slightly beaten
2 cups corn or peanut oil

Trim crust from the bread. Cut each slice into two triangles. The drier the bread, the better. If, however, the bread is fresh, dry it in a 200°F oven for about 1 hour.

Mince the shrimp. If you use a food processor, mince by turning the processor on and off quickly. Mix the shrimp, water chestnuts, salt, sugar, sherry, cornstarch, and beaten egg.

Spread 1 tablespoon of the mixture over each triangle. This can be prepared from 6 to 24 hours ahead and refrigerated.

Heat oil in a deep frying pan or a wok to 375°F. (When the oil is hot enough, a ½-inch cube of fresh bread will brown in about 30 seconds.) Lower the triangles gently into the oil, shrimp-side down. Fry less than a minute and turn over until bread is golden brown. Fry only a few at a time. Do not crowd. Drain on paper toweling and serve immediately. However, if necessary, keep toasts warm in a 200°F oven.

✳ *Suggestions*

- Serve Shrimp Toast on a bed of shredded lettuce for a first course.
- Instead of frying, Shrimp Toast may be baked on a cookie sheet in a 400°F oven for 10 minutes. Moisten the top with a dribble of oil.
- Leftovers refrigerate well for up to three days. Reheat on a cookie sheet at 375°F for 10 minutes.
- For a change, substitute ground chicken, turkey, or Duxelles (page 114) and follow the same directions.

Shrimp in Beer Batter
Serves 8 to 12.

Albert Stockli's Shrimp in Beer Batter is on many restaurant menus and in cookbooks. It is with a very warm memory of Albert, who shared many days of his time with me, that I offer it here. Serve small portions for appetizers, but consider this popular favorite for a main course as well.

2 cups all-purpose flour
12 fluid ounces beer
1 teaspoon paprika
1 teaspoon salt
1 quart corn oil
Additional flour and ½ teaspoon salt
2 pounds raw shrimp, shelled

Combine flour, beer, paprika, and salt to make a smooth batter.

Heat corn oil to 375°F. Use a wok or a deep, 6-quart stew pot. Place a sheet of wax paper near the batter, close to the stove. Heap about ½ cup flour on wax paper and add salt.

When the oil is ready, coat the shrimp with flour, dip into the batter, and then fry in the oil. Fry only three or four shrimp at a time. Fry for about 2 minutes until lightly browned. Drain on paper toweling. Place shrimp on a jelly-roll pan and keep warm in a 200°F oven but for no more than 10 minutes before serving. If the shrimp must be cooked ahead, reheat them in a 425°F oven for 2 or 3 minutes. Serve with the Pungent Fruit Sauce (below).

Pungent Fruit Sauce

3 cups orange marmalade
½ cup orange juice
½ cup lemon juice
2 tablespoons prepared horseradish
1 teaspoon ground ginger
1 tablespoon Dijon mustard
Salt and freshly ground pepper to taste

Beat all ingredients by hand or blend in the food processor by turning it quickly on and off for 30 seconds. Although this will make a large amount of sauce, it keeps very well in a cool pantry or refrigerator.

✸ Suggestions

- Add 2 tablespoons each soy sauce, minced candied ginger, and rice vinegar for a Chinese-style sauce.
- Use the same batter for vegetables or pieces of fish.

Blini
Makes 28 to 32.

Blini are known to us as tiny Russian pancakes served with sour cream and fresh caviar, the ultimate in appetizers. Authentically, they are made with yeast and buckwheat flour. Any seasoned griddle works well, but I own one with seven 3-inch sections; it turns out perfectly round pancakes. Although the skillet is Scandinavian style, it is produced in the United States.

½ cup warm water (105° to 115°F)
1 tablespoon or 1 package active dry yeast
1 cup unbleached all-purpose flour
1½ cups buckwheat flour
½ teaspoon salt
2 cups warm milk
3 eggs, at room temperature, separated
3 tablespoons melted butter, cooled
1 tablespoon melted butter for griddle

Pour warm water into a 1-quart bowl. Sprinkle yeast on top and cover with 1 cup all-purpose flour. Do not mix! Set aside for 10 minutes.

Stir in 1 cup buckwheat flour, salt, and 1 cup milk. Cover the bowl with plastic wrap and let rise until the volume is more than doubled (about 1 hour). Beat in the remaining ½ cup buckwheat flour and 1 cup milk; add egg yolks and 3 tablespoons melted butter. Cover the bowl with plastic wrap again, and let rise for about 1 hour.

Whip egg whites until they hold their shape and cling to the sides of the bowl. Fold them into the batter. Cover the bowl again and prepare to fry the Blini.

Heat a griddle or 7-section griddle on low heat for 5 to 7 minutes. Preheat oven to 200°F so the Blini can be kept warm while all are being fried.

Brush the griddle very lightly with butter. Pour about 2 tablespoons batter onto the heated griddle for each pancake. When the top of the pancake bubbles and dries around the edge, turn it over. Remove to a jelly-roll pan and keep warm in the oven. Serve three or four pancakes to each person. Pass sour cream, caviar, or an assortment of smoked fish.

✳ *Suggestion*
You can simplify the recipe by not separating the eggs. After starting the yeast, add all wet and dry ingredients, including the whole eggs, a little at a time, ending with melted butter.

Whetstone Pancakes (Around the Clock)

The American version of Blini enlists both baking powder and baking soda for raising instead of yeast. Why not try these for appetizers as well as breakfast treats? Jean and Harry Boardman, proprietors of the Whetstone Inn in Marlboro, Vermont, keep a Master Flour Mix on hand. Store it in your cupboard (up to two months), ready to use at a minute's notice.

Master Flour Mix
3 cups whole wheat flour (or buckwheat flour for Blini)
3 cups unbleached all-purpose flour
10 teaspoons baking powder
2 teaspoons baking soda
1 teaspoon salt
4 tablespoons sugar

Sift all ingredients together and store in a covered tin or jar.

Pancakes for Four
1 cup Master Flour Mix
1 egg
1¼ cups buttermilk
3 tablespoons oil

Heat a griddle over low heat for 5 minutes. In the meantime, transfer the Master Flour Mix to a 1-quart bowl. In another bowl, lightly beat the egg, buttermilk, and oil together. Gradually add this wet mixture to the bowl containing the flour mix, mixing with a wooden spoon. Do not overbeat. This procedure is faster than opening a box of commercial pancake mix.

Drop the batter by tablespoonfuls onto the heated griddle. When the batter bubbles on top, turn the pancake over to brown the other side. Serve them with a dab of sour cream or yogurt sprinkled with freshly minced herbs.

✸ Suggestions

- Sometimes I substitute blue cornmeal for whole wheat flour. These pancakes are particularly interesting when served with a dribble of Chili Pepper Paste (page 27).
- Add ¼ cup minced fresh herbs to the batter. Serve with Fresh Tomato Salsa (page 29).

French Pancakes (Crêpes)
Makes twenty 5- or 6-inch pancakes or forty 3-inch crêpes.

¾ cup unbleached all-purpose flour
⅛ teaspoon salt
1 teaspoon sugar
3 eggs stirred with 1 cup milk
4 tablespoons unsalted butter, melted

Mix together flour, salt, and sugar in a 1-quart bowl. In another bowl, lightly beat the egg and milk mixture. Gradually add this wet mixture to the bowl containing the flour mix, and then add 2 tablespoons of the melted butter. The batter must be smooth, so if lumps remain, strain the batter. If using the food processor, add flour, salt, and sugar to the bowl. With the metal attachment, run the processor for 15 seconds. Gradually add the combined eggs and milk, then only 2 tablespoons melted butter. In less than a minute, the batter should be smooth. Transfer the batter to a bowl.

When time permits, allow the batter to rest for 1 hour, which results in more tender pancakes. Batter can be stored in the refrigerator in a closed jar or covered container for up to three days.

To make pancakes, bring batter to room temperature if it has been refrigerated. Stir it for smoothness. Lay out some sheets of paper toweling next to the stove.

Heat the appropriate size skillet for your preference of small, medium, or large pancakes. Before you fry the pancakes, crumple a piece of paper toweling, dip it in oil or butter, and use it as a greasing brush for the skillet.

Hold the skillet with one hand and pour a small amount of batter into the skillet with the other hand. Roll the batter around to cover the bottom. It should dry almost immediately. If there is too much wet batter, tilt the skillet to pour excess back into the bowl of batter.

Use a short spatula or kitchen knife. When the pancake looks lightly browned on the underside, turn it over for just 30 seconds. Then turn it out onto the paper toweling. The pancake should fall out. The pan may or may not need greasing each time. Repeat until you have completed the desired number. Leftover batter can be refrigerated for up to three days.

Hors d'oeuvre Fillings for the French Pancakes

Choose from the following fillings for the French Pancakes: grated Cheddar cheese, Fresh Tomato Salsa (page 29), Duxelles (page 114), minced cooked seafood, or Danish Karse Dip (page 33).

Three Ways to Fill Pancakes

Stack 4-6 pancakes with filling between, then cut in wedges to serve.

Roll in thirds with filling inside.

Fold in half then in half again.

Baked Crêpes with Prosciutto and Porcini Sauce

(Crespelle al Forno con Salsa di Prosciutto e Porcini)

Serves 6 to 8.

In 1990 I arranged a gourmet tour to Italy for 11 men and women. In Bologna we had a week of hands-on lessons at the cooking school directed by Mary Beth Clark. Giovanni Greco, chef of Ristorante Alla Grada, was our superb instructor.

One of the highlights of that memorable week was this dome of baked crêpes. It was so good that I made 12 of them last December for the New Year's Eve dinner at our daughter's restaurant. A small wedge of the crespelle was served as one of the first courses.

For the crêpes, use the French Pancakes (Crêpes) recipe. I am sure Giovanni will forgive me. His recipe is almost the same (he used one less egg and an additional ½ cup of milk).

Béchamel Sauce

3 tablespoons unsalted butter
3 tablespoons all-purpose flour
¼ teaspoon freshly ground nutmeg
1½ cups hot milk
¼ cup heavy cream
Salt and freshly ground pepper to taste

Melt butter in a 2-quart saucepan. Add flour and stir to combine, making a roux. Add nutmeg and cook for 2 to 3 minutes, stirring constantly. Pour hot milk into the roux, whisking continuously. (Using hot milk works faster and prevents lumps.) Continue to cook over medium heat, whisking from the bottom and sides, for about 7 to 10 minutes. Pour in cream. Add salt and pepper to taste, and remove the mixture from the heat. Transfer into a bowl. The sauce can be made in advance and refrigerated for up to three days. It may be frozen for a month if you make double for another serving.

Prosciutto and Porcini Sauce

2 tablespoons each olive oil and butter
4 ounces diced prosciutto
1 clove garlic, minced
2 ounces dried porcini mushrooms, soaked and cleaned (reserve liquid)
Freshly ground pepper to taste
½ cup dry white wine
2 tablespoons freshly minced parsley
½ cup freshly grated Parmigiano-Reggiano cheese

Heat 1 tablespoon each oil and butter in a 1-quart saucepan. Sauté prosciutto for 2 to 3 minutes. Transfer to a bowl. Clean saucepan and begin again with 1 tablespoon each oil and butter. Sauté garlic for just 1 minute (do not burn). Add porcini mushrooms and pepper to taste. Pour in wine and add parsley. Simmer for 10 to 15 minutes until only one-fourth of the liquid remains. Combine this sauce with the prosciutto and add a small amount of the reserved porcini liquid. This sauce can also be prepared in advance and refrigerated overnight.

Crespelle

1 recipe French Pancakes (Crêpes)
1 recipe Béchamel Sauce
1 recipe Prosciutto and Porcini Sauce
½ cup freshly grated Parmigiano-Reggiano cheese

Make ten to twelve 8-inch crêpes. If you wish to prepare them a day ahead, slip wax paper between each crêpe as you stack them and cover with plastic wrap. Refrigerate.

To layer the crêpes: Butter a 10- or 12-inch pie pan. Place one crêpe on the bottom of the pan to start. Spread it with 2 or 3 tablespoons Béchamel Sauce, then 1 or 2 tablespoons Prosciutto and Porcini Sauce. Sprinkle about 2 tablespoons grated cheese on top. Place another crêpe on top and repeat the process. At every other crêpe, tear a crêpe into four or five pieces and place it in the center. As you do this the mound in the center will build up to a dome. The top crêpe should cover all. The crespelle will look like a small, round mountain when you are finished.

Spread only Béchamel Sauce on the covering crêpe and sprinkle it with cheese. Reserve any remaining Prosciutto and Porcini Sauce. Layering the crêpes can be done in advance and refrigerated.

Preheat oven to 375°F. Bake the dome of crêpes in the center of the oven for 30 to 35 minutes until uniformly browned. If it is browning too fast, lower the temperature to 350°F. When finished, remove the crespelle from the oven. Use one or two broad spatulas to transfer it to a serving platter. Let it rest before cutting into wedges. Pour any remaining Prosciutto and Porcini Sauce on top.

Crustless Mushroom Quiche
Serves 4.

Mushrooms are a staple in my refrigerator. They set themselves apart as one of the great flavors in cooking.

2 tablespoons oil
3 tablespoons plain bread crumbs

1 clove garlic, minced
1 onion, minced
1 pound mushrooms, wiped clean and quartered
Salt and freshly ground pepper
½ cup crêpe batter, leftover or freshly made (page 48)
¼ cup grated cheese (Cheddar, Parmesan, etc.)
1 tablespoon chopped parsley
1 tablespoon chopped scallions
½ teaspoon paprika
2 egg whites

Preheat oven to 400°F. Grease an 8- or 9-inch quiche pan or shallow casserole with 1 teaspoon oil. Sprinkle bread crumbs on the pan.

Heat a skillet. Add the remaining oil. Sauté garlic and onion for 1 minute. Add mushrooms and sauté to brown quickly. Add salt and pepper to taste. Transfer to a bowl. Stir crêpe batter, cheese, parsley, scallions, and paprika into mushroom mixture.

Beat egg whites with a pinch of salt until they hold their shape and cling to the sides of the bowl. Carefully fold beaten egg whites into the mushroom mixture. Transfer to the oiled, prepared pan. Bake for 15 to 18 minutes until lightly browned. Cut into wedges and serve immediately.

Mozzarella in Carozza
Serves 4.

Melted cheese sandwiches are popular in American households and appear on typical café menus in France as Croque Monsieur. Mozzarella in Carozza, an Italian classic translated to mean "mozzarella in a carriage," is just another version. Serve two triangle halves with caper sauce for appetizers at a formal dinner or quartered triangles for a pick-up hors d'oeuvre.

Caper Sauce
4 tablespoons olive oil or melted butter
1 tablespoon lemon juice
1 tablespoon capers
4 anchovy fillets, minced
¼ teaspoon pepper

Triangles
8 slices bread (square white bread)
2 ounces mozzarella cheese

1 whole egg or 2 egg whites
¼ cup milk
Pinch salt
1 cup oil (corn or your preference for frying)
4 wedges lemon
4 sprigs Italian parsley

Prepare the sauce first. Mix all ingredients in a small saucepan. Set the sauce aside and hold ready to simmer for 2 to 3 minutes just before serving the triangles.

Trim the crusts off the bread slices to make four sandwiches. Slice the cheese to fit neatly inside. Cut each sandwich in half or quarters for triangles to suit your particular occasion. Preheat oven to 200°F.

Beat the whole egg or egg whites with milk and salt until well mixed. Heat oil in a deep skillet or fryer to 350°F. Dip each triangle into the egg mixture, then fry on both sides until golden. Do a few at a time so they fry evenly. Blot on paper toweling. Transfer to a cookie sheet and keep warm in the oven until all pieces are fried.

As an appetizer for a formal dinner, serve two triangles on a heated dish for each person. Spoon the hot caper sauce over each triangle. Garnish with a wedge of lemon and Italian parsley.

For hors d'oeuvres, place the hot sauce for dipping in the center of a tray. Surround it with the small, crisp triangles. Garnish with lemon and parsley.

✳ *Suggestions*

- If you wish to eliminate frying, after dipping the triangles in the batter, place them on an oiled cookie sheet. Bake in a 400°F oven for 10 minutes.
- Consider different fillings—such as Duxelles (page 114), chicken and fish mixtures, sliced smoked meats, and sausage—as substitutes for cheese.

Shredded Spinach and Salad Greens with Warmed Marinated Mushrooms
Serves 6 to 8.

Serve this salad at the table as a first-course appetizer.

Salad
1 pound fresh spinach
1 head romaine or leaf lettuce
1 teaspoon Dijon mustard
3 tablespoons tarragon or wine vinegar
½ teaspoon kosher (coarse) salt

¾ teaspoon freshly ground pepper
½ cup olive oil

Marinated Mushrooms
2 tablespoons lemon juice
2 tablespoons olive oil
2 tablespoons chopped fresh parsley
4 scallions, minced
½ teaspoon each dried thyme and marjoram
Salt and pepper to taste
1 pound mushrooms, sliced

Wash spinach thoroughly and remove all stems. Wash greens. Dry thoroughly. Shred greens and spinach with a sharp knife. Set aside on paper toweling.

Choose a very large salad bowl. Put mustard, vinegar, salt, and pepper at the bottom. Stir well with a fork or small whisk. Add olive oil, whisking constantly.

Pile greens on top of dressing. Do not stir! Cover with paper toweling and refrigerate. Then marinate mushrooms.

Whisk lemon juice, oil, parsley, scallions, herbs, salt, and pepper together in a bowl. Add mushrooms and marinate them at room temperature for a few hours until ready to serve.

When ready, mix salad and divide on individual salad plates. Heat a 10-inch skillet. Sauté mushrooms in the marinade for 2 to 3 minutes. Garnish each salad with the warm mushrooms. Pass the pepper mill.

Unmolded Cheese Soufflés
Serves 8.

There has been an unnecessary and inflated aura surrounding soufflés. Soufflés are one of the most impressive lessons for teachers to demonstrate, especially because students usually report success. I frequently teach Unmolded Cheese Soufflés as a separate lesson to demonstrate two presentations. As an act of dexterity, I enjoy unmolding soufflés at the table. Turning out soufflés in front of guests is a bit of showing off. On the other hand, the following recipe can be prepared several hours or even a day ahead for a handsome presentation with no loss of flavor.

2 tablespoons butter
3 eggs
2 egg whites
1 cup ricotta or cottage cheese
½ cup grated Swiss Gruyère or Cheddar cheese
¼ cup grated Parmesan cheese

½ teaspoon salt
¾ teaspoon freshly ground pepper
½ teaspoon dry mustard
⅛ teaspoon cayenne pepper
½ cup heavy cream
4 tablespoons grated Parmesan cheese

Butter eight 4-ounce china ramekins or Pyrex cups. Place them in a baking pan that is at least 2 inches deep. Place the pan with buttered dishes in the refrigerator.

Separate eggs. Place egg yolks in a 2-quart saucepan. Combine the 3 separated egg whites with the other 2 egg whites in a bowl for beating.

Stir ricotta (or cottage) cheese into egg yolks. Heat over low heat for 2 to 3 minutes, stirring constantly. Add other cheeses and seasonings. Cook over low heat to combine well. Do not be concerned if the mixture is lumpy. Taste and adjust seasoning, if necessary. Remove from heat.

Preheat oven to 400°F. Beat egg whites until stiff. When whites cling to the sides of the bowl, stop beating.

Fold about one-third of the egg whites into the cheese mixture. Then fold the entire mixture into the remaining beaten egg whites.

Remove pan with the ramekins from the refrigerator. Spoon the soufflé mixture into the ramekins almost to the top. Pour hot water into the outer pan halfway up the sides of the ramekins. Place the pan on the stove and bring the water to a simmer. You will see the soufflés rise a bit. Place the pan in the preheated oven for 10 to 12 minutes. The soufflés will rise above the top. Remove the soufflés to a cooling rack.

To unmold: Grease the bottom of a jelly-roll pan or a shallow ovenware dish. Using a small knife, loosen the sides of the soufflés. Turn them over onto the pan, side by side. Cover with greased wax paper until ready to bake, or refrigerate for 24 hours before proceeding.

To serve: Preheat oven to 400°F. Combine heavy cream and 2 tablespoons Parmesan cheese, then spoon mixture over each soufflé. Sprinkle remainder of cheese over all. Bake for 10 minutes or until the tops sizzle and puff. Serve immediately.

Use the same method for preparing dessert soufflés.

✹ *Suggestions*

- If you wish, substitute light cream for heavy.
- The soufflés do not need to be unmolded. They can be served in the ramekins immediately after baking.
- Instead of the cream, use 1 cup Tomato Sauce (page 88).
- Use a 1½-quart soufflé dish for a single large soufflé. Follow the same instructions but bake for 30 minutes at 375°F.

3

Stocks and Soups

I was fortunate to grow up in a household where a busy kitchen and mother's daily cooking were considered the norm. Little did I realize that I was absorbing the many aromas and essences of basic fine cooking. Soups were staples and taken for granted. They were served as one-bowl dinners with chicken, meat, or fish included. There were soups for cold or warm weather, soups for holidays, and special soups that included beans, grains, or noodles.

Broths (or stocks) are the extractions of flavor from combined ingredients. They are the basis for countless soups as well as sauces. In general, soups are economical and nutritious. Even the busiest person can find the time to cook a simple soup. There is never a bit of waste considering the ample refrigeration space and freezing units available in most homes. My freezer has a special shelf for soups, always in reach for a quick, light meal or an unexpected guest.

Although I am committed to exact recipes in this book, personal taste will influence you to make changes. After all, soups are water flavored with meats, fish, and vegetables. All sorts of combinations and seasonings are possible for the creative cook.

Recipes for Stocks

The recipe for Mother's Chicken Soup may be called a stock or a broth. There is actually no difference in meaning. There are, however, the classic white and brown stocks, important because they are the mainstays for a number of soups, sauces, and myriad recipes in classic cuisine.

Most people will resort to cans or cubes for time savers but the results will not be quite the same. Improved canned broths can be agreeably used and freshened with a rib of celery, a diced carrot, and parsley, or they can be added to creamy vegetable purées. Cubes and powdered packets of concentrate are not as satisfactory and tend to be too salty.

Since white and brown stocks simmer away by themselves, they require little attention after the initial preparation. The rewards of homemade stocks are certainly worth the effort. Stocks can be refrigerated for up to three days, boiled again for 20 minutes, then cooled and refrigerated for future use. Better still, divide stock into containers for freezing. I call this my treasure bank for "in-depth" flavors.

Although beef can be used as well, I prefer veal and chicken for white stock. The essence of these meats blends well with all meats, poultry, and even seafood.

Mother's Chicken Soup
Makes 2 quarts.

Homemade chicken soup was the first soup that I knew by taste alone. It was the very first soup that I cooked as a young bride without a recipe. How quickly I learned that too much water would result in a thin flavor and that boiling it down would concentrate the liquid for strength. The chicken in the pot became our dinner as well.

A roaster cooks faster and results in a less concentrated soup but is excellent for a one-dish meal, Chicken in the Pot. A fowl or stewing chicken (hen) needs longer cooking, best for concentrated stocks. Whether for a stock or a main course, Mother's Chicken Soup will serve you well.

One 4- to 5-pound roaster or fowl (whole or in parts)
Extra necks, gizzards, or backs (no livers)
1 tablespoon kosher (coarse) salt
2 to 3 quarts water (or water to cover)
1 onion
1 rib celery
1 large carrot, scrubbed

1 parsnip, peeled
½ teaspoon freshly ground pepper
1 sprig fresh parsley
1 sprig fresh dill (optional)

Place chicken and extra parts, if you have them, in a 6- or 8-quart soup pot. Add salt and enough water to cover the chicken well. Bring to a boil. Skim off the resulting accumulated foam. Add vegetables and seasonings. Add more water, if necessary. Bring to a boil again. Remove accumulated foam again. Wipe around the inside of the pot with paper toweling to remove any residual foam on the sides.

Simmer partially covered for 2 to 3 hours. If the chicken is a roaster, it will be cooked in less than 2 hours. A stewing chicken needs longer cooking but will produce a more concentrated soup.

Remove the chicken to a bowl for other uses. Strain the soup and discard the vegetables. Cool soup rapidly by placing the bowl of strained soup in a pan of ice water. Remove the fat on top when it separates. If time allows, refrigerate the soup until the fat coagulates on top. It is easily removed at this point.

✳ *Suggestion*

Make Chicken in the Pot, a one-bowl meal. After the soup is strained, with fat removed, add fresh sliced carrots, parsnips, small or halved onions, and perhaps leeks. When these vegetables are cooked but still firm, add portions of the reserved cooked chicken. Serve each person chicken, vegetables, and soup in a deep bowl. For this dinner use a 4-pound roasting chicken to serve four.

White Stock
Makes about 4 quarts.

2 pounds veal (any inexpensive cut)
4 pounds veal bones (knuckle or shin sawed in small
    pieces)
3 or 4 pounds necks, gizzards, or chicken carcasses
About 4 quarts cold water to cover well
6 carrots
2 onions
1 rib celery
Bouquet garni
1 leek, split and washed (optional)
8 peppercorns (preferably white)

Bouquet Garni
(Thyme, Bay Leaf and Parsley)

*Fold over and tie together
with string*

*(Cutting ends releases
aroma!)*

Or fill a celery rib.

Place meat and bones in an 8- or 12-quart soup pot. Cover with water and bring to a boil. Pour off water and rinse meat and bones (this first boil reduces the accumulation of foam). Cover meat and bones again with 4 quarts cold water and bring to a boil. Skim and then add all other ingredients, except peppercorns.

Simmer, partially covered. If the liquid reduces, add another cup cold water. Bring to a boil and skim again for a clear broth. Simmer for 5 or 6 hours. Add peppercorns for the last hour of cooking.

Set the pot aside to cool, uncovered. Use the meat for a salad if it is not too soft; otherwise discard it with the vegetables. Strain the broth through a strainer lined with cheesecloth. Refrigerate or freeze the broth in amounts for your preferred use. Fat can easily be removed when it hardens.

✳ Suggestions

- Retrieve the veal knuckle before straining the broth. Veal knuckle contains gelatin, which takes 8 to 10 hours to dissolve. Refrigerate or freeze the veal knuckle to be used in another stock.
- Cool stock quickly by placing the pot in the sink filled with cold water. Always cool stock uncovered.
- Collect necks and gizzards of chickens and turkeys. Freeze them for additions to your stock pot.

Brown Stock
Makes 2 to 3 quarts.

3 to 4 pounds shin of beef with meat on it
4 pounds beef bones (sawed into small pieces)
Extra chicken backs or frames, necks, and gizzards
2 onions, unpeeled and quartered
3 carrots, sliced on the diagonal
2 ribs celery, diced
4 to 6 mushrooms, sliced
5 or 6 quarts water to cover
2 ripe tomatoes, fresh or canned
2 or 3 large garlic cloves
Bouquet garni
10 black peppercorns

Preheat oven to 475°F. Place beef shin and beef bones on a shallow baking pan. Place chicken parts, onions, carrots, celery, and mushrooms on another shallow roasting pan. Dividing parts and vegetables into two pans ensures even browning. Roast in the oven until well browned, but be sure to stir occasionally so the vegetables do not burn. In the meantime, boil 4 quarts water in a 12-quart soup pot.

When the meat and vegetables are browned, transfer beef and beef bones to the boiling water. Ladle some boiling water into the browned pan. Scrape the pan to remove all crusted, browned bits (it will also help to clean the pan). Pour all into the soup pot. Repeat with the second pan.

Add tomatoes, garlic, bouquet garni, and 1 cup cold water. Bring to a boil. Remove any scum, and simmer partially covered for about 4 hours. As the stock cooks, the liquid may evaporate below the bulk. Add just enough water to cover. Skim as much as possible for a clear, glossy stock. Add peppercorns in the last 30 minutes of cooking.

✳ *Suggestions*

- Many fine cooks and restaurant chefs will use other types of meat, veal knuckles, and bones of veal instead of beef. These meats require very long cooking (up to 12 hours), but they produce a stock with a gelatinous consistency and a beautiful brown gloss.
- Notice that salt is omitted in stocks. It can be added as personal tastes require. Salt is also omitted because when the stocks are further reduced for sauces, they become too salty.
- Ends of ham, rinds of pork fat, and parboiled bacon enhance flavor and color. They may be added when browning the meat.

Fish Stock
Makes 2 quarts.

3 to 4 pounds fish bones and heads of lean, white-fleshed fish
1 tablespoon unsalted butter or oil
1 rib celery, sliced
1 onion, sliced
1 carrot, scrubbed and sliced
¼ pound mushrooms (leftover stems will do)
8 cups cold water
2 cups white wine or ½ cup mild vinegar
2 teaspoons salt
Bouquet garni

Wash the fish bones and heads in cold water. Be sure that gills and livers have been removed.

Use a 4- to 6-quart soup pot. Heat butter or oil, and sauté celery, onion, carrot, and mushrooms for just 2 to 3 minutes. Add fish, water, wine or vinegar, salt, and bouquet garni. Bring to a boil and simmer partially covered for 25 minutes.

Strain broth and discard the bulk. For future use, refrigerate the stock for up to three days or freeze for up to three months.

Vegetable Stock
Makes 1½ quarts.

Vegetable stock is very useful as an addition to creamed puréed soups and as a base for poaching small cuts of meat or fish. Most often, economical cooks save broth as they cook daily vegetables. Be careful not to include vegetables from the strong-flavored group—the broccoli and cabbage family.

1 tablespoon olive oil
2 onions, unpeeled, washed, and quartered
2 ribs celery, diced
2 carrots, scrubbed and diced
Stems of mushrooms, if you have them
1 leek, split and washed well
Bouquet garni
2 quarts water

Heat oil in a 4- or 6-quart pot. Sauté onions, celery, carrots, and mushroom stems for a few minutes, just until glazed, not browned. Add leek, bouquet garni, and water. Bring to a boil and simmer for 45 minutes, partially covered.

Strain. Discard vegetables. Cool, then divide into containers for refrigerator or freezer.

✹ *Suggestions*

- The oil and initial sautéing can be omitted but the broth will not be as flavorful.
- If you cook the broth in larger amounts and freeze it, you will always have a wonderful base for poached breast of chicken and poached fish.
- Salt and pepper are omitted in the recipe, to be added to taste when the broth is used.

❧❧❧

Recipes for Soups

Matzo Ball Soup
Serves 6 to 8.

Mother's Chicken Soup can be garnished with fine noodles, rice, and julienne-sliced leeks and carrots, but matzo balls are truly the best of all garnishes.

The recipe for Matzo Ball Soup was handed down from my husband's grandma. Most recipes call for simmering the dumplings in water. Cooking them in soup gives them a richer flavor, but it also diminishes the soup. When I use soup for cooking the matzo balls, I always make a double quantity. An auxiliary pot of soup simmers on the back burner for ample helpings.

> ½ matzo square, broken up and soaked in ½ cup water until soft
> 2 tablespoons rendered chicken fat
> 3 eggs
> ½ cup matzo meal
> 1 teaspoon kosher (coarse) salt
> ½ teaspoon white pepper
> 3 quarts water, chicken soup, or a combination
> 2 quarts Mother's Chicken Soup (page 58)

Press most of the water from the soaked matzo, leaving it slightly wet.

Using a 1-quart bowl, soften the chicken fat. Beat in the eggs, one at a time, then add matzo meal, wet matzo, and seasonings. Cover with aluminum foil and refrigerate for at least 8 hours or for up to 2 days.

When ready to cook, bring water or soup to a boil. Lower heat to simmer. Moisten your hands in cold water. Form balls (about 1½ inches) of the cold matzo mixture, one at a time, dropping each one gently into the simmering liquid. Cover the pot and simmer for 20 to 25 minutes.

Bring Mother's Chicken Soup to a boil. Serve two to three matzo balls with each bowl of soup.

Wonton Soup
Serves 6.

For a quick change from West to East, you can easily convert Mother's Chicken Soup to Chinese Wonton Soup. Some may wish to make their own dough, but supermarkets are well stocked with Chinese food products so wontons can become a staple in your kitchen.

½ pound ground pork (you may substitute beef, veal, chicken, or even fish)
1 tablespoon dry sherry
1 tablespoon soy sauce
¼ teaspoon sugar
18 wonton skins (the dough wrappings are called "skins")
4 quarts water
2 quarts Mother's Chicken Soup (page 58)
1 cup greens (escarole, bok choy, watercress, mustard greens, or scallions, chopped or sliced)
Soy sauce to taste

Mix pork, sherry, soy sauce, and sugar. Place a small bowl of water to the side of your work area. Place less than a teaspoon of the mixture in the center of a wonton skin. Dip your finger in the bowl of water, and moisten all around the edges of the wonton(A). Fold the wonton skin into a triangle, enclosing the filling, and seal the edge(B). Bring the two outer points of the triangle together and fasten one around the other by pinching them together(C).

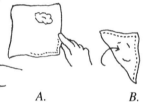

A.   *B.*   *C.*

Boil 4 quarts water. At the boiling point, add the wontons. Bring to a boil again. The wontons will float to the surface. Add 1 cup cold water and bring to a boil. This last boil makes sure that the filling is cooked. The wontons are ready when they float to the surface again. Drain and set aside.

Bring Mother's Chicken Soup to a boil. Add greens and season with soy sauce to your taste. Drop in wontons gently, and simmer for 3 minutes before serving.

✳ *Suggestions*

- Cubed tofu may be added.
- Use leftover wontons for a side dish. Brown them in a skillet with oil, minced garlic and ginger, soy sauce, and sherry.

Consommé
Serves 6 to 8.

8 ounces very lean ground beef
1 onion, diced

1 carrot, peeled and diced
1 egg white, slightly beaten
1 eggshell
6 peppercorns
2 quarts White Stock (page 59) or Brown Stock (page 60);
   without fat

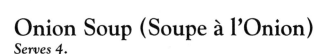

If possible, use a tall 5- to 6-quart soup pot with a small circumference. Mix beef with vegetables in the pot. Add egg white, eggshell, peppercorns, and broth.

Bring to a boil, stirring constantly. When the broth starts to boil, remove the pot to the side to stop boiling. Lower heat and simmer again for 30 minutes, uncovered. Do not stir.

Strain through triple cheesecloth without stirring. Reheat and season with salt, if necessary. Serve piping hot. Pass a decanter of Madeira or port wine around the table for an elegant touch.

Onion Soup (Soupe à l'Onion)
Serves 4.

Three important flavoring vegetables—onion, celery, and carrot—are used repeatedly in soups and stews. Concentrating on the onion in the world-famous Onion Soup is a lesson in itself. Learn to peel and cut an onion. Watch it become limp, sweat, and then brown on heating. The sugar in the onion will caramelize the color. Be careful—do not allow the onion to burn!

4 Spanish or red onions (about 2 pounds), thinly sliced
2 to 4 tablespoons unsalted butter or oil
5 cups Brown Stock, homemade (page 60) or canned
½ cup dry white or red wine
Four ½-inch slices French bread, toasted
6 ounces Swiss Gruyère cheese, thinly sliced to cover each soup bowl
½ cup freshly grated Parmesan cheese

Use a 5- or 6-quart stew pot. Heat butter or oil and add onions. Allow onions to glaze and brown slowly over medium heat, with pot partially covered. This process may take 15 or 20 minutes. If you wish to omit butter or oil, place onions in the heated pot, without the butter or oil, and cover. The water in the onions will bring up steam and the sugar in the onions will glaze them. Check frequently to make sure they do not burn. Stir occasionally.

In the meantime, heat stock. When the onions are browned, add wine to deglaze the onions and extract all color. Add 1 cup stock and reduce over heat for 2 or 3 minutes. Add the remaining stock. Simmer for 20 minutes.

Preheat oven to 400°F. Place four ovenproof soup bowls on a jelly-roll pan. Set one slice of toast in each bowl. Pour the soup over the toast. Top with Gruyère cheese and a sprinkling of Parmesan. Bake for 5 minutes or until the cheese is bubbling. Serve immediately.

✳ Suggestions

- The soup may be prepared up to three days in advance and reheated before adding the cheeses and baking in the oven.
- The toast will be more delicious if rubbed with garlic and baked or sautéed in butter or oil, instead of toasting.
- Onion soup is delicious served piping hot out of the pot, with merely the garnish of toast. Also, the basic peasant soup is cooked with water rather than broth. Why not try vegetable broth?
- For a spectacular finish, top the soup with a soufflé. To make a sauce, melt 1 tablespoon butter and stir in 1 tablespoon flour. Add ½ cup warm milk and salt and pepper to taste, whisking well until thick. Remove from heat. Beat 2 egg whites with a pinch of salt until stiff. Fold egg whites and ¼ cup grated Parmesan cheese into the sauce. Spoon mixture on top of each bowl of soup before baking at 425°F for 5 minutes.
- If you buy Parmesan and Gruyère by the pound, always save the rind. It is pure cheese. Simmer it in water or broth for 20 minutes. Add the cheese-flavored liquid to onion soup or other soups.

Carrot Soup
Serves 6 to 8.

There are many good methods for creating creamed soups. Generally, we call them creamed, but it is a misnomer because so often they look and taste creamed with barely a touch of cream. Some soups are based on puréed vegetables. Thanks to the food processor, the "creamy" texture is achieved in minutes (be cautious when using a food processor to purée potatoes—they may become gluey in the machine). Some creamed soups are achieved with a small amount of flour-thickened sauce, such as Béchamel Sauce (page 82) or Sauce Velouté (page 83), or cooked with rice or potato for texture. No one will contest the fact that an appropriate amount of cream added to any of these soups borders on perfection.

2 tablespoons unsalted butter or oil
1 onion, diced

6 medium carrots (about 1 pound), scrubbed and sliced
2 tablespoons flour
3 cups chicken stock, homemade or canned
Bouquet garni
½ teaspoon salt
Freshly ground pepper

Melt butter or heat oil in a 4-quart soup pot. Add onion and cook over low heat for 3 to 4 minutes. Add carrots and continue to cook until glazed, about 3 minutes.

Stir in flour and cook for a minute. Add chicken stock, stirring well. (If canned stock is used, substitute water for 1 cup stock.) Add bouquet garni and salt. Cover and simmer for 30 minutes.

Taste for additional salt and add freshly ground pepper. Discard bouquet garni. Use a food processor to purée the soup. If the soup is too thick for your personal taste, add more stock, water, milk, or light cream.

✸ *Suggestions*

- Use this recipe for vegetables other than carrots. Make use of the tough ends of asparagus. Use a combination of lettuce greens. In some cases you can use 1 cup leftover cooked vegetables (cauliflower, broccoli, spinach, peas, and so on), plus 1 onion, 1 carrot, and 2 cups broth or water.
- Experiment with different seasonings by adding, for example, a touch of nutmeg, curry, or cumin. Add fresh herbs in season or dried herbs in the colder months.

Leek and Potato Soup
Serves 8 to 10.

This Leek and Potato Soup deserves its great popularity. Even though the leek should be celebrated on its own merits, in soups it adds flavor without being intrusive. Leeks are used extensively in Europe, so supply and demand bring prices to a normal level. Here in the United States, however, leeks are a luxury item, reasonably priced only in the summer when they can be obtained from local farms. If you prefer using leeks in all your broths, as I do, buy them in large quantities when they are readily available or grow them in your own garden. Wash and dry them thoroughly. Package for the freezer.

Leek and Potato Soup is also known as Parmentier, named after the

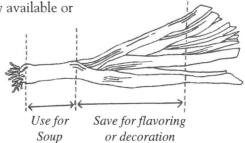

Use for Soup   *Save for flavoring or decoration*

eighteenth-century agronomist who introduced potatoes to the French. The early Romans held that leeks improved the clarity of the voice. This soup is frequently served in our daughter's restaurant because it is her father's favorite.

    2 tablespoons unsalted butter or oil
    1 onion, diced
    4 to 5 leeks, diced (about 2½ cups)
    4 potatoes (about 1 pound), peeled and sliced
    1 carrot, scraped
    1 sprig fresh parsley
    1 sprig fresh dill
    4 cups chicken stock (homemade or canned) or water
    Salt and freshly ground pepper to taste
    1 tablespoon minced fresh chives and parsley

Melt butter or heat oil in a 4-quart soup pot. Add onion and leeks. Cook for about 5 minutes, until vegetables are glazed, not browned. Add potatoes, carrot, parsley, dill, and stock. Cover and cook for 35 to 40 minutes.

It is preferable to purée the mixture through a food mill. If you use a food processor, work it off and on. Sometimes potatoes acquire a pasty texture when they are beaten too long in the processor. Taste and adjust seasoning. Homemade stock will probably require salt, whereas canned broth will not. Return soup to soup pot and heat. Serve with a sprinkling of chives and parsley.

✹ Suggestions

- Vichyssoise is the cold version of leek and potato soup. Chill the soup well. Thin it with 1 or 2 cups light cream. Garnish with chopped chives. Calorie counters can thin with broth and garnish it with a spoonful of yogurt.
- Leeks and potatoes simmered in stock are excellent vegetables for poached fish or boiled beef dinners.
- For a lighter soup, either hot or cold, substitute cucumber and omit potatoes. Garnish with sour cream or yogurt.

Tomato Bisque with Orange
Serves 8 to 10.

If you grow tomatoes or live near a farm, you can cook this Tomato Bisque as a seasonal soup. Fresh, ripened-on-the-vine tomatoes should be used for best results. Bisques are traditionally associated with seafood, and this soup has something of that texture.

3 tablespoons unsalted butter or oil
2 onions (about 1 pound), diced
2 ribs celery, sliced
2 cloves garlic, minced
2 large carrots, diced
¾ teaspoon cumin
¼ teaspoon cinnamon
4 tablespoons flour
8 cups ripe tomatoes, quartered
2 seedless oranges, peeled and diced
1 cup water
2 sprigs parsley
1 bay leaf
½ teaspoon thyme
⅛ teaspoon cayenne pepper
3 tablespoons brown sugar
1 cup light cream or yogurt
Salt and pepper to taste
Thinly sliced orange for garnish

Heat butter or oil in a 6-quart soup pot. Add onions, celery, and garlic. Cook until the onions wilt. Stir in carrots, cumin, and cinnamon. Cook for 3 to 4 minutes, stirring constantly.

Mix in flour and continue to cook for 2 to 3 minutes. Add tomatoes, oranges, water, parsley, bay leaf, thyme, and cayenne pepper. Bring the mixture to a boil. Lower heat and simmer partially covered for 40 minutes.

Strain through a Foley food mill or sieve into another pot. Add brown sugar. Stir in cream or yogurt. Taste and adjust seasoning with salt and pepper. Serve piping hot with a slice of orange on each serving.

✳ *Suggestions*

- Omit the sugar. Season with ¼ teaspoon red pepper flakes and 1 teaspoon Worcestershire sauce. Add ½ cup crabmeat or minced cooked shrimp for a Seafood Tomato Bisque.
- In the height of fresh corn season, add 2 cups corn kernels (I use leftovers from cobs). Add a touch of curry powder.

Garden Vegetable Soup
Serves 8 to 10.

Although our markets offer more and more vegetables out of season, you will be the judge of which ones you prefer. Omit, substitute, or add as you desire. Vegetable soups are fun to cook when you can create your own combinations. Use the following as a guide.

2 tablespoons unsalted butter or oil
1 cup diced onion
1 cup diced carrots
½ cup diced celery
2 to 3 potatoes (about 8 ounces), peeled and diced
½ cup diced leeks (when available)
1 cup diced green beans or peas
6 cups chicken or vegetable stock (canned broth, if used, should be diluted)
¼ teaspoon ground cumin
Bouquet garni
1 cup milk or light cream (optional)
Salt and freshly ground pepper to taste

Heat butter or oil in a 5- or 6-quart soup pot. Cook onion until glazed, then add all the vegetables. Cook for a few minutes, stirring occasionally. Add stock, cumin, and bouquet garni. Bring to a boil, then simmer partially covered for 30 minutes.

Purée soup in the food processor. Add milk or cream if desired. More may be added if a thinner consistency is preferred. Adjust seasoning with salt and pepper.

✹ Suggestions

For Five-Day Vegetable Soup, make the following changes to Garden Vegetable Soup.

First day: Do not purée soup. Serve soup with diced vegetables.

Second day: Add to the puréed soup ½ cup each diced parsnips, green beans, and zucchini with additional stock or water.

Third day: Purée soup and serve with croutons and cheese.

Fourth day: Add milk or cream to the puréed soup to preferred consistency; serve chilled.

Fifth day: For texture, add shredded greens, spinach, peas, corn, or green beans to the creamed soup. Readjust liquid and seasoning.

Seventy-Calorie Vegetable Soup
Makes 10 cups (70 calories per cup).

   1 tablespoon unsalted butter or oil
   1 onion, diced
   2 carrots, peeled and diced
   2 ribs celery, diced
   ½ cup vegetables (yellow squash, zucchini, peas)
   1 potato, peeled and diced
   One 28-ounce can tomatoes
   1 quart stock (chicken, white, brown, or vegetable)
   Sugar, salt, and pepper to taste
   ½ cup orzo (rice-shaped pasta found in specialty food stores)
   1 tablespoon chopped fresh parsley

Heat butter or oil in a 6-quart soup pot. Sauté onion until glazed, not browned. Add all vegetables and stock. Bring to a boil. Cover and simmer for 30 minutes.

Taste and season with sugar, salt, and pepper. Very often canned tomatoes need a touch of sugar, and salt content will vary with the product. Add orzo and cook for 5 minutes. The soup can be prepared ahead and reheated, with orzo added just before serving. Garnish with chopped parsley.

Soupe au Pistou
Serves 10 to 12.

Soupe au Pistou is both a soup and a meal. The pistou, a basil sauce, is essentially the French version of the Italian pesto. Notice the added touch of tomato. Cook this soup wherever you are as long as you can obtain the best fresh vegetables.

Pistou
   4 cloves garlic
   ½ teaspoon salt
   ¼ cup chopped fresh basil or ½ teaspoon dried basil
   4 to 6 tablespoons olive oil
   ¼ cup tomato purée
   ½ cup freshly grated Parmesan cheese

Soup
   1 cup dry white beans (northern, navy, or small kidney)
   4 cups water

½ cup olive oil
1 cup diced onion
2 cups ripe tomatoes, peeled and coarsely chopped
4 quarts water
1 tablespoon salt
2 cups each diced carrots, leeks, and potatoes
1 cup chopped celery, with leaves
2 cups each diced green beans and zucchini
¼ cup broken vermicelli
⅛ teaspoon powdered saffron
¼ teaspoon freshly ground pepper
1 cup freshly grated Parmesan cheese

Prepare the pistou first. Pound garlic with salt to make a smooth paste. (Use a mortar and pestle or a bowl and wooden spoon.) Mash in basil alternately with olive oil. Use the food processor, on and off, if you like, to this point. Remove to a bowl and stir in tomato purée and Parmesan cheese. You may want to double the recipe if you prefer more seasoning in the soup or if you wish to store it for future use. It can be refrigerated for up to three days or frozen for up to two months.

Wash beans and bring them to a boil in water. Boil for 2 to 3 minutes. Cover. Turn off heat and allow to soak for 1 hour. Bring to a boil again and simmer partially covered for 1 to 1½ hours or until beans are tender. Drain beans and reserve liquid. (For another method, soak beans overnight in enough water to cover, then simmer and drain, reserving the liquid.)

Heat oil in an 8-quart soup pot. Add onion and cook until it turns golden. Stir in tomatoes; boil briskly and stir. Add water and salt, and again bring the mixture to a rolling boil. Mix in carrots, leeks, potatoes, and celery, and cook for 15 minutes at a simmer. Add green beans, zucchini, vermicelli, saffron, and pepper. Simmer again until the vegetables are cooked. Add drained beans, using reserved cooking liquid only if the soup needs thinning.

Just before serving, ladle ½ cup soup into a small bowl. Beat into it one-half of the pistou, and stir the mixture back into the soup. Taste and adjust seasoning. Pour soup into a heated tureen and serve. Pass the remaining pistou and Parmesan cheese separately. Pass around hot French bread or hard-toasted bread rounds (fried or toasted in olive oil).

Beet Borscht
Serves 6 to 8.

I know it is time for Borscht when my husband displays a broad smile and hands me a basketful of garden beets. Borscht is universally considered one of the great soups, whether served hot or cold. What a bonus to know that beets are healthful as well! Borscht, the national soup of Russia, is cooked differently in every part of that vast country.

6 medium beets (about 1 pound)
3 cups water
3 tablespoons sugar
½ teaspoon salt
1 teaspoon sour salt (citric acid), or ¼ cup lemon juice plus salt to taste
Garnish of small boiled potatoes and sour cream

Scrub beets well. I prefer not to peel them before cooking. Cook them in about 3 cups water (or enough to cover the beets) for 25 to 30 minutes or until tender.

Strain the liquid into a bowl. Transfer the beets to another bowl. Pour beet liquid into a pot, being careful not to include any sand that may have settled to the bottom. Add sugar, salt, and sour salt (or lemon juice) and heat slightly until the seasoning has dissolved.

Remove the skins of the beets (they will slip off easily). Slice beets by hand in julienne style, or use a processor with the appropriate attachment. Add sliced beets to the liquid in the pot. Taste to adjust seasoning with a balance of sugar, salt, or lemon juice.

Serve Borscht hot with small boiled potatoes and sour cream on top, or refrigerate and serve very cold with the same garnishes.

Mushroom Barley Soup
Serves 8 to 10.

Even though I use whole turkeys throughout the year, the Thanksgiving turkey is always used to the last drop—of bone. The carcass makes a strong broth and then becomes the basis of our Mushroom and Barley Soup.

1 roasted turkey carcass (or other cooked poultry parts)
3 to 4 quarts water (depending on size of the carcass)
Bouquet garni
1 ounce dried mushrooms
½ cup barley
1 cup each diced onion, celery, carrot, and potato
1 pound fresh mushrooms, diced
Salt and freshly ground pepper to taste

Place turkey carcass, whole or broken up, into a 6- to 8-quart soup pot. Cover with water. Add bouquet garni. Bring to a boil and simmer uncovered for 1 hour.

In the meantime, soak dried mushrooms and barley, separately, in enough hot water to cover each. The water can be used in the soup, but watch for sand in the mushroom bowl.

Strain the turkey broth and discard bones. There should be about 2 quarts of broth.

Combine the remaining ingredients with the broth in the same pot. Simmer for 40 to 50 minutes. Season to taste with salt and pepper.

✹ *Suggestions*

- The choice of vegetables (you might add parsnip and turnip, for example) and the amount of broth is flexible. Dried mushrooms and barley are essential ingredients, however.
- Substitute chicken stock or canned broth for the cooked turkey carcass stock.

Pumpkin-Lentil Soup
Serves 8 to 10.

In the early 1960s I introduced Pumpkin Soup to our family at the Thanksgiving table. I brought it to the table in a scooped-out pumpkin used as a tureen. The children loved the idea and everyone enjoyed the soup. The lentils in combination with the pumpkin add another dimension for taste and nutrition.

        2 to 4 tablespoons unsalted butter or olive oil
        2 large onions, diced
        1 rib celery, sliced
        1 carrot, sliced
        ½ cup lentils, rinsed in water
        5 cups chicken stock
        1½ cups cooked or canned pumpkin
        ¼ teaspoon marjoram
        ⅛ teaspoon thyme
        ¼ teaspoon freshly ground pepper
        Dash Tabasco sauce
        1 cup half-and-half (optional)
        Salt to taste

Melt butter or heat oil in a soup kettle. Add onions and cook until lightly colored but not browned. Add celery and carrot; cook for another minute. Stir in lentils and chicken stock. Add pumpkin, herbs, pepper, and Tabasco. Simmer about 1 hour.

Allow to cool, then purée in a food processor. At this time, the soup can be refrigerated for up to three days or frozen for up to two months.

Add half-and-half when you reheat the soup before serving. Adjust seasoning.

✳ *Suggestions*

- The pumpkin may be used as a tureen. Cut across the pumpkin 2 inches below the top. Scoop out the seeds and pulp. Warm the pumpkin in a 300°F oven for 5 minutes before filling with soup. Use the pumpkin top as a cover. Serve at the table, ladling out portions.
- Of course, Pumpkin-Lentil Soup is delicious year-round. Add tiny meatballs for a one-bowl dinner.
- Since lentils contain a fair amount of protein, this soup is a favorite with vegetarians. Substitute Vegetable Stock (page 62) or water for cold chicken stock.
- Additions of rice or canned corn niblets are interesting variations.

Cuban Black Bean Soup
Serves 8 to 10.

Lillian and Peter Zilliacus were innkeepers and our first friends in Vermont. Thirty years later, they are still our dear friends and the memories of their dinners years ago remain with us. Peter's Cuban Black Bean Soup is an exception to his otherwise very delicate classic cuisine.

    1 pound black turtle beans
    2 quarts water
    2 tablespoons salt
    ½ cup olive oil
    1 onion (about ½ pound), diced
    2 green peppers (about ½ pound), seeded and diced
    5 cloves garlic
    ½ tablespoon cumin seeds
    2 tablespoons dried oregano
    ¼ cup white vinegar
    1 quart additional water, if necessary

Wash black beans in cold water. Add beans to a 6-quart soup pot. Add water to cover the beans. Boil for a few minutes. Remove from heat and allow to soak for 1 hour. (For another method, soak beans in water overnight.) Add more water if necessary. Season with salt, and simmer partially covered until the beans are very tender, possibly 2 to 3 hours.

While the beans are simmering, sauté the onions and green peppers in olive oil until the onions are lightly browned.

Crush garlic, cumin seeds, and oregano by hand or in a food processor. Mix the seasonings with white vinegar and add to the sautéed onions and green peppers. Cook together on low heat for 5 minutes.

Stir the seasoning mixture into the cooked black beans and simmer for 10 minutes, stirring occasionally. Purée three-fourths of the mixture using a food mill or processor, but save the remainder to be added for texture. Return the purée to the pot and warm over low heat. If it is too thick, add more water. Serve hot with a spoonful of rice garnish (see below).

Rice Garnish

¼ cup minced onions
½ cup cold cooked rice
½ cup olive oil
2 teaspoons white vinegar

Marinate onions and rice in olive oil and vinegar. Reserve until ready to serve.

✳ Suggestions

- An alternate garnish for Cuban Black Bean Soup is sliced hard-cooked egg and lemon.
- Use the Cuban Black Bean Soup recipe for a casserole. Reduce the amount of water and allow it to evaporate. The casserole without meat is vegetarian, a full meal and nutritionally balanced if served with rice. Add sausage, parts of roast chicken, or duck, if desired.

New England Clam Chowder
Serves 8 to 10.

Clam chowders are among the best of our American soups, provided the clams are fresh and plentiful. New England clam chowder is my favorite, but my husband likes Manhattan Clam Chowder as well, so I cook both.

3 to 4 dozen cherrystone clams
½ pound salt pork or slab bacon, cut into ½-inch dice
3 onions (about 1 pound), thinly sliced
2 leeks, diced
2 ribs celery, diced
1 large carrot, diced
2 potatoes, diced
½ teaspoon thyme (or 1 sprig fresh thyme)
1 sprig parsley

1 bay leaf
½ teaspoon dry mustard
½ teaspoon freshly ground pepper
2 cups water
2 tablespoons unsalted butter
2 tablespoons flour
3 cups scalded milk or light cream

Scrub clams with a stiff brush to clean thoroughly. Place clams in a pot with just ½ inch of water, cover, and simmer. Shake pot occasionally for 3 to 5 minutes or until the clams open (discard any that do not open). Remove clams; allow clam broth to settle (any sand will settle to the bottom). Dice clams coarsely and set aside. Strain the clam broth.

In a soup pot, fry salt pork or slab bacon to render fat. Add onions and sauté until the onions are golden. Add leeks, celery, carrot, and potatoes. Sauté all for 2 to 3 minutes. Remove salt pork or bacon, if you wish. Add seasonings and water. Cook for 10 minutes or until potatoes are tender.

In a small saucepan, melt butter, add flour, and stir to make a roux. Add a small amount of milk or cream to make a smooth paste, and then add the remainder. Add the mixture to the vegetables. Stir in clam broth and clams. Bring all to a simmer and serve hot.

☀ Suggestions

- Substitute ¼ cup olive or corn oil for the salt pork or bacon, if you wish. Salt pork and bacon are the traditional fats used in the chowder.
- For Manhattan Clam Chowder, omit butter, flour, and milk. Add 2 cups crushed tomatoes to the sautéed vegetables, clam broth, and clams. Bring to a simmer. Serve piping hot.

Oyster Bisque Parisienne
Serves 4 to 6.

Many years ago I taught this Oyster Bisque recipe in a chafing dish class. It can be fun to cook in front of a few guests. Choose a sturdy table and a proper chafing dish.

1 pint fresh shucked oysters
2 cups chicken stock
1 medium onion, minced
2 ribs celery with leaves, minced
½ cup plain bread crumbs

2 sprigs parsley
1 sprig fresh thyme (or ¼ teaspoon dried)
1 whole clove
2 cups hot half-and-half
Salt and freshly ground pepper to taste
Dash freshly grated nutmeg
Croutons (toasted slices of French bread)

Strain oysters over a soup pot. Add chicken stock, onion, celery, bread crumbs, parsley, thyme, and clove to oyster liquor in the soup pot. Simmer covered for 30 minutes.

Strain soup into a bowl and then return the strained soup to the pot. When ready to serve, heat soup. Add oysters and hot half-and-half. Bring to a simmer. Taste and adjust seasoning with salt and pepper. Add a dash of nutmeg and serve immediately. Pass the croutons around the table.

Cheese Soup from Uri
Serves 4 to 6.

My neighbor, Hannie Ramsey, is a native of Basel, Switzerland. She remembers this Cheese Soup from Uri (a canton in central Switzerland) as a basic family lunch dish. She cautions that aged Gruyère or Cheddar should be used. A young cheese becomes stringy when cooked at too high a temperature and does not melt properly.

1 tablespoon unsalted butter
5 tablespoons flour
3½ cups warm water
1 tablespoon caraway seeds
1 clove garlic
1 cup milk
1½ cups grated Swiss Gruyère or aged Cheddar
½ teaspoon grated nutmeg
Salt and pepper to taste

Melt butter in a 3-quart soup pot. Add flour and stir with a spoon for several minutes until the mixture becomes slightly brown. Take off heat; whisk in water. Return to heat, and keep whisking until mixture thickens and boils.

Add caraway seeds and garlic. Simmer over low heat for 10 minutes. Take off heat and remove garlic (if you can find it). Add milk and cheese. Stir until cheese is melted, then season with freshly grated nutmeg and salt and pepper to taste. Heat well, but do not boil. Pour into a heated tureen and serve at the table. At lunch in

Switzerland the soup was traditionally served with rye bread, a mixed vegetable, ham salad, and an apple dessert.

Icy Melon Soup
Serves 10 to 14.

Although fruit soups are popular in many countries, I have not been partial to them in my menus. When temperatures are high and melons are sweet, I favor this refreshing soup. It is particularly appropriate for large parties or organizational brunches and suppers.

6 cups cantaloupe or honeydew melon (3 cups cut into neat
   ½-inch cubes, 3 cups coarsely chopped)
2 cups fresh orange juice
¼ cup lemon juice
¼ cup lime juice
¼ cup maple syrup
2 cups dry white wine
Dash of club soda
Mint leaves
Strips of lemon and lime rinds

Reserve the melon cubes. Purée the coarsely chopped melon in a food processor with the juices and maple syrup. Pour into a bowl, then stir in white wine and reserved melon cubes. Chill for several hours.

Just before serving, add the club soda and stir gently. Serve in a chilled bowl or stemmed glass. Garnish each serving with a mint leaf and a strip of lemon or lime rind.

4

Sauces for Every Day and Holidays

Think of a sauce as a touch of seasoning and flavor—not as a cover-up. What magic occurs when a few spoonfuls of White Sauce connect with a cup of cooked spinach! What eye appeal when chicken is glazed with a winey Brown Sauce! The list of sauces is extensive, but most cooks need only a few for their individual styles of cooking. Recently, salsa, an uncooked vegetable relish, has topped the list of sauces for dips, fish, pasta, and almost everything else. But there certainly is more to sauce making than that, with so many easy options available.

In my mind and for teaching, I divide the most useful and savory sauces into colors—white, brown, red, and green. Basically, the white (Béchamel or Velouté) is built on milk or light-colored stock; the brown on browned meat, poultry, and bones; the red on tomatoes; and the green on herbs.

81

Wine sauces are all prepared by the same method. Compare the White Wine Sauce for Seafood (page 84) and the Béchamel on this page. The wine is always reduced with flavorings (shallots, garlic, herbs, and so forth) until it is practically evaporated. The sauce is stirred into this essence, then simmered and strained. The one exception is an addition of wines known as fortified wines—sherry, port, and Madeira. These may be added in small amounts to the sauce at the end. They act as flavoring and need not be reduced by evaporation.

What follows is hardly an Escoffier rendition, but at the very least it will provide you with an ample number of interesting sauces.

Recipes

White Sauce (Béchamel)
Makes 1 ¾ cups.

Many American cooks do not give White Sauce the respect it deserves, so when I led some students on a cooking tour of northern Italy, I was pleased when we found our teaching chefs featuring casseroled vegetables *alla besciamella* as specialties. You can make a truly exceptional white sauce by first steeping a bouquet garni or onion in the warmed milk. Instantly you have added flavor.

2 cups milk
Bouquet garni (or half an onion, studded
   with clove and bay leaf)
4 tablespoons butter
3 tablespoons flour
Salt and pepper to taste

Heat milk with bouquet garni or onion in a saucepan. Bring to a simmer. Turn off heat.

In the meantime, melt butter in a heavy-bottomed saucepan. Add flour and stir over low heat for a few minutes. This mixture is called a roux.

Discard the bouquet garni or onion from the milk. Add the hot milk to the roux and whisk the mixture to smoothness. If the milk had been cold, you would have added it gradually to avoid lumps. Simmer for 4 to 5 minutes to rid the sauce of any floury taste. Season to taste with salt and pepper.

✴ *Suggestions*

- When chefs make a large amount of White Sauce, involving perhaps 2 or 3 quarts of milk, they simmer the sauce for about 1 hour. Long cooking thoroughly rids the sauce of any floury taste.
- Naturally, cream (light or heavy), whole eggs, or egg yolks can each be added for richness and creaminess.
- Cook a homemade Cheese Sauce for macaroni. While you boil ½ pound of macaroni, make the White Sauce. Add 1 cup grated Cheddar cheese and a dash of dry mustard to the sauce. Combine with drained macaroni. Serve immediately or bake in a casserole for a crispy topping.
- Cook a double or triple recipe of White Sauce. Freeze it in 1-cup containers for up to three months. Use it as a thickener for creaming soups or in combination with cooked fish, chicken, or vegetables.

Sauce Velouté (Sauce with White Stock)
Makes 1 ¾ cups.

Velouté is the French term for a white sauce made with a light broth, not milk. There is no equivalent name in English for this sauce. It is a velvety, light-colored sauce used in a number of appropriate recipes. Occasionally, onion, carrot, celery, and even mushrooms are sautéed before adding flour and broth. These additions expand the flavor to suit a particular combination. For example, if you were cooking a sauce for Chicken Pot Pie (page 222), Sauce Velouté would be perfect with chicken stock as a base.

    3 tablespoons butter
    4 tablespoons flour
    2 cups hot chicken stock (or fish or vegetable stock)
    ¼ cup dry sherry (optional)
    Salt and pepper to taste

Melt butter in a heavy-bottomed skillet. Add flour and stir well for 2 to 3 minutes. Stir in hot stock. Bring slowly to a simmer. It will thicken quickly. Add sherry and salt and pepper to taste. Simmer for 5 to 7 minutes.

✴ *Suggestion*

The addition of sautéed diced onions, carrots, and mushrooms is especially good for pot pies.

Sauce Zingara
Makes 6 cups.

If you are already a master of Velouté and Béchamel sauces, you probably have created this very sauce with mushrooms, ham, and chicken stock. My dear friend, Georges Pouvel, a leading teacher of cuisine in France, taught at my Vermont school for several summers. He demonstrated the Sauce Zingara as his special favorite for pasta. We served the sauce with beet (red), spinach (green), and egg noodles (white). Indeed, very Italian.

Sauce Zingara is a perfect example of a sauce combining the stock-based Velouté (page 83) with cream or milk.

> 5 tablespoons butter
> 4 tablespoons flour
> 4 cups hot homemade chicken stock (or canned stock diluted with equal parts water)
> 1 cup cream (heavy or light)
> ¼ pound mushrooms, julienned
> ¼ pound cooked ham, julienned
> Salt and pepper to taste

Prepare a Sauce Velouté with 4 tablespoons butter, flour, and hot chicken stock. Add cream and simmer for 5 minutes.

Melt the remaining 1 tablespoon butter in a skillet. Add mushrooms and cook to barely soften them. Add mushrooms and ham to the Velouté and adjust the seasoning.

✳ Suggestions

- Just think how delicious the sauce would be over shirred or scrambled eggs for a special brunch!
- Create your own sauce with ingredients on hand. Omit ham. Use leftovers of chicken or seafood or perhaps a small amount of cooked meat from the previous night's dinner.

White Wine Sauce for Seafood
Makes 2 cups.

Ask your fish dealer for the bones of any white-fleshed fish to cook Fish Stock for Velouté. As a substitute, use diluted bottled clam juice (2 parts clam juice with 1 part water). You may refer to Chapter 8 for specific fish recipes, but think of this sauce as a basis for several different possibilities. It will even glamorize a can of tuna or clams for a tasty sauce over pasta.

   ¾ cup milk or light cream
   Bouquet garni
   4 tablespoons butter
   2 shallots, minced
   ¾ cup dry white wine
   3 tablespoons flour
   1½ cups hot Fish Stock (page 61), or diluted bottled clam juice (2 parts clam
      juice with 1 part water)
   ⅛ teaspoon freshly grated nutmeg
   Pinch cayenne pepper
   Salt and pepper to taste

Combine the milk or cream with the bouquet garni and set aside.

Melt 1 tablespoon butter in a small saucepan. Add shallots and cook until glazed. Add wine. Bring to a boil and continue boiling until barely 1 tablespoon of wine remains.

In the meantime, cook the Velouté: Melt the remaining 3 tablespoons butter in a saucepan. Stir in flour and cook for 2 to 3 minutes, then add hot Fish Stock or clam juice. Whisk until smooth. Transfer sauce to the reduced wine and shallots. Simmer for a few minutes. Add milk or cream (with bouquet garni removed), then nutmeg and cayenne pepper. Taste for seasoning and adjust with salt and pepper. Simmer for 2 to 3 minutes. Strain!

Sauce Beurre Blanc
Makes a scant ½ cup.

With its velvety texture and slightly acidic flavor, this "white butter" sauce traditionally has been matched to the superb fish of the Loire River. A classic sauce, it once required flour and egg yolks. In the 1970s the great chefs of France adapted the sauce to suit chicken and veal as well. Supposedly they lightened the composition by omitting flour and egg yolks. That may very well be true, but the beautiful texture of Sauce Beurre Blanc is based on pure butter. If you are attempting to lower fat content, you will probably skip this recipe, but do try it once for saucing a freshly caught fish.

   2 tablespoons minced shallots
   ½ cup vinegar or dry white wine
   ½ pound lightly salted butter, room temperature and cut into eight pieces

Cook shallots and vinegar or wine in a 1-quart saucepan at a simmer until the liquid is reduced to barely cover the bottom of the pan. Remove the pan to the counter. Whisk in one piece of the soft butter at a time, waiting for each piece to melt completely before adding the next. After all the butter has been whisked in, the sauce should still be warm and the consistency should coat a spoon. Strain the sauce into a warmed bowl and place over simmering water, never over direct heat.

✳ *Suggestion*

In place of butter, add ½ cup each of Fish Stock (page 61) and heavy or light cream. Boil for 3 to 4 minutes to reduce. Strain into another saucepan. This sauce can be reheated directly over low heat.

Quick Brown Sauce I
Makes 2 cups.

Brown sauces are basic. A few tablespoons will enhance any pan juice. If you are pushed for time, you can rely on the following recipe for a Quick Brown Sauce. Even if you use canned beef stock, the addition of fresh vegetables will perk up the taste.

    2 tablespoons butter or oil
    1 onion, diced
    2 shallots, minced
    ½ cup mushrooms, diced (stems will do, if you have them)
    1 carrot, diced
    1 ripe tomato, diced, or 2 tablespoons canned crushed tomatoes
    3 tablespoons flour
    3 cups hot Brown Stock (page 60) or canned beef stock diluted with ½ cup water

Melt butter or heat oil in a heavy-bottomed saucepan. Sauté onion and shallots until limp and glazed. Add mushrooms, carrot, and tomato. Stir and cook for 2 to 3 minutes. Sprinkle flour on top and blend well. Cook over a low flame for a few minutes, stirring constantly. Add hot stock and bring mixture to a simmer. Simmer partially covered for 30 minutes.

Strain the mixture into another saucepan. Cover top of sauce with a greased wax paper to fit or small bits of butter or oil. This will prevent a skin from forming.

Refrigerate sauce in a covered container if not being used at once or freeze it for up to three months.

Quick Brown Sauce II
Makes 2 to 3 cups.

If you save necks, tips of wings, and other small pieces of poultry, you probably bag them for the freezer as I do. Sometimes I use them for my stocks and other times for the following Brown Sauce. Since the essence of chicken bones is extracted so much faster than that of veal or beef bones, this recipe is an excellent shortcut.

2 pounds chicken parts (necks, wing tips, stomachs, etc.)
1 onion, unpeeled, cut in half
2 onions, diced
2 carrots, diced
2 ribs celery, diced
1 cup diced mushrooms (stems will do)
2 tablespoons butter
½ cup flour
6 cups homemade stock, or combination of 4 cups canned chicken or beef broth and 2 cups water
1 onion, cut in half and studded with 4 cloves and 2 bay leaves
2 cloves garlic
4 sprigs fresh parsley
1 teaspoon dried thyme or 2 sprigs fresh thyme
2 fresh, ripe tomatoes or ½ cup canned crushed tomatoes

Cut chicken parts into small pieces. Place on a jelly-roll pan and brown for at least 45 minutes at 425°F. Distribute unpeeled onion, diced onions, carrots, celery, and mushrooms on another pan. Place in a 425°F oven, and allow vegetables to brown for about 15 minutes. Dot with butter and sprinkle with flour. The flour will color to light brown after 20 to 30 minutes. Turn occasionally so that flour does not burn.

In the meantime, heat the stock. When the chicken parts are brown, remove them to a soup pot. Deglaze the browned pan (from chicken) with a few cups stock. Scrape all the browned particles off the pan and pour broth into the soup pot. Do the same with the vegetables and browned flour. Add all the stock and remaining ingredients. The broth should just cover the ingredients. If not, add some water. Simmer partially covered for 1 hour.

Strain the sauce through a fine strainer; discard bulk. The sauce can be further reduced to make it stronger, if desired, but be sure to skim it for clarity.

Brown Wine Sauce with Green Peppercorns
Makes 3 cups.

In the early 1970s I was observing a class that my daughter was attending at L'Ecole Hoteliere in Paris. Her teacher, Georges Pouvel, asked me to assist. I was given the menial job of picking green peppercorns from their stems. The Madagascar peppercorns were just beginning to be marketed in the United States, but I had never seen them fresh. The morning's lesson included this sauce for roast duckling, and thus green peppercorns in sauce made their formal entrance into my cuisine. This is the classic technique for wine sauces.

    1½ cups dry white or red wine
    ½ cup cognac or brandy
    ½ cup minced shallots
    2 tablespoons green peppercorns (crushed)
    1 tablespoon whole green peppercorns
    3 cups Brown Sauce (page 86 or 87)
    1 cup hot stock (meat or chicken)
    ½ to 1 cup heavy or light cream (optional)

Cook wine, cognac or brandy, shallots, and 2 tablespoons crushed green peppercorns at a boil for about 10 minutes or until the liquid is almost completely evaporated. Add Brown Sauce and bring to a simmer. Add ½ cup stock and simmer for 10 minutes. If the mixture is too thick, thin it with more stock. Strain into another saucepan. Add remaining whole green peppercorns. Then add cream if you wish to enrich the sauce.

Tomato Sauce
Makes 2 cups.

Tomato sauce is a staple in my kitchen. The number of authentic recipes pile high in my folder, but I rely on the fastest and the easiest for everyday use. Of course, in the summer garden tomatoes come fresh to the pot, but through the nongrowing season I rely on a supply of canned crushed tomatoes. Brands vary, so test them to find your own preference.

    1 tablespoon olive oil
    1 onion, diced
    1 clove garlic, minced
    One 28-ounce can crushed tomatoes or 3 to 4 pounds ripe tomatoes, peeled,
        seeded, and diced

½ cup dry white wine or dry vermouth
⅛ teaspoon red pepper flakes
½ teaspoon dried oregano or basil (or 2 sprigs fresh)
1 tablespoon freshly chopped parsley
Salt and pepper to taste
Pinch of sugar

Heat a heavy-bottomed 3-quart saucepan with olive oil. Add onion and garlic. Cook until wilted and glazed. Stir in tomatoes, wine or vermouth, red pepper flakes, and herbs. Simmer for 15 to 20 minutes. Adjust to taste with salt, pepper, and sugar. Simmer for 2 to 3 minutes more. Serve on spaghetti or other pasta, or use as a base wherever tomato as a sauce is indicated.

✸ *Suggestions*

- Unless you freeze or can your own garden tomatoes, canned crushed tomatoes can be a quick assist in a busy household.
- There is no need to buy the more expensive jars of sauces when this easy sauce can be adjusted with your own favorite seasonings.
- Add mushrooms, celery, and carrots to the Tomato Sauce, and use it as a baking accompaniment for fish.
- Add Chili Pepper Paste (page 27) for a spicier result—a great filling for omelets.
- In addition to being basic for stews, a spoonful of Tomato Sauce adds color and interest to soups, sauces, and dips.

Ragu alla Bolognese (Bolognese-style Meat Sauce)
Serves 6 to 8.

Some years ago I had a student who lived in Bologna while her husband attended medical school there. They were fortunate to live above one of the city's famous restaurants. It was a wonderful beginning for a young couple with an interest in eating well. Their friendship with the proprietors reached great heights when the chef was persuaded to share this recipe with them, now handed down to me.

4 tablespoons olive oil
3 tablespoons butter
½ cup minced onions
2 cups minced carrots
2 cups minced celery

2 pounds ground chuck
½ pound sausage (optional)
¼ pound chicken livers (optional)
2 cups red wine
2 teaspoons salt (if homemade stock is not salted)
1 quart White or Brown Stock, preferably homemade (pages 59 and 60)
12 ounces tomato paste
½ teaspoon freshly grated nutmeg
Salt and pepper to taste

Heat oil and butter in a 5- or 6-quart saucepan. Cook onions until wilted and glazed. Add carrots and celery. Stir and cook for at least 5 minutes for vegetables to glaze without browning. Add ground meat (and sausage and liver, if you wish). Crumble the meat with a fork to break it up, and cook until it is no longer pink. Add wine. Simmer over low heat until the wine evaporates. Add salt, stock, tomato paste, and nutmeg. Bring to a boil, then turn down heat to simmer. Cover and cook slowly for about 3 hours. Taste and adjust seasoning.

✳ *Suggestions*

- Take time to cook the Ragu in advance. Refrigerate for up to three days or freeze for up to three months.
- In Bologna lasagne is layered with Ragu, *Besciamella* (White Sauce), and grated Parmesan cheese. Thin layers of pasta might number to 11 or 12.
- Ragu is excellent with the heavier pastas, such as macaronis, shells, and rotelli. These pastas hold the sauce well and can be reheated in casseroles without becoming too soft.
- Blend Ragu with risotto for an oven casserole.

Spinach Sauce
Makes 3 cups.

Green sauces depend on the freshest of garden greens and herbs. It is no wonder that spinach is a principal ingredient in sauces for fish, shellfish, chicken, and veal. The contrast in color and texture appeals to the eye as well as the palate. The Scandinavians definitely prefer dill. The Italians have put pesto on almost every American table, whether fresh or out of a jar. Whether you use these exact recipes or not, think of each green and herb as a boost in seasoning your foods.

2 cups spinach
½ cup fresh parsley, stems removed
½ cup watercress, stems removed
¼ cup scallions (white and green portions)
1 tablespoon butter or oil
1 onion, minced
2 tablespoons flour
½ cup milk or light cream
Salt, pepper, and nutmeg to taste

Place spinach, parsley, watercress, and scallions in a food processor. Pulse the machine on and off until the mixture is coarsely minced.

Melt butter or oil in a saucepan. Sauté onion until glazed. Add chopped greens. Stir and cook for 1 to 2 minutes. Sprinkle flour on top and stir well. Add milk or cream. Simmer while you stir for a few minutes. Taste and adjust seasoning with salt, pepper, and nutmeg. Serve with fillets of sole or breast of chicken—baked, broiled, or poached.

✹ *Suggestions*

- Extend the sauce by adding ½ cup fish or chicken stock. Use with baked fish, chicken, or veal.
- For a vegetarian casserole, combine Spinach Sauce with macaroni and top with grated Parmesan cheese, or use it as a filling for lasagne.
- Add 1 tablespoon minced garlic to the greens; this makes an excellent addition to grilled shrimp.
- Spinach Sauce is similar to the classic Spanish green sauce for fish and seafood. Use olive oil and omit the milk.

Sorrel Sauce
Makes 1 cup.

Sorrel is a sour grassy weed that grows wild and is abundant when cultivated. I have cooked sorrel mainly for a cold summer soup, which in Russia is known as Schav. The French favor a hot, creamy sorrel soup. If you grow sorrel or can buy it young, omit the blanching step in the recipe that follows.

2 cups sorrel, stems removed
¾ cup heavy or light cream
1 shallot, diced
1 clove garlic, diced

Sorrel

Bouquet garni
Salt and pepper to taste

Wash the sorrel. Separate the leaves from the stems. Reserve and use the stems for a broth. Bring 2 to 3 quarts water to a boil. Immerse the sorrel leaves in the boiling water for just 1 minute (this procedure is known as blanching). Transfer to a strainer and press out as much liquid as you can. Put leaves in a food processor, pulsing it on and off to roughly mince the sorrel.

Simmer cream with the shallot, garlic, and bouquet garni until the cream is reduced by about half. Strain cream into a 1-quart saucepan. Stir in sorrel. Taste and adjust flavor with salt and pepper.

✹ *Suggestions*

- Sorrel wilts immediately when it is cooked and turns dark green. Cut young sorrel into strips and sauté it in oil or butter.
- Sorrel stems can be cooked for a broth. The broth will extend the sauce into a soup. Add 1 cup Sauce Velouté (page 83) instead of cream, if desired.
- The summer cold soup, Schav, is a combination of cooked sorrel, lemon juice, sugar, salt, and garnishes of cucumber and sour cream. Sometimes it is enriched with an egg.

Cucumber Sauce
Makes 2 cups.

2 pounds cucumbers
2 tablespoons white vinegar
1 teaspoon kosher (coarse) salt
¼ teaspoon sugar
2 tablespoons butter
2 tablespoons minced shallots
1 tablespoon flour
1 cup stock (fish, chicken, or vegetable)
2 tablespoons chopped fresh parsley
2 tablespoons chopped fresh dill
Salt and pepper to taste

Peel cucumbers, but leave small strips of green peel for color. Cut the cucumbers in half, lengthwise. Scoop out the seeds with a spoon or melon cutter and discard. Cut the cucumbers into thin slices or juliennes.

Mix vinegar, salt, and sugar in a bowl. Add cucumber slices and allow them to marinate for at least 10 minutes. Drain and dry on paper toweling.

Melt butter in a saucepan. Add shallots and cook for 2 to 3 minutes until glazed. Stir in cucumbers to cook for another few minutes. Sprinkle flour on top. Blend all together. Pour in stock and cook until the mixture thickens. Add herbs, salt, and pepper to taste.

✳ *Suggestions*

- The sauce can be enriched with a mixture of 1 egg yolk and ½ cup heavy or light cream. Cook to a simmer and serve with fish or breast of chicken when you would rather have a taste treat than count calories.
- For a lovely presentation, use Cucumber Sauce for cooked fish and seafood. Add fresh dill for garnish.

Dill Sauce
Makes 3 cups.

When you see fresh dill and basil in your market, buy them. They both keep well in the refrigerator for three to five days, so you need not rush to make the sauces. Both Dill Sauce and Pesto (this page) are uncooked sauces and take only minutes to prepare.

1 bunch dill (at least 1 cup)
2 cups sour cream (you may substitute light sour cream or yogurt)
1 tablespoon horseradish (preferably freshly grated)
Salt and pepper to taste

Dill does not usually require washing. Discard the lower stems. Chop the dill and mix it with sour cream and horseradish. Season with salt and pepper. Serve at room temperature with poached fish, chicken, or beef.

✳ *Suggestions*

- Another version of this sauce calls for regular cream, whipped, instead of sour cream.
- You may also consider a teaspoon of Dijon mustard as an additional flavoring.

Pesto
Makes 1¼ cups.

You can, of course, buy Pesto in nearly every supermarket, but once you make it fresh, you will taste the difference.

3 large cloves garlic
2 cups basil leaves

¼ cup pine nuts (pignoli)
1 teaspoon salt
½ teaspoon pepper
⅔ cup olive oil
½ cup freshly grated Parmesan cheese

Place garlic cloves in a food processor. Pulse the machine on and off. Add basil, pine nuts, salt, and pepper. Run the machine for about 15 seconds. Gradually add olive oil. When mixed in, stop the machine and transfer ingredients to a bowl. Add cheese only if you are ready to use the Pesto. I prefer to refrigerate or freeze Pesto without the cheese if it is being made in advance. Stir in cheese before serving.

✹ Suggestion

You will probably have read many recipes for Pesto made with other varieties of greens—even with sun-dried tomatoes and olives. Why not? The choice is yours.

5

Vegetables

I always explore vegetable markets in my travels. The markets in small towns tell the story of surrounding farms and seasonal growth, which naturally influence local cooking. Cities have their large wholesale-retail markets where they merchandise produce from nearby farms alongside the year-round global imports. The choices are vast. I usually roam the stands as I would a museum. They are a feast of color. Each vendor shows his wares in a particular style, a still life at every turn.

On a recent trip to southern France, our friend Madeleine Resen and I made an early morning visit to the great Cannes Market. Madeleine, who lives close by in Mougins, ushered me in to see her favorite fresh flower displays. I quickly moved her to the vegetables. What choices! Leeks, artichokes, wild mushrooms, many varieties of potatoes and tomatoes filled our basket for a sumptuous dinner that evening.

Now that we live in Vermont throughout the year, we have our own garden. Vegetables begin with a show of chives and asparagus, the first in early spring, and finish with winter squash in October. It all started one weekend in 1963. On querying Chef-Innkeeper Peter Zilliacus about his vegetables and berries, he directed us to Mary and Frank Hickin of Mountain Mowings Farm. Imagine an oasis

95

of farming hidden in the upper hills of East Dummerston, Vermont. In those years, we were amazed to find a great number of varieties of salad greens, pea pods, baby squash, husk tomatoes, and many more than I could possibly list. The germ of a persistent thought was satisfied when I started my summer cooking school in Vermont. Mary and Frank provided me with an instant herb garden. They supplied me with the best of greens, vegetables, and berries as they grew them. Part of the fun in cooking is handling a beautiful product, and my students appreciated that.

Vegetables are, perhaps, the most useful, healthful, and versatile of all the fresh foods in a kitchen. I advise the beginner cook to stock onions, carrots, and celery as she or he would stock sugar and salt. These three vegetables are the basic flavor in so many different recipes. Together or separately, they can each make an excellent side dish. Each one combines well with rice, grains, and pasta. Never discard leftover vegetables. They extend salads as they do stews. Some children even love to snack on cooked vegetables rather than dine on them!

Methods for cooking vegetables embrace all the techniques of cooking, most of which will be used in the recipes that follow. Although steaming has been strongly suggested as a way to preserve nutrients, I always advise students to vary the methods of preparation. Sturdy green vegetables retain their bright color when they are quickly cooked at a rolling boil. A quick stir-fry or sauté has its advantages. Deep-fried vegetables can be a special treat. Braising is practiced for all the small leftovers of cauliflower, eggplant, broccoli, and other vegetables that sometimes pile up in the refrigerator.

The microwave oven has become a popular technology for cooking vegetables, but since machines differ in voltage, consult your owner's manual. Many of the following recipes can be prepared using the microwave.

Recipes

Asparagus
Serves 2-4.

Spring has arrived when we see the first asparagus shoot through the earth. Those early ones never see the pot—we eat them raw.

    1 pound asparagus
    1 tablespoon lemon juice
    1 tablespoon olive oil
    Salt and freshly ground pepper to taste

Lightly rinse asparagus. Some soils produce sand under the scales. Such spears must be peeled and washed. Crack off the bottom end of the asparagus where it breaks easily (the ends can be reserved for soups or purées). Peel asparagus to expose the tender flesh, if you wish, but I never do that with our garden variety.

I prepare asparagus with what I call my boil-and-steam method. Boil an inch of water in a skillet large enough to accommodate the length of the asparagus. Water should not cover asparagus completely when you place them in the skillet. Cook uncovered for 3 to 4 minutes, turning them over into different positions.

Pour off liquid from the skillet. Pour on lemon juice and olive oil; salt and pepper to taste. Place four asparagus alongside a main course on a heated plate.

✺ Suggestions

- Wrap cooked cold asparagus in prosciutto or Carpaccio (page 40) for an appetizer or luncheon salad.
- Place an asparagus spear in a leaf of endive. Sprinkle with your preferred dressing or just good vinegar.
- Alternate four or five asparagus spears with strips of cooked chicken. Serve with Green Dressing (page 136).

Stir-Fry Asparagus
Serves 4.

1 pound cleaned asparagus
1 tablespoon oil
¼ cup water or chicken stock
½ teaspoon chervil
½ teaspoon chives
Salt and pepper to taste

Cut the asparagus into 2-inch lengths. Sauté or stir-fry in a heated wok or skillet with oil. Add water or chicken stock. Cook uncovered for 2 to 3 minutes. Season with chervil and chives; salt and pepper to taste. Serve at once.

Buffet Asparagus
Serves 8.

1 French bread (baguette)
2 pounds asparagus, rinsed
3 egg whites
¼ teaspoon salt
Pinch cream of tartar
¼ teaspoon pepper
¼ teaspoon paprika
¼ cup freshly grated Parmesan cheese
2 tablespoons grated sharp Cheddar cheese

Slice the bread on the diagonal to make eight long slices. Toast bread on one side. Place bread, toasted-side down, side by side in a shallow casserole. Follow directions for cooking asparagus, but boil for no more than 2 minutes. Refresh in cold water and drain on paper toweling. Place asparagus, evenly divided, on each slice of bread. Prepare hours ahead or a day in advance and refrigerate.

Two hours before serving, bring the ingredients to room temperature. Set them on a convenient counter. Preheat oven to 400°F.

Twenty minutes before serving, beat the egg whites with salt and cream of tartar until just stiff and clinging to the sides of the bowl. Fold in pepper, paprika, and Parmesan and Cheddar cheeses. Spread mixture evenly over each serving of asparagus on toasted bread. Place the casserole in the oven for 15 minutes, time enough to set out other buffet dishes.

Boiled Artichokes (Hot or Cold)
Serves 4-6.

Cooked artichoke in its simplest form is served with melted butter or Basic Vinaigrette Dressing (page 135). Prepare artichokes ahead and refrigerate for up to two days, but always serve them hot or at room temperature, never cold.

4-6 medium-size artichokes
2-3 tablespoons fresh lemon juice
2-3 teaspoons salt
1 medium-size onion, sliced (optional)
1 bay leaf (optional)
1 clove garlic, peeled (optional)

Wash artichokes, then cut off ½ inch across the top and discard. Rub the cut surfaces with half of a lemon. Cut stem straight across from the bottom (A). Rub the cut portion with the lemon and remove any lower petals that appear discolored. Snip the sharp tips of the remaining petals (B).

Fill a saucepan with enough salted water to cover the artichokes. Add the lemon juice and salt and bring to a boil, adding the optional ingredients if desired. Drop the artichokes into the boiling water, weighting them down if they float. Cook, uncovered, for 30 to 40 minutes, depending on size.

Test them for doneness by pulling off a bottom leaf; it should come away easily. Also pierce the bottom of the heart with a fork to check softness. Remove the artichokes from the water with tongs or a slotted spoon, turn them upside down on a plate, and squeeze them gently to drain off the water (C).

To serve the artichokes, gently open the center and twist out the cone of soft leaves; use a spoon to scrape off the fuzz on the bottom of the vegetable, trying not to dent the bottom. Turn the cone of leaves upside down on top of the artichokes so that it will resemble an opened flower. Serve hot or cold.

✸ Suggestions

- Remove the choke from cooked artichokes and stuff with hot or cold salad mixtures.
- Artichoke Provençale is a perfect choice for buffet service, hot or at room temperature.

Artichokes with Piquant Dressing
Serves 4.

I am so enthusiastic about artichokes that I once carried a bag of 25 of them on a flight returning home from California. The whole bag cost about $1 in Castroville, the hometown of artichoke farms.

Artichokes can be steamed or boiled, stuffed and baked, braised or fried. Many children are intrigued with the artichoke. Picking off the petals, dipping them in butter or vinaigrette, then scraping off the flesh against their teeth becomes a fascinating ritual.

2 large artichokes
1 lemon, cut in half

1 tablespoon flour
1 clove garlic
1 rib celery, cut in chunks
Salt and freshly ground pepper
¼ cup mayonnaise
¼ cup Basic Vinaigrette Dressing (page 135)
¼ teaspoon dry mustard
⅛ teaspoon cayenne pepper

Wash artichokes, then cut off ½ inch across the top and discard. Rub the cut surfaces with half of lemon. Cut stem straight across from the bottom. Rub cut portion with lemon. Remove any lower petals that appear discolored. Snip the sharp tips of the remaining petals (see illustrations page 99).

Use a saucepan that will tightly accommodate the artichokes so that they do not float. Fill with water to about 3 or 4 inches. Mix in flour. Add garlic and celery; salt and pepper to taste. Place artichokes in water stem-side up; cover and simmer for 20 minutes. Turn artichokes over and simmer for another 15 to 20 minutes, depending on the size of the artichokes. Remove the artichokes and drain upside down on a rack or plate.

Mix the remaining ingredients for the dressing. When the artichokes are cool enough to handle, remove center leaves to expose the choke. Gently scrape the choke off the heart with a teaspoon. Fill the cavity with dressing or serve the dressing on the side.

Artichoke Provençale
Serves 4.

4 large artichokes or 12 tiny artichokes
1 lemon, cut in half
2 tablespoons olive oil
2 cloves garlic, minced
1 medium onion, minced
1 pound ripe tomatoes, peeled, seeded, and diced (or canned if fresh is not available)
2 tablespoons chopped fresh basil (or 2 teaspoons dried)
Salt and freshly ground pepper
½ cup olives and Italian parsley for garnish

Wash artichokes. Cut or break off stems. Snap off tough or discolored leaves. Snip the sharp tips of the petals. Cut large artichokes into quarters and small ones in half. Rub every cut side and bottom with the half of lemon. Scrape out the choke of large artichokes only.

Heat oil in a 3-quart Dutch oven or large skillet. Sauté artichokes for about 5 minutes. Add garlic and onion. Stir together and cook for another 2 to 3 minutes.

Add tomatoes and basil. Heat, then add salt and pepper to taste. Cover and simmer for 15 to 20 minutes or until artichokes are tender. Stir occasionally. If tomatoes cause sticking, add ½ cup water or broth. Garnish with olives and Italian parsley.

✹ *Suggestion*

As an alternative to simmering for 15 to 20 minutes, bake in the oven at 350°F for 30 minutes.

Green or Yellow Beans and Shallots
Serves 4 to 6.

1 pound fresh green or yellow beans
1 tablespoon butter or oil
¼ cup minced shallots
Salt and pepper to taste

Wash the beans. Snap off stems and tips. Bring 3 quarts water to a boil. Salt the water, if you wish.

In the meantime, melt butter or heat oil in a 10- or 12-inch skillet. Add shallots, and cook over low heat for 2 to 3 minutes until shallots are glazed, not browned. Set aside.

Immerse beans in the boiling water. When the water comes to a boil again, the beans should be finished in two or three minutes. Test for doneness by tasting a bean. Drain and add beans to the skillet with the shallots. Stir and heat just before serving. Add salt and pepper to taste.

✹ *Suggestions*

- Cut the beans diagonally, in 1- or 2-inch pieces, or lengthwise in slivers for faster cooking or stir-fry.
- Add or substitute minced garlic for shallots.
- Use olive oil, garlic, basil, and ½ cup peeled, chopped fresh tomatoes for a Provençale-style dish.
- Slice beans and stir-fry with 1 tablespoon oil, two slices fresh ginger root, ¼ cup chicken stock, and soy sauce to taste.

Beets
Serves 3 to 4.

I prefer our garden beets to any other, but after the last one from the garden is eaten, I am obliged to buy them from the market. They are healthful and easily cooked to be served hot or cold. Look for beets with fresh green tops. That's a bonus!

> 6 or 7 beets (about 1 pound)
> Pinch salt
> 1 tablespoon lemon juice
> Pinch sugar
> Additional salt to taste

Wash and scrub beets well. Cut off greens and dry them. Refrigerate the greens in a plastic container if you are not using them at once.

Cook beets with a pinch of salt in water to barely cover. Cover the pot and bring to a simmer. After 15 to 20 minutes, test beets with a fork. The fork should easily pierce the center. Transfer beets into a strainer over a bowl to catch the liquid.

When the beets are cool enough to handle, slip off the skins. Pour the liquid slowly from the bowl into a saucepan. Be careful not to include any sand that may have settled to the bottom.

Slice the beets and add them to the beet liquid. Season with lemon juice, a pinch of sugar, and salt to taste. Serve hot as a side dish for any meal.

✳ Suggestions

- Add a pronounced sweet-and-sour taste by mixing 1 tablespoon white vinegar, ½ teaspoon salt, and 2 teaspoons sugar to 1 cup beet liquid. Taste and add more vinegar, salt, and sugar if desired. The sweet-sour balance is a matter of preference.
- Serve beets cold by adding two or three strips each of lemon and orange to the sweet-and-sour variation described above. Marinate beets, either sliced or julienned, in the liquid. At times you may want to add thinly sliced onion, as well. This salad will refrigerate well for up to five days.

Broccoli
Serves 4 to 6.

Broccoli belongs to the group of vegetables known as cruciferous, all related to the cabbage family, whose members also include brussels sprouts, cauliflower, and kohlrabi. These are the superstar vegetables of nutrition, according to recent health reports.

> 2 pounds broccoli
> Freshly grated Parmesan cheese

Wash homegrown broccoli very well, a precaution against tiny garden creatures. Otherwise, a quick rinse will do. Cut broccoli just below the flowerets. Peel the stems and reserve them for use in stir-fries, soups, and purées.

At times I prepare broccoli with the stems — just remove the tip ends of the stem. This is a quick preparation, with floweret and unpeeled stems used at once.

Boil broccoli in 3 quarts briskly boiling water for no more than 3 minutes, to prevent loss of the green color. Serve very hot with a sprinkling of grated Parmesan cheese.

✷ *Suggestion*

If steaming is your favorite method, the cooking time will take almost twice as long. There will be a slight loss of color but some gain in nutritional value.

Broccoli Raab
Serves 4 to 6.

As part of the cabbage family, broccoli raab is very assertive, hardly delicate. It grows mostly leaves and small flowerets.

> 2 to 3 pounds broccoli raab
> 2 tablespoons olive oil
> 2 cloves garlic, minced
> ¼ teaspoon red pepper flakes
> ½ cup grated Parmesan cheese
> Salt and pepper to taste

Wash the broccoli raab. Trim off the tough ends, but keep flowers and tender leaves. Cut into spears. While you boil at least 3 quarts water, heat olive oil in a skillet. Sauté garlic and red pepper flakes. Do not scorch the garlic. Set the skillet aside.

Boil broccoli raab for 3 to 4 minutes, uncovered. Test for doneness to your taste. Drain off water. Transfer the vegetable to the skillet and heat thoroughly before serving. Add cheese and salt and pepper to taste.

✷ *Suggestion*

Add cut leaves and flowers to a boiling pasta during the last 3 minutes of cooking. Drain and mix with heated olive oil, garlic, and cheese for a super fast dinner.

Cauliflower—White or Purple
Serves 4 to 6.

In my childhood, our family enjoyed vegetable dinners every Thursday. Cauliflower cooked and mashed with butter (no food processor back then) produced the texture we now call purée. Alongside we had sliced carrots, fresh spinach garnished with hard-cooked egg, and crisp-skinned baked potatoes. The white cauliflower added creamy texture to the colorful and beautiful dinner plate. If you were to research the vitamins, minerals, and fiber found in cauliflower, you would discover a mighty good nutritional balance.

> 2 pounds cauliflower, white or purple
> Salt and freshly ground pepper

Cut around the bottom of the center base and remove core to expose the divisions of the stalks. Cut into preferred portions, keeping the greens if they are fresh. Rinse lightly.

Immerse cauliflower pieces and some greens in boiling water just to cover. Tightly cover to retain color for white cauliflower, and simmer for 4 to 5 minutes. The purple variety will turn green. Salt and pepper to taste.

✳ *Suggestions*

- At another time, mix 1 tablespoon olive oil or butter with 2 tablespoons each lemon juice and mixed herbs (parsley, chives, scallions, and marjoram). Pour over the cauliflower before serving.
- For everybody's favorite topping, toast plain bread crumbs and minced fresh garlic, slowly, in an oiled or buttered skillet. Be careful not to burn.

Chinese Cabbage with Sesame Seeds
Serves 4.

Chinese cabbage has a mild flavor. It stores extremely well in the refrigerator and is a good staple for use in mixed salads as well as slaws, American or Chinese. Cook it like cabbage, or stir-fry it Chinese style.

> 3 tablespoons corn or peanut oil
> ¼ cup sesame seeds
> 2 slices ginger root (peeled and sliced to the thickness that suits your taste)
> 4 cups diced Chinese cabbage
> 1 cup diced fresh mushrooms
> 1 tablespoon soy sauce
> 1 tablespoon sherry or dry vermouth

¼ cup chicken stock
Salt and pepper to taste
1 teaspoon sesame oil

Warm a serving platter in an oven at the lowest temperature. Heat 1 tablespoon oil in a wok or skillet. Add the sesame seeds to coat and toast them evenly, then transfer them to a dish.

Add 1 tablespoon oil to the wok or skillet. Heat and add the ginger root slices. Brown them, then add the cabbage and stir-fry. Transfer cabbage to a warm platter.

Heat 1 tablespoon oil in the same skillet and add the mushrooms. Cook for 1 minute. Add the cabbage to the mushrooms and cook for another minute. Add soy sauce, sherry or vermouth, and chicken stock. Stir-fry on high heat for 1 minute. Adjust seasoning with salt and pepper, and sprinkle with sesame oil and toasted seeds. Serve immediately on the warm platter.

Green Cabbage
Serves 4 to 6.

When cabbage is cooked traditionally for boiled dinners, it is cut into thick wedges. But for preserving its excellent nutritional value, it should be shredded.

    2 pounds green cabbage, shredded
    1 tablespoon butter or oil
    Salt and freshly ground pepper
    1 teaspoon caraway seeds

Steam or cook cabbage, covered, in ½ inch water with a small amount of salt (personal taste) for 5 to 7 minutes. Turn it once; then test for doneness—it should be cooked through but still crunchy. Add pepper and caraway seeds for the last minute of cooking. Serve hot with robust meats or with grilled fish.

✳ *Suggestion*
For a creamy texture, draw off the cooking liquid if there is much remaining after the cabbage is almost finished. Add ½ to 1 cup light cream, sour cream, or yogurt. Simmer uncovered until liquid reduces.

Sweet and Sour Red Cabbage
Serves 6.

Choose this favorite recipe for a preprepared vegetable dish. Refrigerate for up to five days or freeze for up to one month. Serve with game, duck, pork, ham, or smoked sausage.

2 pounds red cabbage
2 tablespoons butter or oil
2 medium-sized onions, sliced
2 apples, peeled and diced
2 tablespoons lemon juice
2 tablespoons salt
2 tablespoons flour
3 tablespoons sugar
4 tablespoons vinegar

Trim off the bottom of the cabbage and discard it. Cut the cabbage in half and wash it well. Shred it by hand, with a chef's knife, or in a food processor.

Heat the butter or oil in a Dutch oven or stew pot with a tight-fitting lid; cook the onions, uncovered, until just glazed and lightly browned. Add cabbage, apples, lemon juice, and salt. Firmly cover and cook for 20 minutes.

Make a paste of the flour, sugar, and vinegar, and add it to the cabbage. Cover and cook for 20 to 30 minutes more. Adjust seasoning to your taste—some people like more tartness, some more sweetness, and some more saltiness.

Brussels Sprouts and White Onions in Creamy Sauce
Serves 8 to 10.

Brussels sprouts, generally regarded as one of the healthiest vegetables, are not the most popular. At Thanksgiving, I combine them with small white onions to create an interesting and tasteful mixture that entices even the most skeptical members of our family.

1 pound brussels sprouts
1 pound small white onions
1½ tablespoons butter
3 tablespoons flour
1 cup hot liquid reserved from cooking onions
1 cup hot milk
1 cup grated Cheddar or Monterey Jack cheese
½ teaspoon each dry mustard and paprika
Salt and freshly ground pepper to taste

Wash brussels sprouts. Cut off just the very ends, and clip off any dry, loose leaves. Using a knife, cut a cross at the bottom of the stem to decrease cooking time.

Wash onions but do not peel them. Cut a cross at the bottom of the root side to make peeling easier after parboiling.

Simmer brussels sprouts and onions in separate pots. Brussels sprouts will be tender in about 8 or 9 minutes. The cooking liquid for the sprouts can be discarded.

Simmer onions for 5 minutes. Strain and reserve the liquid. Refresh onions under cold water and then peel them. Boil the onions in the reserved liquid until tender. Again, reserve the onion liquid. Place the brussels sprouts and onions in a shallow oven casserole or a 3-quart stew pot.

Melt butter in a 2-quart saucepan. Add flour and stir over low heat for 1 minute. Whisk in the reserved hot onion liquid and then the hot milk. Raise heat slightly. Because the liquid is hot, the mixture will thicken in about 1 minute. Lower heat and simmer for a few minutes, stirring occasionally. Add cheese, dry mustard, and paprika. Taste. Add salt and pepper, if necessary. Simmer for another minute.

Pour the sauce over the vegetables. Preheat oven to 375°F. Bake the casserole for 15 to 20 minutes before serving. If using a stew pot, heat the creamed vegetables very slowly, stirring occasionally to prevent sticking.

✴ *Suggestion*

When using advance preparation and refrigeration, always bring refrigerated vegetables to room temperature before heating. If this recipe is prepared ahead and frozen in a casserole, it will require at least 45 to 50 minutes to defrost in a 400°F oven. Test the center with a fork. The tines should come out piping hot.

Kohlrabi
Serves 4.

Look for kohlrabi in your market. It looks like a bulb with leaves attached. Kohlrabies are usually green but vary in color to a lovely violet. They are so mild that they can be served raw as chips for dipping or stir-fried in Oriental dishes.

1 pound kohlrabi
1½ cups chicken broth diluted with water
1 teaspoon butter
1 teaspoon chopped fresh basil
1 teaspoon chopped fresh parsley
Salt and freshly ground pepper

Trim the leaves off kohlrabi. They can be cooked if they are very fresh, but the bulb is the usable portion. Peel the bulb and slice or cut into chunks.

Simmer the peeled and cut kohlrabi in ½ inch of diluted chicken stock for 7 to

8 minutes. Cover pan while cooking. Uncover and increase heat to high to reduce liquid to about 1 tablespoon. Add butter, basil, and parsley. Season with salt and freshly ground pepper.

✳ Suggestion

For creaminess, add ½ cup White Sauce (page 82) or add ¼ cup light cream and 1 tablespoon dry sherry. Simmer for sauce to thicken.

Stalks of Swiss Chard
Serves 4.

Swiss chard was the winner in our garden last summer. The shredded crisp leaves added another dimension to our salads. At another time, I cooked the leaves as I would spinach. Not a bit was wasted. Even the mild, sliced stalks were delicious when combined with a sauce or seasoned with herbs.

4 cups Swiss chard stalks
2 cups water
½ teaspoon salt
1 tablespoon butter
1 tablespoon flour
⅓ cup reserved cooking liquid combined
     with ⅓ cup warm milk
¼ teaspoon dry mustard
Salt and pepper to taste

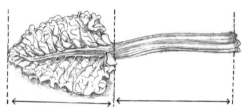

Plunge leaves in boiling water for a few minutes. Serve immediately!

Cut stalks to 2" pieces, cook 3-5 minutes in a saucepan or stir-fry. Use in this recipe.

Rinse stalks. Cut them into 2-inch pieces to make 4 cups. Combine Swiss chard stalks with water and salt in a saucepan. Cover and cook 3 to 5 minutes to desired crispness.

Strain liquid into a bowl. Measure ⅓ cup of the liquid (reserve the remainder for another use) and mix with warm milk. Set aside.

Melt butter in the same pot. Add flour and stir over low heat to make a roux. Then blend in warm liquid mixture and dry mustard. Stir for 2 to 3 minutes until the mixture thickens. Taste and adjust seasoning with salt and pepper. Serve as a side dish.

✳ Suggestions

- Make double the amount and freeze for up to one month.
- Use Swiss chard in stir-fry recipes.
- Wash and dry fresh leaves of Swiss chard. Pack suitable amounts in plastic bags for the freezer. To defrost, plunge the leaves into boiling water. Continue to cook for a few minutes or to your taste. Serve immediately with seasonings to taste.

Marinated Herbed Cucumbers
Serves 4.

Cucumbers grow abundantly in home gardens and they are always available in stores. Think of them as a staple. Once marinated, use cucumbers cold or hot as a side dish.

> 3 or 4 cucumbers (1 to 1½ pounds)
> ¼ cup vinegar
> ½ cup water
> 1 teaspoon salt
> 1 teaspoon sugar
> ½ cup chicken or vegetable stock
> 2 scallions, minced
> 1 tablespoon each minced fresh parsley and tarragon

Peel cucumbers, leaving small strips of green for color and texture. Cut in half, lengthwise. Scoop out seeds with a melon cutter or teaspoon if the seeds are large. Cut the cucumbers into slices.

Mix vinegar, water, salt, and sugar. Marinate cucumbers in this mixture for a minimum of 10 minutes. Add some ice cubes to keep them crisp. Cucumbers may be served cold at this point.

Drain cucumbers and dry on paper toweling. Heat stock with scallions. Add cucumbers and herbs. Simmer for 2 to 3 minutes, and then serve.

✳ *Suggestions*

- For another interesting cold salad, drain the liquid from the marinade. Add up to 1 cup yogurt or sour cream and 1 tablespoon minced chives or cilantro.
- Use Marinated Herbed Cucumbers as garnishes for hot or cold soups.
- Add ½ cup Marinated Herbed Cucumbers to tossed tomato and green salads or as a garnish for poached fish.

Purée of Root Vegetables
Serves 4 to 6.

We inherited a root cellar with our 1843 home when we moved to Vermont. I realize now how necessary root cellars were for the early settlers. They provided cold storage for basic vegetables—the staples in all cooking. Onions, carrots, potatoes, turnips, and winter squash were always on hand. Although we use it for an overflow of these vegetables, it has also become our wine cellar because of its ideal temperature.

2 medium potatoes (½ pound)
2 large carrots (½ pound)
1 parsnip
1 turnip (optional)
1 rib celery, roughly diced
1 small onion, quartered
1 tablespoon butter or oil
Salt and pepper to taste

Peel the potatoes, carrots, parsnip, and turnip and cut into thick slices.

Place the vegetables, along with the celery and onion, in a 2-quart saucepan with water to barely cover. Cover the saucepan and bring to a boil. Cook for 7 to 8 minutes. Test potatoes. As soon as the vegetables soften, drain off the liquid and reserve for vegetable stock or another use.

Purée the vegetables with butter or oil in a food processor, switching on and off briefly, until just smooth. Transfer to a bowl and adjust seasoning with salt and pepper.

To serve, form an oval mound next to a main course on a heated dinner plate. Run the tines of a fork over the top of the mound to make a design. If the purée is cooked hours ahead, transfer to a bowl covered with greased wax paper. Heat over warm water, double-boiler style.

✳ *Suggestions*

- You may refrigerate or freeze purées for other uses. Add to chicken stock for a soup.
- Add 1 tablespoon tomato paste for color.
- Cook purée with 1 or 2 cloves garlic.
- Experiment with different combinations of vegetables.
- Cook the purée with celeriac, when available. (Celeriac is a root vegetable with an intense celery flavor. See page 30.)

Braised Carrots and Apricots (Tzimmes)
Serves 6 to 8.

Every Jewish family has its own favorite recipe for tzimmes. *Tzimmes* in this reference means "combination." In our home, my children favor their grandmother's recipe that is usually served during Passover. Although this is a very old and delicious recipe, the idea of mixing fruits and vegetables has been gaining in popularity among cooks worldwide.

3 pounds carrots
½ pound dried apricots
2 cups chicken stock
½ teaspoon salt
½ cup light brown sugar

Peel carrots and cut into slices. Soak apricots in water to cover.

Combine carrots, apricots in water, chicken stock, and salt, with more water to barely cover the mixture in a saucepan. Cook, covered, at a simmer for 45 minutes. Uncover and continue to cook until all the broth has been absorbed. Sprinkle the top with sugar (less can be used), and place under the broiler for 45 seconds.

✹ *Suggestions*

- For a variation, add or substitute pitted prunes and sweet potatoes for the apricots. Bake in a casserole at 350°F for 1¼ hours.
- Prepare double the amount and freeze leftovers.

Baked Onion in Red Wine
Serves 4.

Consider this: An onion is a good source of vitamins A and C and contains a fair amount of calcium, phosphorus, potassium, and sulfur, with a count of only 8 calories per ½ cup. We all use onions in cooking, but why not use them as a solo accompaniment, perfect with grilled chicken, grilled chops, or that favorite hamburger.

3 large Spanish or Bermuda onions (3 pounds), sliced
1 cup hot stock (chicken, veal, beef, or vegetable)
1 cup dry red wine
2 sprigs Italian parsley, minced
½ teaspoon dried marjoram
1 tablespoon oil or butter (optional)
Salt and pepper to taste

Preheat oven to 400°F. Using a nonstick shallow pan or lightly greased pan, scatter onions on the pan. Bake for 15 minutes. Stir once or twice so the onions do not burn.

When the onions are evenly browned, pour on hot stock and ½ cup wine. Bake for another 10 minutes. Raise the temperature to 425°F. Add remaining wine, minced parsley, and marjoram. Bake for another 10 minutes or until almost all the liquid has evaporated. Blend in oil or butter if you wish. Salt and pepper to taste. Serve next to grilled chicken or meat.

Braised Leeks
Serves 4.

Leeks are elegant members of the onion family. Unless you grow them in your own garden or live in a climate where they are grown, leeks may be extravagantly priced. They lend their unique flavor to soups and fish stews, but for a special treat serve them braised, sometimes in a casserole or as a salad. The dark green leaves of the leeks are sometimes used for flavoring stocks and oftentimes used for decorations after they are blanched.

4 to 6 medium leeks
1 cup chicken or vegetable stock
Salt and pepper to taste

Trim the leeks by cutting them 1 to 2 inches below the white portion. Split the leeks lengthwise and then in half. Wash thoroughly under running water to release sand.

Use a skillet or a deep sauté pan. Cook leeks in ½ inch chicken or vegetable stock. Cover tightly and simmer for 7 to 8 minutes. Uncover and reduce the stock until it just coats the pan. Season with salt and pepper to taste, if necessary.

✳ *Suggestions*

- Serve hot as a side dish.
- Serve cool with a salad dressing on greens.
- Cut into 1-inch pieces and toss into potato or pasta salad.
- Purée Braised Leeks in the food processor with some of the stock. Use them as a base for fish dishes or as an addition to soups.

Mushrooms

The mushroom is a hidden treasure in all good cooking. I would be remiss not to stress its importance. There is hardly any waste, since even the ugly tip ends can be used in stocks, soups, and sauces. The flavor of mushrooms adds a complexity to the final results of dishes that we often take for granted.

Substitute mushrooms for carrots in the recipe for Carrot Soup (page 66). For a low-calorie, low-fat hors d'oeuvre, bring out your stored chafing dish and fill it with steamed mushroom caps and minced herbs. Marinate sliced raw mushrooms in balsamic vinegar, oil, salt, and pepper and toss with salad greens or distribute over sliced ripe tomatoes. Stuff the ample cavities of whole, large mushrooms (reserve the stems for Duxelles, page 114) with cheese, herbed bread crumbs, or minced leftovers—simmer these caps in a small amount of broth (or bake in the oven at 400°F for 10 minutes).

Mushrooms are always available and reasonably priced in fall and winter, perishable and expensive in summer. In today's markets cultivated mushrooms come either packaged or loose. Choose them carefully. They should be firm and white; this is easier to judge when they are sold loosely by the pound. Refrigerate them in an aerated paper box, a cloth bag, or paper toweling, never in plastic wrap.

Unless they are very dirty, do not wash mushrooms. Wipe the mushrooms clean. If you must, give them a quick rinse, then pat them dry.

Today, the cultivation of mushrooms is practically a science. There is also an increased demand for the wild and unusual varieties. One company in northern Massachusetts grows shiitake mushrooms in an old warehouse and they are, indeed, very good. Wild mushrooms grow all around us, but unless you are very knowledge-able, do not pick them yourself for culinary use.

Sautéed Mushrooms
Makes 2½ - 3 cups.

2 pounds mushrooms
1 tablespoon olive oil or butter
2 tablespoons minced shallots or onions
salt and pepper to taste

Heat a skillet slowly and then add the oil or butter. Sauté shallots for 1 to 2 minutes until glazed, and then add mushrooms. Shake pan to brown them evenly and salt and pepper to taste. Use as an accompaniment for any hot dish.

You can freeze mushrooms for up to six months—there is always some loss in flavor and texture, but that can be adjusted with seasonings. Cover small batches of mushrooms with chicken or vegetable broth and freeze.

Duxelles
Makes about 1 cup.

Use Duxelles as a basic vegetable flavoring.

1 pound mushrooms, minced
¼ cup minced shallots
1 tablespoon butter
Salt and pepper
Touch of Madeira or sherry (optional)

Sauté minced mushrooms and shallots in butter. Mushrooms will produce liquid, so sauté until the pan is practically dry and liquid has evaporated. Season with salt and pepper. A touch of Madeira or sherry may be added. Refrigerate in a covered container for up to four days or freeze for up to one month.

✳ Suggestions

- Serve Duxelles as a side dish or spread on toasted French bread for a light lunch or appetizer.
- Use Duxelles as fillings for pancakes and omelets.

Szechwan Eggplant in Chili Garlic Sauce
Serves 3 to 4.

Peggy Berg was a special friend and teacher in my Great Neck Cooking School program. She was so dedicated to Chinese cooking that she had a special wok burner installed in her kitchen. However, her Szechwan Eggplant can be cooked in a skillet as well.

Eggplant Mixture
1 large eggplant (about 2 pounds)
1 small sweet red pepper
1 clove garlic, minced
1 scallion, diced
1 cup oil
¼ teaspoon red pepper flakes
1 teaspoon sesame oil

Chili Garlic Sauce
1 teaspoon chili paste with
    garlic (found in specialty
    food shops)
1 tablespoon soy sauce
1 teaspoon brown sugar
¼ teaspoon salt
1 tablespoon sherry

Wash the eggplant. Cut off stem, but do not peel. Cut the eggplant in half and then into strips about 3 inches long and 1 inch wide.

Remove the seeds and white membranes of the red pepper. Cut it into cubes. Place the eggplant, red pepper, garlic, and scallion on a sheet of wax paper.

Mix the sauce ingredients in a small bowl.

Heat oil and red pepper flakes in a wok or skillet until the temperature is 375°F. Add only a few strips of eggplant at a time so that the temperature of the oil does not fall below 325°F. Stir-fry, moving the pieces of eggplant so they touch the hot surface of the wok or skillet. Cook about 5 minutes, until the eggplant is wilted but not falling apart. Drain the eggplant through a colander placed over a bowl. The oil can be reused if it has not darkened in color.

Return 1 tablespoon of the oil to the heated wok. Add red pepper, garlic, and scallion. Stir-fry until lightly glazed. Add sauce and heat until bubbling. Return eggplant to the wok and carefully stir with the sauce until hot.

Place on a heated dish. Dribble sesame oil on top.

✹ *Suggestion*

Instead of frying the eggplant, cut the eggplant in half. Score deep gashes, 1 inch apart on the cut side. Steam until soft. This procedure eliminates the first stir-fry. Cut the flesh of the eggplant into strips and proceed with the next step in the directions above.

Eggplant Manicotti
Serves 6.

The oval slices of eggplant in this recipe are substitutes for crêpes or manicotti noodles. If time permits, fry or broil double the amount, enough for leftovers for another use.

    1 eggplant (about 2 pounds)
    A sprinkle of kosher (coarse) salt
    2 cups olive or corn oil
    1 pound cottage, ricotta, or pot cheese
    ¼ pound Parmesan cheese, freshly grated
    1 teaspoon oregano
    Salt and pepper to taste

Trim off the stem and bottom ends of the eggplant. Do not peel. Use a sharp knife to cut even slices (about ¼ inch) lengthwise. The slices will look like ovals. Place the slices on a sheet of wax paper. Sprinkle them with kosher salt. Cover with another sheet of wax paper, and weigh them down with heavy objects. (I keep a few bricks on hand for this purpose.)

After 20 to 30 minutes, rinse the eggplant in cold water and dry thoroughly. I sometimes omit this step if the eggplant does not have too many dark seeds in the flesh.

Heat oil in a deep sauté pan or fryer. If very little oil is used, the eggplant will absorb all the oil. If you fry in more oil, the eggplant slices will brown and cook quickly. The remaining oil can be reused if it is not allowed to scorch. Therefore, I recommend 2 cups oil to a 9-inch sauté pan to fill to a depth of about ½ inch. Keep the temperature of the oil no higher than 375°F.

Fry two eggplant slices at a time. Do not crowd the pan. Drain immediately on paper toweling.

Mix cheeses, oregano, and salt and pepper to taste. Place 3 to 4 tablespoons of the mixture down the middle of each eggplant slice, lengthwise. Roll up each slice as you would a crêpe. Place seam-side down in a greased casserole.

Preheat oven to 400°F. Bake the casserole for 15 minutes. Serve two slices per person on a heated dish. Tomato Sauce (page 88) or Ragu Sauce (page 89) can be used as a base or as a spread on top of each serving.

✸ *Suggestions*

- You may broil the eggplant instead of frying it. Lightly brush both sides of each slice with olive oil. Broil until the eggplant is lightly browned and soft.
- Combine one 10-ounce package of frozen chopped spinach, defrosted and squeezed dry, with the cheese filling. More eggplant can also be used for additional filling.

Four-Vegetable Pie
Serves 6 to 8.

If you have not yet read the preceding recipe for Eggplant Manicotti, read it now. You will not only learn how to prepare eggplant, but you will understand my suggestion for cooking more than you need for one recipe. Eggplant is very versatile and can be prepared up to three days in advance and refrigerated. In the following arrangement, eggplant is used as a crust for the pie.

> 1 eggplant (about 2 pounds)
> Kosher (coarse) salt
> 4 medium zucchini (about 1½ pounds)
> 1 teaspoon salt
> 1 tablespoon olive oil
> 1 clove garlic, minced
> 2 tablespoons chopped fresh parsley
> ½ teaspoon each thyme and marjoram
> Freshly ground pepper
> 4 tablespoons plain bread crumbs
> ½ cup Duxelles (page 114)
> 8 to 12 cherry tomatoes, cut in halves

Cut unpeeled eggplant into ¼-inch slices. Salt and fry or broil as described in the recipe for Eggplant Manicotti.

Peel the zucchini, unless it is garden fresh and young. Grate the zucchini and transfer to a colander set over a bowl. Mix with 1 teaspoon salt and set aside to rest. The salt will extract water from the zucchini. After 10 minutes, press the zucchini and collect liquid in the bowl. Save the liquid for another use.

Heat 1 tablespoon olive oil in a skillet over medium heat. Sauté zucchini and garlic for 2 to 3 minutes. Add herbs. Add freshly ground pepper to taste. Remove from heat.

Preheat the oven to 400°F. Use a 9-inch quiche pan or a shallow ceramic baking pan. To assemble the pie, place overlapping slices of eggplant to cover the bottom of the pan, bringing some slices up around the sides to form a shell. Sprinkle 2 tablespoons bread crumbs over eggplant.

Spread a layer of Duxelles and then a layer of zucchini. Sprinkle the remainder of the bread crumbs to cover the top. Place the halves of the cherry tomatoes, cut-side up, evenly over the bread crumbs.

Bake for 15 to 18 minutes. Cut into wedges and serve piping hot.

☀ Suggestions

- Beat together 1 egg and ½ cup light cream. Pour the mixture over the top of the pie before baking.
- Place very thin slices of fontina, Gruyère, or mozzarella cheese on top for the last few minutes of baking time.
- For a multivegetable pie, parboil thinly sliced potatoes with sliced onion. Drain them well and place them on the bottom of the baking pan before lining it with the eggplant.

Stuffed Peppers Barese (Pepperoni Imbettiti alla Barese)
Serves 8.

During our travels, I have found that the most dependable regional recipes were given to me by friends whose families still cooked with old-time authenticity rather than by professional chefs. Marie Agresti supplied this one.

    8 green frying peppers
    1 cup plain bread crumbs
    12 oil-cured black olives, pitted and diced
    One 2-ounce can flat anchovy fillets, diced
    1 clove garlic, minced
    ½ teaspoon oregano
    ½ cup minced Italian parsley
    1 tablespoon freshly grated Romano cheese
    ½ teaspoon pepper
    1 tablespoon dry white wine
    2 tablespoons olive oil
    ⅓ cup cold water
    Olive oil for baking

Wash and dry peppers well. Use a small, sharp knife to neatly cut around the stem of each pepper. Set the stems aside. Remove seeds from the cavities.

Mix in a bowl bread crumbs, olives, anchovies, garlic, herbs, cheese, pepper, wine, olive oil, and water. Stuff the peppers. Place the stems back to fit each pepper.

Preheat the oven to 400°F. Oil a shallow casserole and place peppers side by side so they fit snugly. Brush each pepper with olive oil as you place it in the baking dish. Cover with aluminum foil and bake for 20 to 25 minutes. Uncover and bake just to brown tops.

Serve hot or at room temperature as an appetizer or side dish, perfect for a buffet.

Potatoes Anna
Serves 6 to 8.

On our first trip to Europe in 1959, a friend introduced us to the potato chef on the SS *United States*. He was in charge of a kitchen where only potatoes were prepared. We were fortunate to be able to place special orders, even for potatoes. Potatoes Anna was my choice with one of the dinners. This classic is no more than sliced potatoes, properly layered with melted butter to turn out a beautifully glazed potato cake.

6 to 8 medium potatoes
¼ pound (8 tablespoons) unsalted butter, melted
Salt and freshly ground white pepper

There are special pans for Potatoes Anna, but I use a 9-inch-round, straight-sided sauté pan. Butter the pan lightly and place on low heat.

Peel the potatoes. Work quickly. Do not soak them in water, since they would lose much of their starchiness. Cut two at a time into ⅛-inch slices, evenly stacked. Starting at the center, place one slice and continue to overlap slices in a ring. Then overlap this ring going in the opposite direction. Continue until the bottom of the pan is covered. The bottom layer is most important, because when the potato cake is turned over, it becomes the top. Cut enough slices in half to build an outside edge by placing the cut-side flat against the rim of the pan.

Continue to make layers, dribbling some melted butter on each layer and sprinkling with salt and pepper. There should be a total of four or five layers. Place a round of heavy aluminum foil on the potatoes. Press down and then cook until you can smell the browning butter. Shake pan so the potatoes do not stick to the bottom. Cover pan.

If the pan is ovenproof, place it in a 400°F oven for 20 to 30 minutes. If the pan is not ovenproof, lower the heat on the stove and cook for 15 minutes.

Pour off excess butter. Reserve for another use. Place a 12-inch-round serving platter upside-down over the pan and invert the pan on the dish. Cut into wedges and serve at once.

An All-Time Favorite: The Crisp Potato (Other than French Fries)

Use whichever variety of potato you prefer, including sweet potatoes. Minimize the oil and you will enjoy one of the healthiest of all treats. Choose from the following three recipes.

The Crisp Potato I
Serves 4.

4 medium potatoes
1 teaspoon oil

Cut unpeeled potatoes in half. Drop oil in the center of a shallow baking pan. Dip the cut side of the potato into the oil. Move the potato to the side of the pan. Repeat with the other halves of the potatoes, cut-side down. Preheat oven to 400°F. and bake the potatoes for 30 to 40 minutes or until they feel tender and the cut side is crisp.

The Crisp Potato II
Serves 4.

4 medium potatoes
Oil for baking

Grease a shallow baking pan with oil. Cut unpeeled potatoes into ¼-inch slices. Rub each side of the potatoes in the oil as you place the slices in the pan. Bake for 20 to 25 minutes at 450°F. Sometimes they puff! Do not let them burn.

The Crisp Potato III
Serves 4 to 6.

This recipe is perfect for small and large parties.
Increase the amount as necessary. Use a roasting pan
for larger amounts and prepare a few hours ahead. Reheat before
serving.

 6 medium potataoes (about 2 pounds)
 2 tablespoons oil
 ½ teaspoon paprika
 ¼ teaspoon each salt and pepper

 Cut unpeeled potatoes into chunks. Use a shallow baking pan and add oil,
paprika, and salt and pepper. Mix with the potatoes. Preheat oven to 400°F. Bake
potatoes for 30 to 40 minutes, stirring occasionally.

Potato Pancakes
Serves 6 to 8.

I will never forget the time my mother spent grating potatoes by hand. To this day,
I am still trying to match the texture she was able to achieve. Although until recently
I grated half by hand and minced the remainder in the food processor, I have now
succumbed to the method that follows.

 6 medium potatoes (about 2 pounds)
 1 onion, quartered
 1 cup boiling water
 2 eggs
 1 teaspoon salt
 ½ teaspoon freshly ground pepper
 ¼ cup flour, matzo meal, or cracker crumbs
 ½ cup oil
 2 tablespoons butter

 Peel potatoes and cut into chunks. Place the metal blade in the food processor.
Place half the potatoes and the onion in the machine. Pulse on and off. Change the
blade to the grater and grate the remainder of the potatoes. Transfer to a strainer over
a bowl. Pour boiling water over the potatoes and onion. Mix briefly to press out some
of the moisture. The boiling water will prevent the potatoes from discoloring
quickly.

Pour off the water in the bowl. There may be some starch at the bottom of the bowl, but leave it there. Beat the eggs in the bowl. Add potatoes, seasonings, and flour, matzo meal, or cracker crumbs. Mix.

Heat oil and butter in a skillet. Drop potato mixture into the hot oil and butter by heaping tablespoons. Brown on both sides. Keep pancakes in a 300°F oven until all the batter is used. Serve warm with applesauce.

✳ *Suggestion*

Substitute zucchini for potatoes. Salt zucchini in a strainer. After 15 minutes press out the liquid. Mix with beaten eggs, seasonings, and flour. Fry as directed.

Mashed Potatoes
Serves 3 to 4.

You can never go wrong when you serve mashed potatoes, especially if gravy accompanies the main course. Certainly it is easy enough to boil or bake potatoes in preparation.

> 3 medium potatoes (about 1 pound), peeled and quartered
> Salt and pepper to taste
> Splash hot milk or vegetable stock
> 1 tablespoon butter or oil (optional)

Boil peeled and quartered potatoes in salted water. Use a pot with a tight-fitting cover and test for doneness after 7 or 8 minutes. Pour off liquid, but reserve it for stocks and other uses. Place pot over low heat, stirring for 1 minute to reduce moisture. Bake the potatoes instead of boiling if your oven is already in use or if baking is your preference.

In either case, mash potatoes with salt and pepper to taste. Use a small amount of hot liquid (never cold), such as milk or vegetable stock, for creaminess and 1 tablespoon butter or oil if you choose.

Note that if you must use a food processor for mashing, pulse it on and off briefly. Potatoes become gummy if beaten too long. I use a perforated flat kitchen tool. A potato ricer, food mill, or wooden spoon and a strong arm will each do the same.

✳ *Suggestions*

- Add 2 tablespoons Roasted Garlic (page 27) to the potatoes.
- Make half the amount of Bagna Cauda (page 41) and add hot to mashed potatoes.
- Add ¼ cup sautéed shallots and ¼ pound sautéed shiitake mushrooms.
- For a special celebration, fold in thinly sliced white or black truffles.

Ma's Potato Paprikash
Serves 4 to 6.

I could never write about potatoes without including the family's choice: my mother-in-law's Hungarian specialty.

3 tablespoons butter (use less if you must)
2 to 3 medium onions, diced
1 large green bell pepper (about ½ pound), diced
3-5 medium potatoes (about 1½ pounds), peeled and sliced
1 pound fresh, ripe tomatoes, peeled and seeded, or 1 cup canned
1 teaspoon Hungarian sweet paprika
Salt and pepper to taste

Prepare all ingredients before starting to cook. Use a skillet with a tight-fitting cover.

Melt butter in the skillet. Sauté onions until golden, not burned. Add green peppers. Stir and cook for 2 to 3 minutes. Add potatoes; mix with the onions and green peppers. Cover the skillet and cook for 15 to 18 minutes over low heat. Do not allow potatoes to scorch.

Uncover and add tomatoes and seasonings. Cook for another 10 minutes and stir to combine all ingredients. The final mixture will be soft, perhaps mushy, but it will be most delicious.

Country Kitchen Parsnips
Serves 4 to 6.

Americans may sometimes use parsnips in a soup or stew, but few use it as a solo vegetable. Parsnips cook faster than carrots or potatoes, and they are particularly delicious with a touch of cream.

6 to 8 parsnips (about 2 pounds)
½ teaspoon salt
¼ cup plain bread crumbs
½ cup chicken stock
½ cup light cream (or half-and-half)
½ teaspoon marjoram
1 tablespoon chopped fresh parsley

Peel parsnips. Cut into round slices or lengthwise into quarters. Place in a saucepan with water to cover. Add salt and cover the saucepan. Bring to a boil and simmer for 5 minutes.

Preheat oven to 350°F. Spread 2 tablespoons bread crumbs on the bottom of an 8- or 9-inch shallow casserole.

When the parsnips are ready, strain off the liquid. Place parsnips in the casserole. Mix stock, cream, marjoram, and parsley in a bowl. Pour the mixture over the parsnips. Sprinkle the top with the remaining bread crumbs. Bake for 30 to 40 minutes until the liquid is absorbed and the top is browned.

Baked Yellow Squash or Zucchini
Serves 6 to 8.

If you have a vegetable garden, you know how summer squash plants take over in the garden. The large leaves cover the ground as the first lovely flowers blossom. The flowers are edible and decorative on salads. The Italians fry and sometimes stuff them. We use the matured small squash when we can find them hidden under the large leaves, but often my husband surprises me with a jumbo that grew hidden from sight. The big ones are perfect for puréed soups.

    8 to 10 small yellow squash or zucchini (about 2 pounds)
    2 tablespoons olive oil
    ¼ cup minced shallots
    ½ cup plain bread crumbs
    1 teaspoon marjoram
    Salt and pepper

Scrub the squash. Parboil it in at least 3 quarts boiling, salted water for 2 minutes. Refresh in cold water and drain well. Cut each squash in half lengthwise and score the flesh three times, about ⅛ inch deep.

Heat a skillet with 1 tablespoon olive oil. Sauté shallots for a few minutes until glazed. Do not burn. Remove from heat and add bread crumbs, marjoram, and salt and pepper to taste.

Grease a casserole with the remaining oil. Sprinkle half the bread crumb mixture on the bottom of the casserole. Place squash halves side by side over the bread crumbs. Criss-cross the halves of squash for a second layer, if necessary. Sprinkle the remaining bread crumbs on top. Cover with aluminum foil. This dish can be prepared one day ahead or in advance on the same day and refrigerated.

Preheat oven to 350°F. Bake the squash for 20 minutes. Uncover and bake for 10 minutes more.

Butternut Squash
Serves 2 to 3.

All winter squash deserve special attention. Store them in a cool place and they will last for months. Butternut squash is only one of many varieties, including pumpkin. They can all be prepared similarly. Treat them as you would potato—peeled, cut, and broiled or boiled whole and unpeeled. You can bake them, as well, in a small amount of water. Of course, no matter which way you choose to prepare them, always remove the seeds and stringy pulp before serving.

> 1 small squash (about 1½ pounds)
> Dash salt
> 1 tablespoon lemon juice
> Brown sugar or maple syrup to taste

Cut the squash in half lengthwise and then peel it. Use a sharp potato peeler, a harp or square type, not the long swivel one. Remove the seeds and stringy pulp.

Place peeled, 2-inch chunks in a saucepan with water just to cover. Add a dash of salt. Simmer for 8 to 10 minutes, testing for doneness with a fork. Pour off water. Add lemon juice and brown sugar or maple syrup to taste.

✸ Suggestions

- Try baking pieces of squash in a greased casserole with a sprinkling of lemon juice, brown sugar, and bread crumbs. Dot with butter or oil for flavor and browning. Bake at 350°F for 25 to 30 minutes.
- Or cut unpeeled squash lengthwise. Place it cut-side down in a baking pan with ½ inch water. Bake at 375°F for 30 to 40 minutes. Add more water if it evaporates during baking. Test for doneness by pressing top for softness. Transfer squash to a plate and remove and discard seeds and stringy pulp. Scoop out squash and mash with a few tablespoons hot milk and a very small amount of cinnamon. Add salt and pepper to taste.

Acorn Squash
Serves 3 to 4.

Most often we bake acorn squash in halves with the seeds and stringy pulp removed. Generally, the cavity is filled with butter and a sweetener, but why not try chicken broth for fewer calories and less fat! The preparation below is different. It is practical for faster cooking, smaller portions, and a special presentation.

   1 medium acorn squash (about 1½ pounds)
   Peas or Purée of Root Vegetables (page 109) for filling

Trim off the ends of the acorn squash, then cut the squash into 1-inch slices. Remove seeds and strings. You will probably get four or five rings from a 1½-pound squash.

Preheat oven to 350°F. Place the rings of squash in a shallow pan filled with ½ inch water. Bake for 20 to 25 minutes. Test for doneness.

Serve one ring per person. Fill the cavities with peas or Purée of Root Vegetables.

Vegetable Custard with Zucchini
Serves 8.

There are those special occasions that call for richness, creaminess, and a totally different use for vegetables. This smooth custard can stand alone as a perfect complement to grilled fish. You can also serve it on a bed of tomato purée with crusty bread as a lunch or light supper.

   1 or 2 zucchini (each about ½ to 1 inch wide)
   2 cups Purée of Root Vegetables—carrot, potato, winter squash, parsnip, or
      celeriac (page 109)
   ¼ teaspoon ground cumin
   Salt and pepper to taste
   2 eggs
   ½ to 1 cup heavy or light cream (more cream produces a lighter texture)
   Butter or oil for greasing ramekins

Blanch zucchini for 30 seconds in boiling water, then immediately refresh in cold water. Drain and dry on paper toweling. Cut into very thin slices without peeling.

Grease eight 3- or 4-ounce ramekins or Pyrex molds. Line the bottom and sides of each with slices of zucchini. Place the ramekins or molds in a baking pan that is at least 2 or 3 inches deep.

Preheat oven to 350°F. Beat purée, seasonings, eggs, and cream in a food processor for just 30 or 40 seconds until smooth. Fill the ramekins with the purée mixture. Pour boiling or very hot water into the baking pan, enough to fill halfway up around the molds.

Bake for 25 minutes, at which point the custard should be set.

Gently slip a table knife around the zucchini in each mold. Invert custards onto a heated serving dish. If you prepare the custards in advance, place a greased sheet of wax paper over the molds. Add boiling water to the outside pan to reheat the custards.

Steamed Spinach
Serves 3 to 4.

Spinach appears in baby foods as well as haute cuisine. Baked potato with spinach has long been a recommended combination for toddlers, and mothers have thrived on the leftovers. On the other hand, spinach is used in the sophisticated Oysters Rockefeller and in Florentine recipes.

Fresh spinach is actually easier to cook than to clean. Always break off the heavy stems and discard them. Fill the sink with cold water and swirl spinach around in the water. Let it rest for a few minutes until the sand settles. Sometimes it may need another rinse. Transfer the spinach to a colander or directly into a pot for cooking.

Prewashed spinach is available in bags, but even then you should break off the stems and rinse the leaves. There are some good frozen chopped spinach products that will work well when time is short.

1 pound spinach, washed
Salt, pepper, and nutmeg to taste

After washing spinach, pile it into a 3- or 4-quart saucepan while it is still wet. Cover and turn heat on high. When the cover feels hot to your touch, remove the cover. Reduce heat to low. Stir the spinach and cook for 3 to 4 minutes. Season to taste.

✹ Suggestions

- Add 1 tablespoon butter or ¼ cup light cream to the steamed spinach.
- Add ½ cup sautéed onion or ¼ cup sautéed shallots to the steamed spinach.
- Add ½ cup ricotta cheese or 2 ounces cream cheese to the steamed spinach.
- Chop spinach coarsely in a food processor, then fold in ½ cup sautéed onion and ½ cup yogurt or sour cream.

Quick Creamed Spinach
Serves 3 to 4.

1 tablespoon butter or oil
1 medium onion, diced
1 pound spinach, steamed and chopped
1 tablespoon flour

½ cup milk or cream
Salt, pepper, and nutmeg to taste

Heat a skillet with butter or oil. Sauté onion and add chopped spinach. Turn off heat. Sprinkle flour on the spinach, then stir in milk (cream is even more delicious), salt, pepper, and nutmeg to taste. Cook over low heat until the liquid is absorbed and the spinach is creamy. When preparing in advance, transfer the creamed spinach to a bowl, cover with greased wax paper, and heat over simmering water before serving.

Spinach Soufflé
Serves 4 to 6.

3 tablespoons butter
3 tablespoons flour
1 cup hot milk
2 tablespoons freshly grated Parmesan cheese
1½ pounds fresh spinach, cooked, or one 12-ounce package frozen chopped spinach (defrosted and squeezed dry)
1 teaspoon salt
¼ teaspoon each pepper and nutmeg
Pinch cayenne pepper
3 eggs, separated
3 extra egg whites
⅛ teaspoon cream of tartar
Pinch salt

Preheat oven to 375°F. Grease a 1½-quart Pyrex or soufflé dish with 1 teaspoon butter.

Melt the remaining butter in a saucepan. Add flour to the butter and stir to make a roux. Add hot milk and whisk well. It will thicken quickly. Add cheese, spinach, and seasonings. Remove from heat to the counter. Whisk in egg yolks, one at a time.

In a bowl, beat all egg whites with cream of tartar and pinch of salt until the egg whites cling to the bowl and are stiff.

Fold half of the beaten egg whites into the spinach mixture until well blended. Fold in the remaining egg whites quickly to keep the lightness.

Pour into the soufflé dish and bake for 25 minutes.

Use a large spoon and fork to cut the soufflé into wedges for serving. If the center is somewhat moist or wet, serve it as a sauce over the dry portion. It will all be well cooked.

✸ *Suggestion*
Substitute Swiss chard greens or even broccoli or corn for the spinach.

Spinach Flavored with Vegetables and Cheese
Makes 3 cups.

This is my basic filling for crêpes, manicotti, ravioli, spinach molds, vegetable lasagne, and many other dishes. The mixture can be made ahead and refrigerated for up to three days or frozen for up to one month.

1½ pounds fresh spinach, coarsely chopped, or one 12-ounce package frozen
    chopped spinach
1 tablespoon olive oil
2 to 3 medium onions, diced
½ cup each diced celery and carrot
2 cloves garlic, minced
¼ teaspoon salt
¼ teaspoon each ground cumin and red pepper flakes
½ teaspoon ground allspice
¾ pound mushrooms, sliced
¼ teaspoon freshly grated nutmeg
1 egg
1 egg yolk (reserve white for another use)
⅓ cup flour
½ cup ricotta cheese
½ cup freshly grated Parmesan cheese
Salt and freshly ground pepper to taste

Wash spinach and cook for only 1 minute, following directions for Steamed Spinach (page 127). Transfer to a strainer. Press out liquid. If frozen chopped spinach is being used, defrost completely and press out liquid.

Heat a skillet with 1 tablespoon olive oil. Sauté onions for 1 minute. Add celery, carrot, garlic, salt, cumin, red pepper flakes, and allspice. Sauté over low heat for 4 to 5 minutes until all vegetables are glazed. Transfer to a food processor but do not run at this point.

In the same skillet, sauté mushrooms for 3 to 4 minutes, adding a drop more of oil if necessary. Season with nutmeg. Mix in spinach and stir for a minute or two until any spinach liquid is evaporated. Transfer to the food processor with the other vegetables. Add egg, egg yolk, and flour. Run the food processor on and off for 3 or 4 seconds. The mixture should be coarse, not puréed. Transfer to a 1-quart bowl. Blend in cheeses. Taste and adjust seasoning with salt and pepper.

✳ Suggestions

- The spinach filling can be used as a filling for vegetable ravioli.
- Make a casserole with the spinach filling. Top with bread crumbs and mozzarella cheese. Bake for 20 minutes at 375°F.
- Use the spinach filling to fill large pasta shells or crêpes. Bake in a 375°F oven on a base of fresh Tomato Sauce (page 88) or buttered bread crumbs.
- Prepare lasagne with alternating layers of the spinach filling, Tomato Sauce, and Béchamel Sauce (page 82).
- Use the spinach filling as a stuffing for fish and breast of chicken.

Ratatouille
Serves 8 to 10.

Ratatouille (translated as "coarse stew") has become a familiar food word in our homes. This popular vegetable stew originated in kitchens along the Mediterranean where eggplants, peppers, zucchini, herbs, and garlic grow in abundance. No wonder there are so many different recipes! Many years ago I was advised by my friend Paula Peck to cook the vegetables separately for best results. It is definitely worth the effort.

1 eggplant (about 1½ pounds)
1 tablespoon kosher (coarse) salt
3 to 4 zucchini (1 to 1½ pounds)
½ cup olive oil
3 medium onions, diced
2 green peppers, seeds and white membranes removed, roughly diced
3 cloves garlic, minced (about 1 tablespoon)
2 pounds fresh, ripe tomatoes, skinned and seeded, or 2 cups canned crushed
    tomatoes
½ teaspoon each thyme, basil, and tarragon (double amount if using fresh herbs)
1 bay leaf
Salt and freshly ground black pepper
2 tablespoons chopped fresh Italian parsley

Wash eggplant and cut off stem end. Do not peel. Cut into 1-inch chunks. Place on a sheet of wax paper and sprinkle with about 1 teaspoon coarse salt. Set aside for 20 to 30 minutes. Scrub zucchini. Do not peel.

In the meantime, heat 2 tablespoons oil in a 4- or 5-quart ovenproof stew pot. Add onions and sauté for 3 to 4 minutes until golden. Mix in green peppers and garlic. Continue to cook for 2 to 3 minutes. Add tomatoes and herbs. Cover and simmer for 15 to 20 minutes. While the mixture is cooking, rinse eggplant and dry well with paper toweling.

Heat a skillet with 2 tablespoons oil. Add eggplant and brown over high heat for 1 to 2 minutes, shaking the pan to prevent sticking. Cover skillet, lower heat, and cook for 3 to 4 minutes. Transfer the eggplant to a bowl.

Add 2 tablespoons oil to the same skillet. Sauté zucchini for a few minutes until cooked but not mushy. Lightly combine the zucchini and eggplant with the pepper-tomato mixture.

Taste and adjust seasoning with salt and pepper. Add Italian parsley. Serve hot as an all-purpose side dish.

✳ *Suggestions*

- Ratatouille can be prepared up to two days in advance. Bake it in a casserole and serve buffet style.
- Serve it at room temperature in the summer. Sprinkle with balsamic vinegar and olive oil.
- Prepare ahead and use it as a filling for omelets and crêpes. It is especially good for brunch and lunch and as a contribution for fundraising events.

Braised Bean Curd with Fresh Parsley and Mushrooms (Ma Gu Don Fu)
Serves 4.

Florence Lin, a fine Chinese cook and teacher, has shared many recipes with me. This is one that I especially requested for vegetarian friends and students.

1 large piece bean curd (tofu), about 5" x 4" x 2"
10 ounces fresh mushrooms
2 tablespoons corn oil
2 teaspoons ginger root, peeled and minced
¼ teaspoon kosher (coarse) salt
¾ cup chopped Chinese parsley (cilantro), including tender stems
1 tablespoon Maggi sauce
1 tablespoon light soy sauce
½ cup water or chicken stock
1½ tablespoons cornstarch combined with 3 tablespoons water
2 teaspoons sesame oil

Dice the bean curd into ½-inch pieces and place in a strainer. Rinse mushrooms lightly and slice them. Measure all ingredients and place them near the cooking area.

Heat a wok or a straight-sided sauté pan over moderate heat until hot. Add corn oil and swirl to coat the pan. Add ginger, then mushrooms. Stir-fry for 2 minutes.

Add salt and ½ cup of the parsley. Mix well. Transfer to a heated dish on the side.

Place bean curd in the same heated wok or pan. Add Maggi sauce, soy sauce, and water or stock to the bean curd. Bring to a rapid boil and mix gently. Simmer for 2 to 3 minutes.

Return mushrooms to the wok or pan. Pour in the cornstarch-and-water mixture. Combine gently until a glaze is formed. Add sesame oil.

Transfer to a heated serving dish and garnish with the remaining parsley. Serve piping hot.

6

Dressings and Salads

Salads include all categories of foods, yet we usually associate them with vegetables and greens. Add today's leftover of fish or chicken to a tossed salad and it becomes tomorrow's dinner. Refrigerate cooked green beans for two or three days and include them in the popular Salad Niçoise. Rice, grains, and beans combine with various foods for wonderful summertime salads.

I begin this chapter with salad dressings because they play such an important role in flavoring the salads. Sample the vinegars and oils for personal preference: You may prefer lemon juice to vinegar. Calorie-counters may want to use yogurt or tofu instead of oil. If herbs or spices are new to you, try a pinch of this and that until you are sure that you do indeed want more.

133

Some Pointers Concerning Dressings and Salads

- It is easy to mix salad dressing as you need it. If you prepare a large quantity in advance, store it, tightly sealed, in a cool place or in the refrigerator.
- My favorite method, a French family style, is practical for preparing salad hours ahead. Pour the dressing into the bottom of the salad bowl or whisk dressing ingredients together in the bowl. Place the washed and dried greens loosely on top of the dressing. Do not mix! Cover with paper toweling and refrigerate. At serving time, toss salad and dressing together and serve.
- When you include raw garlic in salads, always remove the green sprout in the clove of garlic. It may have some disagreeable effects on digestion and may also be bitter. It is not necessary to remove the sprout with garlic that is cooked.
- Cheese is a tasty and popular addition to salad dressings. Any variety of the blue-veined cheeses, Gruyère, Cheddar, Parmesan, and feta are suitable choices.
- Salads are perfect for using small amounts of raw vegetables. Leftovers of cooked foods combine well with greens, too.
- Salads are attractive in color, so they make ideal choices for buffets.
- Appetizer salads with strips of warm duck, lamb, or seafood have become popular in fine restaurants. I prefer to use such leftovers for lighter main courses or summertime meals.
- With a little imagination, every salad can be turned into a snack, brunch, lunch, dinner, or late supper.
- When beans, rice, and wheat products are included in salad, the combinations will make the salad a complete, well-balanced meal. Tofu (soybean curd) can be added for more protein.
- Cold pasta salads are commonly served for summer meals and picnic parties. Be sure they are kept in coolers.
- If you are concerned about using raw egg in salad dressings, substitute ¼ cup commercial mayonnaise.

Recipes for Dressings

Basic Vinaigrette Dressing
Makes ¾ cup.

I usually whisk this Basic Vinaigrette Dressing in the bowl before adding my salad. Dijon mustard is not only a good seasoning, it also acts as an emulsifier. After you learn these proportions, and if you like the dressing, making it will become second nature to you. You will probably be able to measure with hand and eye.

    1 teaspoon Dijon mustard
    ½ teaspoon salt
    ¼ teaspoon freshly ground pepper
    2 to 3 tablespoons tarragon or wine vinegar
    ½ cup olive oil (or oil of your choice)

    First, whisk by hand or beat together in a food processor the mustard, salt, pepper, and vinegar (the seasonings will dissolve best in vinegar, not oil). Add the oil slowly, continuing to beat well. Taste and adjust seasoning, if necessary. You may prefer a pinch of sugar as well.

Creamy Dressing
Makes 1¼ cups.

For those who are cautious about raw eggs, I have word from George K. York of the University of California Davis School that acid in combination with eggs will counteract their health risks if you refrigerate for 24 hours before using. You can also substitute commercial mayonnaise for raw eggs.

    1 egg (or ¼ cup mayonnaise)
    2 tablespoons lemon juice
    2 tablespoons tarragon or wine vinegar
    1 teaspoon Dijon mustard
    1 shallot
    ¾ teaspoon salt
    ½ teaspoon pepper
    ⅔ cup olive oil (⅓ cup if you are using mayonnaise)

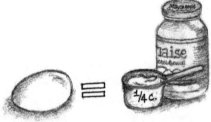

Place egg (if you are using mayonnaise, do not add it until the end), lemon juice, vinegar, mustard, shallot, salt, and pepper in a food processor. Beat for 30 seconds. Gradually add the oil. Add mayonnaise at this point if you are not using the egg. Taste and adjust seasoning.

Green Dressing
Makes 2 cups.

¼ cup each fresh parsley, spinach, and watercress
1 clove garlic, cut in half (green sprout removed)
1 sprig each fresh thyme and marjoram (or ¼ teaspoon, dried)
1 recipe Creamy Dressing (page 135)

Blanch greens in boiling water for 30 seconds. Refresh in ice water, then dry well in paper toweling. Chop greens and garlic in a food processor for a few seconds. Add Creamy Dressing and beat again for 10 to 20 seconds. Adjust seasoning to taste.

Cheese Dressing
Makes 3 cups.

½ cup Basic Vinaigrette Dressing (page 135)
½ cup Creamy Dressing (page 135)
1 cup coarsely chopped cheese (blue, Roquefort, or feta)
1 cup light sour cream or yogurt
½ teaspoon freshly ground white pepper

Combine the two dressings and ½ cup of the cheese in a food processor. Beat for a few seconds until creamy. Transfer to a bowl. Blend in sour cream, remaining cheese, and pepper. Adjust seasoning if necessary.

Fresh Tomato Dressing
Makes about 2 cups.

1 small onion, diced
1 clove garlic, unpeeled
1 tablespoon olive oil
1 pound fresh ripe tomatoes, diced (or 1 cup canned crushed tomatoes)
1 sprig each fresh parsley and thyme
1 recipe Basic Vinaigrette Dressing (page 135)

1 tablespoon cognac (optional)
Salt and freshly ground pepper

Cook onion and garlic in olive oil until the onion is golden (use medium heat so the onion wilts and glazes). Add tomatoes. Cover pan and simmer for 15 minutes. Strain through a food mill or sieve. Cool the tomato essence.

Combine the tomato essence with the Basic Vinaigrette Dressing and cognac. Adjust to taste with salt and pepper.

Tofu-Yogurt Dressing
Makes ¾ cup.

2 shallots
2 tablespoons lemon juice
½ teaspoon salt
¼ teaspoon dry mustard
1 square tofu, about 5"x4"x2"
½ cup yogurt
1 tablespoon each minced fresh parsley and chives (or scallion)
Freshly ground pepper to taste

Place shallots, lemon juice, salt, dry mustard, tofu, and yogurt in a food processor. Run machine for about 45 seconds. Transfer to a bowl and add parsley and chives. Add pepper to taste.

Charles Virion's Dressing
Makes 4 to 5 cups.

Charles used this dressing for his French classic beet and endive salad but my friends and family enjoy it on tossed greens. Although you can prepare half the amount, I find that it keeps well in my refrigerator for two weeks.

6 or 7 shallots
6 large cloves garlic (green sprouts removed)
1½ tablespoons salt
½ tablespoon black pepper
1 tablespoon sugar
1 tablespoon Dijon mustard
¾ cup tarragon vinegar
3 to 4 cups olive oil and corn oil, combined
2 tablespoons hot water

Whirl the first seven ingredients in the food processor until the shallots and garlic are minced. Add oil gradually and process until the dressing is smooth (about 1 minute). Then add water and process briefly again.

✳ *Suggestions*

- Use ½ cup of this dressing as a base for other dressings.
- Creamy Dressing: Add ¼ cup mayonnaise and 1 tablespoon herbs.
- Russian Dressing: Add 1 tablespoon ketchup or chili sauce and 2 tablespoons each mayonnaise and diced pickle.
- Quick Caesar Salad Dressing: Add 2 mashed anchovies, ¼ cup each mayonnaise and grated Parmesan cheese.

Recipes for Salads

Caesar Salad
Serves 4.

In the 1960s I had the most fun teaching a course called "Barbecue Cooking for Men Only." That course went out when women's lib came in. Attracting men to a cooking class in those years was not easy, but the men's barbecue class was always oversubscribed. Although we cooked outdoors, a full menu was planned, including salads. The Caesar Salad and Green Dressing (page 136) were then, and still are, very popular.

Croutons
4 slices white bread
2 tablespoons olive oil
2 cloves garlic, minced

Salad
1 tablespoon lemon juice
2 tablespoons wine vinegar
1 clove garlic, minced
½ teaspoon Dijon mustard
½ teaspoon salt
¼ teaspoon pepper
One 2-ounce can anchovy fillets, mashed
1 egg, coddled (bring water to a boil and remove egg)

½ cup olive oil
2 pounds romaine lettuce, washed, dried, and broken into pieces
½ cup freshly grated Parmesan cheese

Make the croutons first. Cut crusts from the bread; cut bread slices into tiny cubes. Heat a skillet and add oil, then garlic and bread cubes. Toast cubes over medium heat so the garlic does not burn and cubes become crisp. Alternatively, you can toast bread cubes and garlic on an oiled pan in a 300°F oven for 30 minutes. Use only 1 tablespoon oil in this case.

When making the salad, use a large salad bowl for easy tossing. Whisk together lemon juice, vinegar, garlic, mustard, salt, pepper, and anchovies. Add egg, then gradually add oil, whisking constantly. Place greens in the bowl and toss to coat the leaves. Add Parmesan cheese and croutons. Toss once again before serving.

✹ *Suggestion*
If you omit the coddled egg, use ¼ cup mayonnaise and reduce olive oil to ¼ cup.

Spinach and Lettuce Salad
Serves 6 to 8.

Do not pass up iceberg lettuce because some sophisticates consider it tasteless. Yes, it is not distinctive in taste, but it stays crisp when cut, stores very well, and is inexpensive. Spinach certainly lends a contrast in taste and color. When both greens are finely shredded, they are attractive and fluff up to extend the portions.

1 pound spinach
½ head iceberg lettuce
1 bunch scallions, minced (white portions only; save the greens for another use)
½ cup Basic Vinaigrette Dressing (page 135)

Wash spinach thoroughly. Tear off roots and heavy stems. Dry thoroughly and refrigerate in cotton dish toweling or paper toweling. This may be done one day ahead or several hours ahead.

Pile 12 spinach leaves on top of one another. Shred the leaves with a sharp knife. Continue until all the leaves are finely shredded. Do the same with the iceberg lettuce (do not pull the lettuce leaves apart). It is simple to shred iceberg lettuce because the head holds together.

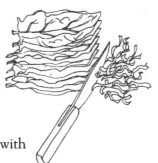

Toss spinach, lettuce, and scallions with Basic Vinaigrette Dressing.

☀ *Suggestions*
- Add 1 cup of any of the following: cooked shredded chicken, flaked tuna fish, freshly cooked fish, toasted croutons or almonds, finely sliced mushrooms.
- Add 1 cup bean sprouts and ½ cup crisp, minced bacon.

Papagallo's Fresh Spinach Salad
Serves 6.

Papagallo's was once a Long Island, New York, restaurant that featured this unique appetizer salad. Try it out before you serve it to guests. The ingredients are simple, but the technique is the test of a quick hand and experience.

1 pound fresh spinach
½ pound mushrooms
Juice of ½ lemon
1 tablespoon olive oil
2 cloves garlic
6 slices bacon, each cut into eighths
¼ cup wine vinegar
½ teaspoon salt
Salt and freshly ground pepper

Remove the stems from the spinach. Wash leaves thoroughly and dry. Tear spinach into bite-sized pieces. Store the spinach in a plastic box or wrap in toweling.

Rinse mushrooms. Dry and slice thinly. Sprinkle with lemon juice.

Ten minutes before serving, combine the mushrooms and spinach in a salad bowl. Bring the bowl to the table or close by. Choose a skillet whose rim measures the same as the bowl, since it will be briefly used as a cover for the bowl.

Hot skillet over cold salad bowl

Heat the skillet, then add oil and garlic. Cook on medium heat. Add bacon and fry until crisp. Discard garlic and pour off all but 1 tablespoon of the rendered fat. Add vinegar to the skillet. Cook for 30 seconds. Bring the skillet to the table. Invert it over the salad bowl and hold there as a cover for just 1 minute.

Uncover. Add salt and freshly ground pepper to the salad. Toss well. Serve at once.

Lentil Salad
Serves 8 to 10.

Lentils cook differently than other legumes. They do not need soaking, and they cook in much less time. Make more than you need to use hot or cold and keep refrigerated for up to one week for other uses.

> 1 pound lentils, rinsed
> 5 cups water
> 2 teaspoons salt
> 2 tablespoons red wine vinegar
> 1 teaspoon black pepper
> 6 tablespoons olive oil
> 4 scallions, white portions only, minced
> ½ cup canned crushed tomatoes (use fresh ripe tomatoes, if available)
> 1 tablespoon minced fresh parsley

Put lentils in a saucepan with water and salt. Bring to a boil. Cover and simmer for 28 to 30 minutes. Test a lentil for doneness. Drain well.

Stir vinegar with black pepper. Add oil, scallions, tomatoes, and parsley. Fold in lentils. Prepare in advance so the seasoning can mellow.

Serve cold with sliced smoked meats or serve hot with sausage.

Three-Bean Salad
Serves 8 to 10.

Canned beans are a handy shelf item, a great asset for the busy homemaker. Use any one of these combinations or all three for more servings.

> One 16-ounce can fava beans, drained and rinsed
> 1 teaspoon paprika
> 1 red onion, diced
> 2 tablespoons lemon juice
> One 16-ounce can cannellini beans, drained and rinsed
> 2 ribs celery, diced
> 2 slices prosciutto or other smoked meat
> 2 scallions, minced
> 1 tablespoon olive oil
> One 16-ounce can kidney beans, drained and rinsed
> 1 small green pepper, seeds removed and diced
> 2 anchovies, minced

1 tablespoon wine vinegar
Salt and freshly ground pepper to taste
Head of escarole
1 sweet red pepper, seeds removed and julienned

Set out three bowls. Mix fava beans with paprika, onion, and lemon juice in one bowl. Mix cannellini beans, celery, prosciutto (or other smoked meat), scallions, and olive oil in the second bowl. Mix kidney beans, green pepper, anchovies, and vinegar in the third bowl.

Season each mixture with salt and pepper. Arrange escarole greens on a large tray. Place mounds of beans side by side with strips of red pepper to separate them.

Orzo, Wheat Berry, and Bulghur Salad
Serves 6 to 8.

The tiny oval-shaped pasta known as orzo looks almost like long-grained rice. Its petite size and semisoft texture mixes well with wheat berries, bulghur, and so many other grains. A variety of mix-and-match combinations make ideal salads for garden parties or picnic baskets. Basic Vinaigrette Dressing (page 135), mayonnaise, or even complex dressings will suit any of the preferred combinations. Small leftovers of chicken, meat, or fish may be tossed in at your discretion. Setting up for these salads is made simple by cooking the grains ahead of time in large batches. Follow the directions on the box for cooking. The precooked grains, without dressing, can be refrigerated for up to four days or frozen for up to one month.

2 tablespoons cottage cheese
¼ cup yogurt or sour cream
2 ribs celery, diced
1 small sweet red pepper, diced
2 scallions, minced
1 teaspoon prepared horseradish
⅛ teaspoon cayenne pepper
1 cup each cooked orzo, wheat berries, and bulghur
Kosher (coarse) salt and freshly ground pepper to taste
Thinly sliced red onion for garnish

Mix cottage cheese, yogurt or sour cream, celery, red pepper, scallions, horseradish, and cayenne pepper.

Mix orzo with wheat berries and bulghur in a salad bowl. Stir in the mixed cottage cheese dressing. Adjust seasoning with salt and pepper.

Mound the salad on a platter. Garnish with red onion slices on top. Individual portions can be divided into containers for picnic parties.

✳ *Suggestion*

If desired, the salad can be wrapped in blanched spinach or Boston lettuce leaves for a different presentation at the table.

Quinoa and Cucumber Salad
Serves 4 to 6.

In South America, specifically in the Andean Mountain region, quinoa (pronounced Ki-noh-ah) is a grain known as the "mother grain." Quinoa is light and tasty, very high in protein, and easy to prepare. At present it is being marketed in health food stores. The grain's production is small, so the price is still high; however, quinoa is worth the cost for its versatility and rich nutrients.

> 1 cup quinoa
> 2 cups water
> 1 cup diced cucumber
> 1 cup bean sprouts
> ¼ cup diced scallion greens
> 1 tablespoon soy sauce
> ¼ cup rice or white vinegar
> ½ teaspoon salt
> 1 teaspoon sugar
> 1½ teaspoons pepper

Rinse quinoa thoroughly. Use a strainer to run fresh water through the grains to remove the bitter outer coating. Place quinoa and 2 cups water in a 1½- or 2-quart saucepan. Bring to a boil. Lower heat to a simmer and cover. Cook until all the water is absorbed—about 15 minutes. The grains will turn transparent from opaque white. Remove to a bowl and allow to cool. (One cup raw quinoa yields about four cups cooked quinoa.)

Stir the remaining ingredients in another bowl. Add 2 cups of the cooked quinoa and blend in gently. Serve at room temperature. Reserve the remainder of the cooked quinoa for another use.

Tabbouleh (Cracked Wheat Salad)
Serves 8 to 10.

When I started to make this middle eastern salad many years ago, I was able to buy the fine-cut bulghur. It was then called #1 bulghur. Now I use a coarser grain. It is the only one I can find marketed. I enjoy this salad best in the summer season when vegetables, herbs, and tomatoes are fresh from the garden.

1 cup bulghur
½ cup lemon juice
1 to 1½ teaspoons salt
½ teaspoon pepper
¾ cup olive oil
1 cucumber, peeled, seeded and finely diced
1 green pepper, seeded and finely diced
1 cup minced scallions
1 cup minced fresh Italian parsley leaves
½ cup minced fresh mint leaves
Romaine lettuce leaves and wedges of tomato (for serving platter)

Cover the bulghur with cold water in a bowl and soak for 1 hour. Drain and press out excess water.

Mix lemon juice with salt and pepper in another bowl. Gradually whisk in olive oil. Combine the remaining ingredients and bulghur with the olive oil dressing. Mound on lettuce leaves and garnish with wedges of tomato.

Green and Red Cabbage Salad
Serves 8 to 10.

1 pound each green and red cabbage
2 tablespoons lemon juice
2 teaspoons salt
1 onion, cut in half
1 red onion
2 oranges
2 ribs celery, shredded
2 carrots, scrubbed and shredded
1 apple, peeled and shredded
½ cup Creamy Dressing (page 135) combined with ½ cup yogurt and 3 tablespoons honey

Shred cabbages in a food processor. Transfer to a large decorative bowl. Add lemon juice and salt, and toss well. Place onion halves in the salad. Cover with wax paper. Set aside for 30 minutes or longer, if it suits your timing.

Shred half the red onion. Slice the other half for garnish. Peel and dice one orange. Slice the other orange, unpeeled, for garnish.

Discard the onion halves in the cabbage. Mix the celery, carrots, apple, shredded red onion, and diced orange with the cabbage. Blend in the combined dressing. Place slices of orange and red onion around the outer edge of the salad.

Greek Salad with Chunky Feta Cheese Dressing
Serves 8.

The recipe committee of the St. Paul Greek Orthodox Church on Long Island took lessons with me in the 1970s to broaden their scope in cuisine. They brought some interesting Greek recipes with them. We shared recipes and began a firm friendship.

Salad
3 heads of a variety of greens
3 fresh, ripe tomatoes, cut into wedges
1 sweet red pepper, seeded and sliced
1 green pepper, seeded and sliced
1 cucumber, sliced
1 red onion, sliced
1 cup Greek olives
One 2-ounce can anchovies, drained of oil (optional)

Dressing
2 cups mayonnaise
2 cloves garlic, minced
½ cup red wine vinegar
2 teaspoons oregano
3 tablespoons olive oil
2 to 2½ cups feta cheese (washed if it is too salty)

Arrange all salad ingredients in a large serving bowl. Mix all ingredients for the dressing in a food processor, pulsing on and off so the cheese remains in small chunks.

Toss the salad with the dressing or arrange the salad on individual dishes and pass the dressing around the table. This salad can be served as an appetizer or a light supper.

Chicken and Mango (or Cantaloupe) Salad
Serves 4.

2 cups water
1 small onion, cut in half
1 rib celery, coarsely diced
½ carrot, coarsely diced
1 sprig fresh tarragon (or parsley, marjoram, or cilantro)
½ bay leaf

8 or 10 leaves of green or red leaf lettuce
1 mango or cantaloupe
½ pound seedless grapes
4 halves chicken breasts, boned and skinned
¾ cup buttermilk
2 tablespoons honey
1 tablespoon freshly chopped parsley
½ teaspoon freshly ground pepper
2 tablespoons toasted sesame seeds

Combine water, onion, celery, carrot, tarragon, and bay leaf in a 10-inch skillet. Bring to a boil. Cover and simmer for 10 minutes to make a broth for poaching the chicken. While it is simmering, set out four dinner plates. Make a base of leafy lettuce on each plate.

Peel and slice mango (or cantaloupe). Place a few slices of the mango or cantaloupe and a few seedless grapes on one side of the lettuce on each plate.

Place the chicken in the simmering liquid. Cover and cook for 6 to 8 minutes.

Mix buttermilk, honey, parsley, and pepper. Set aside.

Remove chicken from the broth. Reserve and freeze broth for another use. Cut each breast of chicken into four or five slices.

Place 1 sliced breast of chicken on the greens on each plate alongside the fruit. Dribble 1 tablespoon buttermilk dressing over chicken. Top with a sprinkling of sesame seeds. Serve at room temperature. Pass around the remaining dressing.

Endive, Lentil, and Seafood Salad
Serves 4 to 6.

Leaves of endive have just enough of a cavity to hold different savory fillings. For this salad I have chosen to use lentils in combination with seafood—a complete meal. Depending on the occasion, you may want to cook lentils and seafood on the day you will be serving them. On the other hand, all parts of this combination can be finished one day in advance and refrigerated. There may be times when lentils and cooked fish are leftovers. Now there you have a bonus.

1 cup lentils, rinsed
2½ cups water
½ teaspoon salt
2 tablespoons lemon juice
2 tablespoons olive oil
2 scallions, chopped
Freshly ground pepper to taste

⅓ cup tarragon vinegar
1 tablespoon Dijon mustard
2 shallots
¼ teaspoon salt
½ teaspoon freshly ground pepper
1 hard-cooked egg
⅔ cup olive oil
4 cups cooked seafood (shellfish, bass, snapper, halibut)
4 large endive
8 or 10 sprigs Italian parsley
1 lemon, cut into wedges

Combine lentils and water in a saucepan. Add salt. Bring to a boil. Reduce heat to a simmer and cover tightly. Cook for 28 minutes. Test to be sure lentils are tender but not mushy. Drain well and transfer to a bowl. Toss lightly with lemon juice, olive oil, scallions, and pepper. Set aside.

Use a food processor to make the dressing. Mix vinegar, mustard, shallots, salt, pepper, and egg. Process for 30 seconds, gradually adding oil. Remove to a bowl.

In another bowl, flake fish and cut shellfish into chunks (a combination would be excellent). Add only 1 cup dressing and toss to coat the seafood. Reserve the balance of the dressing for the table.

Cut the bottom of the endive so that the leaves separate easily. Fill each endive leaf with lentils. Place filled endive around the outer portion of a large, round tray, leaving the center empty. Mound the seafood in the center. Decorate with sprigs of parsley and lemon.

7

Rice, Grains, Beans, and Pasta

Recipes Using Rice and Grains

Rice is a basic ingredient in cuisines from around the world. In some countries it is a mainstay of the daily diet. What has always intrigued me is the great number of cooking methods for rice, each adapted to its own local agriculture. Although there are excellent cooking instructions on box packages, I would like to share some techniques for the favorite varieties of rice that line my shelf.

Long-grain rice, in both white and brown varieties, is four to five times longer than it is wide. Long-grain brown rice takes twice as much time to cook as white but is more nutritious. Use them interchangeably in recipes. Indian basmati rice is long-grain, beautifully textured, and aromatic. Although it is expensive, it is worth the treat.

Medium- and short-grain rice are round and cook to a softer consistency; they are most often used in Oriental dishes and rice desserts. Arborio rice is an Italian short-grain variety and is preferable for Italian rice recipes.

Converted rice is very popular for pilafs and for cooking in general. Converted rice employs a method whereby the unhulled rice is soaked, pressure-steamed, and dried before milling. The nutrients of the bran and germ are returned to the heart of the kernel and the starch is gelatinized. A separated rice grain is the result after cooking.

Wheat berry is not a berry as we know a fruit berry. It is a hard, small whole grain that, when cooked, is crunchy and chewy and has a nutlike flavor. Wheat berry is ground to make cracked wheat, which can be ground fine, medium, or coarse and is used mostly as flour and cereal.

Cracked wheat that is first steamed and dried is called bulghur. I had cooked bulghur many years ago, but back in 1960 bulghur was hard to find even in New York, and the wheat berry was unknown in our cooking circles. Today, you can find both in specialty and health food stores.

I stock many varieties of rice in my pantry, so my rice dishes are always slightly different, suitable for a particular menu and the accompanying recipes.

Cooking Rice: The Chinese Method
1 cup uncooked rice makes 3 to 4 servings.

Rice is required as an accompaniment to most Chinese dishes and is absolutely necessary with stir-fry dishes. My Chinese mentors have advised me to serve soup for a Chinese dinner and to use the same bowl for the rice that follows. A few spoonfuls of the soup should be reserved in the bowl to which a portion of the rice is then added. If the rice is a bit sticky, it will separate in the broth.

1 or 2 cups long-grain white or brown rice
Cold water to cover

Add rice (brown rice can also be used and is gaining in popularity) to a saucepan, and add cold water to cover by 1 inch. I never bother measuring the rice, because leftovers are quite useful. The saucepan should measure at least four times the volume of raw rice. Be sure the pan has a tight-fitting cover.

Cook the rice uncovered on high heat by allowing the water to come to a boil until it evaporates. Air bubbles, which the Chinese call "fish eyes," will show on top. Lower the heat, cover the pot, and simmer for 17 minutes (add 10 more minutes for brown rice). Turn off heat.

If you are not serving at once, do not uncover the saucepan. Rice will retain heat for at least 30 to 40 minutes.

✳ *Suggestions*

- Cook more rice than needed. It can be refrigerated for up to four days or frozen for up to three months.
- Use leftover rice in stuffings, casseroles, soups, cold salads, and especially for Fried Rice (below).

Fried Rice (Chou Fom)
Serves 4.

Ten-minute Special!

Fried rice is listed as a special course in the menus of Chinese restaurants. In your home, it can be one of your best leftovers. Two cups refrigerated or defrosted cooked rice, combined with vegetables and your choice of additions, will stir up a hot dinner in about 10 minutes.

Although proper preparation is important in all cooking, it is particularly necessary in Chinese-style cooking. There are many ingredients, and since the cooking is done very quickly, each needs to be ready and at hand.

1 egg
3 tablespoons peanut or corn oil
¼ teaspoon salt
4 scallions, minced
1 cup diced mixed vegetables (celery, water chestnuts, bean sprouts)
1 to 2 cups diced leftover meats, chicken, or seafood
2 cups cooked rice
1 tablespoon soy sauce
½ teaspoon sugar
¼ teaspoon freshly ground pepper
¼ cup chicken or vegetable stock

Lightly beat the egg with 1 teaspoon oil and salt. Set out the scallions and other foods.

Heat a wok or skillet with 1 tablespoon oil. Add egg and scramble briskly for 15 seconds. Transfer to a heated serving platter.

Add 1 tablespoon oil to the wok or skillet. Stir in scallions, mixed vegetables, and leftover meat, chicken, or seafood. Stir-fry until thoroughly heated. Transfer to the serving dish with egg.

Add the remaining oil to the wok and stir-fry the rice. Season with soy sauce, sugar, pepper, and stock. Stir vigorously to separate grains. Add scrambled eggs and vegetable-and-meat mixture. Stir together on high heat until the stock is absorbed. Serve immediately.

Iranian Steamed Rice
Serves 6.

Rice cooked as in the following recipe was served to us by neighbors who lived in Iran for several years. The cooking is slightly more involved but worth the effort. The long, white grain retains its shape and texture.

    1 quart water
    1 tablespoon salt
    1¼ cups long-grain white rice
    2 to 4 tablespoons unsalted butter

Boil water with salt in a 2- or 3-quart saucepan. Add rice to boiling water. Cook uncovered for 8 minutes. Drain the rice, running warm water through it.

Melt 2 tablespoons butter in the saucepan. Place rice in the saucepan, mounding it in a pyramidlike shape. Cover the rice with a tea towel or paper toweling. Using a tight lid, set the saucepan over very low heat for 30 minutes. The covered rice will keep hot for up to an hour after cooking. Run remaining butter through the rice before serving, if you wish.

✳ *Suggestion*
The amount of salt can be reduced and oil can be substituted for butter.

Basmati Rice
Serves 4 to 6.

Basmati rice is usually imported from India. Recently, however, it is also being grown in the United States. Basmati is unique in aroma. For me, it has the perfect consistency: firm yet well cooked. Although my Indian colleagues have long cooking instructions for basmati, I prefer the Iranian method of preparation.

    1 quart water
    1 tablespoon salt
    1¼ cups basmati rice
    2 to 4 tablespoons unsalted butter

Rinse the rice. Rub the grains through your hands and pick out any green, unripened grains.

Follow the cooking instructions for Iranian Steamed Rice (page 152), but allow to cook a few extra minutes. Always taste for doneness.

Stockli's Rice
Serves 4 to 6.

This is a recipe that Chef Albert Stockli used as an accompaniment to saucy dishes.

  2 quarts water
  1 teaspoon salt
  1 cup rice (long-grain or converted)
  1 tablespoon oil

Bring water and salt to a boil. Add rice and boil uncovered for 15 minutes. In the meantime, preheat oven to 375°F. Grease a jelly-roll pan with oil.

When the rice is finished, strain off the water. Spread the rice on the oiled pan. Cover with greased wax paper and bake for 10 minutes, until the rice is dry and separated. The rice can be cooked in advance and reheated in a bowl over simmering water.

✹ *Suggestion*

Add currants, raisins, and nuts as accompaniments to curries, venison, and game fowl.

Rice Pilaf
Serves 4.

I included Rice Pilaf in the first lessons I ever taught. The method is foolproof for beginners and flexible enough for busy cooks. Cook pilaf either in the oven or on the burner. Substitute wheat berries, barley, or bulghur, or use combinations of grains and rice. Although pilaf has a long historical and international background, I prefer to begin with the basic American style using converted rice. Once you've accomplished it, you will recognize this technique in many great rice and grain casseroles.

  2 cups chicken or vegetable stock
  2 tablespoons butter or oil
  1 cup converted rice

Preheat oven to 350°F if you plan to cook pilaf in the oven. Heat stock in a 1-quart saucepan, or a casserole, with a tight-fitting cover. Melt butter or heat oil in a skillet. Add rice to the skillet and stir for 2 to 3 minutes until the grains are glazed. Transfer rice to the heated stock. If you are using a casserole, cover it and bake in the oven for 25 minutes. If you are cooking the pilaf in a saucepan, cover it tightly and cook for 20 minutes.

✺ *Suggestions*

- To add subtle seasoning, place a bouquet garni on the rice before covering the saucepan.
- Try using wheat berries, barley, or bulghur instead of rice. Wheat berries and barley should be rinsed and soaked, using the same method used with dried beans (page 160). Cooking time for wheat berries and barley is about 15 minutes longer than for rice. Bulghur cooks like rice.

Wild Rice
Serves 4 to 6.

Wild rice is not really a rice at all. It is the long-grain seed of a marsh grass. Until recent years wild rice was harvested exclusively by the Native Americans of the Great Lakes region. It is now grown commercially in the United States and Canada. Even so, wild rice commands a very high price. Use it wisely with game, Cornish hens, duck, and roast pork. Avoid the seasoned package mixes. Use your imagination to extend the serving by combining it with mushrooms, nuts, raisins, and currants. A small amount of another grain will not detract from the earthy flavor and chewy texture of this unusual grass seed.

> 1 cup wild rice
> 2 tablespoons butter or oil
> 2 or 3 shallots, minced
> 3 cups hot stock or water
> Salt and freshly ground pepper to taste
> Bouquet garni

Rinse the wild rice well. Soak in hot water for 1 hour or parboil in salted water for 3 to 4 minutes. Pour off water.

Heat 1 tablespoon butter or oil in a 2-quart saucepan. Add shallots and cook for 2 to 3 minutes without browning. Add wild rice. Stir over low heat until all the grains are glazed, about 2 to 3 minutes. Add hot stock or water and salt and pepper (if stock is not salty). Place bouquet garni on top and cover the saucepan. Cook for 40 to 50 minutes, depending on personal taste, and add remaining butter or oil.

✳ *Suggestions*

- Instead of cooking on the stove, bake in a covered casserole at 375°F for 1 hour.
- Another interesting way to prepare wild rice: After rinsing, soak rice in boiling water until the water cools. Repeat this procedure three or four times. The wild rice will open and be ready to eat as a side dish or to use in salads.
- Use cooked wild rice for stuffing Cornish hens and game poultry.
- A small amount of orange or pineapple juice can be substituted for some of the stock or water.

Risotto
Serves 8 to 10.

One of my treasured memories of our first visit to Rome in 1959 was an introduction to a classic Risotto. The rice was cooked to an exquisite creaminess, perfectly textured to carry small succulent shrimp. Arborio rice—a plump, short-grain rice, Italian in origin and uniquely creamy in texture—is classically used in cooking Risotto.

You may think it bothersome to follow these directions for stirring and adding hot liquid, but you will certainly applaud the result.

2 tablespoons each butter and olive oil
1 onion, minced
¾ cup dry white wine
2 cups Arborio rice
5 cups hot chicken stock
Salt and freshly ground white pepper to taste
½ cup grated fresh Parmesan cheese

Heat a 4- or 5-quart heavy-bottomed saucepan. Add 1 tablespoon each butter and olive oil. Stir in onion, and cook for 2 to 3 minutes until glazed but not browned. Add wine, and boil until the wine is reduced to just glaze the onion. Stir in rice and sauté until the rice turns golden.

Pour in 1 cup hot chicken stock. Simmer and stir occasionally until the liquid is absorbed. Add another cup chicken stock. Continue adding the stock, at intervals, for about 20 to 30 minutes or until the rice is softened to your taste.

Season with salt and pepper, keeping in mind that the stock was properly seasoned. The rice can be slightly wet at the end. Cover with paper toweling and keep at a simmer for 8 to 10 minutes. Blend in remaining butter, oil, and Parmesan cheese before serving.

✳ *Suggestions*

There are several variations for Risotto.

- Italians traditionally add a few tablespoons marrow when sautéing the onion.
- Flavor the stock with saffron for an exquisite seasoning. The Risotto is then labeled Alla Milanese.
- Sauté 2 or 3 cloves garlic (minced) and minced parsley in 1 tablespoon olive oil. Stir in 1 pound raw medium shrimp, shelled and deveined. Cook for 2 to 3 minutes. Set aside. Combine cooked shrimp with rice for the last 10 minutes when cooking Risotto. This dish can be served as a complete main course.
- Risotto with peas, Risi e Bisi, is an especially good combination if fresh garden peas are available, but frozen peas can be a good enough substitute. Render a few strips of bacon with the butter and omit the oil. Add 2 to 3 cups green peas and 2 cups stock. Cook for 10 minutes, then add rice and more stock. Continue as you would when making Risotto. Italians consider Risi e Bisi a soup, but they eat it with a fork. A great informal meal for Super Bowl evenings!

Bomba di Riso (Ring Mold of Rice)
Serves 8.

I had a propitious meeting with an Italian woman during a trip to Bologna. As we were waiting in a hairdressing shop, we began a conversation. Her English was excellent, and we struck up an instant friendship. When I returned with a group of students the following autumn, I called Maria Barbaresco and she invited me to dinner at her home. We numbered eight around her beautifully appointed table and savored a home-cooked Bolognese meal. Bomba di Riso was merely an accompaniment to the main course.

4 tablespoons butter
4 tablespoons flour
2¼ cups hot milk
4 ounces cooked and diced ham (Parma, if you can get it)
2 cups Arborio rice (or long-grain white rice)
4 cups boiling salted water
½ cup plain bread crumbs
⅓ cup grated Parmesan cheese

¼ cup grated Gruyère cheese
1 cup fontina cheese, cut into small cubes

Make a Béchamel Sauce by melting 3 tablespoons butter in a 1-quart saucepan. Add flour and stir over low heat for 1 to 2 minutes. Add hot milk and stir vigorously. The sauce should thicken very quickly. Stir in the ham. Simmer over very low heat, stirring occasionally while you cook the rice.

Add rice to boiling salted water and boil for 10 to 12 minutes, until slightly underdone.

Grease an 8-cup ring mold with the remaining butter. Coat the inside of the mold with bread crumbs. Preheat oven to 400°F.

Strain rice. Mix the rice with the cheeses and the Béchamel Sauce. Taste and add salt and pepper if necessary. Spoon the rice mixture into the mold. Pat the mixture down to even the top. Bake for 25 to 30 minutes.

Work around the edges of the mold with a table knife to loosen it. Place a round serving platter on top. Turn the mold upside down on the platter to unmold. CAUTION: Use pot holders.

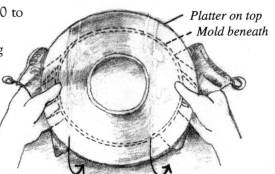

Platter on top
Mold beneath

Place serving platter on top of mold. Turn far end upside down towards you to unmold. Use pot holders!

✹ *Suggestions*

- The Northern Italians do not stint on butter. I confess that I reduced the butter somewhat, so add more if you wish.
- At the Barbaresco home, the ring mold was filled with peas.
- Fill the ring mold with sautéed shiitake, porcini, or cultivated mushrooms.
- Bomba di Riso may be made in a casserole, with or without the ham. I have made it, in a casserole, one or two days in advance, thus saving last-minute work before company dinners.

Zucchini and Rice Casserole
Serves 8 to 10.

Every gardener has some joke about zucchini. They grow like weeds. Camouflaged under broad leaves, they grow to gargantuan size before we see them. No snobbery in our kitchen! We use them small or large, raw or cooked. This particular recipe is the number one favorite among students, family, and friends.

3 or 4 medium-sized zucchini (about 3 pounds)
1 tablespoon salt
2 quarts water
Dash salt
1 cup long-grain white or brown rice
2 tablespoons butter or olive oil
1½ cups minced onions
3 cloves garlic, minced
2 tablespoons flour
1 cup hot milk or light cream
1 cup extracted zucchini juice
¾ cup freshly grated Parmesan cheese
Salt and pepper to taste

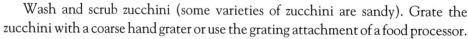

Wash and scrub zucchini (some varieties of zucchini are sandy). Grate the zucchini with a coarse hand grater or use the grating attachment of a food processor.

Place the grated zucchini in a colander set on a bowl to catch the juice. Stir salt into the zucchini and set aside for about 10 minutes. The salt will extract the juice.

Boil water with a dash of salt. Drop rice into the boiling water and boil vigorously for 5 to 6 minutes (cook brown rice a few minutes longer). The rice will still be firm in texture. Drain and set aside.

Press juice out of the zucchini with a large spoon. Reserve 1 cup of the juice for this recipe. The remainder may be refrigerated or frozen for soups, stews, and sauces.

Grease an oblong (13" x 9" x 1½") casserole or a 12-inch round, shallow casserole with 1 tablespoon butter or oil. Preheat oven to 400°F.

Heat a 10-inch skillet. Add 1 tablespoon butter or oil. Sauté onions until they are glazed. Stir in garlic and cook for another minute or two. Mix in zucchini. Stir and blend and cook for 3 to 4 minutes. Sprinkle flour over all and stir again. Gradually add hot milk or cream and then zucchini juice. Simmer for just about 2 minutes. Remove from heat.

If the skillet is deep enough, add the rice and ½ cup cheese. If not, mix zucchini, rice, and cheese in a large bowl. Season with salt and pepper to taste.

Spoon the mixture into the prepared casserole. Sprinkle remaining cheese on top. Bake for 30 to 35 minutes. The top should be crisp and lightly browned.

✳ Suggestions

- If you wish, this recipe can be divided in half before baking. One casserole with half the amount can be baked for immediate use and the remainder stored in the freezer for up to one month.

- Once you learn the procedure for the initial salting and reduction of liquid, you can use the grated zucchini for pancakes, stir-frying, and other combinations.

Wheat Berry Pilaf
Serves 4.

About 10 or 12 years ago, while I was visiting Mountain Mowings in Dummerston, Vermont (my favorite nursery and farm), the owner Frank Hickin handed me a bag of brownish hard nuggets. In a sharp and dogmatic tone of voice he ordered, "Libby, go home and cook these wheat berries." I was impressed with my gift, one of his homegrown goodies. I certainly did cook them, soaking them first because the berries were as hard as tiny pebbles. The crunchy, chewy texture and nutlike flavor of this seed from ordinary wheat appealed to my love of grains.

> 1 cup wheat berries
> 4 cups cold water
> 2 tablespoons butter or oil
> 1 onion, minced
> 2 cups stock or water (preferably hot)
> Bouquet garni
> Salt and freshly ground pepper to taste

Either soak the wheat berries overnight in the cold water or bring them to a boil in the cold water. Simmer for 3 minutes, and, with the heat off, leave covered for 1 hour. Drain well. The water may be reserved for cooking the berries.

Melt butter or heat oil in a 3-quart saucepan. Add onion and cook until wilted. Add wheat berries and stir until they are coated with butter.

Add stock or water. Place bouquet garni on top. Cover and cook for 40 to 50 minutes. Season to taste.

✳ *Suggestion*
Add ½ cup each bulghur and rice for the last 15 minutes of cooking—an interesting combination.

Grits Casserole
Serves 6 to 8.

Lillian Zilliacus brings this casserole to our yearly Christmas Day brunch. She introduced her North Carolina dish to us years ago, and we have adopted it as one of our favorite brunch casseroles.

1 cup grits (regular, not instant)
1 quart boiling water
2 eggs, beaten lightly
6 tablespoons butter
2 cups grated Cheddar cheese
2 tablespoons grated Parmesan cheese
¼ cup sour cream
Salt and freshly ground pepper to taste

Gradually stir grits into boiling water. Return water to a boil. Cover and cook over low heat for 15 to 20 minutes, stirring occasionally. Remove from the heat and let stand for a few minutes.

Stir in the remaining ingredients, reserving ½ cup Cheddar cheese. Transfer to a 1½-quart casserole. Sprinkle ½ cup Cheddar cheese on top. Bake at 375°F for 20 to 30 minutes until the top is crusty.

Recipes Using Beans

Nutritional research has finally elevated the bean to a food of importance, a protein food now included in balanced diets. Good family cooks have always used the dried bean, an economical and filling food, for making wholesome meals.

A busy person can stock any number of canned bean products for an easy and quick assist. However, the preparation of dried beans by soaking and cooking is well worth the effort.

1. Soak beans overnight in water to cover by one inch. Shorten the soaking time if you wish, but then cooking time may be longer. (In the summertime, refrigerate the soaking beans.) An alternative method to overnight soaking is to place beans in a saucepan with water to cover by one inch. Bring to a boil and cook for 3 minutes. Cover the pot and set aside to soak for 1 hour. Change the water after soaking, especially before cooking, to reduce the possibility of poor digestion and resulting gasiness.

2. Cook beans covered by 1 inch of liquid or according to recipe. Slow cooking over low heat or in the oven gives the best results. Always keep beans submerged in water. Add a small amount of warm water if the water reduces too much. The cooking time will depend on the length of time the dried beans have been stored. The longer dried foods are stored in warehouses, the longer they take to soften. After cooking, the beans should have kept their shape and be thoroughly soft inside. Taste and test.

3. Prepare more beans than needed. Refrigerate leftover beans for up to four days or freeze for up to three months.

Black Beans and White Rice
Serves 4.

Many people, vegetarians or not, have discovered the beans and rice combination, long known to Cubans and Puerto Ricans. From a nutritional point of view, it is perfectly balanced for protein and complex carbohydrates. Best of all it is delicious and satisfying.

1 cup dried black beans (sometimes called turtle beans)
1 cup long-grain white rice
1 tablespoon salt
2 tablespoons olive oil
2 onions, diced
3 or 4 cloves garlic, minced
1 tablespoon dried oregano
¼ cup chopped fresh Italian parsley or cilantro
1 red and 1 green sweet bell pepper, seeded and julienned
1 scallion, chopped
½ cup sour cream or yogurt

Cilantro is fresh coriander, also called Chinese parsley.

Follow the directions for soaking and cooking beans (page 160).

Cook the rice, using salt, by following your favorite method. Keep the pot covered until ready to serve. Covered rice will remain hot for up to 30 or 40 minutes.

Heat a 10-inch skillet. Add olive oil. Sauté onions and garlic until wilted, not browned. Add oregano and parsley or cilantro. Stir this mixture into the cooked black beans and simmer for 10 to 15 minutes.

Serve each bowl of Black Beans and White Rice garnished with the julienned sweet bell peppers, scallion, and a spoonful of sour cream.

Santa Fe Pinto Beans
Serves 4 to 6.

If you truly enjoy bean dishes, take the time to cook the speckled, tannish pinto beans. With slow cooking, the skins stay intact but become almost as soft as the interior. The liquid reduces to creaminess, a sauce in itself. Pinto beans are available in specialty stores and some supermarkets. The vegetable and flavoring additions in this recipe can be applied to the other dried bean varieties and to the canned ones as well.

1 cup pinto beans, rinsed thoroughly
2 teaspoons salt
½ onion, studded with bay leaf and clove
½ rib celery, tied with bouquet garni
1 carrot, scrubbed and cut in half
½ cup each diced green and red sweet peppers
¼ pound mushrooms
3 cloves garlic, sliced
1 pound fresh, ripe tomatoes, skinned and seeded, or ½ cup canned crushed
    tomatoes
⅛ teaspoon cumin
1 teaspoon chili powder or ¼ cup Chili Pepper Paste (page 27)
Salt and pepper to taste
Sprigs cilantro or Italian parsley

Soak beans in water to cover by ½ inch (about 3 cups) in a 3-quart saucepan for 8 to 12 hours. Rinse beans and again add water to cover by ½ inch. Add salt, onion, celery, and carrot. Cover and bring to a boil, then lower heat to simmer for at least 2 to 3 hours. Taste and test for softness. Discard onion, celery, and carrot. Add sweet peppers, mushrooms, garlic, tomatoes, cumin, and chili powder or Chili Pepper Paste.

Continue to simmer for 1 hour. The liquid should be practically absorbed, so stir occasionally. The timing will vary, depending on the dried beans. Before serving, season with salt and pepper to taste and garnish with sprigs of cilantro or Italian parsley.

✷ Suggestions

- Use leftover beans in vegetable soup.
- Serve with fried eggs and tortillas for company brunch.

Boston Baked Beans
Serves 6 to 8.

New Englanders have always considered baked beans to be a once-a-week main dish. I have recently combined two recipes. One was given to me by a former neighbor, Fran Blumenschein, the other by a New Englander, Phyllis Grossbaum. They are practically the same, both tried-and-true recipes.

1 pound white navy beans
1 teaspoon baking soda
1 onion, diced

1 tablespoon salt
1 tablespoon vinegar
1 teaspoon dry mustard
¼ cup dark brown sugar
½ cup molasses
¼ cup ketchup
¼ teaspoon black pepper
½ pound salt pork, cut into strips

Wash the beans thoroughly. Soak overnight in a 4- or 5-quart saucepan. Drain. Cover with fresh water to reach 1 inch over the beans. Add baking soda and bring to a boil. Preheat oven to 250°F.

Place onion and all other ingredients (except salt pork) into the beanpot to be used. Mix in the hot beans and their liquid. Add more boiling water to amply cover the beans. Lay strips of salt pork on top. Cover tightly and bake for 12 to 16 hours, or until beans become tender. Uncover and bake for 1 hour longer to crisp the salt pork.

✹ Suggestions

- If you own a Crockpot, cook beans on low for 24 hours. The salt pork will not crisp. Blend it in with the beans.
- Use other varieties of dried beans if you wish.
- Boston Baked Beans may be prepared in advance. Refrigerate for up to four days or freeze for up to three months.
- Use Boston Baked Beans in a casserole with sausages or leftovers of roast pork, beef, or game.

Bean and Vegetable Chili
Serves 6 to 8.

Chili contests have become a community event. Vegetarians will welcome the spicy lift that chili peppers give to mild vegetables and beans. Choose your heat: shall it be fresh chili peppers, Chili Pepper Paste, or chili powder?

¼ cup olive oil
3 large onions (2 cups), diced
¼ cup minced garlic
3 or 4 hot peppers or ¼ cup Chili Pepper Paste (page 27)
6 fresh, ripe tomatoes, peeled, seeded, and diced, or 2 cups canned tomatoes
2 ribs celery, diced with leaves

2 carrots, scraped and diced
1 red and 1 green sweet bell pepper, diced
2 small zucchini or yellow squash, diced
½ teaspoon each marjoram, thyme, and basil
¼ cup minced fresh parsley
¼ teaspoon cumin
2 tablespoons wine vinegar
3 to 4 cups cooked kidney, pinto, or black beans
Salt and pepper to taste
½ cup grated Cheddar or Muenster cheese

Set out all ingredients. Heat oil in a Dutch oven or a stew pot over moderate heat. Add onions, garlic, and hot peppers or Chili Pepper Paste. Stir-fry for a few minutes until glazed. Add tomatoes, celery, carrots, and red and green peppers. Stir gently and raise heat for 2 or 3 minutes. Add zucchini or yellow squash, then all the herbs, cumin, and vinegar. Cover and cook for 12 to 15 minutes.

Stir in beans; adjust seasoning to taste with salt and pepper. Cover and cook for another 15 minutes. Garnish with cheese before serving.

✹ *Suggestions*

- Substitute or omit a vegetable, depending on availability.
- Be careful when cleaning hot peppers. The inner membranes are extremely irritating, so use gloves if necessary. Do not touch your eyes as you are cleaning the peppers.
- One tablespoon chili powder or red pepper flakes can be substituted for the hot peppers.

Chick-Peas in Casserole
Serves 6 to 8.

1 pound dried chick-peas
1 onion, peeled and studded with 2 cloves
1 carrot, scraped and diced
6 Italian plum tomatoes, cut into quarters, or 1 cup canned tomatoes
1 rib celery, tied with bouquet garni
Choice of ham bone, ¼ pound salt pork, or ¼ pound bacon
Salt and pepper to taste

Preheat oven to 300°F. Follow directions for soaking dried beans (page 160).

Strain off water. Place chick-peas in a 3-quart casserole with a fitted cover. Add water to cover by 1 inch. Place all other ingredients on top, except salt and pepper. Cover and bake for at least 1 hour. Taste and test for doneness. Discard onion, celery, and bouquet garni. Add salt and pepper to taste.

Cook casserole well in advance, since the flavor improves on reheating.

✳ Suggestions

- Cook the same amount even if you are serving only one or two. Refrigerate the leftovers for up to five days or freeze for up to one month.
- Use leftovers in Chick-Peas and Pasta (below).

Chick-Peas and Pasta
Serves 4 to 6.

Although cooked chick-peas are used in the following recipe (possibly a good leftover from Chick-Peas in Casserole, page 164), feel free to substitute any of the other bean varieties. For an instant dinner, use the canned beans of your choice. You will find this recipe an interesting change for pasta.

1 pound ziti or elbow macaroni
3 tablespoons olive oil
1 onion, diced
2 cloves garlic, minced
⅛ pound ham or leftover chicken or other meats, minced
2 cups cooked (or canned) chick-peas
½ teaspoon sage
½ teaspoon marjoram
Salt and pepper to taste
½ cup freshly grated Romano cheese

Boil water for ziti or macaroni. Add pasta and boil to desired doneness. In the meantime, warm a deep bowl for serving.

Heat 2 tablespoons olive oil in a skillet. Add onion and garlic. Cook until the onion and garlic are glazed, then add ham or other meat, ½ cup chick-peas, and herbs. Crush chick-peas in the skillet to make a paste. Add the remaining chick-peas with 1 tablespoon olive oil. Blend gently over low heat. Adjust seasoning with salt and pepper.

Drain pasta. Transfer to the warmed serving bowl and toss with the chick-pea mixture. Garnish with grated cheese.

Recipes Using Pasta

After all is said and done, Pasta is only the Italian designation for all forms of noodle. Our dictionary describes the word as a paste made to a form, as for spaghetti. Noodles are used around the world. As I was growing up, my mother made noodles routinely in our kitchen, but she did not scoff at buying boxed noodles for a quick lunch or dinner. How delicious were those hot lunches of freshly boiled noodles and cottage cheese!

Pasta
Makes 1 pound of dough.

If you ate pasta every day, you could choose a different shape for each day of the month. Best of all, these many varieties are easily available. The one shape you cannot purchase before filling is Ravioli, which must be fresh and pliable. Once you master this recipe for Pasta you can easily progress to Ravioli. Since I make Pasta often and in large quantities, I save time by using both the food processor and a pasta machine.

  2⅓ cups all-purpose flour
  ½ teaspoon salt
  3 eggs
  1 tablespoon oil

Processor and pasta machine method: Place flour and salt in a food processor. Beat eggs and oil with a fork in a 2-cup measure. Run the food processor for a few seconds, then gradually add beaten egg into the flour. The mixture will start holding together. It does not have to cling to the blades in a ball, because then it will be too soft. The dough should hold together and be very firm in texture.

Transfer the dough to a lightly floured board. Press it into a rounded sausage shape about 8 inches in length. Cut it into eight equal pieces. Knead each piece for just a few seconds to smooth the dough. Cover the dough with a bowl or cloth to rest for about 15 to 20 minutes.

To roll out the dough with a machine (I use the Altea), always begin with the widest opening (#8 on my machine). Roll the dough through. Fold to measure about 2½ inches and roll through again. That takes care of all the necessary kneading. From then on, decrease the setting one notch at a time to desired thinness, which generally is achieved at setting #2.

Noodles

2⅓ cups all-purpose flour
½ teaspoon salt
3 eggs
1 tablespoon oil

Follow the instructions for making and rolling out Pasta (page 166). After the dough has passed through the widest opening twice, set the machine to the setting that will produce the desired thinness.

For medium and thin noodles, allow dough to dry for about 5 to 7 minutes before cutting noodles. Children love to feed the machine and to catch the noodles as they roll out. Let them help you. Adults like it too, so invite them over for a noodle party.

✹ Suggestion

The simplest way to keep homemade noodles is to dry them for 12 or more hours—they must be thoroughly dry. Then store in a covered container.

Spaghetti with Vegetables
Serves 4 to 6.

Quick and delicious vegetarian favorite

This is one of our quick and delicious meals if you use dried spaghetti (or spaghetti out of a box) combined with any random vegetables on hand. The vegetables boil in the same pot, and with proper timing, the result is just right.

6 quarts water
1 tablespoon salt (optional)
1 bunch broccoli, broccoli raab, green beans, or other vegetable (enough for 4 to 6 servings)
¼ cup olive oil
4 cloves garlic, minced
1 tablespoon mixed minced herbs (basil, thyme, oregano, marjoram)
1 recipe Noodles (this page) or 1 pound dried spaghetti
½ cup grated cheese (your choice)
Freshly ground pepper

Bring water with salt to a boil in a large pot. In the meantime, trim and cut vegetable into serving size.

Heat oil in a small saucepan. Add garlic and herbs and cook over low heat. Do not brown.

Add spaghetti and vegetable to boiling water. Stir and let water come to a boil again and cook for 3 to 4 minutes. Most cut vegetables will cook in 3 or 4 minutes, so subtract that amount of time from the cooking time of the spaghetti. (If the spaghetti is to finish in 10 minutes, add vegetable 6 or 7 minutes after spaghetti has started to cook.) Time it to your preference.

Strain spaghetti and vegetable through a colander and return them to the same pot while still hot. Stir in the sautéed garlic and herbs with the oil and then add cheese. Stir thoroughly but gently so you don't break up the vegetable.

Divide onto warmed plates and serve immediately. Offer more cheese, if you wish, and freshly ground pepper.

✳ Suggestions

- Vary the vegetable. Add arugula and escarole for the last 2 minutes of cooking time.
- For a richer sauce, add ½ cup ricotta cheese to olive oil and garlic.

Spinach and Vegetable Ravioli
Makes 24 to 30 ravioli.

Most of my Italian friends have always, as a matter of tradition, used cheese or meat for ravioli fillings. After trying various combinations, I chose the Spinach Flavored with Vegetables and Cheese recipe as an excellent vegetarian filling.

1 recipe Pasta dough (page 166)
½ cup semolina (coarsely ground durum wheat, found in specialty shops)
½ recipe Spinach Flavored with Vegetables and Cheese (page 129)
1 egg white, slightly beaten
2 tablespoons olive oil or butter
¼ cup chopped fresh parsley

Follow the recipe for making Pasta to the point where you have about 1 pound of Pasta cut into eight pieces. The pieces should rest under a bowl or plastic wrap.

Roll out two pieces at a time. Following directions on the pasta machine, always start at the widest opening (setting #8 on my machine) by rolling and folding for the kneading process. Turn down one notch each time you roll from then on until you reach setting #2. At the end, the strips of dough generally measure about 22 inches long by 2½ inches wide, but that will always vary somewhat.

Spread semolina lightly over your work area. Place two strips of dough on the counter near and parallel to you. Using two teaspoons, drop heaping teaspoonfuls of filling on one strip of the dough nearest you, spacing each spoonful about 1½ inches apart. These dollops should stand up like little balls. Brush a small amount of egg white on both sides of the fillings, down the length of the dough (A).

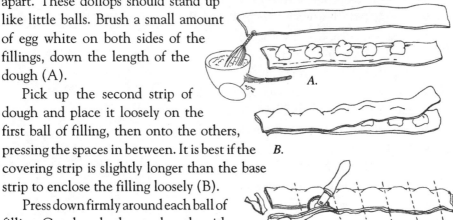

Slightly longer strip away from you.

A.

B.

C.

Pick up the second strip of dough and place it loosely on the first ball of filling, then onto the others, pressing the spaces in between. It is best if the covering strip is slightly longer than the base strip to enclose the filling loosely (B).

Press down firmly around each ball of filling. Cut along both outer lengths with a fluted pastry cutter. Trim off ends and set aside. Cut in between the fillings to separate each ravioli. If you prefer round ravioli, (C) press the dough firmly around the filling, then cut rounds with a cookie cutter that is ½ inch larger in diameter than the filling. As you trim the ravioli, there will be bits and ends. Dry them on a tray and store them as you would spaghetti; save for a future dinner. Place the Ravioli on a board or cookie sheet strewn with semolina.

If you intend to cook them the same day or within two days, keep them refrigerated until ready to use. When ready, let them dry for a few hours.

Use at least 4 or 5 quarts of salted, vigorously boiling water to cook ravioli. If the ravioli is freshly made, they will cook in 3 or 4 minutes. If the ravioli is dried or frozen, it will take twice as long. Always test one corner for doneness according to personal taste. If a large quantity of ravioli is being cooked, boil only 12 to 16 at a time. Remove them with a slotted spoon to a warmed bowl and toss lightly with olive oil or butter. Keep warm in a 250°F oven until all are cooked. Serve with a garnish of fresh chopped parsley.

✸ Suggestions

- For convenience, first freeze the ravioli, separated in one layer on cookie sheets; then box them. Freeze for up to one month.
- Use your imagination to create additional fillings. Choose the cheeses and cooked foods you enjoy most and have on hand. Use your leftovers, but be sure they are cold before you fill the dough.
- Cook ravioli in advance. Line the bottom of a casserole with a preferred sauce. Place the cooked ravioli one next to the other in one layer. Dribble some olive oil or sauce on top. Sprinkle with grated fresh Romano or Parmesan cheese. Bake at 375°F for 20 minutes.

- If time is short and a pasta machine is not one of your tools, do what some well-known chefs do. Use wonton skins! Place the filling in the center of one skin. Moisten the edge. Cover with another skin. Press firmly down around the filling. Cut in desired shapes as described above.

- When you are not counting calories, steep ¼ teaspoon saffron threads in 1½ cups heavy cream. Simmer to reduce cream slightly. Season with salt and pepper, then spread hot sauce on a heated plate. Top with three ravioli for an individual serving. Pass the grated Parmesan cheese. Serves four.

Spinach and Vegetable Lasagne
Serves 6 to 8.

If you have made the full amount of Spinach Flavored with Vegetables and Cheese to make the Spinach and Vegetable Ravioli dish on page 168, you may decide to use the leftover filling for a vegetarian lasagne. Or prepare the Spinach Flavored with Vegetables and Cheese filling specifically for the recipe below. Both the filling and the lasagne can be frozen for up to three months.

    1 recipe Pasta dough (page 166)
    2 cups Tomato Sauce (page 88)
    ½ recipe Spinach Flavored with Vegetables and Cheese (page 129)
    4 ounces mozzarella cheese, cut into strips
    1 cup Béchamel Sauce (page 82)
    ½ pound soft, fresh cheese (ricotta, cream, or cottage cheese)
    ½ cup grated fresh Parmesan cheese

Roll dough through the pasta machine as you would for ravioli. You will have eight long strips of dough, about 2½ inches wide.

Boil 4 to 6 quarts salted water. Place a large bowl of cold water close by. Boil two or three lengths of dough at a time. If the dough is freshly made, it will soften in about 1 minute. If the dough has been dried, cook for 3 to 4 minutes. Use tongs to remove the boiled dough to the bowl of cold water then to a dampened towel or wax paper. Continue until all the dough is cooked.

Use a rectangular casserole, about 13" x 9". Casseroles may vary in size, but this is not very important since the procedure for layering the pasta and filling is very flexible. Always begin by spreading a few tablespoons Tomato Sauce to cover the bottom of the casserole. Fit lengths of dough side by side in one layer. Use scissors to cut them to the size of the casserole. Spread the fillings. Start with the spinach filling, using only about ½ cup, then spread the Tomato Sauce followed by mozzarella cheese. Use a mixture of Béchamel Sauce and the soft cheese for another filling. Each filling should be enough for two layers. Save some Tomato Sauce and the Parmesan cheese for the top. Since the dough is thin, there should be at least eight layers of dough.

Bake at 375°F for 35 to 40 minutes.

✳ *Suggestions*

- Sometimes I make lasagne in an oval or round casserole for a different look and then serve it cut into wedges.
- Improvise with leftover fillings and pasta. Prepare cannelloni. Fill 4-inch lengths of pasta. Wrap the dough around the filling into a tubular shape. Bake at 350°F for 25 minutes on a base of Tomato Sauce or Ragu alla Bolognese (page 88 or 89). Garnish with cheese.
- Add cooked rice or a grain to the Spinach Flavored with Vegetables and Cheese. Bake in a casserole until piping hot.
- Fill large cooked pasta shells with the same filling. Dribble olive oil on top and bake in the oven at 350°F for 20 minutes.

Lawrence Street Noodle Pudding
Serves 8 to 10.

My mother's do-ahead weekend pudding was the simplest combination of cooked noodles, beaten eggs, and some oil. We all loved the crispy surface when it was baked, whether it was hot or nibbled on out of the refrigerator.

If you prefer a mildly sweet pudding that doubles for a main course accompaniment or even dessert, try the following. Our friend, Blanche Siegelbaum, popularized her recipe, and it became the favorite on our street.

Pudding
1 pound medium egg noodles
One 12-ounce can evaporated milk
3 eggs, lightly beaten
½ cup sugar
Juice and grated rind 1 large lemon
¼ teaspoon salt
¾ cup raisins
4 tablespoons melted butter

Topping
2 tablespoons softened butter

½ cup brown sugar
Pinch salt
½ cup chopped walnuts or almonds

Preheat oven to 325°F. Set out a 12-inch rectangular baking pan. Boil noodles as directed on the package. While noodles are boiling, mix all pudding ingredients in a large bowl.

In another small bowl, use a fork or your fingers to rub butter, brown sugar, and salt into small particles for the topping. Add nuts.

Drain noodles and run cool water through them. Add drained noodles to the egg mixture. Pour into baking pan. Spread topping evenly over noodles. Bake for 40 to 45 minutes until lightly browned.

✹ *Suggestions*

- Add 1 cup crushed pineapple or 1 cup applesauce.
- Add segments of tangerine when tangerines are in season.
- Substitute ½ cup maple syrup for the sugar in the pudding.

Buckwheat Groats and Bow-Tie Noodles (Kasha Varnishkes)
Serves 6 to 8.

My own most-favored noodle dish registers at the top of the list of recipes for the current true-to-health vegetarian craze. Although buckwheat is technically not a grain, it contains both proteins and carbohydrates. Team it with noodles for Kasha Varnishkes, an excellent buffet casserole.

1 cup buckwheat groats (kasha)
1 egg, lightly beaten
1½ cups boiling water in a 3-quart saucepan
½ teaspoon salt
3 to 4 tablespoons butter, oil, or reduced chicken fat
1 pound onions, minced
½ pound bow-tie noodles (farfalle), cooked
Salt and freshly ground pepper

Kasha

Mix buckwheat groats with beaten egg. Heat a skillet on medium heat. Add groats and stir until groats are dry and separated. Transfer the groats to the boiling water with salt. Cover and simmer for 15 minutes. In the meantime, melt 2 tablespoons butter, oil, or fat in the skillet. Sauté the onions until they turn color, lightly browned.

Combine onions with bow-tie noodles and groats. Add remaining butter, oil, or fat to the desired amount. Season with salt and pepper.

Transfer to a casserole. Bake for 20 minutes at 350°F before serving. Toss once or twice to keep noodles separated.

✸ *Suggestions*

- Varnishkes may be served immediately after combining noodles and kasha. I prefer the additional baking time to separate and crisp the noodles and grains.
- Add mushrooms when sautéing the onions.
- Use kasha by itself with sautéed onion and mushrooms as an accompaniment to stews. Also use it as a filling in meat loaves, blintzes, and strudels.
- Do not try to omit egg when drying kasha. It will cook to a mushlike cereal. You can try 2 egg whites for 1 whole egg.

8

Fish and Shellfish

Slowly but surely American families are beginning to include fish in their weekly menus. Not only does fish add a healthy dimension to a good diet, it fills the need for fast cooking. A last-minute cook can bake, broil, or poach fish or shellfish in fewer than 10 minutes. Add a vegetable, salad, and crusty bread and the meal is complete in no more than 20 minutes.

It is most important to locate a responsible fish market. Acquaint yourself with the salesperson. Ask questions about source and freshness. New varieties with baffling names seem to be arriving from around the world. Purchase a small quantity of a new variety and cook it at the same time as you cook a familiar one. It will be a lesson worth learning for your next purchase.

When our children were very young, I would often cook a combination of fish and shellfish. My idea was to include a favorite variety and then add one or two new tastes.

There are many excellent recipes that follow in this chapter, but most often I simply bake fish with minced shallots and ½ cup white wine (or dry vermouth), lightly covered with oiled wax paper. At other times, I am lucky enough to find a

175

container of chicken or clam broth in my freezer. Then I can poach fish in the heated broth. Fish steaks and meaty fish slices are perfect for broiling, but they must be carefully timed to avoid overcooking.

I do enjoy handling sweet-smelling, very fresh fish, and that's the way I always buy it. I never make a selection before consulting the fish dealer. Whatever fish or shellfish you decide to prepare, buy only the freshest.

Notes on Cooking with Fish

1. Remove fish from its wrapping as soon as possible. Rinse it in cold water. If the fish is not to be cooked promptly, store it in a shallow casserole or pan. Salt it lightly with kosher or sea salt. Fill a plastic bag, loosely, with ice cubes. Tie the end of the bag well so that any melted water will not leak through. Place the ice bag over the fish to cover it completely. Store up to 24 hours in the refrigerator, if necessary.

2. Serving portions of fish vary with individual appetites. Roughly figure on 8 to 10 ounces of raw fish with bone per person, or 4 to 6 ounces of filleted raw fish per person.

3. When fish is skinned, it leaves a darker side. Always use this side for stuffing.

4. An addition of lemon, vinegar, or dry wine is necessary for all fish during cooking and/or serving.

5. Always preheat the oven before broiling or baking fish.

6. Fish cooks rapidly, especially when broiled or baked at high temperatures. Allow 10 minutes for each inch of thickness as a good measure for timing. Many people prefer tuna and salmon medium-rare. Use your fingers to test. Firmness and resistance to touch indicate that the fish is well done. If your fingers depress the flesh, it is rare. Check doneness by cutting into the center if you do not trust your experience.

7. Fillets of fish are always available. The busy cook can reach for the simplest of ingredients for seasoning a variety of fish—red snapper, sole, haddock, cod, and others. If the fillets are large, cut them into portions of 4 to 6 ounces. Remember that when bones, head, and skin are removed from the fish, some of its flavor is lost.

8. Heads and bones supply the greatest flavor to fish dishes. Cook the fish whole whenever possible.

9. Ask for bones and heads at your market to make fish stock (see Chapter 2 for stock recipes). Fish stock is a fat-free flavoring for all fish dishes. It strengthens the flavor of one-bowl fish dishes and is used as a base for sauces and chowders. Refrigerate or freeze the stock in small quantities for future use.

10. Canned clam broth can be used instead of fish stock, but dilute it with water if it is too salty. A light chicken stock is also a good substitute.

11. Parmesan cheese is an excellent addition to fish dishes. Buy a wedge and grate it as needed or refrigerate ½ cup grated Parmesan cheese in a covered container for instant use.

Recipes

One-Bowl Fish and Vegetables
Serves 4.

The basic techniques of cooking fish have remained the same for years. Boiling fish, which we prefer to call poaching today, is the simplest way to cook a fish meal in one pot. When I was a child, it was a favorite in our home. Based on techniques learned in "the old country," fish was simply covered with water. Vegetables such as onion, celery, carrot, and potato were then added. The final touch was a generous dab of butter dropped on the steaming hot soup before it was served. It was a flavor I will never forget. Just a few additions in the recipe below reflect our changing tastes.

2 tablespoons olive oil
4 small onions, cut in half
2 ribs celery, diced
2 carrots, scraped and diced
4 medium potatoes, peeled and thinly sliced
2 leeks, white parts only, cut in half vertically
1 quart boiling water
2 tablespoons lemon juice
½ teaspoon each thyme and oregano (or use 1 tablespoon each of fresh if available)
¼ cup chopped fresh parsley
2 to 3 pounds red snapper, bass, haddock, or cod with bone or 1½ to 2 pounds fillet of fish
Salt and freshly ground pepper to taste

When ready to cook, set all the cut vegetables on the counter closest to the stove. Use a 6-quart Dutch oven or other good cooking pot with a cover.

Heat the oil in the pot over moderate heat. Add onions, celery, and carrots. Cook for a few minutes, stirring occasionally, until vegetables are glazed. Add potatoes and leeks. Stir lightly together, cover, and cook for 7 to 8 minutes on low heat.

Pour in water; add lemon juice, thyme, oregano, and half of the parsley. Place fish on top of the vegetables. Sprinkle with a small amount of salt and pepper. Bring heat up to a simmer, then cover the pot and cook for 7 to 10 minutes. The fish is finished if it flakes easily when poked with a fork.

Divide vegetables and fish into four heated soup bowls. Pour broth on top. Serve with crusty bread or rolls.

Fish Stew Provençale
Serves 4.

French influence expands upon the simplicity of the previous recipe by using aromatic herbs and spices. First, choose the freshest fish in season and the herbs you know best. Add a pinch of an unfamiliar one. No spice or herb should be overwhelming.

Croutons (Toasted Sliced Bread)

1 loaf French or Italian bread
2 or 3 cloves garlic
2 tablespoons olive oil

Stew

2 to 4 tablespoons olive oil
2 onions (about ½ pound), sliced
2 ribs celery, diced
2 large carrots, scraped and diced
2 tablespoons roughly diced garlic
2 leeks, white parts only, diced
4 or 5 strips orange rind
½ teaspoon saffron threads, soaked in 1 quart hot water
1 cup fresh (or canned) tomatoes, skinned, seeded, and diced
1 cup dry white wine
½ teaspoon each thyme and marjoram
¼ cup chopped fresh parsley
½ teaspoon fennel seed (1 diced fresh bulb of fennel may be substituted and added with the celery)
Salt and freshly ground pepper to taste
2 to 3 pounds grouper, halibut, whole bass, or monkfish or 1½ to 2 pounds fillet of fish

½ cup grated Parmesan cheese
8 croutons

Prepare the croutons in advance so they are ready when the fish is ready. Preheat oven to 375°F. Cut bread into 1-inch slices. Cut cloves of garlic in half. Rub garlic on each slice of bread. Use a jelly-roll pan to accommodate the bread in one layer. Spread oil over the pan. Turn slices of bread in the oil to cover both sides. Bake for 20 minutes, turning the bread over once. The bread should be lightly toasted when finished.

Place all ingredients on the counter next to the stove when ready to cook. If you wish to serve at the table, use a suitable 6-quart Dutch oven or a handsome covered soup pot. Heat 2 tablespoons oil in the pot. Add onions; stir and cook over low heat just to glaze and sweat them (do not brown). Use more oil if you wish. Add celery, carrots, garlic, and leeks. Cook uncovered over medium heat for 3 to 5 minutes, stirring occasionally.

Add orange rind. Add hot water with saffron. Cook uncovered until the liquid is reduced by half. Add tomatoes, white wine, thyme, marjoram, 2 tablespoons parsley, and fennel. Season with a desired amount of salt and freshly ground pepper. Add more hot water, if necessary, to cover the vegetables by ½ inch. Cover and cook for 5 minutes.

Place fish on the vegetables (the liquid should just cover the fish). Cover pot and simmer for 10 minutes. Sprinkle ¼ cup Parmesan cheese and the remaining parsley on top, and take to the table. Place two croutons in each of the four soup bowls. Divide vegetables and fish among the four soup bowls equally, pouring the broth on top. Pass the remaining Parmesan cheese at the table.

Braised Fish with Clams
Serves 4.

If clams are available in your area, take advantage of the extraordinary flavor they add to other varieties of fish. Braise almost any variety of fish (except, perhaps, mackerel and bluefish) with clam broth. This light but hearty fish soup is a dinner today and every bit as good tomorrow.

12 littleneck clams
1 medium onion, quartered
2 medium carrots, scraped and cut in half
4 small red-skinned potatoes
1 leek, white part only, washed and cut in large dice
1 quart water
1 cup white wine

1 rib celery, tied with bouquet garni
¼ teaspoon red pepper flakes
½ teaspoon ground white pepper
1½ pounds bass, red snapper, halibut, haddock, grey or lemon sole, or other firm-
	fleshed fish

Scrub clams well. Sometimes I soak them in a sinkful of water with ¼ cup cornmeal before scrubbing. The soaking seems to release sand.

Place clams and all other ingredients, except fish, in a 5- or 6-quart Dutch oven or heavy stockpot. Cover and bring to a boil. Lower heat and simmer for about 15 minutes. If some clams have not opened, shake the pot and cook for another minute or two (shaking the pot sometimes opens the slow ones). Transfer the clams to a bowl, discarding any that have not opened.

Remove clams from their shells and place on a warmed side dish. Broth will accumulate as you do this. Add the broth to the vegetables in the pot. Set clams aside.

Place the fish on top of the vegetables in the pot. Cover and simmer for 7 to 8 minutes depending on the thickness of the fish.

Add clams to the fish and vegetables. Simmer for another minute. Taste and adjust seasoning, adding salt if necessary.

Divide the fish, clams, and vegetables equally on warmed dinner dishes or in soup bowls. Spoon some broth over all. Pass crusty bread and broth around the table.

✹ *Suggestion*

Sometimes when clams are in abundance I cook up a huge potful. Some are for the day's dinner and some go into a pasta sauce the next day. Clam broth is always much in demand, and any excess is frozen for future use. The broth may be used wherever liquid is needed in fish recipes and sauces.

Fried Smelts
Serves 4 to 6.

Frying is the quickest cooking method for small fish, fillets, and shellfish. Many people love the crust as much as they do the fish. When these tiny morsels are fried properly, they absorb little fat, thus satisfying our constant concern for good health. Substitute any shellfish, mollusks, or small fillets for the smelts in the recipes below.

In the winter months, my neighbor, Roy Betit, fishes for smelt through the ice in the lake nearby. Roy enjoys his fish at its freshest and best, so he immediately cleans them and prepares them for dinner in his heated bobhouse on the ice.

    1 cup oil (¼ butter or bacon fat may be used in part)
    1½ cups flour, cornmeal, or plain bread crumbs
    Salt and freshly ground pepper
    24 smelts, cleaned and with heads left on
    1 lemon, cut into wedges
    Sprigs fresh parsley

Slowly heat the oil in a straight-sided skillet or a 3-inch-deep stew pot. In the meantime, spread flour, cornmeal, or bread crumbs, or any combination of the three, on a sheet of wax paper. Add salt and pepper. Dredge each fish in the dry breading mixture and set aside.

Test the hot oil with a cube of white bread—it should become golden brown in 30 seconds. Fry the fish in the oil for about 3 minutes on each side, being careful not to crowd the fish so they fry evenly. Remove to paper toweling and continue until all the smelts are fried.

Serve immediately or keep warm in a 250°F oven until ready to serve. Fried smelts are best when served within 20 minutes of frying. Garnish with a wedge of lemon and a sprig of fresh parsley.

Fresh Smelts Savory
Serves 4 to 6.

Many years ago, Leon Lianides, the celebrated New York City restaurateur of the Coach House, was a guest lecturer at one of my classes. Leon, who is of Greek background, taught the following recipe for smelts. They are fried as in the above recipe but are presented quite differently.

    24 smelts
    Salt and pepper
    1½ cups flour
    2 cups olive oil
    2 bay leaves
    3 cloves garlic, chopped
    3 tablespoons wine vinegar
    1 onion, sliced thin
    1 tablespoon rosemary
    1 tablespoon chopped parsley

Season fish with salt and pepper and roll in the flour to dredge. Heat the oil in a deep frying pan to 350°F. Add fish, a few at a time, and fry them for about 3 minutes on each side until crisp and golden brown. Drain the smelts on paper toweling.

Pour off all but about ½ cup oil. Add the remaining ingredients to the oil in the skillet. Simmer for about 5 minutes for a delectable sauce.

Place the smelts on a platter, and strain the sauce over the fish. Sprinkle parsley on top and refrigerate for 3 or more hours. Serve on lettuce greens for a salad dinner or as a first course.

Baked Halibut, Monkfish, Salmon, or Swordfish

Serves 4 to 6.

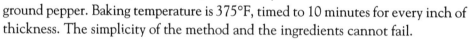

Baking fish is almost foolproof. Whenever in doubt about a cooking method for the variety of fish on hand, baking is always my choice. When baking fish, I can rely on my supply of basic ingredients—shallots, white wine, choice of olive oil or butter, coarse salt, and freshly ground pepper. Baking temperature is 375°F, timed to 10 minutes for every inch of thickness. The simplicity of the method and the ingredients cannot fail.

    2 to 3 pounds halibut, monkfish, salmon, or swordfish
    2 to 3 tablespoons olive oil or butter
    Kosher (coarse) salt and freshly ground pepper
    2 tablespoons diced shallots
    ½ cup dry white wine or dry vermouth
    Lemon wedges and fresh parsley sprigs for each portion

Fish should be baked in one piece and cut into portions after baking. Preheat oven to 375°F.

Oil or butter a shallow baking dish that will accommodate the fish. Sprinkle salt, pepper, and shallots over the bottom of the dish. Place the fish in the dish and pour wine or vermouth on top. Cover the fish with a sheet of greased wax paper. Bake for 10 to 15 minutes, depending on the thickness of the fish. Test with a fork in the thickest portion. If the middle is still translucent, cook a little longer (unless you like fish slightly underdone). Garnish with lemon wedges and parsley before serving.

✳ *Suggestion*
Haddock and cod are available almost year-round in many areas. They can be substituted for the fish in the above recipe. Onions or the white portions of scallions can be used when shallots are not available.

Quick-Baked Fillets of Fish
Serves 4.

If you are looking for a quick dinner, this is the easiest and most basic one for fish. You can dress it up with yogurt, sour cream, a slice of tomato, and a sprinkling of cheese. However, it can really be delicious without the extra dressing if your fish is fresh and sweet.

    4 fillets of fish (4 to 6 ounces each)
    1 to 2 tablespoons olive oil or butter
    Kosher (coarse) salt and freshly ground pepper
    ½ cup plain bread crumbs
    2 to 3 tablespoons fresh lemon juice (about ½ lemon)
    4 lemon wedges (about ½ lemon)
    Sprigs parsley

Rinse fillets in cold water, and set aside on paper toweling. Preheat oven to 450°F. Use a shallow baking dish or jelly-roll pan large enough to accommodate the fish in one layer. Grease the pan with only as much oil as necessary. Sprinkle a small amount of salt and pepper over the oiled sheet.

Spread bread crumbs on wax paper. Dredge both sides of the fish in bread crumbs and place on the oiled baking dish or pan. Spoon fresh lemon juice and the remaining oil over the fish.

Bake for 5 to 7 minutes. If not brown enough, set fish under the broiler for 30 seconds. Garnish with lemon wedges and parsley before serving.

Fillet of Fish with Cheese and Wine
Serves 4.

    4 fillets of fish (about 4 ounces each)
    Salt and freshly ground pepper
    ¼ cup flour
    ¼ cup grated cheese (Parmesan, Gruyère, or Cheddar)
    1 tablespoon each oil and butter
    ½ cup dry white wine (or chicken or vegetable stock)
    ¼ cup each chopped fresh parsley and scallion greens
    4 lemon wedges

Sprinkle fillets with salt and pepper. Dredge fish in flour and shake off excess. Divide the cheese by placing a mound on the skin (darker) side of each fillet. Fold fish over, point to point, making a double layer and enclosing the cheese.

Heat the skillet over low heat. Add oil and butter. When hot, add one fillet at a time. Sauté for 3 minutes on each side. Remove to a heated platter and cover with aluminum foil. Keep warm in a 250°F oven until ready to serve.

Swirl wine in the skillet to deglaze it. Heat to reduce the liquid to half. Add scallions and parsley for just a few seconds. Spoon the mixture over the fish when ready to serve. Garnish each fillet with a lemon wedge.

Baked Fillets of Fish with Smoked Salmon
Serves 4.

Fish

4 fillets of fish (4 ounces each)
4 very thin slices smoked salmon
Freshly ground black pepper
½ cup plain bread crumbs
2 tablespoons olive oil or softened butter
Salt and pepper
¼ cup minced shallots
½ cup dry white wine
1 pound spinach or Swiss chard leaves

Sauce

1 tablespoon butter or olive oil
1 tablespoon capers
¼ cup lemon juice
4 scallion greens, chopped
2 tablespoons chopped parsley

Spread fillets on a sheet of wax paper in one layer. Cover each fillet with a slice of smoked salmon. Grind some black pepper over all. Sprinkle about 2 tablespoons bread crumbs over the slices of salmon, and roll each fillet to enclose the salmon. Refrigerate the fish if this dish is being prepared in advance.

Preheat oven to 475°F. Grease a small, shallow casserole with oil or butter and sprinkle with some salt and pepper. Spread shallots and 2 tablespoons bread crumbs over the bottom. Place the fillets side by side in the casserole. Sprinkle the remaining bread crumbs over the fillets. Pour white wine around the fish. Bake for 10 minutes.

While the fish is baking, steam the spinach (page 127); then make the sauce.

Melt butter or heat oil in a pan. Add capers, lemon juice, scallions, and parsley.

Mix and heat the sauce just before serving.

To serve, spread the spinach, equally divided, on each plate. Place a fillet on top of the spinach. Spoon hot sauce over each fillet.

Braised Fillets of Fish with Sesame Seed Stuffing
Serves 4.

½ cup sesame seeds
¼ cup plain bread crumbs
2 tablespoons minced shallots or 2 tablespoons scallions (white portions only)
½ cup minced sweet red pepper
2 tablespoons chopped parsley
½ teaspoon each marjoram and thyme
Pinch cayenne pepper
1 egg white, lightly beaten
Salt and pepper to taste
4 fillets of fish (4 to 6 ounces each)
1 cup fish or chicken stock
½ cup each dry white wine and water
1 rib celery tied with bouquet garni

Toast sesame seeds on a cookie sheet in a 350°F oven. Set aside ¼ cup of the toasted sesame seeds, and mix the remainder with the bread crumbs, shallots or scallions, red pepper, parsley, marjoram, thyme, cayenne pepper, and egg white for a stuffing. Season with salt and pepper to taste.

Place fillets, skin-side up, side by side on a sheet of wax paper. Spread the stuffing, equally divided, on each fillet and roll them up to enclose the stuffing.

Heat the stock, wine, water, and celery in a straight-sided skillet. When the liquid comes to a boil, lower heat. Place fillets, fold-side down, into the simmering liquid. Cover and simmer for 10 to 12 minutes. Serve with a sprinkling of sesame seeds.

✹ Suggestion

- Freeze leftover broth for future use. For example, use the broth for White Wine Sauce for Seafood (page 84).
- For a creamier sauce, mix 2 tablespoons each softened butter and flour (to make a mixture called *beurre manié*). Add the mixture a little at a time to the simmering broth, which will thicken as it cooks.

Fillets of Fish with Fresh Tomato Mousse
Serves 6.

I adapted the following recipe from *Cooking With the Young Chefs of France* by Elizabeth Lambert Ortiz. Georges Paineau of Brittany was the young chef who developed this recipe. This recipe is best when tomatoes are in season and ripe.

6 medium-sized ripe tomatoes (about 2 pounds), peeled, seeded, and chopped
Salt and pepper to taste
3 tablespoons butter
2 tablespoons minced shallots
3 egg whites
6 fillets of fish (6 to 8 ounces each)
⅓ cup dry white wine
½ cup heavy cream
Golden caviar for garnish

Cook tomatoes slowly in a small saucepan, stirring occasionally, until the mixture is thick. Season with salt and pepper. Transfer to a bowl and cool thoroughly. Preheat oven to 400°F.

Use 1 tablespoon butter to grease an ovenproof dish large enough to accommodate the fish, doubled over, in one layer. Scatter shallots over the surface of the dish. Sprinkle with salt and pepper.

Beat egg whites to a light frothiness, and fold into cooled tomato mixture. Spread the mixture over each fillet, then fold over gently, point to point. Transfer fish into the baking dish. Pour wine and cream over the fish. Cover with greased parchment paper, and bake for 10 to 12 minutes. Carefully remove fish to a heated platter or individual serving dishes. Cover to keep warm.

Strain the cooking juices into a saucepan. Reduce by half over high heat, then stir in remaining butter bit by bit. Spoon the sauce over the fish. Place 1 teaspoon golden caviar on top of each fillet.

✳ *Suggestions*

- Calories can be reduced by omitting the butter and cream. Use shallots and white wine instead.
- Serve with a julienne of steamed carrots, zucchini, and leeks.

Fillets of Sole in Phyllo
Serves 4.

Fillets of Sole in Phyllo makes a lovely presentation that looks like it took hours of work, but it didn't. The dish can be totally completed much in advance for a perfect company dinner. Keep it in mind, too, as a first course (using smaller 3-ounce fillets) for a celebration dinner.

>   4 fillets of sole (4 to 6 ounces each)
>   Salt and pepper
>   4 sprigs cilantro or Italian parsley
>   Four 1-ounce cubes halibut, swordfish, or salmon (you can also use shellfish)
>   8 sheets phyllo dough (available in specialty food shops)
>   8 tablespoons (¼ pound) clarified butter (unsalted)
>   4 tablespoons plain bread crumbs

Preheat oven to 400°F. Rinse fillets in cold water. Place on wax paper, skin-side up, and sprinkle lightly with salt and pepper. Place 1 sprig cilantro or parsley on each fillet and then a cube of fish on top. Roll up to enclose the cube of fish, and place fillets

Bake rolled fillets 10 minutes.

in a lightly buttered baking dish. Bake for 10 minutes. Remove from the pan and allow to cool thoroughly.

Keep the phyllo covered with plastic wrap or a damp cloth while you work with each sheet. Brush one sheet phyllo with clarified butter. Sprinkle some bread crumbs over it. Place another sheet of phyllo on top. Brush it with butter and sprinkle with bread crumbs. Place a cooled fillet in the center of the sheets of phyllo.

Prepare phyllo.

Enclose cooled fillet.

Gather and twist.

Crisp in oven 10-12 minutes before serving.

Gather the phyllo around the fish to enclose it with a twist of the phyllo. Repeat with the other fillets. At this point, the wrapped fillets can be refrigerated or they can stay at room temperature for about an hour. If the fillets have been refrigerated, bring them to room temperature 30 minutes before baking.

Preheat oven to 400°F. Place fillets on a lightly buttered, shallow pan and bake for 10 to 12 minutes, until browned and crisped. Serve immediately on a bed of rice.

Steamed Whole Sea Bass with Broccoli
Serves 4.

There are times when I am enticed to cook a whole fish with head and tail, in which case not a bit of flavor is lost. Since I own a Chinese steamer, I opt for an aromatic Oriental seasoning, perfect for steaming. Of course, you can use any steamer or poacher or even a covered roasting pan as long as it has a rack.

2 to 3 pound sea bass (or try red snapper or other whole fish)
1 tablespoon soy sauce
2 tablespoons sherry
½ teaspoon pepper
2 teaspoons cornstarch
1 tablespoon corn oil
4 dried Chinese mushrooms
4 slices fresh ginger root, diced
2 cloves garlic, minced
4 scallions, cut in 3-inch lengths and julienned
2 cups broccoli flowerets
1 tablespoon sesame oil

Rinse the fish in cold water, inside and out. Score it at 2-inch intervals by cutting through the skin on top.

Mix soy sauce, sherry, pepper, cornstarch, and oil. Rub this seasoning on both sides of the fish and marinate for about 30 minutes, or do this ahead and refrigerate the fish overnight.

Soak dried mushrooms in hot water for 30 to 40 minutes. Discard the stems if they are tough. Cut mushrooms into thin slices.

Transfer the fish on a dish that will fit in the steamer, or line the steaming rack with greens to replace the dish. Place the fish on the dish or rack. Spread mushrooms, ginger, garlic, and scallions over the fish. Steam over simmering water for 20 to 30 minutes. Place broccoli around the fish for the last 10 minutes of cooking.

Transfer the whole fish to a heated oval platter. Surround it with broccoli. Trickle sesame oil over the broccoli.

Baked Bluefish with Summer Squash
Serves 4.

When we lived on Long Island, my friend, Ricky Torella, shared his fresh catch of bluefish with us. I confess that the only bluefish I ever truly enjoyed were those caught by Ricky in the Montauk waters, then cooked in my kitchen the very next day. That summer I grilled one fish on our barbecue, crisp and charred, then saved another one for baking.

2 tablespoons olive oil
3- to 4-pound bluefish (or other whole fish)
Kosher (coarse) salt and black pepper
6 slices lemon
1 medium red onion, sliced
1 sweet bell pepper (red or green), sliced
2 ripe tomatoes, sliced (or ½ cup canned tomatoes)
1 medium-sized yellow squash, sliced
1 medium-sized zucchini, sliced
¼ cup chopped fresh basil
¼ teaspoon red pepper flakes
2 to 3 cups warm mashed potatoes
4 sprigs Italian parsley

Preheat oven to 375°F. Grease an oval or rectangular casserole with 1 tablespoon olive oil. Make sure that the casserole is at least 2 inches longer than the fish.

Score the top of the fish six times, cutting through the skin ¼ inch deep. Lightly salt the top and inside of the fish. Grind some black pepper on top. Insert a slice of lemon into each cut.

Place the fish in the oiled dish. Spread onion, pepper, tomatoes, yellow squash, and zucchini evenly around the fish. Sprinkle basil and red pepper flakes over the vegetables.

Dribble the remaining olive oil over the fish. Lightly cover with aluminum foil or parchment paper. Bake for 25 minutes. Remove fish from the oven.

Preheat the broiler. Use two spoons to drop small mounds of mashed potatoes around the edge of the dish on top of the vegetables, or use a pastry bag to pipe out a fancier border. Broil for 3 to 4 minutes until potatoes turn light brown. Garnish with parsley.

Trout
Serves 4.

Trout have always been considered very special in fish cookery, but not many of us have been privileged to have our own pond with fresh trout. Recently we discovered a trout farm close to us in South Newfane. There may be a difference between nature's bounty and fish farming, but at least the freshness can be present in both.

There are many ways to enhance the flavor of trout, but the following recipe is the fastest and simplest.

4 medium-sized trout, boned
Salt and pepper
¼ cup flour
¼ cup untoasted, fine, plain bread crumbs
½ cup corn or olive oil
2 tablespoons butter
¼ cup minced shallots
½ cup dry vermouth or white wine
¼ cup chopped fresh herbs (parsley, chives, tarragon)
2 tablespoons lemon juice

Rinse the trout in cold water. Season inside and out with salt and pepper. Mix flour and bread crumbs on a sheet of wax paper. Dredge fish in the mixture. Preheat oven to 375°F.

Heat a skillet with oil and 1 tablespoon butter. Add two fish at a time if the skillet is not large enough to hold four. (If you crowd them, they will not brown and crust properly.) Turn the fish as they brown, about 2 minutes on each side. Transfer them to a baking pan large enough to hold all the fish in one layer.

Pour off remaining oil in the skillet. Wipe it if the flour and crumbs are blackened. Add remaining butter to the skillet. Sauté shallots until glazed. Add vermouth or wine, herbs, and lemon juice. Boil for 2 minutes to reduce the liquid. Spoon the mixture over the trout.

Bake the trout for 10 minutes. Serve immediately.

✳ Suggestions

- Instead of frying, after dredging the fish in the flour and bread crumbs, place the trout on a baking pan that has been spread with shallots and wine or stock. Add herbs and lemon juice. Bake for 25 minutes at 375°F.
- Fill the cavity of each trout with Duxelles (page 114). Bake as above.
- Fill the cavity of each trout with a julienne of sautéed leeks and carrots. Instead of frying, poach the fish in broth for 15 minutes. Transfer fish to a dish. Remove the skin of each fish, and wrap the fish in blanched escarole or other leaf lettuce. Place in a baking pan while you make the sauce, and keep fish covered and warm at 250°F. Pour the broth into a saucepan. Reduce broth, then thicken it or enrich it with cream and butter, or thicken it with a mixture of 2 teaspoons cornstarch and 2 tablespoons water.

- Fill the cavity of each trout with a mousse of salmon or shellfish (page 37). Bake on a buttered or oiled baking pan at 375° F. for 30 minutes. Serve with Sauce Velouté made with fish broth (page 83).

Scallops au Gratin
Serves 4.

When I guided a group on a cooking tour through France some years ago, we were given a splendid lesson by my friend Georges Pouvel. Georges never fails to add something to my cooking knowledge. At that time it was a technique for cooking scallops. It is absolutely foolproof.

1¼ pounds scallops
¼ cup minced shallots
Bouquet garni tied in a 3-inch rib of celery
2 cups fish, vegetable, or chicken stock
½ cup dry vermouth or white wine
Salt and white pepper
2 leeks, washed
2 tablespoons butter
2 tablespoons flour
¼ teaspoon dry mustard
Pinch cayenne pepper
1 ounce fresh salmon caviar for garnish

Be sure to remove the muscle from the scallops if your fish dealer has not already done so. Place the scallops, shallots, and bouquet garni in a skillet large enough to fit them in one layer. Add stock and vermouth or wine to just cover. Sprinkle lightly with salt and white pepper if your stock is not salty.

Start heat on low and gradually increase. As soon as the liquid simmers, remove the pan to the side. Do not boil. At this point, the scallops are edible and can be used in any scallop dish.

Cut leeks ½ inch below the white portion. Discard or reserve the greens for other use. Cut the white portion of the leeks into 1-inch pieces. Cook them in water to cover for 5 to 7 minutes.

Discard bouquet garni and strain the scallops over a bowl. Keep the liquid for a sauce. Transfer the scallops to a shallow 8- or 9-inch baking casserole. Distribute the cooked leeks among the scallops.

Melt the butter in a saucepan over medium heat. Stir in flour, mustard, and cayenne pepper. Cook for 2 minutes. Gradually add liquid from the scallops, stirring constantly. Simmer for a few minutes until it comes to a boil. Taste for additional seasoning.

Pour the sauce over the scallops. Heat the casserole in a 350°F. oven for 20 to 25 minutes. For a beautiful garnish, place a teaspoon of salmon caviar in four places on top before serving.

Baked Shrimp
Serves 4.

Shrimp have become America's favorite seafood. They are very low in fat and high in cholesterol, so one balances the other. If you can afford the price, use shrimp for its quickness and for its adaptability. This crustacean can be deliciously cooked with seasonings ranging from fruity to tart to spicy and sharp.

Follow the directions for using each seasoning.

Four Optional Seasonings:

Orange and Chardonnay Wine

    1½ to 2 pounds shrimp, shelled and deveined
    1 cup fresh orange juice
    1 cup Chardonnay wine
    1 tablespoon each orange and lemon zest
    2 tablespoons minced shallots
    ½ teaspoon kosher (coarse) salt
    ¼ teaspoon white pepper
    ½ cup light cream
    Sprigs Italian parsley

If you have the time, marinate the shrimp (from 15 minutes to 6 hours, refrigerated) in all the ingredients except the cream and parsley.

When ready to cook, preheat oven to 400°F. Place shrimp in a shallow baking pan and pour marinade into a 1½-quart saucepan.

Bake shrimp for 7 to 8 minutes, turning each one after 3 minutes. If the shrimp are small, they will cook more rapidly.

In the meantime, boil the marinade to reduce the liquid volume by half. Add cream and simmer. Strain the sauce, if you wish.

Divide the shrimp equally on four warmed dinner plates. Pour sauce over the shrimp. Garnish with Italian parsley and serve with rice.

Garlic and Herbs

1½ to 2 pounds shrimp, shelled and deveined
4 large cloves garlic, minced
1 tablespoon each minced fresh parsley, thyme, and marjoram
1 tablespoon each vinegar and lemon juice
½ teaspoon kosher (coarse) salt
¼ teaspoon pepper
2 tablespoons olive oil

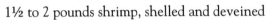

Mix all ingredients together. Marinate shrimp from 15 minutes to 6 hours, refrigerated. Preheat oven to 400°F. Bake shrimp for 7 to 8 minutes in a shallow baking dish with the marinade. Turn each shrimp after 3 minutes. If the shrimp are small, they will cook more rapidly.

Mustard and Yogurt

1½ to 2 pounds shrimp, shelled and deveined
2 tablespoons Dijon mustard
1 teaspoon prepared horseradish
1 cup yogurt (substitute light sour cream or mayonnaise, if you wish)
½ cup minced scallions
½ teaspoon kosher (coarse) salt
¼ teaspoon white pepper

Follow directions in the recipe for Garlic and Herbs.

Tomato and Feta Cheese

1½ to 2 pounds shrimp, shelled and deveined
1 cup canned crushed tomatoes
1 tablespoon each basil and chopped fresh parsley
1 teaspoon oregano
¼ teaspoon red pepper flakes
2 tablespoons lemon juice
½ teaspoon kosher (coarse) salt
¼ teaspoon white pepper
½ cup crumbled feta cheese

Marinate the shrimp in all the ingredients, except the cheese. Follow the directions in the recipe for Garlic and Herbs. Before serving, sprinkle feta cheese on top and broil for 30 seconds.

✹ *Suggestion*

In each case, shrimp can be skewered, baked as suggested, broiled or grilled over charcoal.

Shrimp in Lobster Sauce
Serves 4.

Shrimp take longer to clean than to cook, but I still prefer to buy them in their shell for maximum flavor. If you bathe them in your favorite seasoning, you can steam, stir-fry, or broil them. They will be ready to serve in about five minutes. One of my favorite sauces for shrimp is the Oriental Lobster Sauce. The name of the sauce is somewhat misleading, since there is not a bit of lobster in it. However, the sauce is traditionally served with Lobster Cantonese—hence the name. The same sauce can be served with softshell crabs, clams, and oysters.

1 pound shrimp (20 to 24), shelled and deveined
2 teaspoons fermented black beans (soaked in water to cover for ½ hour)
2 large cloves garlic, minced
2 tablespoons corn oil
¼ pound ground pork
1 tablespoon sherry
1 tablespoon soy sauce
½ teaspoon sugar
½ cup water
1 tablespoon cornstarch dissolved in 2 tablespoons water
1 egg, slightly beaten
2 scallions, diced

Wash and drain the shrimp. Drain water from the black beans. Crush the black beans and mix with garlic.

Heat the corn oil in a wok or a straight-sided skillet. Add the black beans and garlic. Stir for 30 seconds. Add pork. Stir-fry until the pork turns white, about 2 to 3 minutes. Add shrimp, stirring constantly and heating until the shrimp turn opaque. Stir in sherry, soy sauce, and sugar. Cook for 1 minute. Add water. Cover and cook over low heat for about 2 minutes.

Uncover. Stir in cornstarch mixture and cook until the sauce thickens. Add beaten egg and stir again. Turn off heat immediately after the egg has been added. Scatter scallions on top. Serve at once.

✳ *Suggestion*

Fermented black beans can be purchased in Chinese food stores and specialty food stores. They store for months in a covered jar.

Pan-Fried Oysters
Serves 2.

When the first oysters arrive at the fish market, my husband and I have no resistance. All other plans are set aside. We must dine on oysters that very day, turning dinner for the evening into an oyster treat.

  10 to 12 oysters, shucked, or one 8-ounce container fresh oysters
  1 tablespoon soy sauce
  1 tablespoon Worcestershire sauce
  Dash Tabasco sauce
  2 cups shredded lettuce
  2 tablespoons butter or oil
  ¼ cup port wine

Drain liquid from the oysters and reserve. Marinate the oysters in soy, Worcestershire, and Tabasco sauces for 15 to 20 minutes. Cover a serving dish with shredded lettuce.

Heat a skillet and add 1 tablespoon butter or oil. When the butter is melted or the oil is heated, add the oysters. Sauté for 2 to 3 minutes, shaking the pan and turning the oysters over.

Place the oysters on the shredded lettuce. Add port wine and reserved liquid to the hot skillet for 30 seconds. Turn off heat. Add remaining butter or oil, bit by bit, until all is incorporated. Pour the sauce over the oysters. Serve immediately.

Deep-Fried Oysters
Serves 2.

  10 to 12 oysters, shucked, or one 8-ounce container fresh oysters
  ½ cup flour
  1 egg
  ¼ cup buttermilk
  ½ cup cornmeal
  Salt and freshly ground pepper
  2 cups oil

Drain liquid from the oysters. Spread flour on a sheet of wax paper. Beat the egg and buttermilk in a shallow dish and place alongside the flour.

Spread cornmeal on another sheet of wax paper next to the beaten egg mixture. Sprinkle a little salt and pepper into the cornmeal.

Dip each oyster first in the flour, then in the egg mixture, and then in the cornmeal. Place oysters on a cookie sheet, leaving space between each oyster. Allow the breaded oysters to rest about 20 to 30 minutes. They can be prepared in advance, in the morning, and refrigerated.

Heat oil in a small saucepan or a wok. Frying temperature should be 350°F. Lay out a few sheets of paper toweling for draining the oysters.

Fry a few oysters at a time one minute on each side. Drain on the paper toweling. The oysters may be kept warm in a 300°F oven if you are frying large amounts.

Serve with the following Mustard Sauce on toasted French bread or shredded lettuce.

Mustard Sauce

1 cup mayonnaise
2 tablespoons lemon juice
1 tablespoon Dijon mustard
½ teaspoon dry mustard
2 tablespoons prepared horseradish
2 tablespoons chopped stuffed olives
⅛ teaspoon cayenne pepper

Mix all ingredients together. Serve with oysters.

Fried Oyster Hero
Serves 2.

The story goes that years ago husbands who arrived hours late for dinner brought home these oyster sandwiches to cajole their wives. Call this a modern hero and enjoy it without excuses.

1 large French or Italian bread
1 recipe Mustard Sauce (this page)
Shredded lettuce (enough to cover bread)
1 recipe Deep-Fried Oysters (page 195)
Sour pickles for garnish

Slice the bread lengthwise. Preheat oven to 375°F. Remove some of the doughy section from the bottom half of the bread.

Spoon some Mustard Sauce on the bottom half of the bread. Cover with shredded lettuce and then place the oysters evenly on top of the lettuce. Dribble sauce over and around the oysters. Cover with the top half of the bread.

Place on a cookie sheet and bake for 5 minutes. Cut into four sections. Serve immediately with sour pickles.

Baked or Charcoal-Broiled Stuffed Lobster
Serves 4.

Whether you cook indoors or out, lobster is a warm-weather celebration. Although steaming or boiling a lobster is the "Maine-iac" way, I sometimes dress it with stuffing, then bake or barbecue it. The additional stuffing substitutes for butter with just a minimum of olive oil.

Four 1½-pound lobsters
1 small onion or 2 shallots, minced
1 clove garlic, minced
1 small sweet red pepper, minced
¾ cup plain bread crumbs
1 tablespoon chopped fresh parsley
2 tablespoons grated Parmesan cheese
Salt and freshly ground pepper to taste
2 tablespoons olive oil
¼ cup white wine
4 lemon wedges

To prepare a live lobster, do not remove the wooden pegs or rubber bands on the claws. Hold the lobster steady with a dish cloth under your hand or wear a glove. Turn the lobster on its back. Plunge a sharp knife into the middle of the body. Cut down through the tail without cutting the shell. Hold the lobster on either side and crack the shell open. Remove the sac (stomach) between the eyes and discard. Open it flat. Do not remove the liver (tomalley) or the coral, if there is any. If you are cooking the lobster the same day, your fish dealer will handle this procedure for you.

For baking, preheat oven to 450°F. Mix onion or shallots, garlic, red pepper, bread crumbs, parsley, and cheese. Season with salt and pepper to taste. Moisten with olive oil.

Place the lobsters on shallow baking pans. Fill the cavities with the stuffing and spread some over the flesh of the tail. Sprinkle the tops with white wine.

Bake for 15 minutes or until the shells are quite red. Then broil, at least 4 to 6 inches away from the heat, for just 1 or 2 minutes. Serve with wedges of lemon. **To charcoal broil:** Mix all the ingredients for the stuffing, including 1 tablespoon olive oil. Package the stuffing securely in heavy aluminum foil in the shape of a thick pancake.

When the burning charcoal turns gray and is hot, place the lobsters, shell-side down, on the grill. Place the package of stuffing to the side of the lobsters. Grill the lobsters for about 12 to 15 minutes, brushing them once or twice with olive oil and white wine. In the meantime, turn the package of stuffing over to cook it evenly.

Just before serving, turn the lobsters over to broil on the flesh side for 2 to 3 minutes. Open the package of stuffing carefully because steam will escape. Fill the cavities of each lobster with some stuffing and spread some on the flesh of the tail. Serve at once with wedges of lemon.

If your barbecue grill has a cover, simply place the lobsters on the grill and cover it. Cook the lobsters and the packaged stuffing about 20 minutes. Baste the flesh with oil and wine once or twice. Proceed to stuff as if charcoal broiling. Serve at once with wedges of lemon.

Fish Dumplings of Pike (Quenelles de Brochet)
Serves 4 to 6.

I will probably never forget my first taste of Quenelles de Brochet. In 1959, when my husband and I toured France for the first time, we agreed that nothing in our eating experience had matched the silken, creamy, and delicate flavor of this French fish dumpling. Since we chose our inns and restaurants from Michelin's best, we were traveling on the royal path of gastronomy.

I was familiar with the bony pike, since my mother had used it for her weekly Gefilte Fish. Imagine, she boned the fresh fish herself and chopped it by hand!

Good cooks around the world are clever with their methods for turning out the tastiest fish balls, dumplings, and loaves with the boniest fish. The fish is so well chopped, sieved, and cooked that nary a bone can be found.

The pike is a lean fish, but with the addition of egg whites, cream, and sometimes bread or flour, the texture turns into a gossamer dumpling, an haute cuisine specialty.

3 pounds pike (or halibut, flounder, or lemon sole)
½ teaspoon salt
¼ teaspoon white pepper
¼ teaspoon nutmeg
½ cup milk
3 tablespoons butter
½ cup flour
2 eggs, separated
½ cup whipping cream
1 teaspoon butter for the skillet
½ teaspoon salt

Have the fish filleted to make 1½ pounds of boneless fish. The bones and scraps may be saved for fish stock. Mix the salt, white pepper, and nutmeg for a seasoning.

Make a *panade* as follows: Heat the milk with butter in a saucepan until the milk starts to simmer and butter is melted. Add flour and mixed seasonings. Stir briskly until a ball is formed and comes away from the sides of the pan. Remove from flame and beat in one egg yolk at a time. Cool mixture on a plate in the refrigerator.

Cut fish into small pieces. Grind four or five pieces at a time in a food processor. Refrigerate the fish in the food processor bowl for at least 30 minutes. Be sure that the ground fish, egg whites, cream, and *panade* are very cold.

Beat the ground fish in the food processor, adding the *panade* a little at a time. Add egg whites a little at a time, and then gradually beat in cream.

Boil 1 cup water in a small saucepan. Test a tiny ball of fish by cooking it in the boiling water for 2 minutes. Taste it for seasoning. Add more salt and pepper to the fish mixture, if necessary.

Butter a large skillet. Prepare a bowl with hot water, two oval soup spoons, and 2 quarts boiling water. Dip the spoons in hot water. Scoop a spoonful of fish in one spoon and shape it with the other to make a ball (or *quenelle*). Make each one the size of a large egg. Place the quenelles in the greased skillet, one next to the other.

Slowly pour boiling water down the side of the skillet to just cover the quenelles. Add ½ teaspoon salt to the water. Cover the skillet and simmer for 15 minutes. Remove the quenelles to a buttered baking dish with a slotted spoon. Coat them with one of the sauces below, and heat in the oven before serving.

Sauce Variations

- Make a fish stock with the bones and scraps saved from the fish. Then choose a Sauce Velouté made with fish broth (page 83) or Sauce Beurre Blanc (page 85).

- For a quick sauce, thicken 2 cups fish stock with a *beurre manié* as follows: Mix 2 tablespoons softened butter with 3 tablespoons flour. Drop bit by bit into simmering fish stock. Add a tablespoon of dry sherry. For a special treat, add ½ cup crabmeat or diced cooked shrimp to the sauce.

Gefilte Fish
Makes 18 to 22 pieces.

Gefilte Fish are boiled dumplings of ground pike and lake whitefish, softened with eggs but without cream. The rich lake whitefish adds great flavor and texture.

The results are certainly very different from the French quenelles. In both cases, though, good cooks will settle for nothing less than the freshest fish. That is their common ground.

Stock

3 medium onions, sliced
3 medium carrots, scraped and sliced
1 tablespoon kosher (coarse) salt
½ teaspoon white pepper
Bones and heads of fish
1 carp head (if available)
1 quart water

Fish

6 to 7 pounds combined lake whitefish and pike
3 whole onions
¾ cup water
4 eggs
½ cup matzo meal or cracker meal
1 tablespoon kosher (coarse) salt
½ teaspoon white pepper
1 teaspoon sugar
1 carrot, peeled and cut into thin slices

Your fish dealer will bone and sometimes even grind the fish for you, but be sure that he gives you the bones and head. These are important for flavoring the stock.

Prepare an enameled or noncorrosive 6- to 8-quart pot with a tight-fitting cover and a rack to fit the bottom. Place all the ingredients for the stock in the pot. Place rack on top. Simmer for 15 to 20 minutes while you prepare the fish.

Chop the 3 whole onions with ¾ cup water in a food processor for 1 minute. Transfer to a measuring cup with a pouring lip.

If your fish dealer has not ground the fish, cut it in pieces and grind in a food processor or a grinder. Put the ground fish in the bowl of an electric mixer. Beat at low speed, gradually adding the onion with water, then the eggs (one at a time), matzo meal or cracker meal, and seasonings. Beat for 3 to 4 minutes. The mixture should be pasty and adhere to a spoon.

Drop a tiny ball of the mixture into the simmering stock. Cover and cook for 2 minutes. This is your test for seasoning. Do not taste the fish raw. Cool the little ball and taste. Add more salt and pepper to the raw fish mixture, if needed.

With two large tablespoons, first dipped in water, form the fish mixture into a large oval shape in the spoon. Move the fish from spoon to spoon to shape the oval. Gently place the fish balls on the rack of the pot in one layer. Place a thin slice of carrot on each ball of fish. It will be necessary to make two to three layers of fish balls, so cover the pot and cook the first layer until the fish is firm, about 5 minutes. Proceed to the next layer and do the same. Always keep the spoons wet as you form the oval balls. When all are in the pot, cover and simmer for 1½ hours.

Allow the fish to cool before removing each piece to a deep bowl. Strain the broth. Press down on the bones to obtain every bit of essence and natural gelatin. Pour the broth over the fish and refrigerate. Some people like the fish warm, but most enjoy it cold with beet horseradish. Gefilte Fish is best made two or three days ahead to intensify the flavor and gelatinize the broth.

Turban de Sole
Serves 6.

There are many different versions for preparing the basic quenelles and I have tried dozens. This one is called a turban because a fillet of fish is wrapped around the ground fish mixture. What I like best is the easy technique of poaching this simple sausage shape. Credit for this recipe goes to Monsieur Rey, a most talented teacher at Le Notre, the renowned school in France.

    1 tablespoon butter, softened
    ½ teaspoon kosher (coarse) or sea salt
    ¼ teaspoon white pepper

3 fillets of lemon sole or flounder (4 to 6 ounces each)
12 fresh asparagus spears
4 ounces pike, halibut, or other white-fleshed fish, very cold
2 ounces scallops, very cold
2 ounces shrimp, shelled and deveined, very cold
1 egg or 2 egg whites, very cold
½ cup whipping cream, very cold
¼ teaspoon salt
⅛ teaspoon white pepper
Pinch cayenne pepper

Prepare a sheet of heavy aluminum foil, measuring 12" x 14". Spread softened butter over the surface almost to the edge. Sprinkle salt and pepper over the butter.

Cover each sole or flounder fillet with wax paper and pound lightly to even the thickness. Place the fillets on the aluminum foil, touching side by side and positioned lengthwise toward you. Transfer the fish on the foil to a tray and refrigerate.

Spread softened butter, salt and pepper on heavy foil.

Save asparagus tips for garnish.

Parboil asparagus for 2 minutes uncovered. Immerse in cold water immediately. Drain and dry well. Preheat oven to 400°F. Prepare a 12-inch baking pan by adding simmering water to the depth of 1 inch.

All ingredients should be very cold. Grind pike or other white-fleshed fish, scallops, and shrimp in the food processor. Next blend in the egg or egg whites, and then gradually add the cream and seasonings. Spread half the mixture over the middle surface of the fillets. Cut two or three lengths of asparagus and place in one line across the center of the fillets. Save the tips for a garnish. Spread the remaining mixture to cover asparagus.

Don't allow foil to roll under fish.

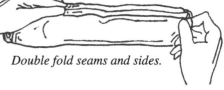

Double fold seams and sides.

Holding the outer ends of the foil, roll the filled fillets in the aluminum foil to form a sausage shape. Double-fold the seam and sides of the foil to enclose the fish well. Place the fish in the pan with the simmering water and bake for 1 hour.

Transfer fish to a platter, opening the foil carefully because steam will escape. Spread one of the following sauces on heated dishes. Place two 1-inch slices on each dish with a garnish of asparagus tips.

Sauce Variations

- Use Red Pepper Sauce (below), a Sauce Velouté made with fish broth (page 83), or Sauce Beurre Blanc (page 85).
- For a change, soak ¼ teaspoon saffron threads in fish stock before making Sauce Velouté. The exotic flavor and color are great contrasts to the fish.

❋ Suggestions

- Leftover Turban de Sole makes a very special appetizer.
- Prepare Turban de Sole specifically for cold summertime dinners. Serve it on tossed greens with Vinaigrette Dressing (page 135) or yogurt with grated fresh horseradish.

Fish Terrine with Red Pepper Sauce
Serves 6.

My friend, Gregory Usher, taught this delicate fish terrine to a very receptive group in my kitchen. Although it is typically French, again related to the quenelles, we in the United States would call it a fish loaf. Salmon and any number of white-fleshed fish are always available to us. Winter or summer, hot or cold, this loaf is more than just ordinary.

Terrine

2 teaspoons butter
1 medium sweet red pepper, cored, seeded, and diced small
½ pound salmon fillet
1½ pounds whiting or other whitefish fillet
3 egg whites
Salt and white pepper
1 cup whipping cream

Red Pepper Sauce

2 medium sweet red peppers
3 tablespoons white wine vinegar
3 tablespoons dry white wine
2 shallots, finely chopped

2 sticks (½ pound) unsalted butter, cut into cubes
Salt and white pepper

Preheat oven to 350°F. Butter a bread loaf pan with 1 teaspoon butter.

Blanch the red pepper in boiling, salted water. Remove from the boiling water, rinse in cold water and drain. Pat dry with paper towels.

All ingredients should be kept very cold. Cut the salmon fillet into ¾-inch squares. Purée the whiting or other whitefish in a food processor. Beat the egg whites lightly, and gradually add the egg whites, salt, pepper, and cream to the fish purée in the food processor. Poach a spoonful of the mixture and taste for seasoning. Adjust seasoning in the mixture, if necessary. Transfer the mixture to a bowl.

Gently fold the diced red pepper and salmon pieces into the fish mixture. Spoon the mixture into the prepared bread loaf pan. Use remaining teaspoon butter on wax paper to cover terrine. Set the loaf pan in a pan of water and bring to a boil on top of the stove. Transfer to the oven and bake for about 30 minutes or until a skewer inserted in the terrine comes out clean.

The Red Pepper Sauce can be made in advance if it is more convenient. Broil the peppers until blackened, cool them in a paper bag, then peel them. Discard the core and seeds. Purée in a food processor. Boil the vinegar, wine, and shallots in a small saucepan until the liquid is almost evaporated. Reduce the heat to low and gradually whisk in the butter, moving the pan off the heat if it gets too hot, so a smooth sauce is formed. Season with salt and pepper. Strain the sauce into a bowl and blend in the red pepper purée.

To serve, set a slice of terrine on each plate and pour some of the sauce around it. If the sauce is not warm, pass the plate under the broiler for a few seconds before serving.

9

Poultry

Winter or summer there is no other food that has the versatility of chicken. Buy it whole or in parts. Poach it, roast it, stew it, broil it, or sauté it. Combine chicken with vegetables, fruit, grains, rice, noodles, or beans. Dice it or slice it for salads; cream it for pancakes, pot pies, and casseroles. Think ahead to cook double quantities. Use cooked chicken for salads and sandwiches, especially in warm weather.

The whole chicken is among the most economical purchases in the marketplace and among the fastest to cook. Just think about the fringe benefits, too. Necks, gizzards, and livers can be frozen to be used for stocks, stuffings, and pâtés.

Poaching results in a cooked chicken that is tender and lightly flavored; roasting produces a crisp skin and succulent flesh. Figure on 1 pound of chicken per person.

Always unwrap a chicken when you bring it home and, if you are not cooking it at once, store it as follows: Fill a small plastic bag with five or six ice cubes. Tie the bag to enclose the ice cubes. Place the bag of ice cubes in the cavity of the chicken. It can be refrigerated this way for up to two days. (This applies to other small birds, ducks and turkeys.)

Recipes for Chicken, Cornish Hen, Quail, and Duck

Roast Chicken with Vegetables
Serves 4.

The seasoning for roasting a chicken varies from a little to a lot, from simple to complex, from one locale to another and from person to person. The following recipe is a one-pan roast chicken dinner. Sometimes I substitute a cut orange and onion for the herbs in the cavity. Reach into your shelves for handy seasonings to suit your preferences.

One 3- to 4-pound roasting chicken
Kosher (coarse) salt and freshly ground pepper
2 sprigs each tarragon and thyme or ½ teaspoon each dried
1 pound red-skinned potatoes, unpeeled and cut into quarters
1 pound white onions
2 large carrots, scraped and cut in thick slices
2 leeks (white portion only), cut in thick slices
1 pound mushrooms, quartered
½ cup Madeira
½ cup chicken stock or water

Preheat oven to 450°F. Dry chicken and remove all fat. Sprinkle with salt and pepper inside and out. Place tarragon and thyme in the cavity of the chicken. Slip the tips of the chicken wings under the breast. Tie the legs closely together to keep the chicken in shape. Place the chicken on a rack to fit inside a roasting pan that is just large enough to accommodate the vegetables heaped around it.

Strew potatoes, onions, carrots, and leeks around the chicken. Roast for 30 minutes, turning the chicken occasionally.

Lower the oven temperature to 350°F. Distribute the mushrooms on the vegetables. Add Madeira and chicken stock or water. Roast for another 30 to 40 minutes. Allow the chicken to rest for 5 to 7 minutes before cutting into portions.

✳ *Suggestions*

- With or without herbs, place halves of lemon or orange in the cavity of the chicken before roasting.
- Vary vegetables by using parsnips, squash, and turnips.

- Add fresh tomatoes when they're in season locally, as well as red and green peppers.
- Roast two or three chickens without vegetables for cold summertime dinners, picnics, and easy-to-eat leftovers.

Roast Chicken Stuffed Under the Skin
Serves 4.

One 3- to 4-pound roasting chicken
Kosher (coarse) salt and freshly ground pepper
2 tablespoons butter or olive oil
¼ cup minced shallots
1 tablespoon minced garlic
1 pound mushrooms, minced
2 tablespoons Madeira or sherry
1 tablespoon fresh thyme or ½ teaspoon dried
2 tablespoons minced Italian parsley
½ teaspoon salt
½ teaspoon freshly ground pepper
¼ cup toasted bread crumbs
½ cup white wine
½ cup chicken stock

Rinse and dry the chicken; season with a sprinkling of salt and pepper.

Heat butter or oil in a skillet. Add shallots and garlic. Cook until wilted, about 2 to 3 minutes. Add mushrooms and Madeira or Sherry. Cook on high heat to reduce moisture, but do not allow to burn. Add thyme, parsley, salt, pepper, and bread crumbs to form a paste. Cool thoroughly.

Starting at the neck of the chicken, separate the skin from the flesh by gently working your fingers below the skin. Loosen the skin from the entire breast and legs. Stuff the chicken with the cooled, prepared mixture. Push the stuffing under the skin to cover legs and breast. Slip the tips of the wings under the breast. Tie the legs closely together to keep the chicken in shape.

Preheat oven to 425°F. Roast the chicken for 30 minutes. Reduce heat to 350°F. Baste chicken with wine and stock about every 10 minutes. Roast for 30 minutes more. Allow chicken to rest for 5 to 7 minutes. Using a sharp knife or poultry shears, cut the chicken into portions and serve. Pass the pan liquid as a sauce.

Serve the following Port Wine Sauce for a special dinner. Prepare while the chicken rests.

Port Wine Sauce

1 cup dry white wine
¼ cup minced shallots
2 cloves garlic, minced
½ bay leaf
1 cup pan liquid
¼ cup tawny port wine
Salt and pepper to taste
1 tablespoon cornstarch stirred with 2 tablespoons water

Reduce wine, shallots, garlic, and bay leaf until just a tablespoon of liquid remains. Add the pan liquid from roasting the chicken and the port wine. Strain into another saucepan. Taste to adjust seasoning with salt and pepper. Bring to a boil. Add cornstarch mixture slowly to barely thicken the sauce, enough to coat the spoon.

✳ Suggestions

- To omit butter or oil, heat a skillet for 3 to 5 minutes over moderate heat. Add shallots, garlic, and mushrooms. Cover the skillet and cook for 2 to 3 minutes to produce moisture from the mushrooms to cook the mixture. Uncover and cook until moisture is evaporated. Add herbs and bread crumbs, then salt and pepper to taste.
- To remove fat from the pan liquid, pour pan liquid into a stainless steel bowl fifteen minutes before chicken is finished. Place pan liquid in the freezer. The fat will coagulate to be easily removed. If the fat does not firm up quickly enough, add a few ice cubes to the *cooled* liquid. The ice cubes will be quickly coated with fat. Remove them.

Chicken Breasts in 10 Styles

I might just as easily go on to give you 100 ways to prepare chicken breasts, but let's leave that to current publications. Here, the styles are narrowed down to ingredients that you can reach for in your cupboard or refrigerator—flavorings, herbs, and seasonings on hand.

When chicken breasts are boned and skinned, they lose the best of their succulence. Fill the gap with the suggestions that follow. Be sure to reduce cooking time for so-called chicken cutlets, which are thinly sliced, or substitute turkey cutlets.

4 chicken breast halves, skinned and boned (about 4 to 5 ounces each)
1 teaspoon kosher (coarse) salt
¼ teaspoon white pepper
½ teaspoon dried thyme
¼ cup flour
1 tablespoon each oil and butter

Some chicken breasts are marketed with the tender fillet still attached to one side. It separates easily, so cut it off for a future use. Freeze the fillets for stir-frying or quick skewer grilling.

Pound each chicken breast under wax paper if the thickness is uneven. Season with salt, pepper, and thyme. Dredge in flour on both sides. Shake off excess flour. Preheat oven to 300°F.

Heat a 10-inch skillet over medium heat for 2 to 3 minutes before adding oil and butter. When the butter melts, sauté two chicken breasts at a time for 3 to 4 minutes on each side. Set aside in a shallow oven dish and proceed to do the same with the remaining breasts. Bake all the chicken breasts for 10 minutes with one of the following additions or simmer in the sauté pan as described below.

1. With Lemon: Deglaze the same hot skillet with ¼ cup fresh lemon juice. (Should you find lemon grass in your produce market, dice it and add it with the lemon juice.) Add to chicken and bake. Before serving, garnish each portion with a wedge of lemon and a sprig of parsley.

2. With Mushrooms: Sauté 2 tablespoons minced shallots for 1 to 2 minutes. Add 1 pound sliced cultivated mushrooms or 4 to 6 ounces shiitake mushrooms. Sauté until mushrooms are slightly browned. Pour on ¼ cup each Madeira and chicken stock and 2 tablespoons cognac. Reduce over high heat for 3 minutes. Spread over the chicken and bake. For a special treat, add cream instead of chicken stock.

3. With Shallots, Garlic, and Parsley: Sauté ¼ cup minced shallots and 2 tablespoons minced garlic over medium heat. Be careful not to burn. Spread on chicken and bake. Add ½ cup chopped parsley just before serving.

4. With Tomato and Herbs of Provence: Sauté chicken in olive oil only. Add ½ cup diced onion and 1 tablespoon minced garlic to the hot skillet. Use more olive oil if necessary. When the onion looks glazed, add 1 diced red or green bell pepper and 1 cup ripe, skinned, seeded, and diced tomato (preferably not canned). Stir in ¼ teaspoon each dried marjoram, rosemary, basil, thyme, and parsley. (It will be all the better if you add fresh herbs to your taste.) Add ¼ cup chicken or vegetable stock. Simmer for a few minutes. Taste and adjust seasoning. Serve the baked chicken on a bed the sauce.

5. With Orange and Balsamic Vinegar: Deglaze sauté pan with ½ cup fresh orange juice and ¼ cup balsamic vinegar. Heat and reduce by half. Add ½ cup chicken stock and simmer for 2 minutes. Stir in 1 teaspoon cornstarch mixed with 1 tablespoon water. The sauce will become glossy and slightly thickened. Spoon half over the chicken in the oven dish and bake. Spoon the remaining sauce around the chicken on a heated dinner plate. Garnish with sliced orange.

6. With Spicy Sauce: Sauté 1 tablespoon shallots until glazed. Add 1 cup each chicken stock and white wine, 2 tablespoons canned crushed tomatoes, ½ teaspoon allspice, and ¼ teaspoon each cumin and cracked red pepper. Return chicken to the skillet. Cover and simmer for 3 to 4 minutes instead of baking. Taste to adjust seasoning. Serve immediately.

7. With Mustard, Honey, and Horseradish: Mix ¼ cup Dijon mustard and 1 tablespoon each honey and horseradish with ½ cup chicken stock. Spread over each portion of chicken. Return to the sauté pan. Cover and cook for 5 minutes or spread mixture on chicken and bake in the oven.

8. With Cranberries and Maple Syrup: Combine 1 cup fresh cranberries with ⅓ cup maple syrup in the skillet. Cover and cook over low heat for about 4 minutes until the cranberries pop open. Spread over chicken and bake.

9. With Scallions and Water Chestnuts (Chinese style): Heat skillet with 1 tablespoon corn oil. Sauté chicken breasts for 2 to 3 minutes on each side. Remove to a heated dish. Add 1 more tablespoon oil to the hot skillet. Sauté 1 teaspoon each minced garlic and fresh ginger for 1 minute. Do not burn. Stir in 1 cup diced scallions and ½ cup sliced water chestnuts. Season with 1 tablespoon each soy sauce and sherry and ¼ cup chicken stock. Return chicken to pan and simmer for about 5 minutes.

10. With Curry and Seasonal Fruits: Add 1 tablespoon more oil to the hot skillet. Sauté 1 tablespoon each minced garlic and fresh ginger with 1 teaspoon curry powder. Cook over medium heat for 2 to 3 minutes until aromas develop. Do not burn. Choose fresh fruit in season—peeled and sliced apples, pears, peaches, melon, mango, berries, and so on. Cook the fruit briefly with spices. Bake chicken. Spoon the sauce and fruits onto heated dinner plates. Place chicken on top.

✹ Suggestions

- If you wish to omit the sautéing in the basic recipe, brush the chicken breasts with a little oil. Bake at 350°F for 15 to 18 minutes.

- To ensure moistness, marinate the chicken breasts in a favorite salad dressing, buttermilk, or yogurt before breading.
- Flour, cornmeal, bread crumbs, cracker meal, and nuts are all possibilities for different breadings. Try each alone or in combinations.
- For a heavier crust, dip the chicken first in flour then beaten egg white or whole egg, and then plain bread crumbs. Season flour and crumbs to your preference.

Breast of Chicken, Le Petit Chef
Serves 6.

Many years ago Maurice Champagne, owner-chef of The Mill on the Floss in New Ashford, Massachusetts, shared his recipe with me for chicken Amandine. The batter marinade is particularly good for moistening chicken and holding the crust. My daughter, Betty, combined that technique with pine nuts (pignoli) and grapes instead of almonds. It has been a favorite at her Wilmington, Vermont, restaurant, Le Petit Chef.

  6 halves of chicken breasts, skinned and boned
  ½ cup flour
  ¼ teaspoon salt
  ⅛ teaspoon pepper
  1 egg (or 2 egg whites)
  ⅔ cup milk (or light cream)
  ⅔ cup plain bread crumbs
  ⅓ cup ground pine nuts (pignoli)
  2 tablespoons each oil and butter
  ½ cup sweet vermouth
  ¼ cup whole pine nuts (pignoli)
  1 cup seedless grapes

Cover each chicken breast with wax paper or aluminum foil, and pound to flatten if the thickness is uneven.

Mix flour with salt and pepper. Add egg and milk or cream. This can be done in the food processor. Marinate the chicken in this batter for at least 30 minutes, or marinate refrigerated for up to 2 days.

When ready to cook, heat a 10- or 12-inch skillet over low heat. Preheat the oven to 300°F.

Combine bread crumbs and ground pine nuts on a sheet of wax paper. Use a pair of tongs to coat each chicken breast with the crumbs and pine nuts. Set aside until all are completed.

Add oil and butter to the heated skillet. The butter will sizzle and foam but should stay golden and not turn brown. Fry two or three pieces of chicken at a time so as not to crowd the skillet. Lightly brown the chicken on both sides and then remove to a shallow baking dish. Sprinkle vermouth, whole pine nuts, and grapes over all. Bake in the oven for 15 to 18 minutes. Serve immediately.

Crusty Boned Chicken Thighs
Serves 4.

4 chicken thighs, skinned and boned
Kosher (coarse) salt and pepper
4 teaspoons butter, softened
¼ cup mixed herbs (choice of fresh or dried parsley, tarragon, chives, thyme, basil, and marjoram)
¼ cup olive or corn oil
½ cup flour
1 cup plain bread crumbs
¼ teaspoon each salt, pepper, and paprika
2 egg whites, lightly beaten
½ cup dry vermouth
¼ cup each Dijon mustard and prepared horseradish, mixed together

Pound chicken thighs under foil to flatten slightly. Sprinkle the thighs with a small amount of kosher salt and pepper. Mix butter and herbs. Spread an even amount on each piece of chicken. Roll up to enclose the herb mixture. Set in the freezer for 15 minutes. Preheat oven to 375°F.

Slowly heat the olive or corn oil in a deep frying pan while you proceed. Spread flour on a sheet of wax paper. On another sheet of wax paper mix bread crumbs, salt, pepper, and paprika. Place the bowl of lightly beaten egg whites between the two. Dredge chicken first in flour, then dip in egg white, and finally coat with bread crumbs.

Brown chicken on all sides until crusty. Blot on paper toweling. Place the pieces side by side in a casserole. Pour vermouth around the chicken and bake for 25 minutes. Pass the mustard and horseradish mixture around the table when serving.

Boned and Stuffed Chicken Legs
Serves 6.

This is a fine party main course, whether it be buffet or sit down. Cook it hours ahead and reheat, or simply keep it warm at 275°F for an extra hour. It never fails, even for very late guests.

6 whole chicken legs (drumsticks and thighs)

1 teaspoon kosher (coarse) salt

¼ teaspoon pepper

2 tablespoons butter or oil

3 large shallots, minced

2 cloves garlic, minced

12 plain unsalted crackers soaked in ½ cup chicken stock

1 medium carrot, scraped and grated

1 rib celery, minced

1 pound ground veal (or substitute turkey, chicken, pork, or even shellfish)

⅛ teaspoon each ground cinnamon, cloves, allspice, thyme, and cayenne pepper

Salt and pepper to taste

½ cup each chicken stock and white wine

1 egg white, slightly beaten

½ cup plain bread crumbs, seasoned with salt, pepper, and paprika

Ask your butcher to bone the entire leg (drumstick and thigh). Do not remove the skin. If you would like to try boning them yourself, use a small, sharp knife and your fingers. Start at the top of the thigh bone. Slit the flesh next to the bone. Force the flesh down with your fingers. Sever the flesh carefully around the joint of the drumstick. Then, working close to the bone with the knife, gradually push the flesh down. The flesh will actually turn inside out on the flesh side. Cut it off at the end. Cut off as many visible tendons as possible, then return legs to skin-side shape. Sprinkle with salt and pepper.

To make the stuffing, heat a skillet slowly. Add butter or oil. Sauté shallots and garlic to wilt them without browning. Remove from the heat.

Press out some moisture from the crackers. Combine the crackers with sautéed shallots and garlic. Add carrot, celery, ground veal or other meat, and seasonings. To test seasoning, sauté a teaspoonful of the mixture and taste. Add salt and pepper to taste.

Divide the stuffing evenly into six parts. Stuff each leg to remold the shape. Preheat oven to 350°F.

Choose a shallow casserole to place the legs in one layer, next to one another. Pour stock and wine around the legs. Brush beaten egg white on each leg, then sprinkle seasoned bread crumbs on top. Bake for 1 hour, uncovered. If desired, dribble a bit more oil or butter over the legs for the last 5 minutes of baking.

✳ *Suggestions*

• Garnish each leg with a fresh leaf of thyme, tarragon, or parsley.

- Serve noodles laced with a julienne of zucchini and red pepper to complete a perfect dinner.
- Steamed basmati rice is always a good accompaniment for chicken.

Broiled Rock Cornish Hen or Chicken with Red Wine Sauce
Serves 4.

I always enjoyed teaching this recipe in my classes. It exemplifies the reason for reducing the liquid in cooking to produce a good sauce. If at first the recipe appears long and complicated, break it down into the following simple parts:
1. Broil the birds.
2. Make the sauce.
3. Deglaze and reduce the broiling pan.

> 2 rock Cornish hens or a 2- to 3-pound chicken
> Kosher (coarse) salt and pepper
> Juice 1 lemon
> 1 pound small white onions, unpeeled
> 2 tablespoons oil or 4 ounces bacon, blanched and diced
> 1 tablespoon tomato paste
> 2 cups dry red wine
> 1 pound mushrooms, quartered
> 3 cups veal or chicken stock, preferably homemade, unsalted
> ½ cup minced shallots
> 1 clove garlic, smashed
> Bouquet garni

Cut along both sides of the backbone of each hen or chicken in order to remove the backbone. Use the bone for stock. Remove the center breast bone, if you wish. Open the hen flat, skin side up. Cut a slit through the skin on each side near the thigh. Insert the drumsticks through the slits to keep a good shape. Lightly pound the bird, flesh-side up, to flatten it. Season with salt, pepper, and lemon juice. Place on a broiling pan.

Preheat the broiler with the rack placed at least 7 or 8 inches from the flame. Broil the hens or chicken for 15 minutes on each side.

In the meantime, make the sauce. Make a criss-cross cut on the stem end of each onion. Parboil the onions for 3 minutes. Run through cold water. Drain and peel.

Heat oil or render bacon in a straight-sided sauté pan. Use part oil, part bacon or butter, if you wish. Add onions and cook for a few minutes. Pour off any excess fat. Stir in tomato paste to coat the onions evenly. Cook for 5 minutes over low heat. Add ½ cup wine. Bring to a boil and simmer to reduce slightly. Add mushrooms and reduce again until the liquid is almost evaporated. This slow reduction glazes the vegetables and concentrates flavor. Add 1 cup stock to the onions and mushrooms.

Cook uncovered until liquid is reduced to a glaze. Add a second cup stock and reduce again. Add the last cup stock and cook until the onions are tender. Set aside.

Reduce, Reduce, Reduce!

In a separate pan, combine the remaining 1½ cups wine with shallots, garlic, and bouquet garni. Reduce liquid to about half.

When the hens are done, transfer them to a heated platter or keep warm in a 250°F oven. Pour off any fat in the broiling pan. Deglaze the pan with the wine-shallot liquid. Strain the deglazing liquid into the onion-mushroom sauce. Heat the sauce.

Uncovered, without stirring.

Place half a hen or a portion of chicken on each dinner plate. Surround each with onions and mushrooms and coat with sauce.

✳ Suggestions

- Wheat Berry Pilaf (page 159) or Wild Rice (page 154) are good accompaniments.
- The basic sauce can be prepared hours in advance. Broil hens or chicken 1 hour in advance and keep warm in a 250°F oven. Deglaze the pan and finish the sauce just before serving.

Chicken, Chick-Pea, and Red Onion Stew with Couscous
Serves 4.

Many years ago I was invited to the kitchen of Al Mounia, a newly opened Moroccan restaurant. Hassan Berrada, the restaurateur, was more than cordial with answers to my questions. He carefully explained the traditional methods for cooking couscous. I follow his directions to this day and diligently avoid the instant brands. The following method of cooking couscous allows the tiny semolina grains to swell gradually and plump up.

One 3- to 4-pound chicken, cut into eighths
½ teaspoon salt
¼ teaspoon black pepper

¼ teaspoon each ground cinnamon and allspice
1 jalapeño pepper, seeded and minced
3 cloves garlic, minced
1 cup couscous
1 cup tepid water
2 tablespoons olive oil
4 medium red onions, thinly sliced
½ cup each chopped fresh parsley and cilantro
4 cups freshly cooked chick-peas or canned equivalent
½ cup chopped celery leaves
½ teaspoon saffron threads
2 cups hot chicken stock
½ cup lightly salted water

The couscousiere is the traditional double steamer for couscous. The bottom is the stewing pot and the top is a tight fitting colander, lined with double cheesecloth. If you do not own one, improvise with a colander that fits snugly over one of your deep stew or soup pots. Line the colander with cheesecloth.

Couscousiere

Toss chicken parts with salt, pepper, cinnamon, allspice, pepper, and garlic. Let stand for 30 minutes. This can be done in advance and refrigerated.

While the chicken is marinating, spread couscous on a jelly-roll pan. Pour tepid water on top of the couscous and wet it thoroughly. Let stand for 15 minutes. Run your fingers or a fork through the couscous to break up lumps. Transfer couscous to cheesecloth lined colander.

Heat oil in a stew pot. Add seasoned chicken and onions. Cook over moderate heat, turning occasionally for 5 to 6 minutes to extract the flavors and lightly color the chicken. Mix in parsley, cilantro, chick-peas, celery leaves, saffron, and stock. Cover and simmer for 20 minutes. Uncover. Place colander with couscous on the stew pot. Cook chicken and couscous over moderate heat for 15 minutes, loosely covered.

Remove couscous to one side. Pour lightly salted water on top and allow couscous to cool slightly. Run fingers or a fork through the couscous to aerate and break up lumps.

Set the colander of couscous on top of the stew pot again. Steam again, loosely covered until the chicken is finished—all in all, about 1 hour.

The most important technique in cooking this tiny grain is to repeat the steaming, cooking, and aerating. This gives the grains a chance to swell slowly and separate without lumping. Mound the couscous on a large heated platter and surround with chicken and sauce in the pot.

✳ *Suggestions*

- The chick-peas will soften to create a thick sauce to serve on the couscous as well as the chicken, but if you wish the chick-peas to remain whole, add them only for the last 15 minutes of cooking time.
- Add carrots or turnips to the stew at the beginning for additional vegetables.
- Pass Chili Pepper Paste (page 27) around the table for a dash more spice.
- Use the same technique and seasonings for other long-cooking stews—veal, lamb, pork, and beef.
- Cook couscous separately and serve with Chicken Fricassee (the following recipe).

Chicken Fricassee
Serves 6 to 8.

When I think of Chicken Fricassee, my taste buds recall the fricassees often cooked in our home as I was growing up. The chicken parts—wings, necks, backs, and even the gelatinous chicken feet—were browned and stewed until they almost fell apart. Sometimes tiny meatballs were added and then the combined sauce was truly flavor-intensive. These small parts of chickens are economical and are very often available at the market. Of course, the chicken feet are a thing of the past unless you live near or on a chicken farm.

Fricassee

4 to 5 pounds chicken parts
1 teaspoon kosher (coarse) salt
½ teaspoon pepper
2 onions, diced
½ cup flour
1 teaspoon salt
½ teaspoon white pepper
1 tablespoon paprika
3 fresh, ripe tomatoes, skinned and diced, or 1 cup canned crushed tomatoes
3 cloves garlic, minced
Bay leaf and 2 sprigs parsley
3 or 4 cups hot chicken stock or water

Meatballs

1 pound ground veal, beef, or turkey
1 small onion, grated
1 egg
¼ cup cracker or bread crumbs soaked in ½ cup water
¼ teaspoon each salt and pepper
1 tablespoon oil

Rinse the chicken parts and dry well. Season with salt and pepper. Preheat oven to 425°F.

Spread the diced onions on the bottom of a 6-quart Dutch oven or stewing casserole. Roll the chicken parts in flour mixed with salt, white pepper, and paprika. Place the chicken on top of the onions and place the pot into the preheated oven. Turn the pieces occasionally to brown evenly. This will take about 20 to 30 minutes.

In the meantime, mix all the meatball ingredients, except the oil. Dip your fingers into the oil, which makes it easy to roll small meatballs in your hands. Place them on a cookie sheet. Set the pan in the oven to brown the meatballs.

When the chicken is browned, add the meatballs to the chicken parts. Add tomatoes, garlic, bay leaf, parsley, and enough stock or water to just cover. Place a tight lid on the pot.

Lower oven temperature to 350°F and cook the fricassee for 1 hour. Uncover once or twice to make sure the liquid is not evaporating too much. Add more stock or water, if necessary. Taste and readjust seasoning.

✳ Suggestions

- Serve family style in the center of a ring of rice, bulghur, or noodles.
- Fricassee freezes well if there is enough sauce to cover. Cook enough for freezing and enjoy a bonus meal in the future.

Grace Chu's Millionaire Chicken
Serves 4 to 6.

I had the great pleasure of meeting Grace Chu, a talented and charming woman, in 1962. Her first book had just been published, and I presented her as a lecturer at one of my classes. The original Chinese name of this recipe translates as Odd Flavor Chicken, but Madame Chu changed it when one of her students exclaimed that it was worth a million dollars. I agree with the praise, but I must add high praise for Grace herself.

3 quarts water
1 whole chicken (2½ to 3 pounds)
1 head iceberg lettuce, shredded

Sauce: Group A

4 tablespoons soy sauce
2 tablespoons honey
1 clove garlic
½ teaspoon Szechwan peppercorns, crushed

Sauce: Group B

3 tablespoons corn oil
2 scallions, chopped
4 slices ginger root, minced
¼ teaspoon red pepper flakes

Bring water to a boil in a deep soup pot. Submerge chicken and boil for 15 minutes. Turn off flame, cover pot, and let chicken cool for at least 20 minutes before taking it out of the pot. Arrange the shredded lettuce on an attractive serving platter.

In the meantime, combine the sauce ingredients of Group A in a small bowl. Let stand for 5 minutes. Mix sauce ingredients of Group B in a small pan. Bring to a simmer and cook for 2 or 3 minutes. Pour Group B into the bowl containing Group A.

Drain chicken of liquid and transfer it to a plate. Cut the chicken into 8 to 12 pieces. Bone it, if you wish. Place it on lettuce, leaving a rim of the greens. Pour the combined sauce over the chicken. I prefer serving this dish at room temperature. You can, however, prepare it in advance and refrigerate.

✳ Suggestions

- Serve Grace Chu's Millionaire Chicken with steamed rice and a stir-fried vegetable for a main course.
- Make double the amount of sauce, if you enjoy it as much as we do.
- Keep this recipe in mind for a perfect party buffet dish. Prepare a day ahead, but arrange it on the lettuce the day of the party.

Chicken Wings in Oyster Sauce
Serves 4.

When the China Institute in New York City offered its first courses in Chinese cooking, some of my student friends and I enrolled in the program. The young teacher, Beverly Lee, used many recipes from the book *Chinese Cooking for American Kitchens* by Dr. Calvin Lee. The book is now out of print, but the recipes come alive often. This is one of them.

8 chicken wings
3 scallions
4 thin slices fresh ginger root, peeled
4 tablespoons oyster sauce (available in specialty food shops)
1 teaspoon light soy sauce
1 tablespoon dry sherry
1 teaspoon sugar
Black pepper
2 teaspoons cornstarch
2 tablespoons water
½ cup hot chicken stock
2 tablespoons oil

For Chinese cooking it is especially important to gather all ingredients, each in separate small bowls next to the stove, ready to be used.

Cut each chicken wing into three sections. Cut the green leaves of the scallions into ½-inch pieces and dice the white portions.

Mince ginger. Mix the oyster sauce, soy sauce, and sherry together. Add sugar and a few grains of black pepper. Mix the cornstarch with water. Set aside. Keep the chicken stock hot on the stove. Prepare a warmed serving platter. All of this can be done in advance.

Set a wok or a straight-sided skillet on high heat. Heat until it is quite hot. Add oil, then minced ginger. Stir until brown. Add wings and stir-fry until the skin colors.

Add oyster sauce mixture to coat the wings. Stir-fry for another 2 minutes. Add chicken stock. Cover and lower heat. Simmer for 10 to 12 minutes.

Uncover and turn heat up. Add cornstarch mixture and scallions. Stir until thick. Serve immediately or keep warm in a 225°F oven.

Kotopita (Chicken in Phyllo)
Eight slices in each roll.

Leon Lianides, whom I have mentioned in other sections of this book, has shared recipes with me that I have treasured. This recipe for the Greek Kotopita is practical and delicious. Each pastry roll makes eight ample slices. The preparation is simple if you plan ahead.

  1 cooked chicken, about 4 pounds (see Mother's Chicken Soup, page 58)
  8 to 10 tablespoons butter, melted
  3 medium onions, chopped fine
  4 ribs celery, chopped fine
  1 cup strong chicken stock
  3 eggs
  2 tablespoons chopped fresh parsley
  ¼ teaspoon nutmeg
  Salt and pepper to taste
  10 sheets phyllo (12" x 15") for rolls

Skin and bone the chicken after cooking. Chop it into small pieces. Heat a skillet for 2 to 3 minutes over medium heat. Add 2 tablespoons butter. Sauté onions for 2 minutes, then add celery. Continue cooking until vegetables are glazed, not browned.

Add chopped chicken and stock. Cook until the liquid is absorbed. Transfer to a bowl and cool.

Beat eggs with a whisk until frothy. Fold the eggs into the chicken mixture. Season with parsley, nutmeg, salt, and pepper.

Unwrap phyllo and cover with a damp cloth to keep the sheets from drying out. Brush one phyllo sheet with melted butter. Proceed to build a stack of five sheets, buttering each one (A).

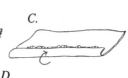

A.

Spread half the chicken mixture on the long side of the first stack of phyllo (B). Flap the dough over to cover it, (C) then fold in the two ends (D). Roll like a jelly roll (E). Place on a jelly-roll pan. Brush with melted butter. Follow the same procedure to make a second stack of five sheets. Repeat with the filling and rolling.

B. *C.*

D.

Preheat oven to 350°F. Bake for 30 to 35 minutes or until lightly browned and crisp. Cool slightly before cutting into slices.

E.

✳ *Suggestions*

- To simplify preparation, cook the chicken up to two days ahead. Refrigerate the chicken and 1 cup stock. Freeze leftover stock for another time.
- If you wish, complete the filled pastry rolls one day ahead and refrigerate. Bake just before serving.
- Bake both pastry rolls for immediate use or freeze one for up to a month for another serving.
- Kotopita is especially good for buffet service.
- Many fillings can be devised instead of chicken. Sautéed vegetables, cooked ground meat, various cooked grains, and leftover turkey are only a few of the possibilities.

Chicken Pot Pie
Serves 4 to 6.

If you enjoy preparing ahead and filling the freezer for future dinners, spend a free rainy day cooking double amounts of Mother's Chicken Soup (page 58). Use the two chickens cooked for the stock for the Greek Kotopita and this American Chicken Pot Pie. You can even switch from using the traditional pie pastry in this recipe to using the remaining phyllo dough from the Kotopita.

One 4- to 5-pound chicken, cooked
4 carrots, scraped and sliced
½ pound small white onions, peeled
2 tablespoons butter
3 ribs celery, diced
5 tablespoons flour
3 cups warm stock (2 cups chicken stock plus broth from carrots and onions)
1 cup milk or cream
½ cup each cooked peas and mushrooms (optional)
1 tablespoon minced parsley
Salt and pepper
1 recipe Basic Pie Crust (page 283) or Biscuits (page 23), or 5 sheets phyllo

Skin and bone the chicken. Cut into large chunks. Place in a bowl and set aside.

Cook carrots and onions in water to barely cover. Place a greased round of wax paper directly on the vegetables. Cover the pot and simmer for 7 to 8 minutes.

Melt butter in a saucepan. Add celery and cook until glazed, not browned. Stir in flour over low heat. Stir for 2 to 3 minutes. Add warm stock. Whisk smooth, then add milk or cream. Pour sauce into the bowl with chicken, then add drained carrots, onions, optional vegetables, and parsley. Taste and adjust seasoning with salt and pepper.

Divide mixture among four to six ovenproof deep dishes, depending on size. Cool thoroughly before covering with Basic Pie Crust, Biscuits, or phyllo. If you are using phyllo, after brushing five sheets with butter as described in the recipe for Kotopita (page 221), cut a round to the size of the deep dish.

Bake the Chicken Pot Pie at 375°F for 25 to 30 minutes, until the topping is crisp and the sauce is bubbling.

✳ *Suggestions*

- Bake the Chicken Pot Pie in a 10-inch shallow casserole.
- If you are planning a big party, prepare three or four casseroles up to four weeks ahead and freeze. Bake frozen pies for double the time. Cover the top lightly with foil so the pastry does not brown too rapidly.

Mexican Chicken in Chili-Tomato Sauce with Summer Vegetables
Serves 6 to 8.

On one of our trips to Mexico, we stayed at Na-Bolom in San Cristóbal. This small inn, which feels like home, is owned by Trudy Duby Blom. After a day or two I acquainted myself with the cook, Beatriz Myangos. She not only used the pick of their vegetable garden, but she was nutritionally innovative. The dining room table seated all the guests and young assistants to Trudy. Joyful dining and conversation completed a day of touring the local towns and markets. Beatriz kindly shared the following recipe with me.

¼ cup Chili Pepper Paste (page 27)
5 to 6 medium fresh, ripe tomatoes (about 2 pounds), skinned, seeded, and chopped
2 to 4 tablespoons olive oil
2 chickens (2½- to 3-pound broilers), each cut into eighths
2 onions, diced
3 cloves garlic, minced
3 to 4 sprigs fresh thyme
1 bay leaf
1½ pounds summer squash, sliced
1 pound kohlrabi, sliced
Salt and pepper to taste

Prepare the Chili Pepper Paste. Mix with tomatoes. Preheat oven to 350°F.

Heat a skillet or straight-sided sauté pan and then add 2 tablespoons oil. Brown a few pieces of chicken at a time and transfer to a casserole with a cover while you sauté onion and garlic in the same skillet. Add more oil if necessary to glaze the onion and garlic. Add chili-tomato mixture. Simmer while stirring for 2 to 3 minutes. Pour over the chicken. Distribute the thyme and bay leaf on top. Cover and bake in the oven for 45 minutes.

Meanwhile, parboil or steam the squash and kohlrabi until they are tender but firm. Gently add the vegetables to the chicken. Taste sauce for seasoning and adjust with salt and pepper. Add a little water or broth if the sauce has evaporated. Serve with rice.

✳ *Suggestion*

Beatriz served this dish with brown rice. I sometimes use the different varieties of rice that I stock. I also mix bulghur or wheat berries with rice.

Quail, Grilled or Braised
Serves 4.

Quail are available at specialty markets in many areas. They are tiny, about 5 or 6 ounces with bone. Therefore, it is a good idea to order two per person. I usually buy eight. I grill them all and have one dinner of four quail for my husband and myself. Then I braise the remaining quail a few days later for a different kind of dinner.

    8 quail
    1 cup red wine
    ½ teaspoon salt
    ½ teaspoon pepper
    ¼ teaspoon dry mustard
    2 tablespoons olive oil
    1 teaspoon mixed dried thyme and rosemary or a few fresh sprigs each

Use kitchen scissors to split the backs of each quail. Cut off the backbone. Press the quail flat. The breastbone can be removed easily if you wish.

Use a large bowl to mix wine, salt, pepper, and mustard together. Stir in the oil and herbs. Marinate the quail in this mixture for 1 hour or refrigerate overnight.

When ready to cook, bring the birds to room temperature while you heat the charcoal grill or kitchen broiler.

Grilling: Discard the marinade and wipe the quail dry. Grill them for 3 to 4 minutes on each side. Cover and cook for 5 to 6 more minutes. Don't overcook. The flesh should remain slightly pink.

Broiling: Broil the quail at least 5 or 6 inches from the heat for 3 to 4 minutes on each side. Then bake at 425°F for 10 minutes. The flesh should be slightly pink.

Braising: After searing the quail on both sides, remove the ones that will be braised at another time. Cool and then refrigerate them. When ready to cook, heat a straight-sided sauté pan. Add one tablespoon olive oil. Sauté 1 sliced onion, 1 tablespoon minced garlic, and 6 cleaned and sliced shiitake mushrooms. When the vegetables are glazed, pour in ½ cup each red wine and chicken stock. Simmer for 2 to 3 minutes until the liquid is reduced. Add the quail and cover the pan. Simmer for 30 to 40 minutes. Sprinkle 1 to 2 tablespoons minced fresh parsley, chives, and chervil on top before serving. If you do not have fresh herbs, use half the amount, dried.

✳ *Suggestion*

- If you find small free-range chickens in your market, do treat yourself. They are just slightly larger than quail and cook quickly. Brown them in olive oil with lots of garlic. Season with salt, pepper, lemon juice, and minced lemon grass. Bake for 20 to 30 minutes in a 375°F oven. Serve with Purée of Root Vegetables (page 109) for an elegant and delicious main course.

Roast Duck
Serves 4.

Although most people tell me that duck is better in restaurants, I do not agree. We have always looked forward to family-style Roast Duck. With napkins tucked under our chins, every last bone is finger-picked. Actually, duck needs minimal preparation. This succulent bird is wrapped in its own savory seasoning, so please do not remove the skin.

One 4- to 5-pound duck
Kosher (coarse) salt and pepper
1 orange or apple, halved

Choose a roasting pan that is closely fitted with a rack. Line the bottom and sides of the pan with heavy aluminum foil for easier clean-up.

Wash and dry the duck, inside and out. The drier the duck, the crispier the skin will be. Season the duck with salt and pepper. Place the orange or apple in the cavity.

Do not truss the duck and do not prick the skin. Without trussing, all parts of the duck will be exposed to the oven heat so that the fat will render from all surfaces. The shape is not important because the duck will be carved in the kitchen.

There are two cooking methods from which to choose. The first is to preheat the oven to 350°F. Roast the duck on the rack for 3 hours. Set aside to cool. Cut the duck in half. Reheat, skin-side up, at 425°F for 10 minutes. Serve.

Alternatively, preheat oven to 425°F and roast the duck for 2 hours. Transfer to a heated platter, then use a sharp knife or poultry shears to cut the duck into 8 to 12 pieces. It is rich enough to serve three or four.

✳ *Suggestions*

- Simple accompaniments of sliced orange, fresh pineapple, or melon are refreshing.
- Use segments of grapefruit warmed in honey or pears poached in wine for another garnish.
- Try using a Brown Sauce (page 86 or 87) or Brown Wine Sauce with Green Peppercorns (page 88).
- In November, serve roasted fresh chestnuts with the duck.

Aromatic Roasted Duck
Serves 3 to 4.

One duck (4 to 5 pounds)
1 tablespoon minced fresh ginger root
2 tablespoons minced garlic
6 scallions, chopped coarsely
2 strips orange rind
2 tablespoons honey
¼ cup soy sauce
1 tablespoon sherry

Wash and dry the duck very well, inside and out. I usually allow the duck to rest on a rack, in a cool place, for an hour. The Chinese hang it and sometimes use a fan

Sew neck securely, or use skewers.

to further dry it. The drier the duck, the crispier the skin.

Mix all other ingredients. Sew the skin together to close the neck of the duck. Place mixed seasonings into the duck cavity. Sew the opening thoroughly so that there is no seepage.

Although the duck can be roasted on a rack at 425°F for 2 hours, I prefer to use my covered charcoal grill. Allow the charcoal to heat up, and add pieces of soaked apple or cherry wood. Move the charcoal and pieces of wood around the edge

Stuff and sew the back cavity.

of the coal rack to leave the center empty. Place an aluminum foil pan in the center to catch the drippings. Refit the top rack and, when it is hot, place the duck over the drip pan. Cover the grill. Turn the duck occasionally to make sure it is cooking evenly and not blackening. Grill duck for 1½ to 2 hours.

✳ *Suggestions*

- While the charcoal is hot, roast sweet potatoes (in heavy aluminum foil) on the side of the grill.
- For a special party, grill hamburgers or chops on the side when the duck is just about finished to make a delicious mixed grill. Shrimp or vegetables on a skewer is another treat for a summer buffet.

Casserole of Black Beans and Duck
Serves 6 to 8.

So many European cassoulets are the results of tradition, but I do not know if there is any tradition attached to this black bean and duck combination. Black beans and roasted duck have each been our favorites, so I combined them. As a special winter treat, this is food for hearty eaters and heavy exercisers.

    1½ cups black beans
    One 4- to 5-pound duck
    Salt and pepper
    2 quarts water with 1 tablespoon salt
    2 onions, diced
    1 green bell pepper, diced
    1 red bell pepper, diced
    3 cloves garlic, minced
    2 teaspoons oregano
    1 teaspoon cumin seeds
    Ham bone or beef bone
    1½ pounds sausages (sweet or hot, as preferred)
    1 cup cubed roast pork or ham
    1 tablespoon olive oil
    ½ cup minced Italian parsley or fresh cilantro

Wash beans in cold water. Cover with water and bring to a boil for 3 minutes. Remove from heat and allow to stand covered for 1 hour.

In the meantime, preheat oven to 425°F. Wash and dry duck well. Season it lightly with salt and pepper. Place on a rack in a roasting pan and roast for 1½ hours.

Drain water from the beans. Cook beans in salted water with onions, peppers, garlic, oregano, cumin seeds, and ham or beef bone for 1 to 1½ hours. The timing is approximately the same as the duck. Beans vary in cooking time, so test for softness.

Cut the sausages into serving slices. Brown them in a hot skillet and mop them on paper toweling. Preheat oven to 375°F.

Cut the roasted duck into eight pieces. Use a deep, ample 4- to 5-quart casserole. Sometimes I use a paella pan. Transfer beans to the casserole, spreading them evenly. Bury pieces of the duck, sausage, and pork or ham in the beans. Dribble a small amount of olive oil over the top and cover loosely with foil. Bake for 1 hour. Stir once or twice but do not mash beans. Garnish on top with parsley or cilantro before serving.

✳ *Suggestion*

This recipe can be accomplished with ease one or two days ahead and refrigerated. Separate the parts of the recipe, if you wish, by cooking the beans one day. Roast the duck on another day, perhaps while you are using the oven for another purpose. Refrigerate for up to three days and then assemble.

Recipes for Turkey

The turkey has finally come into its own. Every part of the turkey is given ample space in all markets, year-round. Even so, there is nothing to replace the whole roasted bird by unanimous vote from this food-opinionated family.

Although I cook fresh and frozen turkey all year, I prefer the fresh turkey for Thanksgiving. Vermont farms breed turkeys for fall and early winter, and they are superb. At Thanksgiving, Roast Turkey is the star, and each year our grandchildren and even their parents ask, "How big is the turkey?" In our kitchen, bigger is better for post-dinner pickings and leftovers.

I am forever surprised that so many people still ask basic questions about roasting whole turkeys. The following are answers to some of the most frequently asked questions.

How large a turkey should you buy?

Estimate 1 pound of turkey per person. However, it is more economical to buy a larger size than is needed for one dinner. Larger turkeys have broader breasts and more flesh in proportion to bone. The leftovers for sandwiches and casseroles provide delicious post-holiday meals.

How do you defrost a frozen turkey?

Defrost a turkey slowly in its original wrapper and in the refrigerator. A frozen turkey will take from two to four days to defrost in the refrigerator, depending on its size. To hurry defrosting, a turkey wrapped in its original bag may be soaked in cold water. The slower you defrost a turkey, however, the less weight it will lose in cooking and the more juices will be retained. Never soak a turkey directly in water. That will result in the loss of proteins and vitamins as well as flavor.

How do you handle a fresh or defrosted turkey before cooking?

First remove the neck, which is usually placed in the cavity, and the bag of liver and stomach found in the crop of the turkey. Rinse the turkey lightly inside and out with cold water. Pat dry with paper toweling. Season the inside with kosher (coarse) salt and freshly ground pepper. Fill a plastic bag with about a dozen ice cubes. Secure the opening of the bag and place it in the cavity of the turkey. Wrap the turkey in aluminum foil and refrigerate for one day prior to cooking.

Should the turkey be stuffed or should the dressing be baked in a separate casserole?

Stuffings vary from one house to another, from one community to another, as well as from East to West and North to South. There were years when I tried a new stuffing each Thanksgiving. I have settled, at recent Thanksgivings, for our family's choice, which always includes chestnuts. At other times, because I roast turkey frequently, we enjoy eating different stuffings. Ritz Cracker Stuffing (page 233) and Bread Stuffing (page 233) are two basic stuffings.

A turkey should be stuffed for the traditional Thanksgiving dinner. The stuffing adds moistness and flavor. However, the answer is also yes for the casserole preparation since that method serves those who prefer a crusty stuffing. Personal preference is usually the answer. You may wish to prepare your choice of stuffing one day ahead, but do not stuff the turkey until just before roasting it. This precaution is advisable since stuffing provides a medium for the growth of bacteria in the turkey. In fact, it is also wise to remove the leftover stuffing from a cooked turkey after serving. Store the stuffing in a separate container in the refrigerator.

How much stuffing is needed to serve various numbers of guests and how much is needed to stuff a turkey?

Approximately ½ cup stuffing will be adequate for each person, and you can estimate ¾ cup stuffing for each pound of turkey weight. Measure the cooked stuffing. If it is not enough to feed your guests or to stuff the turkey, add more of one or two of the basic ingredients on hand. After stuffing the turkey, any excess can be baked in a casserole.

¾ cup cooked stuffing per pound of turkey.

How do you actually stuff the turkey?
First be sure to remove the bag of ice cubes from the cavity. Pat the cavity dry with paper toweling. Spoon the stuffing lightly into the cavity. If possible, stand the turkey on end, holding its legs, and shake the stuffing down; do not pack. Sew up the skin with a large needle and dental floss, or use skewers to close up the turkey. Then go to the other end, which is the crop of the turkey. Turn the turkey on its breast. Fill the area that once held the neck. Use the skin to enclose it. Sew it securely or use skewers. Turn the turkey breast-side up and twist the wing tips under the back to hold them in place. Use a strong white cord and place it at the midpoint under the back. Bring it over the wings along the sides of the turkey to the legs. Tie the legs securely to the body. No matter how you accomplish this, never bring the cord across the breast. The well-tied, compact turkey holds its juices and makes an attractive presentation.

Dental floss

Cord for tying

How can the preparation of gravy be accomplished other than at the last minute?
One or two days ahead, cook the broth ingredients for the gravy. Reserve at least 6 cups broth for basting the turkey. Store in the refrigerator. Then make a thick Sauce Velouté (page 83) and refrigerate until needed for gravy.

On Thanksgiving day, how do you time the roasting and serving?
Always work backward. Set the time for serving the turkey. Allow 1½ hours for predinner drinks, appetizers, or soup. This includes the last hour of roasting time and ½ hour before carving. Estimate the number of roasting hours (see timetable on page 231).

What is the procedure for roasting?
Remove the turkey and the stuffing from the refrigerator several hours before roasting. Follow directions for stuffing and basting the turkey. Preheat oven to 325°F. (I use that temperature for turkeys of all sizes.) If more browning is needed at the very end, raise the temperature to 375°F for 10 minutes.

After seasoning the turkey, set it on a rack in a dry roasting pan. Dip a layer of cheesecloth into the basting broth. Loosely cover the turkey with the cheesecloth. If the turkey weighs less than 14 pounds, it may be roasted breast-side down and turned over after half the cooking time. Larger birds are difficult to turn. Roast the larger ones breast-side up for the full time.

Use the following Turkey Roasting Timetable to roast at 325°F.

Ready to Cook Weight	Amount of Stuffing	Cooking Time
8 to 13 pounds	6 to 10 cups	3½ to 4 hours
13 to 16 pounds	10 to 14 cups	4 to 5 hours
18 to 22 pounds	14 to 18 cups	5 to 6½ hours

After 2 hours, start basting occasionally. Remove the cheesecloth toward the end of the roasting time to baste and brown evenly. When you remove the cheesecloth, also remove the string.

Test for doneness by moving the leg to see if it is flexible and soft. Use an instant thermometer inserted in the center of the breast. It should register 160° to 175°F. The turkey will continue to cook after removing from the oven.

How do you carve a turkey?

Prepare a carving board with a deep well to collect the juices. Be sure to sharpen your favorite knife. Set a heated large platter next to the carving board and a heated bowl for the stuffing. Use a long-tined fork for carving and a long-handled spoon to remove the stuffing.

Place the turkey with legs at the right, for right-handed people. Cut through and separate the entire leg from the breast. It will actually pull away from the back. Do the same at the wing joining the breast. Carve the fleshier parts of the leg and wing. Leave some meat on the bone for guests who enjoy nibbling. Start carving the breast from the corner of the wing joint. Carve down at a slight angle to the breast bone. Carve enough for one serving for all.

Roast Turkey
Serves 12 to 16.

One 12- to 16-pound turkey, defrosted, with giblets
Kosher (coarse) salt and freshly ground pepper
1 onion
1 carrot
1 rib celery
2 quarts water
Seasonings to taste (sprigs of fresh parsley and thyme, dried herbs in small
    amounts)

1 recipe stuffing (pages 233–235)
8 tablespoons (¼ pound) melted butter or oil
1 teaspoon salt
½ teaspoon pepper
1 teaspoon paprika
3 tablespoons butter
5 tablespoons flour
2 cups hot broth

Remove the neck, bag of liver, and stomach found in the crop and cavity of the turkey. Lightly rinse the turkey, inside and out, with cold water. Pat dry with paper toweling.

Place the turkey giblets with onion, carrot, and rib of celery in a soup pot. Cover with water and bring to a boil. Add seasonings to taste. If available, add more giblets and chicken parts for extra flavor. Simmer partially covered for 1½ to 2 hours depending on tenderness of giblets. Strain the broth and dice the turkey giblets to be used either in the stuffing or in the gravy. Reserve at least 6 cups broth for basting the turkey. Store remaining broth in the refrigerator until ready to make the gravy.

Season the inside of the turkey with salt and pepper. Spoon the stuffing into the cavity (do not pack). Sew up the skin or use skewers. Turn the turkey breast-side up and twist the wing tips under the back to hold them in place. Tie the legs securely to the body.

Preheat oven to 325°F. Mix together 8 tablespoons butter or oil, salt, pepper, and paprika. Rub half the mixture over the entire turkey. Add the other half to the broth you will be using for basting.

Set the turkey on a rack in a dry roasting pan. If the turkey weighs less than 14 pounds, it may be roasted breast-side down and turned over after half the cooking time. Larger birds are difficult to turn, so they may be roasted breast-side up for the full time. Dip a layer of cheesecloth into the basting broth. Loosely cover the turkey with the cheesecloth, and place it in the oven.

Follow the Turkey Roasting Timetable (page 231) to determine cooking time. Start basting occasionally after 2 hours.

Remove the cheesecloth and string toward the end of the roasting time to baste and brown evenly. Test for doneness by moving the leg to see if it is flexible and soft, or use an instant thermometer inserted in the center of the breast (it should register 160° to 175°F). The turkey will continue to cook after it is removed from the oven. If more browning is needed at the very end, raise the temperature to 375°F for 10 minutes.

After roasting the turkey, remove it to a carving board. Let it rest for 20 to 30 minutes while you prepare the gravy.

Place the roasting pan on a medium flame. Pour on 2 cups of hot basting broth. This will deglaze the pan as you scrape off all the brown particles. Lower the flame. Melt 3 tablespoons butter in a saucepan. Add 5 tablespoons flour to make a roux. Pour the roasting pan broth into the roux, stirring constantly to cook a thickened gravy. Simmer for 5 to 7 minutes. If it is too thick, add more broth. Taste to readjust seasoning with salt and pepper.

If you have prepared a Sauce Velouté (page 83) in advance, as suggested previously, (page 230), deglaze roasting pan with a cup of broth, scraping off all brown particles. Combine this with Velouté Sauce.

After carving the turkey, remove the stuffing to a heated bowl. Cover slices of turkey with a small amount of very hot gravy. Pass the remaining gravy around.

Ritz Cracker Stuffing (Our Thanksgiving Favorite)
Stuffs one 12- to 16-pound turkey.

3 medium onions, diced and sautéed
3 ribs celery, diced
1 large carrot, scraped and grated
1 pound cooked chestnuts
1 tablespoon chopped parsley
1 pound Ritz crackers, crushed
2 eggs, beaten
1 cup cold water
Salt and pepper to taste

Mix sautéed onions with celery, carrot, chestnuts, parsley, and crackers. This mixture can be prepared one or two days ahead. Mix in eggs, water, and salt and pepper to taste just before stuffing the turkey.

Bread Stuffing
Stuffs one 12- to 16-pound turkey.

4 tablespoons butter or oil
2 to 3 onions (1 pound), diced
4 ribs celery, diced
12 cups dry white bread, torn into pieces or cubed
¼ cup freshly chopped parsley
1 tablespoon mixed herbs (thyme, sage, marjoram)
Salt and freshly ground pepper to taste
1 cup chicken stock or water

Heat butter or oil in a skillet. Cook onions for a few minutes until glazed. Add celery. Stir together and cook for 3 to 4 minutes.

Mix bread, parsley, and herbs in a large bowl. Add onion and celery. Season to taste with salt and pepper. Cover and refrigerate until needed. Add stock or water just before stuffing the turkey.

Virginian Cornbread Stuffing
Stuffs one 12- to 16-pound turkey.

My friend, Jenny Heinbach, a born Virginian, added this stuffing to my collection of favorites.

4 tablespoons butter
1 cup diced onions
½ cup diced celery
6 cups dry white bread, cubed
3 cups Buttermilk Cornbread (recipe below), crumbled
1 cup diced peeled apples
½ cup each sultana (yellow) raisins and walnuts
½ pound sausage
4 ounces diced ham
1 tablespoon chopped parsley
1 cup chicken stock

Melt butter in a skillet. Cook onions and celery until softened and glazed.

Mix white bread, cornbread, apples, raisins, walnuts, sausage, ham, and parsley in a large bowl. Lightly blend in onions and celery.

Just before stuffing the turkey, add chicken stock. Test flavoring by cooking a small ball in a greased skillet. Taste and season, if necessary.

Buttermilk Cornbread

1½ cups white cornmeal
½ cup all-purpose flour
2 teaspoons baking powder
1 teaspoon baking soda
1 teaspoon salt
2 cups buttermilk
2 eggs
3 tablespoons melted butter, oil, or bacon drippings

Preheat oven to 425°F. Oil a 9" x 13" baking pan.

Sift cornmeal, flour, baking powder, baking soda, and salt in a large bowl. Add buttermilk, eggs, and butter, oil, or bacon drippings, stirring well to incorporate all ingredients.

Pour mixture into the prepared pan. Bake for 25 minutes until crusty.

☀ *Suggestions*

- Add 1 pound veal, 1 cup sliced red sweet pepper, and ½ teaspoon nutmeg to the Ritz Cracker Stuffing.
- Add twice as much onion and carrot to the Ritz Cracker Stuffing, as well as diced giblets.
- Substitute other favorite crackers in the Ritz Cracker Stuffing.
- For the Bread Stuffing, add 1 pint oysters to the sautéed onion and celery. Cook the oysters for just 30 seconds.
- Add 1 pound sausage to the Bread Stuffing. Moisten with 1 cup broth before stuffing the turkey.
- Add thinly sliced apples and sultana (yellow) raisins to the Bread Stuffing.

Smoked Grilled Turkey
Serves 15 to 20.

My husband takes to the barbecue and smoker as soon as temperatures permit. We collaborate at the outdoor grill for most of our summer entertaining.

Some years ago, Dot Davis, a student of mine and a teacher in Barre, Vermont, shared this recipe with me. The seasoning is just right and the recipe is perfect for family use. Well wrapped, it can be refrigerated for up to seven days or frozen for up to one month.

    2 teaspoons spice mixture (5 bay leaves, 5 whole coriander seeds, 6 whole cloves, 16 whole black peppercorns)
    1 turkey (about 17 pounds) or 2 turkey breasts
    2 cups salt
    1 cup sugar
    5⅓ teaspoons saltpeter (available at a pharmacy)

Grind the spice mixture in a food processor or spice grinder. You may grind a larger amount for future use.

Use a large plastic container or other container that will fit in the refrigerator and comfortably hold a 17-pound turkey or two turkey breasts. Place the turkey in the container and add cold water to just cover the turkey. Remove the turkey from the container.

Add salt, sugar, saltpeter, and spices to the water in the container and stir until the sugar and salt are dissolved to make a brine solution.

Place the turkey in the container of brine solution. If necessary, weight the turkey down to keep it under the brine. Cover and place in the refrigerator for 2 to 4 days.

When ready to smoke, remove the turkey from the brine. Dry well inside and out with paper toweling.

Start fire in the grill with charcoal. Soak a generous handful of wood chips in water. When coals are burning well, spread them around the side of the coal rack. Place a drip pan in the center surrounded by coals. Strew the wood chips on the coals.

woodchips

charcoal

drip pan

Grill the turkey in the covered grill (with vents open) for 3 to 4 hours. Time depends on the temperature of the fire. A low fire with comparatively few coals will take longer. Turkey breasts smoke somewhat faster. Insert an instant cooking thermometer near the second joint of the leg but not touching the bone. The temperature should register at least 160°F. Do not overcook.

After taking the turkey out of the grill, allow it to rest for a while before carving.

10

Meat

Broiling

As a young and inexperienced cook, some 50 years ago, I depended on the broiler for fast weekday meals. After a working day, broiling a steak, chop, or hamburger was simple—and delicious as well. In addition, I would sometimes pan-broil or sauté small tender cuts. Even as a novice, I could complete a very satisfying dinner in less than 30 minutes, and to this day, I still rely on these methods. If you broil meats often, experience will be your best teacher. Apply the broiling technique to all varieties of tender cuts.

Do not wash the meat. Instead, wipe it with paper toweling. Sometimes machine cutting by the butcher deposits bone splinters on the surface. If you are storing meat in the refrigerator (no more than three days), protect it with a thin coating of oil and wrap it in plastic wrap. It is important to bring meat to room temperature before broiling. Always preheat the broiler before cooking.

Note the timing for broiling beef steak, veal, or pork to your taste. Make observations. Your personal taste will dictate the result you would like to achieve.

Pan Broiling

If you have inherited your grandmother's black iron skillet, use it for pan broiling. Otherwise use a stainless steel-lined aluminum skillet or the black iron griddles that have raised ridges.

When I cooked a tiny lamb chop for my first baby (now 50!), I was advised to heat the skillet, sprinkle a little kosher (coarse) salt on it, and then place the chop on the pan. The salt formed a brown crust. Turned over once and cooked for 2 minutes on each side, the surface of the meat was browned and juicy pink in the center. Try it for yourself.

Pan broiling is fast and works well for small cuts, less than ½ inch thick. Small chuck steaks, paillettes of veal, and center-cut pork slices cook fast with this greaseless method.

Do not overcook. Serve small dishes of soy, balsamic vinegar, mustard, and ketchup for side seasonings.

Sautéing

The French verb *sauter* means to jump and refers to the movement of shaking the pan to keep the food from sticking. Different from pan broiling, a small amount of fat is used in sautéing. As a general rule, flavoring vegetables are added and, sometimes, stock and wine.

Stir-Frying

There are differences in the methods of stir-frying and sautéing. When sautéing, the skillet is only moderately hot, and it is shaken to prevent sticking. Compare the recipes. Notice that the meat and vegetables are stir-fried separately because the timing is different for each. The ingredients are assembled at the finish. When stir-frying, the wok or skillet is quite hot and meat is moved around the pan with large spoons or chopsticks.

Roasting

I think roasting is perhaps the simplest technique for cooking meat. Roasting properly implies dry heat—no covers. The cut of meat does all the work, and it must be a tender section. Of course, the most tender cuts are always the most expensive, so most families splurge on roasts for weekend meals or for special holidays. There is always the bonus of leftover meat for lunch box sandwiches and great weekday snacks; and don't forget leftover bones for stocks.

Facts to remember:

- Always roast on a rack so the bottom of the meat does not sit in drippings, where it would stew and overcook.
- Use an instant meat thermometer to determine exact doneness.
- The roast will continue to cook for at least 5 minutes after removing from the oven. Allow it to rest for at least 10 minutes before carving. Inner juices will disperse more evenly and carving will be easier.
- Add hot stock, wine, or water to the hot roasting pan after removing meat to a carving board to rest. Prepare sauce or gravy with the broth. Even if you are not using a sauce, always deglaze the pan with hot liquid. Save it in the freezer for another use. It also washes your pan.
- Use a sharp knife for carving—one that you are used to handling. It does not have to be a special carving knife.

Broiled Porterhouse Steak
Serves 2.

The porterhouse steak is unique. It includes the strip (or shell) steak and, separated by the bone, the fillet. The fillet is always the most tender cut, the strip (or shell) is the most flavorful. Buy a steak that is at least 1½ inches thick for two servings. After broiling, use a sharp knife to separate each section from the bone; then cut the strip and fillet into ¼-inch slices. Divide the slices of strip and fillet into portions so that each serving has some of each. In our house we toss for the bone.

1 porterhouse steak (1½ to 2 inches thick)
1 teaspoon kosher (coarse) salt
½ teaspoon Worcestershire sauce
Freshly ground pepper to taste

Remove excess fat from the steak, but leave some on the border. Season the steak with salt and Worcestershire sauce. If time allows, place the steak on the broiler pan and set aside for 1 hour. Position the oven rack at 3 to 4 inches from the heat. Broil the steak for 8 or 9 minutes on one side and 5 minutes on the other for rare meat.

Learn to test the steak with your finger like a professional. If your finger easily makes a dent in the steak, it is rare. If it barely pushes through the top, it is medium. If the surface is very firm and your finger makes no dent it is well done.

The meat can be tested more scientifically by inserting an instant thermometer: 120°F is very rare, 130° to 140°F is medium-rare, and so on.

Allow the broiled steak to rest as you place vegetables on heated dinner plates or serving bowls. Carve the steak at the table and serve.

✳ *Suggestions*

- Save the scraps of meat for meat loaf or stuffings.
- Save the bone for soups, stocks, or sauces, if you are not bone nibblers.
- If there is a substantial amount left over, refrigerate for an Oriental stir-fry dinner.

Broiled Veal Chop with Mustard
Serves 2.

Although there is no trick to broiling a veal chop, it does need careful timing and ample seasoning. Overcooking causes dryness, so look for pinkness at the bone. Choice of seasoning is to your taste—anything from salt and pepper to leftover gravy, tomato sauce, a sprinkling of cheese, or, our favorite, Dijon mustard.

1 tablespoon Dijon mustard
⅛ teaspoon dry mustard
½ teaspoon paprika
1 tablespoon warm water
2 loin veal chops, ½ inch thick (about 6 ounces each)
Pepper to taste

Mix Dijon mustard, dry mustard, paprika, and water into a paste. Spread half the mixture on one side of each chop. Place the chops, seasoned-side up, on a broiler pan. Set aside while the broiler is preheating. Be sure the oven rack is set about 3 inches from the heat.

Warm the dinner plates, and start your vegetables before you start broiling the chops.

Broil the chops for 5 minutes on the seasoned side. Turn the chops over and spread the sides with the balance of the paste. Broil for 3 minutes. Turn the chops over to the first side. If you are unsure about doneness, make a small slit near the bone. The meat should be slightly pink. Give it another minute in the broiler. Serve immediately with a dash of pepper.

✳ *Suggestions*

- Use a combination of mustard and honey for another seasoning.
- Garnish the top of each chop with a fresh leaf of an herb.
- When you use a tomato sauce, broil the chop first then cover it with the sauce for the last minute of broiling.
- Marinate the chops with sherry and smashed green peppercorns before broiling.

Broiled Pork Chops with Apple and Hard Cider
Serves 2.

We are lucky to live in a New England town near a fine winery owned by our friend and neighbor Ed Metcalfe. His North River Winery produces a variety of excellent fruit wines as well as Metcalfe's Hard Cider. After uncorking, hard cider keeps well for up to two weeks in the refrigerator. I keep it on hand for extra moistness and subtle flavor in my pork and chicken dishes.

2 pork chops (loin or rib), ½ to ¾ inch thick
1 tablespoon soy sauce
½ cup hard apple cider
1 tablespoon oil
2 shallots, minced
2 apples, peeled and sliced
½ teaspoon white pepper
¼ cup whipping cream (optional)

Marinate pork chops in soy sauce and hard apple cider. Set aside until ready to broil.

Heat an 8- or 10-inch skillet. Add oil. Sauté shallots and some apple slices (reserve 1 sliced apple for garnish) for 3 to 4 minutes. Lower heat so they don't burn.

Preheat broiler. Set the oven rack 3 inches below the heat. Dry chops with paper toweling, then place them on a broiler pan. Save the soy and cider marinade to make the sauce.

Place the chops in the oven. Broil for 6 minutes on one side, 3 minutes on the other side.

In the meantime, add the reserved marinade to the shallots and apple slices. Heat and reduce the liquid to almost half. Season with pepper. Add cream and simmer over low heat.

Spread the apples and sauce on two heated dinner plates. Garnish each chop with an apple slice after the chop has been placed on the sauce.

✳ *Suggestions*

- Seasonings for veal and pork are interchangeable. Try the seasonings in the previous recipe for veal.
- Use a free hand with herbs and spices. Both pork and veal need these added aromatics.
- If you make the Roasted Garlic (page 27) or Chili Pepper Paste (page 27), use a touch of either one on pork chops.

Steak au Poivre
Serves 2.

Steak au Poivre is a classic French preparation for steak, but it is internationally enjoyed. Although there are different versions, fresh coarsely cracked pepper must always be pressed into the steak. Cognac is the accepted great flavoring, but I add a few tablespoons of port wine as well. My husband sometimes adds a dash of cream, and it is delicious. Although the strip, or shell, steak is an excellent cut for this recipe, we like the fillet steak. A 4- or 5-ounce fillet is an ample serving for each person.

    1 tablespoon black peppercorns
    2 fillet steaks, ¾ to 1 inch thick
    ¼ teaspoon kosher (coarse) salt
    1 tablespoon each oil and butter
    ¼ cup cognac
    ¼ cup whipping cream (optional)
    2 tablespoons port wine

The peppercorns must be coarsely cracked. Do not use a pepper grinder. Place the peppercorns inside a folded and sealed sheet of aluminum foil. Smash them with the back of a heavy skillet.

Season the steaks with salt. Open the aluminum foil and press the pepper into both sides of the steak.

Heat an 8- or 10-inch skillet. Add oil and butter. When the butter melts, sauté the fillets. Brown on one side for about 3 to 4 minutes. When the edges start to turn color and the tops of the fillets show juiciness, turn over.

Add the cognac. Tilt the pan so that the flame catches onto the cognac or use a match. The flame might become quite high so stand at arm's length. When the flame in the pan dies down, place each steak on heated dinner plates.

Add cream and port wine to the skillet. Heat and reduce sauce to thicken it slightly. Pour the sauce over each steak and serve.

Bellow Beef Curry
Serves 4.

Cook ahead to let seasonings blend!

Some time ago, when I was laid up with an ailing leg, our friends Janis and Saul Bellow, in consideration for my then-busy cook-and-housekeeper husband, brought dinner for the four of us. The evening was a treat! The recipe is a collaboration of Janis's seasoning and Saul's technique. The technique is a combination of sautéing, stir-frying, and braising. I liked the idea of cooking it a day ahead to allow the seasonings to mellow.

2 tablespoons olive oil
1 Spanish onion, diced
2 ribs celery, diced fine
2 pounds sirloin, sliced thin
½ cup gravy (left over from a roast or stew)
2 cups dry red wine
2 cups canned Italian plum tomatoes
3 cloves garlic, minced
2 heaping tablespoons Madras curry
⅛ teaspoon cumin
1 tablespoon minced fresh ginger root
1 teaspoon Worcestershire sauce
Dash Tabasco sauce (Saul likes it spicy)
2 sprigs each fresh parsley, basil, and cilantro
Salt and pepper to taste

Heat a 10- or 12-inch skillet. Add oil and then onion to brown lightly. Add celery and stir. When the celery is glazed, transfer the vegetables to a dish and set aside.

Turn heat on high. Sear slices of sirloin a few pieces at a time, browning on both sides. Transfer the meat to a platter as you do this.

Return the celery and onion to the hot skillet. Add gravy, wine, tomatoes, garlic, and all the seasonings up to and including the Tabasco sauce. Simmer for 5 minutes.

Return the meat to the skillet with the fresh herbs. Blend together, gently. Add salt and pepper to taste. Remove from heat. Transfer to a shallow casserole and refrigerate overnight.

Before serving, preheat oven to 375°F. Heat for 20 to 25 minutes. Do not overcook. Serve with rice.

✸ *Suggestions*

- Set the table with bowls of accompaniments such as chutney, raisins, almonds, coconut, and so on.
- Add sliced red and green bell pepper to the celery and onion.
- Use fewer tomatoes and add ½ cup Chili Pepper Paste (page 27) as a substitute for Tabasco.

Scaloppine of Veal
Serves 4.

Any small, tender cut of veal, pork, or lamb can be sautéed for quick cooking. You must decide on your seasonings ahead of time because the cooking will be fast. Choose the herbs you prefer, but add them at the end of the cooking time. (To add them earlier would cause the herbs to darken while sautéing.) Give the herbs just enough time to warm and thus release their aroma.

Study the basic procedures below. Although veal will need to be pounded to break connecting tissues in the meat, pork and lamb go straight to the pan. The interchange of seasonings and vegetables are your choice.

1 pound veal, cut for scaloppine
½ cup fine plain bread crumbs
½ cup unbleached all-purpose flour
1 teaspoon salt
½ teaspoon white pepper
¼ teaspoon paprika
2 tablespoons each oil and butter (preferably clarified)
½ cup imported Madeira or Marsala wine
1 teaspoon each dried marjoram and thyme

Place each slice of veal under aluminum foil and pound it to an even thinness. Mix bread crumbs, flour, salt, pepper, and paprika on a sheet of wax paper.

Dredge the slices of veal in the mixture and set aside in one layer. Preheat oven to 275°F.

Heat a 10-inch skillet slowly. When the skillet is hot, add oil and butter. The oil and butter should be moderately hot so the meat does not brown too fast. Sauté 2 or 3 pieces of veal at a time, leaving space between the pieces. Turn them over once. If the pieces are crowded, they will steam instead of cook around the edges. Place the slices on a shallow baking pan as you finish the sautéing.

The flat side of a heavy cleaver makes a good pounding tool... or a steel pounder made just for that purpose.

If the crumbs in the skillet have blackened, wipe the skillet clean with paper toweling. Heat the skillet. Add wine and herbs. Simmer for 2 minutes. Pour over the veal. Place the veal in the oven for 10 minutes before serving. (To prepare an hour in advance, cover the veal with oiled wax paper and place in the oven at 225°F.) Garnish with fresh herbs of your choice.

✳ *Suggestions*

- Sauté ½ pound fresh mushrooms before adding wine.
- Add ½ cup Brown Stock (page 60) with the wine. Thicken the sauce with 1 teaspoon cornstarch mixed with an equal amount of cold water.
- Top slices of sautéed meat with Tomato Sauce (page 88) and a sprinkling of grated Parmesan cheese or thin slices of fontina and Gruyère cheese.
- Place thinly sliced prosciutto and fresh leaves of sage on the sautéed meat.
- A small amount of Brown Sauce (page 86 or 87), sometimes a leftover in the freezer, extends the wine.
- Use curry powder and ground coriander to season pork and lamb. Add the seasoning to the skillet before adding the wine.

Veal with Lo Mein and Vegetables
Serves 4 to 6.

This veal recipe is a good example for learning how to stir-fry. The recipe can also be your guide for substituting ingredients you have on hand. For example, veal is not generally used in Chinese dishes, but I have taken a liberty here.

½ pound scaloppine of veal (shoulder may be used)
2 teaspoons soy sauce
¼ teaspoon pepper
1 tablespoon sherry

1 tablespoon cornstarch

1 tablespoon each minced garlic and fresh ginger root

1 large onion, sliced

½ pound mushrooms (or 4 dried Chinese mushrooms, presoaked), sliced

1 red bell pepper, seeded and cut into strips

1 green bell pepper, seeded and cut into strips

2 cups sliced mixed fresh vegetables (carrots, zucchini, broccoli, cauliflower)

2 to 4 teaspoons oil

½ cup chicken stock

½ pound lo mein noodles or linguini, cooked

1 tablespoon sesame oil

½ cup diced scallions

Cut veal into ¼-inch strips. Marinate the veal in a mixture of soy sauce, pepper, sherry, and cornstarch. Set aside.

Prepare the vegetables. Lay out a sheet of wax paper on the counter nearest the stove. Place garlic and ginger on one corner of the wax paper. Place all vegetables on the wax paper next to each other.

Heat a wok or a large skillet. Pour in 3 teaspoons oil. Add garlic, ginger, and then onion. Stir over high heat for 1 minute, then add veal. Stir again over high heat for another minute or two. Remove all to a heated platter. Add more oil to the wok (or skillet). Stir-fry mushrooms and peppers, then add the mixed vegetables. Stir constantly for 1 minute. Pour in chicken stock. Cover wok and cook for 2 to 3 minutes.

Uncover and add the cooked lo mein or linguini noodles. Toss and blend well together. Finally, mix in veal and onions over very high heat. Serve on a heated platter with a sprinkling of sesame oil and scallions as garnish.

Boiling and Stewing

Both methods require meats to be covered with liquid while they simmer under covers. For brown stews, meats are browned first to produce brown color then covered with liquid.

Boeuf Bouilli (Boiled Beef)
Serves 8 to 10.

This is truly an old-fashioned family dinner. I remember my mother cooking beef, vegetables, and lima beans—my father's favorite dinner. Many years later I encountered Boiled Beef in a more sophisticated setting. Henri Soulé, the renowned restaurateur, served it as a salad in his New York City restaurant, Pavillon. What a perfectly wonderful treat it is, hot or cold, winter or summer.

    4 to 5 pounds brisket of beef (veal may be substituted)
    3 to 5 pounds beef or veal bones, cracked into smaller chunks
    4 cloves garlic
    2 onions studded with 2 whole cloves
    3 ribs celery
    4 to 5 carrots, peeled and cut in half
    Bouquet garni
    1 parsnip, peeled and cut in half
    ½ cup dried lima beans, soaked overnight
    Salt and pepper to taste

Use a 6- or 8-quart soup pot with a tight-fitting cover. Put all ingredients into the pot, except salt and pepper. Pour in cold water to cover. Simmer, partially covered, for at least 1 hour. Skim occasionally if foam has formed on top and if residue clings to the side of the pot. Cover again and cook for 30 minutes. Add salt and pepper to taste. Cook for another 30 minutes or more, until the meat feels tender when tested with a fork.

Serve bowls of hot soup and lima beans. Discard the vegetables and bones with a slotted spoon. Transfer meat to a carving board. Slice and serve it on the side with sharp mustard and horseradish.

Boeuf Bouilli Pavillon Style
Serves 8 to 10.

This is a superb buffet dish, especially when the beef has just been cooked and is served at room temperature.

Boeuf Bouilli

    1 recipe Boeuf Bouilli (page 246), without lima beans
    1 tablespoon each chopped fresh chives and parsley

Sauce Gribiche

    1 hard-cooked egg
    1 egg yolk (or ¼ cup commercial mayonnaise)
    1 tablespoon white vinegar
    1 tablespoon Dijon mustard
    2 shallots

1 small onion
2 sprigs parsley
1 tablespoon fresh tarragon leaves (or 1 teaspoon dried)
¾ cup corn or olive oil
3 drops Tabasco sauce
½ teaspoon Worcestershire sauce
Salt and pepper to taste
1 tablespoon cold water
1 tablespoon each chopped chives and parsley

Omit the lima beans in the Boeuf Bouilli recipe, but cook the beef and vegetables in the same way. Refrigerate or freeze the soup for another time. Allow beef to cool to room temperature before slicing.

In the meantime, make the Sauce Gribiche. Place the cooked egg, egg yolk or mayonnaise, vinegar, mustard, shallots, onion, and herbs in a food processor. Pulse it on and off, then gradually add oil. Transfer to a bowl. Whisk in all other ingredients except chopped chives and parsley.

Slice the meat and arrange on a platter or tray in overlapping slices. Spoon half the sauce over the meat. Garnish the top with chopped chives and parsley. Serve remaining sauce on the side.

Beef and Veal Stew
Serves 4 to 6.

Beef and Veal Stew is a basic browned stew, good for any day of the week. The beef and veal make an excellent combination. Use pork as a substitute for either beef or veal or as an addition.

2 to 3 pounds chuck of beef (with bone)
2 to 3 pounds shoulder of veal (with bone)
Salt and pepper
1 cup diced onions
4 tablespoons flour
1 teaspoon paprika
1 quart water
1 cup red wine
4 cloves garlic, minced
1 cup each diced celery and carrot
1 large tomato, peeled, seeded and diced, or 1 cup canned crushed tomatoes
Bouquet garni

8 or 10 tiny red-skinned potatoes, peeled
Sprigs of Italian parsley for garnish

Preheat the oven to 425°F. Cut beef and veal into large chunks. Include the bones. Season with a sprinkling of salt and pepper. Place the meat, bones, and onion in a shallow baking pan. Bake for 10 minutes.

In the meantime, mix the flour and paprika. Remove the meat and onion from the oven. Sprinkle the mixed flour and paprika on top. Turn the pieces gently to coat them evenly. Return the pan to the oven for another 10 to 15 minutes.

Prepare a stew pot with a tight-fitting cover. Pour in water and bring to a boil. After the meat is browned, transfer it directly to the boiling water.

Pour red wine into the hot baking pan to deglaze and clean the pan of all brown bits that cling to it. Add the wine and scrapings to the meat and water. Mix in garlic, celery, carrots, and tomatoes. Place the bouquet garni on top, for easy removal later. Cover the pot and simmer for 1 hour.

Remove bouquet garni and add potatoes to the stew. Cover and cook for 15 minutes or until the potatoes and meat feel tender when tested with a fork.

Serve portions on heated dinner plates. Garnish the top with a sprig of Italian parsley.

✴ *Suggestions*

- When you cook red-skinned potatoes, strip the skin every half inch to give an attractive striped effect.
- To develop a richer and browner color in the stew, uncover the pot for the last 30 minutes. Keep the stew at a simmer.
- When beets are plentiful in our garden, I cook a Beet Borscht (page 72) and serve it in large soup bowls. We enjoy adding a portion of the stew to the borscht for a one-dish meal.
- Top the stew with a spoonful of sour cream for an interesting look and an added taste.

Lamb Stew with Dill and Yogurt
Serves 6 to 8.

This lamb stew is a winning example of a white stew. The spices and fragrant seasonings combine with the lamb for a perfect finish. Even reluctant lamb-eaters have said an enthusiastic yes to this recipe at our table.

4 to 5 pounds lamb (neck, shoulder, or shank)
1 tablespoon kosher (coarse) salt

½ teaspoon white pepper
¼ teaspoon each cinnamon, ginger, and nutmeg
2 tablespoons oil
3 medium onions, diced
6 tablespoons unbleached all-purpose flour
3 or 4 cloves garlic, minced
1 cup chopped fresh dill
¼ cup fresh lemon juice
2 cups stock or water
Salt and pepper to taste
1 cup yogurt

It is important to choose from the cuts suggested here. The bones with a small amount of untrimmed fat will lend great flavor. Ask your butcher to section the meat into large chunks.

Mix salt, pepper, cinnamon, ginger, and nutmeg on a sheet of wax paper. Turn chunks of meat in the seasonings.

Heat a Dutch oven or stew pot with a tight-fitting cover over moderate heat. Add oil and then onions. Cook for a few minutes to sweat and glaze the onions.

Add meat and cook uncovered for about 10 minutes, stirring occasionally. Sprinkle flour over all, blending it with the meat and onions. Add garlic and ½ cup dill. Pour in lemon juice and stock or water. Mix thoroughly. Cover the pot and simmer for 2 to 2½ hours or until the meat is tender. Taste to adjust seasoning with salt and pepper.

If you are preparing the stew a day or two ahead, cool the pot rapidly in a sink filled with cold water. Refrigerate. Remove the fat when it hardens on the surface.

Before serving, heat the stew and stir in the yogurt. Serve piping hot with a sprinkling of remaining dill.

Braising

Braised meats are either glazed or browned, sometimes in a small amount of fat if the meat is lean. Flavoring vegetables and a small amount of liquid is added. When the meat simmers under cover its flavor and juices combine with the liquid to produce the finishing sauce.

Braised Pot Roast
Serves 8 to 10.

Every family has its very own memory bank for pot roast. Seasonings run the gamut from the simplest salt and pepper to long lists of herbs and spices. Added liquid, if any, can be water, stock, wine, tomato, or even beer. Following this simple recipe will, at least, provide technique and timing and allow for some seasoning choices of your own.

3 to 4 pounds brisket or rump of beef
1½ teaspoons salt
½ teaspoon pepper
½ teaspoon paprika
3 to 4 medium onions, diced
¼ cup unbleached all-purpose flour
1 cup hot water or stock
3 cloves garlic, minced
1 carrot, peeled and grated
2 tablespoons tomato paste or ½ cup canned crushed tomatoes
1 bay leaf, plus 2 sprigs each parsley and thyme, tucked into the cavity of celery and tied
1½ cups dry red wine
2 tablespoons dark brown sugar (optional)

First-cut brisket is the most often used cut for pot roast, but I frequently use the rump of beef as well. The rump is also called the bottom round. Look for the triangular-shaped cut (see also Triangle of Roasted Rump, page 259, for more about rump cuts).

Preheat oven to 425°F. Season the meat with salt, pepper, and paprika. Place on a shallow baking pan. Strew onions around the meat. Brown for 15 to 20 minutes, turning the meat occasionally for even browning. (Of course, you can also brown the meat and onions in a stew pot or Dutch oven on the top of the stove. Follow the directions for adding the flour and then the stock.) When the meat looks browned, sprinkle the flour on top and return to the oven for 10 more minutes.

Transfer the meat and onions to a stew pot. Deglaze the baking pan with the hot stock or water, scraping off remaining browned bits sticking to the pan. Pour onto the meat. Add the remaining ingredients. Cover the pot and simmer for 1½ hours.

Test for doneness with a fork, which should easily pierce the meat. (The meat, however, should remain firm.) Let meat cool for 10 or 15 minutes to make carving easier.

Carve the meat against the grain into thin slices (or as you prefer them). Place the slices back into the sauce. Cover and simmer for 20 minutes. Taste the sauce to adjust the seasoning.

✳ *Suggestions*

- If you prefer a smooth sauce, strain it over the meat.
- Cook Braised Pot Roast two to three days ahead and refrigerate. Remove the congealed fat on top before reheating.
- If you plan a dinner weeks ahead, cook the beef and freeze it in a covered casserole, ready to be reheated.
- All leftovers can be frozen.

Braised Venison
Serves 6 to 8.

People come from miles around to attend the game dinner at the Jacksonville, Vermont, Municipal Center each year. Wild venison is contributed by local hunters. Three shifts of about 100 people arrive at their allotted time to feast on game. Venison in markets and restaurants is sectioned from deer raised on farms, but these diners come to Jacksonville for a true taste of the wild.

Cook venison as you would beef, but remember, it is a lean meat. Marinate venison for essential flavor and some tenderizing. Broil or sauté venison fillets and steaks as described in the beef recipes. They are especially good at the rare and medium-rare stages.

This recipe for Braised Venison takes several days to prepare. Plan ahead.

Marinade

2 cups red wine
½ cup vinegar
½ cup water
1 onion, studded with 4 whole cloves
1 carrot, sliced
2 bay leaves
12 juniper berries, finely crushed
1 teaspoon salt
1 teaspoon pepper

Venison

4 pounds venison, shoulder or rump

½ pound bacon
2 onions, diced
3 ribs celery, diced
2 carrots, diced
4 cloves garlic
3 sprigs fresh parsley
½ teaspoon dried thyme
2 teaspoons salt
½ teaspoon pepper
4 tablespoons flour
1 cup marinade liquid
2 cups venison stock or beef stock
¼ cup currant jelly
2 slices rye bread (with caraway seeds)
¼ cup minced Italian parsley

Combine the marinade ingredients and marinate the venison. The liquid should cover the meat completely. If it does not, add more wine, vinegar, and water proportionately. Marinate for 3 to 5 days in the refrigerator.

On the night you plan to serve the venison, render the bacon in a Dutch oven or a stew pot. Remove the crisp bacon. Crumble it and set it aside. Pour off all but enough bacon fat to cover the bottom of the pot.

Drain the meat thoroughly and reserve 1 cup of the marinade liquid. Wipe the meat dry. Brown the venison on all sides in the bacon fat. Turn meat to brown well.

Add onions, celery, carrots, garlic, parsley, thyme, salt, and pepper. Sprinkle flour over the vegetables and stir until blended. Cover and set into a moderately hot oven (375°F) or cook covered on top of the stove for 30 minutes.

Heat marinade liquid and stock. Add to meat. Continue cooking for about 2 hours, or until the meat is tender. Stir in currant jelly and rye bread until the bread has softened and the mixture is smooth. Taste and adjust seasoning.

Remove meat, cool slightly, and then slice. Strain the sauce over the meat. Heat thoroughly before serving. Sprinkle crisp bacon and parsley on top.

Accompaniments for Braised Venison

- Boil noodles and drain. Mix with 2 tablespoons or more of olive oil and salt and pepper to taste. Add ½ cup currants that have been soaked in Madeira.
- Heat 24 cooked chestnuts in 2 to 3 tablespoons butter. Surround the venison with chestnuts when serving.

- Cover pitted prunes with port wine. Marinate them for 6 hours to 6 weeks or longer. Keep them covered in a cool place and use as a garnish for game, poultry, ham, or use as a dessert.

Braised Pork Tenderloin with Apples and Prunes
Serves 4.

Gregory Usher, Director of the École de Gastronomie Française Ritz-Escoffier in Paris, is an American who has built his career as translator, teacher, writer, and administrator of cooking schools. As he is a longtime friend of mine, I was delightfully surprised to learn that his folks are our neighbors in Whitingham, Vermont. When he was visiting them a few years ago, Gregory gave three days of lessons to a class in our kitchen. What good fortune for students who lived close by. This recipe is one of the excellent main courses he taught.

1½ cups veal or chicken stock or canned broth
8 pitted prunes
2 tablespoons oil
2 pork tenderloins, about 1 pound each
4 cups peeled and sliced Granny Smith apples
2 medium onions, sliced
3 tablespoons Calvados or hard apple cider
1 tablespoon flour
Salt and pepper
2 tablespoons butter
2 tablespoons sugar
⅓ cup heavy cream

Bring the stock to a boil in a saucepan. Soak prunes in the hot stock for about 1 hour to soften them. Strain and reserve both prunes and stock separately.

Heat a skillet. Add oil. Brown the tenderloins on all sides, then remove them to a dish. Use the same skillet to sauté 2 cups apple slices and onions until they are golden.

Return the tenderloins to the apples and onions. Pour in the Calvados or cider and flame. When the flame dies down, lower heat and stir in flour. Add the reserved stock. Season with salt and pepper and bring to a boil. Cover and simmer until the meat is tender, about 40 to 50 minutes, stirring occasionally. At this point, the cooked pork can be refrigerated with its sauce for up to three days or frozen for up to one month. Before serving, reheat the pork with its sauce on the stove or in the oven.

Prepare the garnish before you slice the meat. Heat butter in a skillet. Sauté the remaining apple slices. Sprinkle sugar on top, then turn the apple slices over in the skillet. The sugar will caramelize. Add the prunes and cook for 4 to 5 minutes over low heat.

Carve pork into ¼-inch slices. Arrange the slices on a warmed platter. Strain the apple-onion sauce into a saucepan. Bring to a boil; add cream and boil for 1 minute. Spoon the sauce over the pork. Garnish with caramelized apple slices and prunes.

✳ *Suggestion*
Serve with a pancake of julienned potatoes.

Braised Shoulder Veal Chops with Sweet and Hot Peppers
Serves 4.

Shoulder veal chops are economical and are sometimes even tastier than the more expensive chops. Prepare the following recipe even if you are cooking for only one or two. The overall flavor will be improved with the extra meat and bone. Divide into portioned dinners for the freezer (freeze for up to two months). On the other hand, you also can cook double the amount, well in advance, for a larger dinner party.

    4 shoulder veal chops, ½ inch thick with bone (about ¾ pound each)
    1 teaspoon kosher (coarse) salt
    ½ teaspoon pepper
    3 tablespoons olive oil
    ¼ cup brandy
    2 medium onions, diced
    2 cloves garlic, minced
    1 tablespoon minced fresh ginger root
    2 sweet red peppers, julienned
    1 or 2 hot peppers, seeded, or ¼ cup Chili Pepper Paste (page 27)
    1 tablespoon flour
    2 sprigs each fresh thyme and marjoram or ½ teaspoon each dried
    1 cup fresh tomatoes, skinned, seeded and diced, or 1 cup crushed canned tomatoes
    1 cup chicken stock, veal stock, vegetable stock, or water
    ½ cup Madeira

Preheat oven to 375°F. Prepare a shallow casserole with a cover to accommodate the chops in one layer. If you braise large amounts, you can layer the chops.

Season the veal with salt and pepper. Heat a skillet and add 2 tablespoons oil. Brown the veal on both sides. Brown two at a time so you do not crowd the skillet. Transfer the chops to the casserole as you brown them.

Pour brandy into the skillet to deglaze and clean away all the brown bits that cling to the pan. Add this broth to the chops.

Heat the remaining oil in the skillet. Add onions, garlic, and ginger. Sauté for a few minutes until the onions are limp and aromas build. Stir in peppers. Lower heat. Lightly mix flour into the vegetables. Add herbs, tomatoes, stock or water, and Madeira. Simmer for 2 minutes and then pour over veal chops. Cover tightly and bake for 45 minutes. Serve with rice, bulghur, or noodles.

✸ *Suggestions*

- You can complete cooking on the stove for 30 minutes instead of in the oven if you have a large, deep-sided sauté pan with a cover.
- For an added spark of taste, sprinkle the tops of the veal chops with grated Parmesan cheese before serving. Set under the broiler for 30 seconds.

Osso Buco (Braised Veal Shank)
Serves 4 to 8.

My friend, Ricky Torella, cooked Osso Buco in his successful family restaurant long before it became so popular. I observed him and included the recipe in my *Menu Cookbook for Entertaining* in 1969. My daughter Betty has made some minor changes to the recipe. Essentially, braising in this recipe is no different from braising other meats, but this unique cut of veal, including bone with marrow, simmers to the point of taste perfection.

Eight 1¼-inch veal shanks with bone marrow in center
½ cup flour (approximately)
¼ cup olive oil
4 tablespoons (¼ cup) butter
1 large onion, diced
1 rib celery, diced
1 carrot, diced
2 cups dry white wine
1 cup canned crushed tomatoes or 1 large
    tomato, peeled and seeded
1 clove garlic, minced
1 cup concentrated or canned veal or chicken stock
2 tablespoons each lemon and orange rind

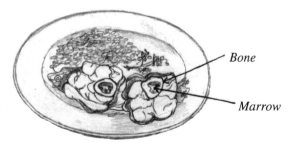
Bone
Marrow

Salt and pepper to taste
¼ cup chopped fresh Italian parsley

Tie each veal shank with a string to hold the bone and marrow in place as it cooks. Dredge the veal in flour.

Use a Dutch oven or an enameled stew pot. Heat the pot slowly; add half the oil and half the butter. Brown pieces of veal on both sides. Do a few at a time so the veal browns evenly. This may take 8 to 10 minutes. Remove all to the side.

Add more oil and butter to the pot. You may vary the amounts. Sauté the onion, celery, and carrot over medium heat for 4 to 5 minutes. Add wine and boil to reduce the liquid slightly. Add tomatoes, garlic, and stock. Return veal to the pot. Cover and simmer for 1¼ hours.

Stir in half the lemon and orange rind. Simmer for another 15 minutes (time may vary). Test the meat with a fork for tenderness. Add salt and pepper, if necessary.

Remove strings. Serve one or two slices per person. Garnish with a sprinkling of lemon and orange rind and parsley.

✳ *Suggestions*

- Traditionally, Osso Buco is served with Arborio rice flavored with saffron.
- If you find only two or three slices of shank in the market, freeze and add more when needed. Cooking larger amounts of meat will develop more flavor in the final sauce.
- Chefs use their own tricks. Ricky used some prosciutto in his recipe. My daughter adds her own veal brown sauce instead of stock and tomato.

Roast Fillet of Beef (Whole Tenderloin)
Serves 8 to 10.

You can never go wrong with a whole tenderloin of beef. Of course, it is company fare, but there is little fuss in preparation. Roast the beef in a preheated oven after all the guests have arrived. There will be enough time for a drink and a simple appetizer. Cook or heat vegetables while the beef rests before slicing. Choose either of the two methods that follow, or try them each at different times.

Method I

1 whole fillet of beef, 4 to 5 pounds, trimmed
2 tablespoons soy sauce
1 tablespoon Worcestershire sauce
1 teaspoon pepper

Make sure the thin membrane covering the beef has been removed from the fillet. The fillet will be thick at one end and very thin at the other. Cut off the very thin end and reserve for stir-frying or ground meat or even for cooking a brown sauce.

Rub the fillet all over with the soy and Worcestershire sauces and pepper. Set it on a rack in a broiling pan. Let it rest at room temperature for at least 2 hours before roasting.

Preheat oven to 400°F. Roast the fillet 30 to 35 minutes for very rare, 45 minutes for medium-rare. Use an instant thermometer to be sure: The inner temperature of the meat will be 130°F for very rare and 145°F for medium-rare.

Transfer meat to a carving board for 8 to 10 minutes while you finish accompaniments. Cut into ¼-inch slices, two or three per person. No sauce is necessary, but you can use the drippings in the pan by deglazing them with 1 cup hot beef stock or canned broth for a quick sauce.

Method II

    1 whole fillet of beef, 4 to 5 pounds, trimmed
    1 tablespoon each soy and Worcestershire sauces
    1 teaspoon pepper
    2 tablespoons olive oil or melted butter
    2 shallots, minced
    1 carrot, finely diced
    2 tablespoons minced fresh Italian parsley
    1 cup dry red wine
    1 cup Brown Sauce (page 86 or 87)

Follow the instructions in Method I for removing the thin membrane and cutting off the thin end of the fillet. Rub the fillet with the sauces and pepper, then cover it with olive oil or melted butter. Strew the shallots, carrot, and parsley in a shallow baking pan. Place fillet in the pan and let it rest at room temperature for at least 2 hours before roasting.

Preheat oven to 400°F. Roast the fillet for 30 to 35 minutes. Remove the fillet to a carving board.

Deglaze the roasting pan with dry red wine. Scrape all bits away from the bottom and sides of the pan. Strain into Brown Sauce. Boil for 5 to 7 minutes to reduce the liquid. Carve the beef into ¼-inch slices, two or three per person. Strain the sauce onto the beef or serve on the side.

Triangle of Roasted Rump
Serves 6 to 8.

Today there is uniformity in labeling meat. By law, every label informs the consumer as to the cut and section of the animal. In many cases, however, the shape and size is more important to the knowledgeable cook.

The rump is the Bottom Round as defined by the label. My butcher friend, Carl, clued me in to a most important fact. The triangular-shaped rump, at 2 to 3 pounds, is the most flavorful and economical cut for rare roast beef. Look for that small *triangular* shape.

Use a paste of ginger and Dijon mustard for seasoning. Omit salt and pepper. The cooking aroma is tantalizing.

> ¼ cup Dijon mustard
> 1 tablespoon powdered ginger
> One 2- to 3-pound rump of beef

Mix mustard and ginger into a paste. Rub the paste all over the meat. Let it rest at room temperature for at least 1 hour if you are roasting the same day. If not, season the beef, wrap in plastic wrap, and refrigerate for up to three days before roasting.

Preheat oven to 400°F. Place beef on a rack in a broiler pan. Roast for 40 to 60 minutes (about 18 to 20 minutes per pound). Doneness also depends on shape. Use an instant meat thermometer—130°F for very rare, 145°F for medium-rare.

Allow the beef to rest for 10 minutes to permit juices to settle evenly throughout. Carve into very thin slices. Start at the pointed end first, but turn the meat to make sure you are slicing against the grain. Serve immediately with any juices that collect as you slice.

✳ *Suggestions*

- Use leftovers for sandwiches or in a stir-fry dish.
- If there is a large, unsliced piece left over, braise it like a pot roast for another meal.
- The rump is a perfect cut for the barbecue.

Roast Leg of Lamb
Serves 8 to 10.

Roast Leg of Lamb is always my choice for simplicity, minimum preparation, and unquestionably good results. When in doubt as to the number of guests, this dish goes the farthest. Bake potatoes at the same time, and the dinner is all but completed.

1 leg of lamb, 6 to 8 pounds
4 or 5 cloves garlic, sliced
10 to 12 sprigs fresh rosemary or 1 tablespoon dried
Kosher (coarse) salt and pepper
2 or 3 tablespoons flour

Cut away any large chunks of fat on the bottom and sides of the leg (or ask your butcher to do this). Leave a small covering of fat on top. Make at least 10 to 12 slits into the flesh or fat on top and bottom. Insert a slice of garlic and a small sprig of rosemary into each slit (use a sprinkling of dried rosemary in each slot if you do not have fresh).

Season meat with salt and pepper, then pat all over with flour. This can be done 1 or 2 days ahead and refrigerated. If not, prepare earlier in the day. Set aside until time to roast.

Preheat oven to 400°F. Roast the lamb for 1 hour; reduce heat to 350°F. Roast for 30 minutes more. Test for preferred doneness with an instant thermometer (130°F for very rare, 140°F for medium-rare, and 160°F for medium). There is great variance in personal preference, but there are always well-done ends if the meat is too rare for some. Set lamb on a carving board for at least 10 minutes before slicing.

Although most of the time I serve Roast Leg of Lamb with its juices, I always deglaze the hot roasting pan with broth, wine, or both. I strain it into a saucepan and heat to reduce the volume of liquid slightly. Serve this sauce separately, or freeze it for another time.

✳ Suggestions

- Bake quarters of unpeeled potatoes in another pan while the lamb is roasting.
- Substitute other herbs for rosemary, if you prefer.
- There is an old technique of roasting the lamb on peeled potatoes. Roast slowly at 300°F for 5 to 6 hours. The lamb will be well done to a crisp with fabulous-tasting potatoes.

Stuffed Boned Leg of Lamb
Serves 8 to 10.

Ask your butcher to bone the lamb for you, butterfly style. Tell him that you are stuffing it, so he should be especially careful to make it as even as possible. Stuff the lamb one or two days ahead. The herbs and seasonings mellow to flavor the meat. Although this dish is best when fresh herbs are available, use half the amount of dried herbs at other times.

¼ cup olive oil
2 cloves garlic, minced

2 to 3 medium ripe tomatoes (about 1 pound) skinned, seeded, and chopped
2 tablespoons each chopped fresh Italian parsley, basil, and thyme
½ cup plain bread crumbs
Salt and pepper to taste
½ pound Swiss chard or spinach leaves
1 leg of lamb, 6 to 8 pounds, boned
¼ cup flour

Mix oil, garlic, tomatoes, herbs, and bread crumbs. Season with salt and pepper to taste. Blanch the Swiss chard or spinach leaves in boiling water for 30 seconds. Refresh in cold water. Dry on paper toweling.

If the thickness of the lamb is very uneven, pound it under aluminum foil to flatten it. Spread the seasoned mixture of tomatoes, herbs, and bread crumbs onto the boned side of lamb. Cover with leaves of Swiss chard or spinach. Roll up (like a jelly roll) and tie with string at ½-inch intervals. Season all over with salt and pepper, then roll it in flour. Place on a rack in a roasting pan.

Preheat oven to 400°F. Roast lamb for 1¼ hours. Test for doneness with an instant meat thermometer, preferably rare (130°F) to medium-rare (140°F). Set aside to rest for at least 10 minutes. Carve into ½-inch slices and serve on a bed of Rice Pilaf (page 153).

✳ Suggestions

- Bake peeled potatoes in the roasting pan or in another pan as an excellent special accompaniment.
- For summertime parties, prepare the lamb ahead and refrigerate. Slice thinly at room temperature and serve with mustard.

Roast Rack of Lamb
One rack serves 2 to 4.

Rack of lamb is definitely a high-budget meat. For members of your family or dear friends who enjoy lamb, choose it for birthday celebrations or other special events.

1 or 2 racks rib lamb chops
Kosher (coarse) salt and pepper
3 cloves garlic
1 cup plain bread crumbs
½ cup minced fresh parsley
1 tablespoon each minced fresh chervil and thyme or ½ teaspoon each dried

Ask your butcher to cut off the chine bone from the rack of lamb. He or she will trim it to make it easier for you to carve. Trim the top fat, but leave a thin coating of the fat.

Score the fat across the front and back of the rack about 2 inches from the end of the bone. Scrape and clean away the fat and meat up to the scored guideline. This will make a separation between the bones but keep the meat portion intact.

Season the lamb with salt and pepper. Rub it well with cut pieces of garlic. Mix bread crumbs and herbs together. Preheat oven to 425°F.

Prepare a shallow roasting pan to hold one or two racks. Roast the rack of lamb for 20 minutes. Sprinkle the bread-crumb mixture on top, pressing it down with a small spatula. Roast the lamb for another 10 minutes. Take it out of the oven and let it rest for 5 minutes. Carve between the ribs for individual portions. The outside ribs will be medium, the inside will be medium-rare. There are choices for all preferences.

If you roast two racks, intertwine the ribs before serving and carving for a special presentation.

✺ *Suggestions*

- Serve duchess potatoes and baked tomatoes as accompaniments.
- Pipe out mashed potatoes enriched with egg yolk onto a greased cookie sheet. Brown in the oven while roasting the rack of lamb.

A Sampling of Ground-Meat Recipes

My freezer always has a supply of ground meat, usually in 4- to 8-ounce packages. The ground-meat category includes beef, veal, pork, lamb, and, of course, the poultry family. It was not easy to choose this small sampling from my recipe file.

Beefburgers with Onion and Thyme
Serves 3 to 4.

This is a hamburger with frills. My one-time student-teacher trainee, Ellen Greene, shared this recipe with me. As Assistant Food Editor of *Woman's Day* magazine, she now shares recipes with people around the United States. How satisfying that is for me! This is her recipe just as she wrote it.

Beefburgers

½ cup finely chopped onion (1 medium-sized onion)
3 tablespoons vegetable oil
¾ teaspoon salt
½ teaspoon dried thyme
¼ teaspoon pepper
1¼ pounds very lean ground beef chuck
1 egg, slightly beaten
½ cup all-purpose flour
1 tablespoon chopped fresh parsley

Sauce

½ cup beef stock
⅓ cup dry vermouth
1 teaspoon cornstarch

Sauté the onion in 1 tablespoon oil in a medium-sized skillet for 3 minutes or until the onion is tender but not browned. Remove from heat. Stir in salt, thyme, and pepper, and let the mixture cool briefly.

Mix beef, egg, and the onion mixture. Shape into three or four 1½-inch thick patties.

Heat the remaining 2 tablespoons oil in the skillet. Dip beefburgers in flour to coat both sides (do this just before frying). Add to the skillet and cook over medium-low heat, 6 to 8 minutes per side for medium.

While the beefburgers cook, mix sauce ingredients in a small bowl. Remove burgers to a plate. Pour off fat, if any, from the skillet.

Pour sauce mixture into the skillet, bring to a low boil, and cook until clear and thickened. Return beefburgers and cook about 30 seconds, turning once to coat both sides with sauce.

To serve, spoon sauce over burgers, then sprinkle with parsley.

✳ Suggestion

I broil an unadorned 4-ounce hamburger without seasoning. For perfection, the meat must be freshly ground. Pass the mustard, ketchup, and other condiments around the table.

Thai Beef Salad
Serves 4.

Thai cuisine was hardly known in the United States in the early 1970s. Joel Levy, a friend of ours, had worked in an officers' mess in Vietnam and came home with a notebook of especially interesting recipes. This Thai Beef Salad is a combination of cold and hot, it is light yet filling, and it is very fast to cook.

1 head romaine lettuce
½ cup water
1 pound ground lean beef
1 medium red onion, sliced thin
1 bunch scallion greens, diced
4 teaspoons fresh lime juice
1 tablespoon Fish Sauce (Nuoi Mam) or soy sauce
2 teaspoons crushed red pepper
1 tablespoon chopped fresh cilantro
Salt and pepper to taste

Separate the lettuce leaves. Wash and dry well. Place them around a large round or oval platter.

Heat water in a skillet. When it comes to a boil, add the beef. Stir with a fork to separate the pieces of beef. When the raw red color is gone, remove the skillet from the heat.

Mix in the remaining ingredients, adding salt and pepper to taste. Mound the beef mixture in the center of the lettuce leaves. Use the lettuce as a scoop. This salad is fun finger food, but forks and knives are also permitted.

✳ *Suggestion*
Serve with a bowl of steaming hot rice.

Tiny Cabbage Rolls
Serves 6.

If you are searching for recipes that cut down on meat, this is a good choice. Adding rice and bulghur extends the meat to make an ample filling for the cabbage leaves. The seasoning is important, so use every bit of it.

1 large cabbage, preferably with outer green leaves
¾ pound ground meat (beef, veal, lamb, or poultry)
¾ cup long-grain rice

½ cup bulghur, soaked in water for 10 minutes and drained
¼ cup minced scallion
1 teaspoon salt
¾ teaspoon freshly ground pepper
½ cup fresh lemon juice
1 cup homemade chicken or vegetable stock or 1 cup canned
¼ cup minced garlic
4 tablespoons melted butter or olive oil

Cut deeply around the core of the cabbage. Remove the core and discard it. This will loosen the leaves when the cabbage is blanched. Immerse the cabbage in boiling water. As the leaves fall apart and soften, place them on paper toweling. Cut each leaf in half in fairly even sizes of about 3 inches.

Mix meat, rice, bulghur, scallion, salt, and pepper. Place a teaspoonful of the mixture in the middle of each leaf. Roll each leaf loosely around the filling to form a tube, leaving room for expansion. Place the cabbage rolls in a Dutch oven or stew pot, one row on top of the other. Pour in the lemon juice and stock, then the garlic and butter or oil. Cover and simmer on the lowest heat for 1 to 1½ hours. If the liquid evaporates completely, add a little water. Serve hot, or serve cold on a summer's day.

✳ Suggestions

- In the Middle East these cabbage rolls are eaten dry as a finger food.
- Use the filling to make tiny meatballs without cabbage. Bake in a casserole with the same seasoning at 375°F for 40 minutes.

Sauerkraut and Meat Patties
Serves 4 to 6.

Choucroute Garni is the delicious Alsatian stewed sauerkraut with smoked meat. With apologies to my Alsatian friends, Claire and Pierre Wagner, I have improvised one of my fast American copies of their classic recipe.

1 can sauerkraut (27 ounces)
1 tablespoon oil
1 onion, diced
1 carrot, scraped and diced
1 Granny Smith apple, peeled and diced
1 cup chicken stock or canned broth
1 cup dry white wine
1 cup water
¾ pound ground beef or pork (chicken and turkey are good substitutes)

2 cloves garlic, minced
1 small onion, grated
½ teaspoon each dried oregano, basil, and paprika
¼ teaspoon each ground allspice and dry mustard
⅛ teaspoon ground anise
⅛ teaspoon cayenne pepper
¼ cup bread crumbs soaked in ¼ cup water
Salt and pepper to taste

Drain sauerkraut in a colander. Run cold water through it to remove the saltiness. Press out the water, then separate the strands.

Prepare a 4- to 6-quart stew pot with a tight-fitting cover. Heat the pot over medium heat. Add oil, then diced onion, carrot, and apple. Sauté until they are softened and glazed, about 3 to 4 minutes.

Add stock, wine, and water, and stir. Boil to reduce the liquid slightly. Cover and simmer for 10 to 12 minutes.

In the meantime, mix the meat with the remaining ingredients, except for the salt and pepper, which you will add after you have tested the seasoning by cooking a tiny ball of meat in the simmering stew for 1 minute.

Divide the meat mixture into 8 or 10 patties. Broil or pan-broil the patties for 2 minutes on each side, just to brown the surface. Place the patties in the sauerkraut. Cover the pot and simmer for 20 to 25 minutes. Serve hot with boiled potatoes, pickles, and mustard.

✷ Suggestions

- Sauerkraut and Meat Patties are just great when served with crusty bread and beer.
- Serve the stewed sauerkraut with grilled frankfurters.
- Add sausage, ham, or smoked pork to the sauerkraut instead of meat patties.

The Lianides's Moussaka
Serves 6 to 8.

Moussaka, the Greek and Middle Eastern casserole of eggplant, meat, and cheese, is found in a number of books. I believe this recipe is the best that I have seen, thanks to Leon Lianides, owner of the Coach House in Manhattan. I have used it in my cooking classes for lessons on eggplant, the reduction of wine, and the sublime finish of white sauce enriched with eggs and cheese. Lessons in cooking go hand in hand with this superb dish.

Eggplant

2 medium eggplants (about 3 pounds)
1 tablespoon kosher (coarse) salt
1 cup flour
½ cup olive oil
8 tablespoons (¼ pound) butter
2 cups dry red wine
3 tablespoons tomato purée
¼ bay leaf
Pinch thyme
Pinch marjoram
2 medium-sized onions, finely chopped
1¼ pounds lean lamb, ground twice (beef may be substituted)
¼ cup chopped parsley
¼ teaspoon cinnamon
¾ teaspoon salt
½ teaspoon pepper
⅓ cup plain bread crumbs
⅓ cup grated fresh Parmesan cheese

White Sauce

4 tablespoons unsalted butter
4 tablespoons flour
2 cups hot milk
½ teaspoon salt
⅛ teaspoon nutmeg
2 eggs, beaten
½ pint ricotta cheese

Cut unpeeled eggplants into ½-inch slices. Sprinkle the slices with salt. Cover with wax paper and weight them down with heavy canned goods or other weighted objects. This will extract the bitter juices. Dry each slice well and then dredge them in flour.

Heat a large, deep skillet with olive oil and 2 tablespoons butter. Brown the eggplant slices on both sides, a few pieces at a time. Drain them on paper toweling.

In a saucepan, reduce the wine to half its volume, about 1 cup. Add tomato purée, bay leaf, thyme, and marjoram. Simmer for 10 minutes. Remove bay leaf and set the tomato-wine sauce aside.

Heat a skillet with 2 tablespoons butter. Sauté onions, then add lamb and cook for 10 minutes. Stir in tomato-wine sauce, parsley, cinnamon, salt, and pepper. Reduce heat and simmer until most of the liquid has been absorbed. Remove from the heat. Season to taste with salt and pepper.

To make the White Sauce, melt 4 tablespoons butter in a saucepan. Add flour to make a roux. Stir in hot milk and whisk to smoothness. Season with salt and nutmeg. Simmer, while stirring, until the sauce is thick and smooth. Remove from heat. Cool for 5 minutes. Thoroughly mix in beaten eggs and ricotta cheese.

Preheat oven to 350°F. Grease a baking pan or casserole (9" x 13" or a 16-inch oval) with the remaining butter. Sprinkle bread crumbs evenly over the bottom. Arrange a layer of half of the eggplant slices. Spread the meat mixture on top. Cover with the remaining eggplant slices. Pour the white sauce over all to cover completely. Sprinkle with Parmesan cheese.

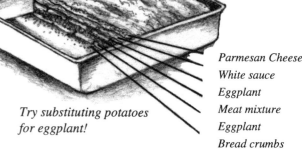

Parmesan Cheese
White sauce
Eggplant
Meat mixture
Eggplant
Bread crumbs

Try substituting potatoes for eggplant!

Bake for 45 to 50 minutes until the top is golden and bubbling. Remove from the oven and cool for a few minutes to facilitate cutting. Divide into squares for number of portions.

✸ Suggestions

- The Moussaka is even more flavorful and can be cut more evenly when allowed to rest for several hours or overnight in the refrigerator. Reheat before serving.
- Use the wine-meat mixture as a filling for rolled crêpes or rolled eggplant slices.

Herb's Chili
Serves 2.

My husband enjoys cooking when I am away. Quite different from his extravagant fillet of beef with cognac and sweet cream is his chili, a fast and simple dinner. He cooks it for two and sometimes for four to six, inviting friends over to join him.

    1½ tablespoons olive oil
    ¾ cup chopped onion
    2 large cloves garlic, minced
    ¾ pound ground beef

4 medium fresh tomatoes, peeled and seeded or 2 cups crushed tomatoes
1 teaspoon chili powder
6 tablespoons tomato paste
⅛ teaspoon paprika
Dash Tabasco sauce
½ cup red wine
One 16-ounce can kidney beans
Salt

Heat oil in a stew pot. Sauté onion, garlic, and beef in oil until onion is translucent.

Add tomatoes, chili powder, tomato paste, paprika, Tabasco sauce, and wine. Bring to a boil. Reduce heat to low and simmer for 30 minutes. Add beans, cover, and simmer for another 30 minutes. Season with salt.

Barbecuing

Early in our married life my husband and I were lucky to be able to rent a lower floor apartment with a little garden out back. We wasted no time in investing in an outdoor grill. For us, the grill meant time spent out in the fresh air, and outdoor barbecuing became a delightful way to cook in the summer. Until then, I had been the kitchen cook. With outdoor cooking, my husband and I collaborated, as we do to this day.

We grill outdoors from early spring through late autumn even in inclement weather. The highlights of a summer season are gatherings of family and friends for Memorial Day, the Fourth of July, and Labor Day. Even though frankfurters and hamburgers are the traditional fare, we often smoke a turkey (page 235), grill a leg of lamb, or cook our favorite ribs. With these larger cuts, we use two grills and always place a drip pan in the center of the gray hot coals. We cover the grill, with the vents open, as the meat cooks. This gives us free time to enjoy appetizers with our guests.

We have found that ribs are favorites at our barbecues. As a finger food they appeal even to the most fastidious knife-and-fork users at outdoor parties. Choose from Lamb Riblets, Beef Short Ribs, Country-Style Pork Ribs, or Spareribs.

Simple Facts for Barbecuing
1. Consider the outdoor grill as a broiling or roasting unit.
2. Wait for the coals to become hot and ash-gray before grilling.
3. For aromatic seasoning, add water-soaked hickory, mesquite, maple, or fruitwood chips to the hot coals.

4. If you are barbecuing larger cuts of meat and poultry, pile the hot coals around the edge of the fire rack. Leave room in the center for a large enough aluminum foil drip pan to catch the drippings. Cover the grill, with vents open, for slow cooking.
5. Use the cover to prevent the fat from flaring. Keep a water sprayer handy for the many times you broil without a cover, causing fat to flame.
6. Most important, be an observant caretaker. Keep your eye and mind on the fire and food. Be careful to avoid burning and overcharring.
7. Take advantage of the fact that the hot coals usually last longer than the meal you have cooked. Plan ahead and grill a chicken or other main dish after the cooking for the day has been completed. Grill a small roast beef or loin of pork on the still-hot coals for the week's summer salads or sandwiches.

Rubs, Marinades, Bastes, and Sauces

Rubs, marinades, bastes, and sauces are essential to the success of barbecued dishes. Rubs are combinations of dry seasonings rubbed into the surface of meats before barbecuing. Marinades are used as tenderizers as well as basting sauces. Bastes range from oil or melted butter to wine, vinegar, and stocks. Sauces are used for dipping or side dishes.

Dry Rub (Seasoned Salt)
Makes a generous ½ cup.

¼ cup kosher (coarse) salt
1 tablespoon pepper
½ teaspoon dry mustard
½ teaspoon allspice
1 tablespoon each thyme and marjoram
¼ teaspoon cayenne pepper

Thoroughly mix together all ingredients. Store in a jar. Use judiciously on chops and roasts, just enough to season all sides. Store with well-marked pantry seasonings in this amount or even double.

Light Marinade
Makes 2 cups.

Use this marinade for shoulder veal, lamb, pork, and poultry.

1 cup chicken stock
1 cup dry white wine
1 tablespoon each chopped fresh parsley and tarragon

1 teaspoon paprika
Salt and pepper to taste

Mix all ingredients together in a dish large enough to accommodate the meat. Marinate the meat for at least 1 hour before barbecuing or refrigerate overnight. After marinating meat, always wipe off excess marinade before grilling, especially marinades with paprika, soy, sugar or tomato — these will burn rapidly at grilling temperatures. Use the marinades at the end of the grilling time as a baste or a sauce.

Apple Cider Marinade
Makes 1 ¼ cups.

Use this Apple Cider Marinade for pork and poultry.

   1 cup apple cider
   2 tablespoons soy sauce
   2 tablespoons maple syrup
   ½ teaspoon dry mustard
   Salt and pepper to taste

Follow the directions in the recipe for Light Marinade.

Chinese Marinade
Makes 1 ¾ cups.

This Chinese Marinade is tasty on ribs, pork, lamb, and beef.

   4 tablespoons Hoisin sauce
   3 tablespoons soy sauce
   2 tablespoons minced garlic
   3 tablespoons sugar
   1 cup canned chicken broth
   1 tablespoon dry sherry

Follow the directions in the recipe for Light Marinade.

Orange-Tomato Marinade
Makes 2 cups.

Use this marinade for pork and veal.

   1 cup orange juice
   ½ cup canned crushed tomatoes

1 tablespoon honey
½ cup chicken or vegetable stock
1 teaspoon each chopped parsley and oregano

Follow the directions in the recipe for Light Marinade.

Tomato Barbecue Sauce
Makes 3 cups.

This Tomato Barbecue Sauce can be used for basting or dipping.

2 cups canned crushed tomatoes in purée
½ cup catsup
2 tablespoons minced fresh garlic
2 teaspoons chili powder
1 teaspoon dry mustard
4 tablespoons brown sugar
1 tablespoon Worcestershire sauce
2 tablespoons red wine vinegar
¼ cup oil
1 teaspoon kosher (coarse) salt
½ teaspoon freshly ground pepper

Stir all the ingredients together and then simmer for 10 minutes.

Sweet and Sour Sauce
Makes 2 cups.

This Sweet and Sour Sauce is excellent for dipping.

1 cup canned chicken broth
1 tablespoon minced garlic
1 tablespoon minced fresh ginger root
½ cup white vinegar
½ cup sugar
¼ cup fresh lemon juice
1 tablespoon grated lemon rind
¼ cup orange marmalade
¼ cup apricot jam
½ teaspoon curry
Salt and freshly ground pepper to taste

Stir all ingredients together in a saucepan and simmer for 5 minutes.

Barbecue Recipes

Barbecued Whole Leg of Lamb
Serves 10 to 12.

One 7- or 8-pound leg of lamb
2 teaspoons Dry Rub (page 270)
4 to 6 cloves garlic, cut in slivers
8 to 10 good-sized branches fresh rosemary

Trim the heavy fat from lamb, but leave a thin coating of fat on top. Cut gashes into the top and bottom of the leg. Insert a sliver of garlic and a few rosemary leaves into each gash.

Before grilling the lamb, place all the rosemary branches on the grilling rack. Set the lamb on top and cover the barbecue (leave vents open). Cook the lamb for about 1½ hours, turning it over once during that time. The heat of the fire may vary, so begin grilling 2 hours before serving. Barbecued lamb is delicious at all stages, rare to well done. Serve with Sweet and Sour Sauce (page 272) or just Dijon mustard.

Lamb Riblets
Serves 4 to 6.

4 or 5 pounds lamb riblets
1 recipe marinade (pages 270–272)
1 recipe Tomato Barbecue Sauce (page 272)

Lamb riblets are cut from the breast of lamb into individual ribs. Marinate them in your choice of marinades and refrigerate overnight.

When ready to grill, wipe excess marinade off each riblet. Reserve the marinade. Grill for 30 to 40 minutes in a covered barbecue (leave vents open). Baste with marinade and serve with Tomato Barbecue Sauce.

Beef Short Ribs
Serves 4.

1 cup dry red wine
¼ cup Dijon mustard

1 teaspoon dry mustard
1 tablespoon minced garlic
1 tablespoon minced fresh ginger root
1 teaspoon Worcestershire sauce
1 teaspoon dried thyme or several sprigs fresh thyme
2 bay leaves, broken into pieces
2 tablespoons minced fresh parsley
Dash Tabasco sauce
4 to 5 pounds beef short ribs
1 recipe Tomato Barbecue Sauce (page 272)

Mix all ingredients, except ribs and sauce, in a large bowl. Place ribs in the mixture; coat them thoroughly. Marinate overnight in the refrigerator.

Before grilling, wipe the marinade off the ribs. When the coals are hot and gray, place the ribs on the rack. Cover the grill with the vents open. The cover should be lifted from time to time so the ribs can be turned to prevent scorching. Complete grilling should take from 1 to 1½ hours.

Serve with Tomato Barbecue Sauce.

Country-Style Pork Ribs
Serves 4 to 6.

Country-style pork ribs are similar to pork chops, although they are laced with more fat and are perfect for barbecuing. The fat renders out over the hot coals, but the meat will remain tender and juicy.

4 or 5 pounds pork ribs
2 teaspoons Dry Rub (page 270)
½ cup sweet vermouth

Season the ribs with the Dry Rub. Grill ribs about 10 minutes on each side. Baste with vermouth.

Spareribs
Serves 4 to 6.

3 or 4 pounds spareribs (one large rack)
1 recipe marinade (pages 270-272)
1 recipe Sweet and Sour Sauce (page 272)

Trim any outside fat on the ribs. Cut the rack in half for easier handling but do not separate the individual ribs. Although some books will advise you to parboil the ribs before grilling, I never do.

Marinate the spareribs in your choice of marinades (my favorite is the Chinese Marinade). Be sure to wipe off excess before grilling and reserve the remaining marinade. Grill about 45 minutes in a covered barbecue (leave vents open). Turn the ribs occasionally. Baste for the last 15 minutes with the marinade. Carve between the ribs. Serve with the Sweet and Sour Sauce for dipping.

11

Pastries, Cakes, and Cookies

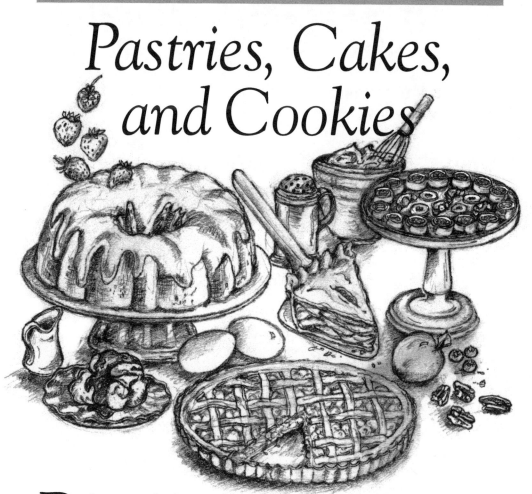

Baking is an absolute joy. Many people tell me that they would rather bake than cook, yet we cannot live on cake alone. Although my husband and I resist the rich and delicious desserts in our everyday menus, holidays and special occasions call for the ultimate. Everyone looks forward to the presentation of the sweet finale.

My first and most rewarding experience in learning to bake started with puff pastry, the most difficult technique of all. The excitement generated by this first performance actually started my career as a teacher of cookery. I was young, confident, and inspired—absolutely convinced that I could teach others to construct these crisp, blown-up, airy pastries. Success breeds success, so I broadened my horizons to include my favorite desserts in this chapter.

Pastry Recipes

Classic Puff Pastry
Makes about 3 pounds.

There are two methods for making puff pastry, the classic method and the quick or rough (so-called) method. Once you learn the technique of the Classic method, you will probably continue to use it as I do. It is the gossamer crust for savory appetizers as well as desserts.

Pointers before starting:
1. Work on a cool day; morning is generally a good time.
2. Prepare space in your refrigerator to rest dough between turns.
3. Roll dough on a cool surface—Corian, Plexiglass, marble, or granite.
4. You will need a heavy rolling pin, a plastic scraper, a steel dough knife, a flour dredger, a dry flour brush, and some good cookie sheets.
5. When you make Classic Puff Pastry for the first time, plan to be available for several hours. With experience you will find that the dough can be refrigerated or frozen at different stages.

> 3 cups unbleached all-purpose flour
> 1 cup cake flour
> 3 ounces unsalted butter, cut into bits (about 12 pieces)
> 1 cup plus 1 or 2 tablespoons ice water and
>   1½ teaspoons salt, mixed together
> 4 sticks (1 pound) unsalted butter, at 60 to
>   65 degrees

Preparation of Basic Dough: Sift both flours into a bowl. Remove ½ cup and set aside. Add 3 ounces of butter to the flour in the bowl. Rub the butter and flour with your fingers into tiny crumbs. Gradually add 1 cup salted ice water to form a dough with your hand. Use a little more water, if necessary. The dough will look rough; do not work it to smoothness. Cover the dough with a cloth and set it aside while you prepare the butter.

Place the 1 pound butter on a smooth surface. Sprinkle with the reserved ½ cup flour on top. Use the heel of your hand to soften butter mixed with flour. Form into a 5- or 6-inch block. Use a plastic scraper to press the block flat and even, about 1 inch thick.

Rolling and Folding: Always dust the rolling surface and the dough with flour. Roll the dough into a round of about 12 to 14 inches in diameter, leaving the center thicker than the edges. Place the brick of butter in the center (A). The butter should have the same consistency as the dough.

Fold two opposite sides of the dough to overlap, enclosing the butter in an envelope of dough (B).

Dust the surface and dough with flour (C). Press the dough lightly with the rolling pin to distribute butter evenly and create a square or oblong shape. Press it again to elongate it to about 10 inches in length (D). Roll it from the center toward the outer end and then from the center toward you. Do not roll over the edge, but keep the thickness even throughout. Always move the dough and use a little dusting of flour to prevent sticking.

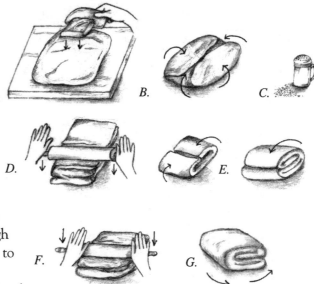

Fold the outer ends of the dough in toward the center. Double it again to make four layers (E). Lightly press the layers together with the rolling pin (F). Change the position of the dough by giving it a quarter turn to the right. It will look like the pages of a book (G).

Flour the dough and the surface. Press the dough down lightly at even intervals with the rolling pin to make it easier to roll. Repeat the rolling as before. Start at the center and roll out in two directions to form a rectangle of at least 20 inches by about 7 inches. Fold both sides toward the center, then over to make four layers. You have now made two turns. You will be making two more turns before completing the dough. Dust with flour, cover, and refrigerate for about 30 or 40 minutes. At this point you can also refrigerate it in plastic wrap or aluminum foil for one day.

Repeat this rolling again. If the dough has become too firm, let it rest at room temperature to soften. Always press the dough evenly with the rolling pin before rolling again. Try to keep shape rectangular.

The dough is completed when it is rolled and folded four times.

Baking: Although a very long chapter can be written on ways and means for using and baking Classic Puff Pastry, the following is one of the simplest.

After the completed dough has rested in the refrigerator, place it on a floured surface. It will be extremely firm. Let it soften for 10 minutes; press it down with the rolling pin. Cut it into four or six even pieces. This will make it easier to handle.

Press down each piece, then roll it into a length of 12 to 18 inches. Always roll it on the smooth, not the cut, side. If you keep the thickness even at ¼ inch, the result will be layers of blown-up pastry after baking. Cut each length into 2- or 3-inch squares or rounds if you wish. Always cut down sharply for best results. Turn each piece over (bottom-side up) onto a cold cookie sheet. Refrigerate before baking or freeze them in a box for up to one month.

Preheat oven to 425°F.

Bake pastries for 15 to 20 minutes. Remove to a rack. When they are cool, slip a knife through each one to cut it in half horizontally. Remove any moist dough inside. Fill each one with fresh berries, sliced peaches, warmed sautéed apple slices, or custards of your choice. Of course, ice creams and frozen yogurts are American favorites.

❋ Suggestions

- A remarkable property of this dough is that it can be made and frozen, unbaked, up to a month. Always bake it on the day to be enjoyed.
- Keep all scraps of dough. Put one next to another to roll into a sheet or place one on top of the other. Freeze, well wrapped. When ready to use, defrost. Roll dough into a ⅛-inch thickness. Use a cookie cutter to form round shapes and press each in grated cheese or sugar, for a savory or a sweet pastry. Bake for 5 to 7 minutes at 425°F.
- Use a cookie cutter to cut out round shapes. Top fish, chicken, and meat pies to form a crust.

Essie's Danish Elephant Ears

If you have mastered "Puff Pastry" (page 278) you will probably use the leftover dough for these gossamer ovals. If not, follow this receipe for a perfect "melt in the mouth" cookie.

½ pound unsalted butter, cold but pliable
2 cups all-purpose flour
7 tablespoons ice water
1 to 1½ cups sugar

Break butter into 16 pieces. Place butter in a bowl with flour. Toss together with your hand. Add water and form a ball. Divide into 2 pieces and refrigerate for 1 hour.

Flour a rolling surface. Roll out dough ⅛" thick. Use a 1½" cookie cutter to cut out rounds. Place these on a plate, overlapping. Reroll scraps. Refrigerate until firm (1 hour).

Preheat oven to 450°F.

Prepare 2 or 3 ungreased cookie sheets. Place sheet of wax paper on your counter. Make a mound of about 2 tablespoons of sugar on the center of paper. Place 3 rounds of dough, side by side on the sugar. Roll them once to elongate them. Turn them over and roll again. Place these on a cookie sheet. Using a fork prick each one many times while you pull to make a longer oval.

Bake cookies for 5 to 6 minutes. Look at them before that. If they have glazed turn them over. Watch at this point because they burn easily but they are well worth your time! Cool on a rack. They keep well in a cookie tin for 2 or 3 weeks and freeze up to 3 months.

Baklava Rolls (Sourota)
Makes 75.

The Greek phyllo dough is certainly a cousin to Classic Puff Pastry. Although I continue to make my own Classic Puff Pastry, I do buy phyllo. There still are people who pull these thin sheets by hand!

Phyllo is always layered, sheet on sheet, with a brushing of melted, preferably clarified, butter. When the layers are baked, they puff and crisp as does Classic Puff Pastry. Dozens of variations are constructed with phyllo but Sourota, a ruffled open cylinder, is the most fun to make.

Some years ago Kathy Boulukas, a student of mine, taught me how to form this pastry. Kathy is chairperson of the Recipe Club of her church. The club has completed two best-selling Greek cookbooks.

Before you start, find or purchase a wooden dowel, measuring about ¾ inch in diameter by 8 inches long. Also, prepare the clarified butter at your convenience. It keeps for at least one month in the refrigerator and can be used in cooking and baking.

Syrup

2 cups sugar
2 cups water
1 tablespoon lemon juice
1 stick cinnamon
⅓ cup honey

Filling

4 sticks (1 pound) unsalted butter
½ pound walnuts, finely chopped
½ cup zwieback crumbs (or plain bread crumbs)
1 teaspoon cinnamon
¼ cup sugar

1 pound phyllo

Combine sugar, water, lemon juice, and cinnamon in a saucepan. Bring to a boil and simmer for 40 minutes. Remove from heat and stir in honey. Set aside to cool.

To clarify butter, melt butter and simmer over low heat for 20 to 30 minutes. Do not allow butter to brown. The milky separation on top will turn to a thin film with long, slow cooking. Strain it for a resulting clear yellow liquid—called clarified butter—which may be stored in the refrigerator for up to four weeks. Clarified butter is often suggested for baking and cooking. Like oil, it can take much higher heat than fresh butter. You will use about ½ cup for this recipe. Refrigerate the remainder for future use.

Combine walnuts, zwieback, cinnamon, and sugar. Use scissors to cut the phyllo sheets into thirds. Cover with plastic wrap or a damp cloth.

Preheat oven to 350°F.

Using one sheet of phyllo at a time, brush each with butter and sprinkle 1 teaspoon filling along the bottom edge of the sheet (A). Fold in side edges about ½ inch, then fold bottom edge over filling (B). Place a dowel on the bottom edge of the phyllo, and roll dough loosely around the dowel to form a tube (C). Push in phyllo along the dowel from both sides to gather it in folds (D). Hold pastry with one hand and pull out the dowel with the other (E). Place

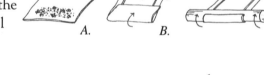

A.   B.   C.

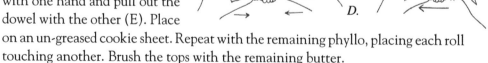

D.   E.

on an un-greased cookie sheet. Repeat with the remaining phyllo, placing each roll touching another. Brush the tops with the remaining butter.

Bake for 15 minutes until golden. Pour cool syrup over the hot pastry. The pastry should sizzle. Immediately remove to a cooling rack.

☀ Suggestions

- These Baklava Rolls can be prepared days in advance, refrigerated for up to three days or frozen for up to one month.
- Make only half the recipe; freeze the other half of phyllo for another time.

Basic Pie Crust
Makes one 8- to 10-inch double crust.

The American pie has always been a great favorite in our homes, and I am sure it will never go out of fashion. I realize that many people are intimidated by this simple pastry that cracks when you want it to roll smoothly. Throw caution to the winds. Ignore the do's and don'ts. Yes, do follow the recipe, but only experience, your hands, and keen observation will bring the best results.

Even if you need only a single crust, prepare the entire recipe. Refrigerate or freeze the extra amount for another time; the basic work has been done.

2½ cups unbleached all-purpose flour
½ teaspoon salt
1 teaspoon sugar
8 tablespoons (¼ pound) unsalted butter, cut into 16 bits
½ cup vegetable shortening
6 tablespoons ice water

Combine flour, salt, and sugar in a bowl. Place butter and shortening in the flour and cut it into tiny beads with a wire pastry blender. If you own an electric mixer, you can do this with a paddle attachment at low speed.

Add water, 1 tablespoon at a time, to form a ball of dough. If it falls apart and feels too dry, add a bit more water.

Divide the dough into two even pieces. Pat each piece into a round shape. Wrap in wax paper and set aside for about 20 minutes. It can be refrigerated at this stage for up to two days or frozen for up to one month.

The dough should be at room temperature when you are ready to roll out the pie pastry. Flour the working surface and the rolling pin.

Press dough into a round shape with your hands. Roll the dough from the center up and then from the center down. Turn and move dough as you work to prevent it from sticking and to keep the round shape. If the dough cracks and breaks, bring it together again into a ball and press it once more into a round shape. Flour your board and start again.

Measure the size by inverting the pie plate on the dough. Trim it 1 inch larger than the plate for a bottom crust. Trim it 1½ inch larger for the top crust to cover the filling.

For an 8- to 10-inch single crust, dust the rolled-out dough lightly with flour. Fold it into quarters and transfer it to the pie baking plate from the center to the rim. Unfold the dough to cover the pie plate loosely. Press the dough down lightly on the bottom and the sides. Fold the edge under the rim and flute it or mark it with the tines of a fork. Refrigerate or freeze for 15 minutes before baking to prevent shrinkage. To bake, line the bottom and sides with aluminum foil and heap 1 pound dried beans on the foil as a weight to keep the bottom flat.

For a double-crust pie, place the bottom crust as described above. Trim the edge around the pie plate. Add the filling. Transfer the top crust over the filled pie. Fold top edge over the bottom crust and under the rim to seal it. Flute the edge or press it with the tines of a fork. Score the top in three or four places to make vents so the steam can escape.

Save all leftover scraps when trimming the dough. They can be used for small pot pies or fancy designs on the top crust. Freeze them for future use.

There are many crusts that need not be rolled out at all. The Brown Sugar Crust, the Rich Pastry Crust, and the Easy Ginger Crust are a few. They vary in flavor and can complement the fillings that you personally choose. Mix the ingredients by hand, with an electric mixer, or in a food processor.

Brown Sugar Crust
Makes one 8- or 9-inch bottom crust.

8 tablespoons (¼ pound) unsalted butter, cold but pliable
½ cup light brown sugar
1 cup unbleached all-purpose flour

Preheat oven to 375°F. Set out an 8- or 9-inch pie pan or a shallow ceramic dish.

Mix all ingredients together quickly but thoroughly. Press the soft dough into the pie plate all the way up the sides of the rim. Place a sheet of heavy aluminum foil to fit on top of the pastry. Press it down lightly.

Bake for 15 minutes. Remove foil and bake for 5 minutes more. Cool thoroughly if a cold filling is being used. If filling is to be baked, spread the filling onto the hot pastry and bake.

Rich Pastry Crust
Makes one 8- or 9-inch bottom crust.

1 cup unbleached all-purpose flour
⅛ teaspoon salt
6 tablespoons unsalted butter, cold but pliable

2 tablespoons sugar
1 egg yolk

Preheat oven to 400°F. Set out an 8- or 9-inch pie pan or a ceramic dish.

Mix flour and salt together in a bowl. Make a well in the dry ingredients and break butter into it in small bits, also adding sugar and egg yolk. Gradually incorporate the flour until it is completely blended and the bowl is clean. Press the soft dough into the pie pan, going up along the sides to cover the surface well. Place a fitted sheet of aluminum foil into the dough. Press it down lightly.

Bake for 15 minutes; remove foil and bake for 5 minutes more. Cool before filling if cold filling is being used. Use directions for filling if it is to be a baked filling.

Easy Ginger Crust
Makes one 8- or 9-inch bottom crust.

3 tablespoons butter
1 cup gingersnap crumbs
½ cup untoasted bread crumbs (day-old bread made into crumbs)
1 tablespoon sugar

Preheat oven to 350°F. Butter an 8- or 9-inch pie pan with 1 tablespoon butter.

Use a blender or a food processor to make gingersnap crumbs. Melt remaining 2 tablespoons butter. Add melted butter to gingersnap crumbs, bread crumbs, and sugar. Mix well.

Press mixture into buttered pie pan, extending up along the sides. Bake for 8 or 9 minutes. Cool thoroughly.

Apple Pie
Serves 8.

Apple pies are most delicious when you use tart cooking apples mixed with Macintosh and Granny Smith apples.

8 cups peeled and sliced apples (5 to 6 pounds)
⅔ cup sugar
¼ cup lemon juice
1 teaspoon cinnamon
1 recipe Basic Pie Crust (page 283), rolled out for a two-crust pie
2 tablespoons each plain bread crumbs and brown sugar

Preheat oven to 425°F. Mix apples with sugar, lemon juice, and cinnamon.

Use a 9- or 10-inch pie plate or a shallow ceramic dish. Line the bottom with a round of pastry dough. Sprinkle bread crumbs and brown sugar over the bottom. Spoon apples evenly onto the dough. Cover with the larger round of dough. Fold top edge over bottom crust to flute it. Score the top in three or four places. Moisten the top with a spray of water and sprinkle with a little sugar.

Bake on the bottom rack of the oven for 10 minutes. Lower temperature to 375°F. Move the pie to the middle rack and bake for 45 to 50 minutes. The filling should be bubbling and oozing, the color of caramel. Remove to a cooling rack. Serve warm or at room temperature.

✸ Suggestions

- Crumble 3 tablespoons butter, ¼ cup sugar, ¼ cup brown sugar, ½ teaspoon cinnamon, 2 tablespoons bread or cookie crumbs, and ⅓ cup flour into small lumps. Add to leftover scraps of dough and place crumbs on top crust before baking.
- Substitute 2 cups cranberries for 2 cups apples. Add ⅓ cup more sugar and 2 tablespoons orange juice.
- When I make this Apple Pie for Thanksgiving, I prepare it well ahead of time and freeze it, unbaked, for up to two weeks. I bake it Thanksgiving morning after defrosting it for 15 minutes. Then I add another 30 minutes to the prescribed baking time.
- If you have one pastry round, bake a deep-dish apple pie with only the top pastry. That, too, freezes well unbaked.

Pecan Pie
Serves 8.

One 9-inch unbaked Basic Pie Crust (page 283), preferably cold
3 eggs
½ cup sugar
Pinch of salt
1 cup dark Karo corn syrup
1 teaspoon vanilla extract
4 tablespoons butter, melted
1½ cups pecans

Preheat oven to 400°F. Line the crust with aluminum foil. Heap 1 pound dried beans on top so the crust does not bubble and shrink. Bake the crust for 5 minutes.

In the meantime, beat eggs with sugar. Add salt, syrup, vanilla, and butter.

Remove foil and beans. Spread pecans on the pie crust. Pour on egg mixture and bake for 10 minutes at 400°F. Lower heat to 300°F and bake for 35 minutes. Serve at room temperature.

✳ *Suggestion*

My neighbor, Elsie Corse, bakes her maple walnut pie with almost the same ingredients. Instead of sugar and Karo syrup, she uses 1½ cups dark maple syrup, and instead of pecans she uses walnuts.

Pumpkin Chiffon Pie
Serves 8.

2 cups canned pumpkin (1-pound can)
2 egg yolks
1 cup evaporated milk
1½ cups dark brown sugar
½ teaspoon salt
½ teaspoon nutmeg
½ teaspoon cinnamon
¼ teaspoon ginger
1 envelope unflavored gelatin mixed with ½ cup cold water
2 egg whites
¼ cup dark brown sugar
One 9-inch *baked* Basic Pie Crust (page 283)

Mix together pumpkin, egg yolks, evaporated milk, sugar, salt, and spices in a saucepan. Cook over low heat, stirring constantly. It takes about 3 to 5 minutes for the mixture to barely simmer. It will be smooth and somewhat like custard. Add mixed gelatin and water to the hot pumpkin.

Transfer to a bowl and either cool over ice or place in the refrigerator. When the pumpkin mix becomes thick and sticks to the sides of the bowl, beat the egg whites, adding dark brown sugar gradually. Fold the egg whites into the pumpkin. Spoon into pie crust; refrigerate.

The pie can be prepared 24 hours in advance and refrigerated. Decorate the top with sweetened whipped cream, if desired. Try a heaping tablespoon of frozen yogurt or vanilla ice cream with it.

Blueberry Pie
Serves 8.

We have had several banner years for blueberries. Our fields have been covered with the tiny wild berries, and our cultivated bushes supplied the large ones. Best of all, I have a husband who has the patience to pick them. Blueberries are the easiest of all berries to work with. They keep their shape even after freezing. Add them to cake batters, muffins, pancakes, and berry sauces, but be sure to bake this pie in fresh blueberry season.

    1 recipe Basic Pie Crust (page 283)
    1 quart blueberries
    ⅔ cup sugar
    2 tablespoons lemon juice
    ½ teaspoon cinnamon
    2 tablespoons unbleached all-purpose flour
    3 tablespoons each plain bread crumbs and light brown sugar, mixed

Preheat oven to 375°F. If you have rolled out the pie crust in advance and refrigerated it, bring it to room temperature.

Mix berries, sugar, lemon juice, cinnamon, and flour in a bowl. Place bottom crust in a pie pan. Sprinkle half the bread crumbs and brown sugar mixture over the bottom. Spread the berries evenly and then cover with the top crust. Score the top in three or four places. Spray it with a little water and sprinkle the top with the remaining bread crumbs and brown sugar mixture.

Bake the pie on the bottom rack of the oven for 20 minutes. Move to the upper rack, and bake for 35 minutes or until the filling is bubbling and the crust is golden.

Coconut Custard Pie
Serves 8.

    2½ cups milk
    4 eggs
    ½ cup sugar
    ½ teaspoon salt
    1 teaspoon vanilla extract
    1 unbaked 8- or 9-inch pie crust, refrigerated
    4 tablespoons unsweetened or sweetened shredded coconut

Preheat oven to 400°F. Heat milk to a simmer. Beat eggs, sugar, salt, and vanilla together. When the milk is hot, gradually add it to the egg mixture.

Place the cold pie crust in a pie plate and put it on the lowest rack of the oven. Then carefully pour milk mixture into the pie crust.

Bake for 30 minutes. Five minutes before baking is finished, sprinkle the coconut over the top. Set back in the oven to complete baking.

✹ *Suggestion*

Omit coconut. After baking, cool the pie on a rack. Place sliced strawberries on top.

Crunchy Meringue Pie
Serves 8.

This pie is definitely the quintessential American dessert. Our daughter serves it at her restaurant, Le Petit Chef, with her homemade ice cream, dark sweet chocolate sauce, and whipped cream. She shares the recipe with her guests, but they continue to order it at the restaurant.

> 3 egg whites (at room temperature)
> 1 cup sugar
> 14 Ritz crackers, crushed
> ½ teaspoon baking powder
> ⅔ cup walnuts

Preheat oven to 350°F. Grease a 9-inch pie pan.

Beat egg whites until frothy; add sugar gradually until the whites stiffen (3 to 5 minutes). Combine the crushed crackers with the baking powder and add to the meringue with the walnuts.

Spread the mixture evenly over the greased pan. Bake for 35 minutes. Cool.

✹ *Suggestions*

- Pile 3 cups whipped cream over the meringue to cover completely. Sprinkle shavings of dark sweet chocolate over all.

- Hull 1 pint strawberries. Cut in halves and soak in ¼ cup kirsch for 1 hour. Blend strawberries with 3 cups sweetened whipped cream and spread on the baked meringue. The kirsch may be omitted if you choose.

- Place round scoops of ice cream all around the edges of the pie. Fill the center with fresh berries or sliced peaches. With a decorating bag, pipe whipped cream around berries and ice cream.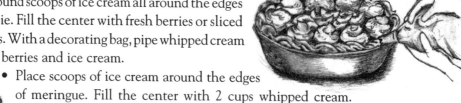
  - Place scoops of ice cream around the edges of meringue. Fill the center with 2 cups whipped cream. Dribble chocolate sauce over all.

Yogurt Pie
Serves 6.

½ pound cream cheese, at room temperature
1 cup yogurt
2 tablespoons honey
1 teaspoon vanilla extract
One 8-inch Easy Ginger Crust (page 285)
1 cup fresh raspberries or strawberries
1 teaspoon unsweetened cocoa

Beat cream cheese until smooth. This is easily done if the cheese is at room temperature.

Blend in yogurt thoroughly and then the honey and vanilla. Spread mixture evenly on the crust and refrigerate overnight.

Garnish the top with a circle of raspberries or strawberries and a sprinkling of the unsweetened cocoa.

Stoltzman's Linzer Torte
Serves 8.

In the early 1970s Sol Schoenbach, our friend and world-renowned bassoonist, and the then-young clarinetist, Richard Stoltzman, played duets as a beautiful finale to a dinner at my Vermont summer school. Richard is now one of the world's leading clarinetists, yet he continues to pursue his hobby of baking. At a lesson in pastry, Richard shared an interesting technique for piping out the lattice strips on a Linzer Torte. I have suggested it to students ever since. Instead of rolling out the rich pastry dough, he beats it soft enough to use a decorating bag.

1 cup flour
2 tablespoons unsweetened cocoa
½ teaspoon cinnamon

¼ teaspoon ground cloves
2 sticks (½ pound) salted butter, softened
½ cup, plus 1 tablespoon, sugar
2 egg yolks
2 cups ground almonds
1 cup raspberry jam
1 egg white
1 tablespoon water
2 tablespoons confectioners' sugar

Mix the flour, cocoa, cinnamon, and cloves together in a bowl and set aside. Cream the butter in an electric mixer and beat in the ½ cup sugar. Beat in the egg yolks. Gradually blend in the almonds and the flour mixture, and continue beating to make a batter that is thick but soft enough to use in a decorating bag.

Using about half the batter, spread an even layer, ⅛ to ¼ inch thick, in the bottom of an 8- or 9-inch round baking pan with a removable bottom. Spread the jam over the batter to within ½ inch of the edge, taking care not to break the layer of batter.

Spoon the remaining batter into a pastry bag fitted with a large tube, ½ inch in diameter. Pipe three to five parallel lines of batter straight across the layer of jam from one edge to the other. Give the pan a quarter turn and pipe three to five more parallel lines across the pastry from edge to edge. Pipe the remaining batter around the edge.

Refrigerate for 1 hour. Preheat oven to 300°F.

Beat the egg white with the remaining sugar and water until frothy. Brush this mixture over the pastry strips and the edge. Place the torte in the oven and bake for 1 hour. Allow to cool completely.

Before serving, sift confectioners' sugar over the top. Remove the sides of the pan and serve.

Cream Puffs (Pâte à Choux)
Makes 72 one-inch puffs; 48 two-inch puffs; or 12 four-inch puffs.

A bakeshop eclair was a special treat for me as a child. I was quite grown up when I learned the secrets of this simple pastry. Cream Puffs are formed from a cooked paste that miraculously puffs up in the oven. The Burgundians serve them unfilled at wine tastings or bake the Gougere, cream puff paste with cheese. In New Orleans they fry them and call them Beignets. The fillings and sauces are limitless, so your choices can range from sweet to spicy. Once you learn to bake these puffs, they will become basic.

8 tablespoons (¼ pound) unsalted butter
1 cup cold water
1 cup unbleached all-purpose flour
⅛ teaspoon salt
4 eggs

Place butter and water in a saucepan over low heat. The water will heat as the butter melts. If the butter is not melted when the water starts to simmer, remove the pot to the side for a few seconds until the butter melts. When the butter is melted and the water is boiling, lower the flame. Add flour and salt. Use a wooden spoon to stir the mixture into a ball. It will come away from the sides of the saucepan. Move it around with the wooden spoon for 2 to 3 minutes.

Transfer the dough to the bowl of an electric mixer. Add one egg at a time at low speed. After the last egg is beaten in, the mixture will be glossy and smooth but pasty.

Preheat oven to 400°F. Lightly grease a cookie sheet. Use two spoons to drop the paste in small balls, 1 inch apart, or use a decorating bag with a ½-inch plain tube to do the same.

Bake for 20 to 25 minutes. Test one puff by cooling it for 30 seconds. If the test puff collapses, give the puffs another few minutes in the oven.

Cool the puffs on a rack. Cut the puffs in half and fill with whipped cream, custard, fresh fruit, or ice cream. Another method is to make a small hole at the bottom or side of the puffs and squeeze in the cream or custard from a decorating bag fitted with a small tube. Serve with a dusting of powdered sugar or rich chocolate coating (page 311).

Dessert Beignet
Makes 72 one-inch puffs.

1 recipe Cream Puffs (page 291)
6 ounces apricot jam
2 tablespoons water
¼ cup Madeira
2 or 3 cups corn oil
½ cup powdered sugar

Follow the instructions in the recipe for Cream Puffs to make the paste and drop the balls on a lightly greased cookie sheet. Refrigerate.

While the Beignet puffs are in the refrigerator, prepare an apricot sauce by mixing apricot jam with water in a saucepan and melting over low heat. Add Madeira and stir. Keep sauce warm.

Heat corn oil in a deep frying pot to 375°F. Take Beignet puffs from the refrigerator and drop them into the oil, frying no more than six or eight at a time. Remove them to paper toweling. Serve with a sprinkling of powdered sugar. Pass the warm sauce around the table.

Gougere
Makes 48 2-inch puffs.

> 1 recipe Cream Puffs (page 291)
> 1½ cups grated Gruyère cheese
> ¼ cup grated Parmesan cheese
> 1 teaspoon Dijon mustard
> Dash each salt, pepper, and cayenne pepper

Follow the recipe for making Cream Puffs, but add Gruyère and Parmesan cheeses, mustard, salt, pepper, and cayenne to the Cream Puff paste. Bake as directed for cream puffs.

Danish Pastry
Makes 4 to 5 dozen.

Danish Pastry and Schnecken are yeast-risen pastries, the most favored finger cookies amongst family, friends and students. Because the recipe makes a quantity, I do freeze them. Then I am always prepared with a fantastic sweet for the right moment.

If you have never used yeast before, read about it in Chapter 1 (page 2). Danish Pastry is related to Classic Puff Pastry, in which softened butter is rolled into layers of basic dough. In this case, the plain dough rises with the help of yeast. Prepare the dough up to three days in advance. Refrigerate it, and bake the shapes on the day of serving. They will be superb.

> ½ cup warm water
> 2 tablespoons active dry yeast
> 3½ cups or more unbleached all-purpose flour
> 3 sticks (¾ pound) butter, at room temperature
> ½ cup sugar
> 2 eggs
> ½ cup milk
> 1 teaspoon vanilla extract
> 1 cup sugar mixed with 1 teaspoon cinnamon
> 1 egg
> 1 tablespoon milk

Pour water in a bowl. Sprinkle yeast on top. Cover with 1 cup flour. Do not mix! Set aside for 10 minutes.

Reserve 4 tablespoons butter. Knead the remaining butter with ½ cup flour and shape it into a block ½ inch thick.

Add the reserved 4 tablespoons butter, sugar, eggs, milk, vanilla, and 2 cups flour to the yeast and water. Beat vigorously with your hand or use an electric mixer with a flat paddle. The dough might be a little sticky, so flour it well.

Transfer the dough to a floured surface. Roll it lightly into a rectangle about 8" x 12". Place the block of butter over the bottom half of the dough. Fold the top of the dough over it to enclose the butter. Press the dough lightly with a rolling pin. Turn the dough a quarter turn to the right, resembling a book with binding on the left. Roll into an oblong, using more flour for the board if necessary. The size of the oblong will not matter. If the dough sticks or becomes elastic, refrigerate it for about 15 minutes. Roll and fold the dough at least three times so that the layers of butter are blended into the dough. Allow the dough to rest in the refrigerator before shaping into forms.

Cut off one-quarter of the dough. Roll it into a rectangle, ¼ inch thick. Sprinkle with sugar and cinnamon, and roll it up as if making a jelly roll. Cut into 1-inch slices and place, cut-side down, on ungreased pans, ½ inch apart. Make other shapes as illustrated.

Allow pastries to rise for 30 minutes. Brush each one with a wash of egg mixed with milk. Sprinkle with sugar and cinnamon.

Preheat oven to 375°F and bake for 15 minutes. Remove to a cooling rack.

Sliced Roll   Crescent   Filled Danish

Cut Danish   Knot   Snail   Twist

✳ Suggestions

- Use other fillings, such as ground nuts, raisins, apricot and prune mixtures, sweetened cream cheese, and almond paste.
- Do not waste any ends. Form twists, snails, and knots. Roll in sugar and cinnamon.
- Drizzle a confectioners' sugar icing on top for a decoration: Mix ½ cup confectioners' sugar with 1 tablespoon water (or orange juice) and a drop of vanilla. Make it as thin or thick as you wish. Use a fork or a decorating tube to make lines on each pastry.
- Use this recipe for coffee rings or other shapes. Larger shapes will require 30 minutes of baking time at 350°F.

Schnecken (Pecan Buns)
Makes 7 or 8 dozen tiny buns.

William Greenberg, Jr. taught me his exact recipe for Schnecken, even though it is one of the most popular items at his shop in New York City. I cut his quantities in half for home use. If you do not own eight or nine petite muffin pans, bake these in two or three batches. The dough keeps in the refrigerator for up to three days.

Dough

2 tablespoons active dry yeast
½ cup warm water
3 sticks (¾ pound) unsalted butter, at room temperature
½ cup sugar
3 egg yolks
½ teaspoon salt
1 cup sour cream
1½ teaspoons white vinegar
5½ cups unbleached all-purpose flour

Filling

2 sticks (½ pound) unsalted butter, at room temperature
2¼ cups (1 pound) packed light brown sugar
1 teaspoon cinnamon
1 tablespoon light Karo corn syrup
Whole pecans (7 or 8 dozen, one for each bun)
Cinnamon and raisins

Dissolve yeast in warm water. Set aside. Cream butter and sugar in an electric mixer. Add egg yolks and salt, then sour cream and vinegar.

Add dissolved yeast, then beat in flour, reserving about 1 cup flour for kneading. Transfer the dough to a floured surface and knead for a few minutes to form a smooth mass.

Place dough in a floured plastic bag, giving it room to expand. Refrigerate for a minimum of 6 hours or a maximum of 3 days.

To make the filling, cream butter and half the light brown sugar along with the cinnamon and Karo syrup. Place 1 tablespoon of mixture in the bottom of each muffin tin. Place one whole pecan, flat-side down, in each one.

Flour a rolling pin and the surface for rolling. Set out remainder of brown sugar, a shaker of cinnamon, and raisins.

Cut dough into four pieces. Roll out one at a time. Roll dough into a rectangle about ⅛ inch thick. Place it with the long side parallel to you. Sprinkle with brown sugar, cinnamon, and raisins. (Bill is very generous with this; there are usually no exact amounts.) Press the sugar and raisins lightly into the dough. Roll up like a jelly roll and then stretch the compact roll slightly. Cut it into ½-inch slices for small buns. Place each bun into the prepared tins. Allow to rise for 20 to 30 minutes.

Preheat oven to 375°F. Place the tins on jelly-roll pans, because the sugar caramelizes and sometimes runs over. Also you will turn the hot buns over directly onto the same pans. Bake for 25 minutes. Turn tins upside down immediately onto the jelly-roll pans, because the sugar hardens quickly. Be careful not to touch the hot sugar. Use two butter knives to handle the buns.

✳ Suggestion

These buns have become a specialty of mine. They freeze perfectly but also can be kept in a covered container at room temperature for up to a week. For a change, bake buns ½ inch apart in a pie tin or casserole to form a cake.

Cake Recipes

Before beginning to bake:

1. Study the recipe. Do you have the ingredients, pans, and uninterrupted time?

2. Bring all the ingredients to room temperature.

3. Be sure to use the flour specified in the recipe. Unbleached all-purpose flour is used in most cakes. Cake flour is a soft flour to be used for delicate cakes.

4. Make substitutions only after following the exact recipes a few times.

5. In most cases sift and measure ingredients on wax paper instead of using bowls.

6. Dot the bottom of the baking pans with oil or butter. Line the bottoms with wax paper to fit. Cakes will turn out easily.

7. Use the electric mixer sensibly. Lightweight and moist ingredients will take faster speeds; heavier ingredients must be started at low speed. Both dry and very wet ingredients will spatter out of the machine if it is not operated on a low speed.

8. Check the oven temperature occasionally with a portable thermometer. Center the cakes on the racks. After a while, you will probably detect the hotter areas in your oven.

9. Always preheat the oven.

10. Fill a cake pan no more than two-thirds full.

11. Test for doneness with a cake tester or toothpick. Insert tester in the center. If it comes away dry, the baking is finished. Butter cakes usually come away from the sides of the pan. Exceptions will be explained in the specific recipes.

Grand Marnier Torte
Serves 10 to 12.

2 sticks (½ pound) unsalted butter, plus 1 tablespoon for greasing pan
1¼ cups sugar
4 eggs
1 cup sifted cornstarch
1 cup unbleached all-purpose flour
1 teaspoon baking powder
2 teaspoons vanilla extract
2 tablespoons Grand Marnier liqueur
Grated rind of 1 orange (about 1 tablespoon)
4 tablespoons confectioners' sugar

Grease a 2-quart tube pan with the 1 tablespoon butter. Preheat oven to 375°F. Beat butter with sugar for about 7 to 10 minutes in an electric mixer. Add the first egg, then beat in ½ cup cornstarch. Add the second egg, continuing to beat and blend the mixture. Add ½ cup flour. Beat in the third egg, then add ½ cup cornstarch. Beat in the fourth egg. Add ½ cup flour mixed with baking powder. Add vanilla, Grand Marnier, and orange rind. Mix thoroughly.

Transfer the batter to a greased pan. Smooth the top evenly with a rubber spatula. Bake for 40 to 50 minutes. Cool on a rack before turning the cake out of the pan. Dust the top with confectioners' sugar.

✳ *Suggestions*

- This cake keeps well wrapped in plastic wrap for up to one week. Freeze it for up to two months.
- Grand Marnier Torte is best enjoyed in thin slices and is especially good when topped with a fruit sorbet.

Sour Cream Cake
Serves 12.

My recipe for this delicious-to-the-last-crumb cake dates back to 1960 in my file. It has been published with various changes in many magazines and books, but this recipe is still the easiest to bake and the most foolproof.

2 cups unbleached all-purpose flour
1 teaspoon baking powder
1 teaspoon baking soda

¼ teaspoon salt

8 tablespoons (¼ pound) unsalted
    butter

1 cup sugar

2 eggs

1 cup sour cream

1 teaspoon vanilla extract

2 tablespoons sugar mixed with
    ½ teaspoon cinnamon

¼ cup chopped walnuts

4 ounces coarsely cut dark sweet chocolate or chocolate bits

Kugelhopf Pan

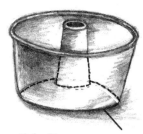

Tube Pan

*Removable
bottom with tub*

Preheat oven to 350°F. Grease a 2-quart tube pan (or fancy kugelhopf pan). Sift flour, baking powder, baking soda, and salt together.

Beat butter and add sugar gradually in an electric mixer for 1 to 2 minutes. Add one egg at a time. Beat in flour mixture and sour cream alternately, beginning and ending with flour. Add vanilla.

Sprinkle half the sugar and cinnamon on the bottom of the greased pan. Pour in half the batter. Sprinkle in the remaining sugar and cinnamon. Spread half the walnuts and chocolate over the batter. Pour remaining batter on top. Sprinkle remaining walnuts and chocolate on top and then smooth the batter evenly.

Bake for 45 minutes. Cool on a rack before turning out of the pan.

Chocolate Cake
Serves 12 to 24.

Jessica Seiden may not remember that she shared this recipe with me, but I can never forget her contribution. It has all the qualities to please our American taste.

3 ounces unsweetened baking chocolate

2¼ cups sifted cake flour

2 teaspoons baking soda

½ teaspoon salt

8 tablespoons (¼ pound) butter

1 pound light brown sugar

3 eggs

½ cup buttermilk (or sour cream)

1 cup boiling water

2 teaspoons vanilla extract

Bake this cake in three 8-inch layer pans or in one 13" x 9" x 2" pan, whichever suits your needs.

Dot the bottom of each pan with oil or butter so that a lining of wax paper will lay flat.

Melt chocolate in a bowl over warm water. Preheat oven to 350°F.

Sift flour, baking soda, and salt onto wax paper. Beat butter in an electric mixer until smooth. Add sugar gradually. Beat for 1 to 2 minutes. Add one egg at a time, incorporating them well.

Stop the machine. Add melted chocolate. Beat at low speed, then alternately add flour mixture and buttermilk, starting and ending with the flour mixture. Turn machine to the lowest speed. Pour boiling water in gradually and then add vanilla. Blend mixture by hand with a rubber spatula to make sure it is well combined. The mixture will be very thin.

Pour into the prepared pan or pans. Bake the layer pans for 20 to 25 minutes and the oblong pan for 40 to 45 minutes. Cool thoroughly on a rack before turning out of the pan.

✳ *Suggestions*

- Spread layers with whipped cream or with one of the icings described later in this chapter. Use it as a celebration cake—for birthdays, holidays, anniversaries, and so on.
- Use two layers and freeze the third for another dinner. Wedges of plain Chocolate Cake are perfect with a spoonful of frozen yogurt or ice cream.
- For a meeting or an organizational party, I cut the oblong cake into 24 squares or slices. The rich portions are very ample.

Chocolate Torte
Serves 12.

This torte is quite different from the preceding Chocolate Cake. The texture is dense with the richness of chocolate, butter, and eggs, but it has no flour.

8 ounces unsweetened baking chocolate
2 sticks (½ pound) unsalted butter, at room temperature
3 cups confectioners' sugar
8 eggs, separated
1 cup chopped walnuts or pecans
Whipped cream for topping or decoration

Preheat oven to 350°F. Dot the bottoms of two 9-inch layer pans with oil or butter. Cut wax paper to line the bottoms.

Melt chocolate in a bowl over hot water. When melted, allow to cool slightly.

Beat the butter in an electric mixer and gradually add confectioners' sugar. When light and fluffy, add the egg yolks, beating constantly. In the meantime, beat the egg whites to a peak. When they hold on to the sides of the bowl, they are ready. Do not overbeat.

Fold the melted chocolate into the butter and sugar mixture. Then fold in the beaten egg whites. Transfer one-third of the mixture to a bowl and set it aside as a filling to be used later.

Stir the chopped nuts into the remaining batter. Spoon equal amounts into each of the layer pans and smooth the tops. Bake for 17 minutes.

Run a knife around the edge of the cakes to loosen them from the pans. Cover the pans one at a time with a rack and, using pot holders, invert the cakes. Remove the wax paper, allowing cakes to cool.

Spoon the reserved filling on top of one of the layers. Cover with the other layer. Serve each portion with a dollop of whipped cream.

✸ Suggestion

For a special presentation, decorate the cake with whipped cream and shaved chocolate.

Basic Sponge Cake
Serves 12.

If you love to bake, memorize this recipe for Basic Sponge Cake. There is something joyful about producing a cake without your head stuck in a book. Although the traditional pan for a sponge cake is the removable tube pan (see illustration page 298), after a while you will be baking it in layers, squares, and sheet pans. It always works.

    6 egg whites (at room temperature)
    ⅛ teaspoon salt
    ½ teaspoon cream of tartar
    1¼ cups sugar
    6 egg yolks, at room temperature
    2 tablespoons orange juice
    2 tablespoons lemon juice
    Finely grated rind 1 orange
    1¼ cups sifted cake flour
    4 tablespoons confectioners' sugar and 1 quart berries

Prepare an ungreased, 10-inch tube pan with a removable bottom. Preheat oven to 325°F.

Beat egg whites with salt and cream of tartar in the large bowl of an electric mixer until frothy. Gradually add sugar, and beat until the whites form a thick meringue (about 3 to 5 minutes).

Use a fork to stir egg yolks with juices and rind. Pour yolks onto beaten egg whites, and mix in by hand. Fold flour in, a little at a time, with a rubber spatula.

Pour the batter into the pan and bake for 1 hour. Invert pan on the counter and cool before removing the pan from the cake.

Serve slices with a dusting of confectioners' sugar and fresh berries.

☀ Suggestions

- Slice the Basic Sponge Cake into three layers. Fill with whipped cream and strawberries, raspberries, peaches, or other fruit.
- Decorate the top and sides of the cake with whipped cream and Chocolate Squigglies (page 312).
- For a variation, add ½ cup sour cream after the flour is blended in. The late Elaine Ross, a friend and fellow cookbook writer, proposed that original idea. It lends moistness and richness.
- Those who observe the Passover holiday can use this same recipe. Substitute 1 tablespoon lemon juice for the cream of tartar. Use ⅓ cup sifted cake meal and ¼ cup sifted potato starch instead of cake flour.

Génoise
Serves 10 to 12.

The Génoise is the French equivalent of our Basic Sponge Cake, with the addition of melted butter. The butter gives it a finer texture and a little more weight, to carry richer buttercream frosting. In some ways the technique is simpler, since there is no separation of eggs.

    6 eggs, at room temperature
    1 cup sugar
    1¼ cups sifted cake flour
    4 tablespoons clarified, melted butter (see instructions page 282)
    1 teaspoon vanilla extract

This recipe will make two 9" x 1½" layers; or one 10" x 3" round cake; or one 17" x 11" x 1" sheet;, or one 13" x 9" x 2" oblong.

Dot the bottom of the pan with oil or butter. Cut wax paper to fit the bottom of the pan. Preheat oven to 350°F.

Place eggs and sugar in the large bowl of an electric mixer. Stir them together. Set the bowl over simmering water for a few minutes. The mixture should be warm and syrupy. Watch carefully so the eggs do not cook! Beat eggs and sugar in the electric mixer for 8 to 10 minutes. The batter will mount to triple volume and become smooth, thick, and ivory in color.

Remove the bowl from the machine. Fold flour into the batter by hand, a little at a time. Add one-fourth of the batter to the clarified butter and mix in well (A). Transfer that mixture to the bowl of remaining batter and fold gently but quickly (B). Add vanilla.

Spread the batter evenly in pans. Smooth top. Bake, allowing 20 to 25 minutes for two layers or a sheet cake; 35 to 40 minutes for one large cake. Remove cake from pans and cool on racks.

✳ *Suggestions*

- Serve slices or squares with fresh fruit or berries, frozen yogurt, ice cream, or sorbet.
- Decorate layers for strawberry shortcake or a Celebration Cake (page 312).

Chocolate Mousse Cake
Serves 10 to 12.

When Gregory Usher was my guest teacher a few years ago, he demonstrated this cake. The cake is the basic Génoise flavored with cocoa. When it is combined with chocolate mousse, it is a superb dessert.

Génoise
3 eggs, at room temperature
½ cup sugar
½ cup sifted cake flour
¼ cup unsweetened cocoa
2 tablespoons clarified butter, melted and cooled (see instructions page 282)

Chocolate Mousse
7 ounces dark sweet or semisweet chocolate
2 cups heavy cream
Unsweetened cocoa

Liqueur Syrup
½ cup sugar
6 tablespoons water
Liqueur to taste (Grand Marnier, Cointreau, or other liqueur)

Dot a 10-inch layer pan with oil or butter. Cut wax paper to fit the bottom. Set out a 9-inch springform pan. Preheat oven to 350°F.

Place eggs and sugar in the large bowl of an electric mixer. Stir them together. Set the bowl over simmering water for a few minutes, but be careful not to cook the eggs. The mixture should be warm and syrupy. Beat eggs and sugar for 8 to 10 minutes. The batter will mount to triple volume and become smooth, thick, and ivory in color. Remove the bowl from the machine.

Sift flour and cocoa together. Fold the flour mixture into the batter by hand, a little at a time. Add one-fourth of the batter to the clarified butter and mix in well. Transfer that mixture to the bowl of remaining batter and fold gently but quickly.

Bake the cake in the 10-inch pan for 20 to 25 minutes. Allow it to cool on a rack before turning it out of the pan.

When the cake is cool, trim it to fit inside the 9-inch springform pan and carefully transfer it to the bottom of the pan.

To make the Chocolate Mousse, melt the chocolate over warm water. Whip the cream until soft peaks form. Pour the warm chocolate over the cream and continue beating until well blended.

Make the syrup by dissolving the sugar in the water over low heat. Add liqueur to taste, if you wish. Brush the syrup over the cake in the springform pan, then pour in the Chocolate Mousse. Refrigerate overnight. Before serving, remove the springform and transfer the cake to a serving dish. Dust the top with cocoa.

Chocolate Roll
Serves 8 to 10.

There is no other Chocolate Roll to compete with this one, inspired and introduced by Dione Lucas. Her one-hour lessons on television in 1948 were my first formal introduction to French cookery. Without conscious realization, I was training in that period for my future career of teaching cooking.

    8 ounces dark sweet chocolate
    7 eggs, separated
    ¾ cup sugar
    2 cups heavy cream
    ¼ cup confectioners' or superfine sugar
    1 teaspoon vanilla extract
    ½ cup unsweetened cocoa

Dot a 17" x 11" jelly-roll pan with oil or butter. Cut and place a sheet of wax paper long enough to cover the bottom of the pan and extending at least 1 inch over the short sides. Preheat oven to 350°F.

Break the chocolate into pieces. Melt over warm water or in a warm oven. Stir with a spoon when it is barely melted.

Beat egg yolks with sugar until they are pale in color and smooth. Use a rubber spatula to blend the warm chocolate into the egg yolk mixture. Beat egg whites until they cling to the sides of the bowl. Do not overbeat. Fold half the beaten egg whites into the chocolate mixture. Then gently fold in the remainder.

Spread the batter evenly in the pan. Bake for 17 minutes.

Remove the pan from the oven. Cover it completely with a damp cloth. Set aside to cool.

In the meantime, beat the cream. When it starts to thicken, add confectioners' or superfine sugar and vanilla, and beat until it clings to the beater. Refrigerate until ready to be used.

Lay out two sheets of wax paper, longer than the pan, on a working surface. Place the sheet nearest you overlapping the other. Sprinkle the unsweetened cocoa generously over the sheets.

Run a knife along the insides of the pan to loosen the cake. Flip the pan over onto the wax paper (A). Remove the pan, then separate the wax paper from the cake, gently. Do not worry if the cake breaks. It can be pushed together when it is filled.

Spread the whipped cream, starting 2 inches from the long end nearest you (B). Flip the long side of the cake over by holding the outer points of wax paper. Roll it over. Pull the wax paper as you roll the cake (C).

A.

B.

Sprinkle with cocoa to cover cracks

C.

D.

Use top sheet of wax paper to start roll

Cut off ends for a clean pattern

Transfer the Chocolate Roll to a long serving board or tray and slip out the wax paper. Dust the top with more cocoa to cover any cracks (D). I always cut a thin, small diagonal slice at either end to show a neat separation of cake and cream. The rough ends are eaten by anyone close by or saved for the next day.

✳ *Suggestions*

- Sometimes I make a Mocha Cream Filling. Blend 2 cups heavy cream with 6 tablespoons unsweetened cocoa, 1 teaspoon instant coffee, and a pinch of cinnamon. Refrigerate for 1 hour, then beat with ½ cup confectioners' sugar and 1 teaspoon vanilla extract.
- For a large party, make this recipe twice. Use two pans or bake it twice, a double recipe. Instead of rolling it, layer one cake on the other. Fill with double the amount of cream. Dust the top with unsweetened cocoa.

Fresh Coconut Angel Cake
Serves 12 to 18.

This cake has become a family tradition on Thanksgiving. My three pies almost take a back seat next to this imposing mountain of white. If you undertake to make it, be sure that you delegate the job of breaking and peeling the coconut. Accomplish that at least a day ahead of time. Be sure to reserve the liquid of the coconut.

Angel Cake

1⅓ cups sifted cake flour
2 cups sugar
2 cups egg whites, at room temperature (about 12 eggs)
2 teaspoons cream of tartar
½ teaspoon salt
2 teaspoons vanilla extract

Frosting

1 cup coconut liquid (use milk if you do not have liquid)
¾ pound marshmallows
2 cups heavy cream, whipped stiff
1 or 2 fresh coconuts, peeled and grated

Use an ungreased 10-inch round tube pan with a removable bottom. Preheat oven to 375°F.

Sift flour with 1 cup sugar onto a sheet of wax paper. Sift at least three times. Set aside.

Beat egg whites, cream of tartar, salt, and vanilla until stiff but still moist. Add the remaining cup of sugar a little at a time, beating constantly.

Sift about one-fourth of the flour mixture over the egg whites and fold it in with a rubber spatula. Fold in the remaining flour by fourths. Transfer the batter to the ungreased pan. Smooth out the top. Bake for 35 to 40 minutes. Invert pan on a rack to cool cake.

To make the frosting, cook coconut liquid or milk with marshmallows over low heat until the marshmallows melt. Cool in a bowl. Refrigerate until the mixture starts to jell.

Beat the jellied mixture until frothy in the electric mixer. Combine mixture with whipped cream.

To assemble the cake: With a knife, loosen cake from around the edges, the bottom, and the tube. Place the cake upside down on a lazy Susan or round serving dish. Carefully remove pan.

Slice the cake across to make three layers. Move the top two layers to the side. Spread a generous amount of cream and coconut on the bottom layer. Continue the same as you replace the other two layers on the cake. Spread cream on top and around the sides. Heap grated coconut all over, filling the middle cavity as well. Refrigerate until ready to serve.

✳ *Suggestions*

- The Angel Cake is a treat even without the cream and coconut.
- Save the egg yolks, well covered, in the refrigerator for up to five days to bake Brioche (page 20), Challah (page 18), or Schnecken (page 295). Use one or two in cookie recipes.
- Poach egg yolks. Use them in salad dressings, over greens, and in chicken and tuna fish mixtures.
- Use egg yolks in meatballs and meat loaves.

Rose Fund's Honey Cake
Serves 12 to 16.

We like to remember the people who were fine home bakers. They knew how to use materials on hand. Every good kitchen had jam, honey, and a supply of apples. Fortunately, we have inherited these hearty, old-fashioned cake recipes. They are used today in our homes and even in restaurants.

4 eggs
2 cups (16 ounces) honey
1½ cups sugar
¼ cup oil
4 cups unbleached all-purpose flour

2 teaspoons baking powder
1 teaspoon baking soda
½ teaspoon salt
1 teaspoon each ground cinnamon and cloves
1 cup strong coffee, at room temperature
½ cup chopped almonds

Preheat oven to 325°F. Dot a 13" x 9" pan with oil. Line the bottom with wax paper.

Beat eggs with honey in an electric mixer, then add sugar and oil. In the meantime, sift the flour, baking powder, baking soda, salt, cinnamon, and cloves. Gradually add the flour mixture to the egg mixture. Set the machine speed on low and add coffee, then nuts. Mix well.

Pour the batter into the pan. Bake for 1 hour. Serve the cake in slices, not in squares. Pass softened cream cheese around for a treat.

Rena Gold's Apple Cake
Serves 10 to 12.

4 cups apples (about 3 pounds), peeled and coarsely chopped (use part cooking apples—Baldwin, Cortland—and part eating apples—Macintosh, Granny Smith)
1½ cups sugar
2 tablespoons lemon juice
2 cups unbleached all-purpose flour
2 teaspoons baking soda
½ teaspoon salt
2 eggs
½ cup corn oil
2 teaspoons vanilla extract
1 cup chopped walnuts or pecans

Oil a 10-inch tube pan. Preheat oven to 350°F.

Mix the apples with sugar and lemon juice. Set aside for 30 minutes. Sift flour, baking soda, and salt together. Beat eggs with oil by hand or in an electric mixer. Add flour mixture, then apples, vanilla, and nuts.

Set machine at low speed or continue mixing by hand for just 1 minute. Transfer batter to the tube pan. Bake for 1 hour. Cool in the pan before turning out.

Serve slices with a dusting of confectioners' sugar or a spoonful of ice cream.

Anita Prichard's Tennessee Jam Cake
Serves 10 to 12.

2 sticks (½ pound) unsalted butter
2 cups sugar
4 eggs
1 cup seedless blackberry jam
1 cup buttermilk
1 teaspoon baking soda
3 cups unbleached all-purpose flour
1 teaspoon each unsweetened cocoa, cinnamon, and nutmeg
¼ teaspoon ground cloves
1 cup each raisins and chopped walnuts

Use a bit of the butter to grease a 10-inch tube pan. Preheat oven to 350°F.

Cream butter and sugar in an electric mixer. Add one egg at a time and beat for 2 to 3 minutes. Then add jam.

Combine buttermilk with baking soda. Sift flour and spices together. Mix 2 tablespoons of the flour mixture with the raisins and nuts.

Add the balance of flour and buttermilk to the batter alternately, starting and ending with flour. Add the raisin and nut mixture. Pour the batter into the pan.

Bake for 1 hour. Cool the cake on a rack before removing to a tray.

The cake is traditionally decorated with a butter frosting, but it is also good unadorned.

Butter Frosting
Makes enough for one 9- or 10-inch cake.

1 pound confectioners' sugar, sifted to remove any lumps
8 tablespoons (¼ pound) unsalted butter, softened
⅛ teaspoon salt
1 teaspoon vanilla extract
3 to 4 tablespoons milk

Cream one-third of the sugar with the butter and salt. Blend vanilla, 2 tablespoons milk, and the remaining sugar into the mixture. Gradually stir in remaining milk until the desired spreading consistency is obtained.

Decorating Cakes

There are many times when celebrations call for decorated cakes. Although we may not be able to emulate the professional confectioner, it is not difficult to artistically finish a cake for a special occasion.

There are any number of basic possibilities for cake decoration. For example, you can choose from icings, creams, frostings, crystallized or fresh flowers, messages piped from decorating bags, and other interesting adornments.

Study the recipes for cake decorations and decide on your preference. You can then prepare the necessary tools and supplies before you start.

Tools:

>   Cooling racks for cakes
>   A turntable or any Lazy Susan
>   Rubber spatulas
>   Steel spatula
>   Large 16- or 18-inch decorating
>   bag with one or two tubes
>   Wax paper or parchment paper
>   for throwaway decorating bags
>   (see diagram)

Supplies:

>   Confectioners' sugar
>   Dark sweet chocolate
>   Unsalted butter, heavy cream, eggs
>   Vanilla extract
>   Fresh flowers (optional)
>   Crystallized flowers

Making a Decorating Bag

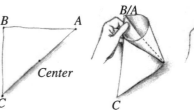 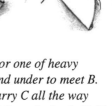

Use two triangles of wax paper or one of heavy parchment. Roll A around, up and under to meet B. Hold securely with left hand. Carry C all the way around the tube to meet A and B from the back. Fold the top to close it securely. Snip the top with scissors to make an opening of desired size.

✳ *Suggestions*

- Poke holes in a warm Basic Sponge Cake (page 300) or Génoise (page 300). Drip fresh orange juice into it for a flavorful moistener. My friend Silvia Allen uses her knitting needles to poke the holes. A cake tester or toothpicks may also be used.

- Make a syrup as in the Chocolate Mousse Cake (page 302). Brush it on layers of Sponge Cake or Génoise to keep them moist.

Whipped Cream
Makes 4 cups.

Use Whipped Cream for an easy and delicious coating.

    1 pint whipping cream
    4 tablespoons confectioners' sugar
    1 teaspoon vanilla extract

Place the bowl, beater, and cream in the refrigerator before whipping. Add confectioners' sugar and vanilla to cream. Beat with a hand beater. (Use an electric mixer if you are beating more than 2 cups.) Stop beating when the cream stiffly holds on to the beater.

Mocha Whipped Cream
Makes enough for 1 three-layer cake.

    1 pint whipping cream
    6 tablespoons unsweetened cocoa
    1 teaspoon instant coffee
    Pinch cinnamon
    ½ cup confectioners' sugar
    1 teaspoon vanilla extract

Mix cream, cocoa, coffee, and cinnamon in a mixing bowl. Refrigerate for 1 hour. Beat cream with confectioners' sugar and vanilla until it holds its shape.

Chocolate Fudge Frosting
Makes enough for 1 three-layer cake.

    4 ounces unsweetened chocolate
    4 tablespoons unsalted butter
    3 cups confectioners' sugar, sifted
    ½ cup warm milk
    1 teaspoon vanilla extract

Melt chocolate and butter in an electric mixer bowl set over a pan of simmering water. When the chocolate and butter are melted, set the bowl in the mixer. Add sugar and milk alternately while mixing; then add vanilla. The more sugar you add, the fudgier the consistency. More warm milk will thin it for a coating.

✳ Suggestions

* Add one egg yolk for a shiny finish.

- Add up to ½ pound softened unsalted butter for a quick buttercream frosting.
- Flavorings of coffee, brandy, or rum are good additions.

Rich Chocolate Coating

6 ounces dark sweet chocolate
1 cup heavy cream

Melt chocolate with cream over low heat while stirring slowly but constantly. Bring to a simmer. The mixture will coat the spoon. Set aside to cool. Pour over the top of a cake and the sides as well.

✳ *Suggestions*

- Add ½ cup coffee or hot water to thin the coating for a sauce.
- Serve Rich Chocolate Coating with filled Cream Puffs (page 291) or poached fruits.

Vermont Sour Cream Icing
Makes about 1¼ cups.

1 cup sour cream
1 cup maple syrup

Mix sour cream and maple syrup in a saucepan. Bring to a simmer. Cook until the mixture coats a spoon. Use it as a coating on plain cakes or yeast cakes.

Chocolate Squares, Rounds, or Squigglies
Makes about 24 2-inch squares.

6 ounces dark sweet chocolate

Chop or shave chocolate into the smallest bits possible so that they melt fast and evenly. Melt half the chocolate over warm water or in an oven at the lowest temperature setting (about 200°F). When the chocolate is melted, add the remaining chocolate and stir until smooth. Do not beat it.

Line two cookie sheets with wax paper. Heap a few spoonfuls of chocolate on each sheet of wax paper and spread into a rectangle about ⅛ inch thick. The sizes will vary. Place the cookie sheets in the refrigerator. When the chocolate firms up but is not brittle, use a knife to cut through into squares, strips, or any imaginative shapes. Use cookie cutters to make round shapes. Do not separate at this time. Refrigerate again until the chocolate is hard and then separate the shapes. Remove the wax paper and use as decorations on cakes or with desserts.

Squigglies: Someone on the staff of our daughter's restaurant named these fancy decorations for cakes and desserts. Makes 3 to 4 dozen.

Cut a 12-inch sheet of wax paper. Double it over to make a triangle and then roll it into a horn shape for decorating (see illustration page 309). Fill it half full with melted chocolate. Snip the very tip with scissors to make a tiny opening. Fold the top to close it securely. Pipe out the chocolate into designs (see illustration) on sheets of wax paper as previously described. Refrigerate until firm. Cut wax paper around shapes. Refrigerate the shapes on the wax paper in a covered container. Slip off the wax paper before using them to decorate a cake or a dessert.

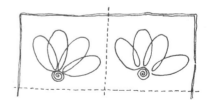

Celebration Cakes

There are a number of combinations for filling and decorating special holiday, birthday, and anniversary cakes. This Celebration Cake is my simplest and quickest.

    1 Basic Sponge Cake (page 300) or Génoise (page 301), two or three layers
    Liqueur Syrup (page 302) or orange juice
    Whipped Cream or Mocha Whipped Cream (page 310)
    Berries or fruit, only if in season
    Rich Chocolate Coating (page 311)
    Chocolate Squares, Rounds, or Squigglies (page 312)

Cut a piece of cardboard to fit the size of the cake. Brush the top of each layer of cake with syrup or orange juice.

Place one layer of the cake on the cardboard. Use a turntable if you have one. Spread a layer of whipped cream and a few cut berries. Place the second layer on the first and do the same. Always think ahead and reserve enough whipped cream for the sides.

Spread the Rich Chocolate Coating on the third layer. Let the chocolate set before moving the layer to the top. Sometimes you will have to trim around the sides of the cake to make it even. Spread the reserved whipped cream to cover the sides of the cake. Place squares, rounds, or squigglies of chocolate, at even intervals, so they adhere to the cream (see photograph on cover).

Decorate the top of the cake with rosettes of whipped cream (use a decorating bag fitted with a star tube), crystallized flowers, or fresh flowers.

✹ *Suggestion*
Use a wax paper bag filled with whipped cream to write a message on top.

Cookie Recipes

An almost empty cookie jar is all the announcement I need that it is time to get busy and bake another batch. With a jar of cookies kept available, we are never caught short for a dessert. The selection of cookie recipes that follow are my basics. Butter cookies store very well in a glass container, always at hand on our dining room buffet. Schnecken (page 295), Pecan Squares (page 314), Cookie Crescents (page 316), and other assortments are packed in boxes for the freezer. Choose your own favorites and bake them well in advance.

Butter Cookies with Variations
Makes 4 or 5 dozen.

2 sticks (½ pound) unsalted butter
¾ cup confectioners' sugar
2 cups unbleached all-purpose flour
¼ teaspoon salt
1 teaspoon vanilla extract

Cream butter with sugar in an electric mixer. Add flour, salt, and vanilla. Beat for 1 to 2 minutes until well combined.

To bake immediately and quickly, preheat oven to 350°F. Roll small balls (about 1 inch) in your floured hands and place them 1 inch apart on a cookie sheet. Press each ball flat with the tines of a fork. Make another shape by poking a small cavity in each ball. Fill the cavity with a dot of jam. Bake for 10 to 12 minutes or until golden. Transfer from the pans to a cooling rack at once.

Variations

- To achieve a different texture, dip each unbaked shape, first in lightly beaten egg white and then in sugar mixed with cinnamon. Bake, sugar-side up, as suggested.
- Add one egg yolk to the recipe; fill tiny tart forms.
- Add one egg and ¾ cup ground almonds or pecans to the recipe. Form small crescents, then bake. Dust them heavily with confectioners' sugar after baking.
- Instead of vanilla, add 1 tablespoon orange juice, brandy, or a sweet liqueur.

- After baking melt 3 or 4 ounces dark sweet chocolate. Use a fork to drizzle the melted chocolate over the top of the cookies. You can also dip a portion of the top of the cookie into the melted chocolate. Always refrigerate cookies dipped in chocolate until the chocolate hardens. They then can be stored layered in boxes. Refrigerate or freeze for up to one month.
- Prepare sliced almonds and ground nuts. After dipping the cookies in melted chocolate, dip the coated portion on the nuts.
- Sandwich two thin cookies with melted chocolate or jam.

✳ *Suggestion*

Try another baking method. Cut the dough into four pieces. On a floured surface, roll each piece into the shape of a salami, 1½ inches in diameter. Wrap in wax paper; refrigerate or freeze. When ready to bake, cut each piece into ¼-inch slices. Place the slices on cookie sheets and follow the baking directions above.

Pecan Squares
Makes 20 to 24 squares.

8 tablespoons (¼ pound) unsalted butter
½ cup sugar
1 cup flour
2 eggs
1 cup brown sugar
1 cup chopped pecans
3 tablespoons flour
Pinch salt
1 teaspoon vanilla extract

Preheat oven to 375°F. Prepare a 9-inch square pan.

Cream butter with sugar in an electric mixer. Beat in 1 cup flour. Spread mixture over the bottom of the pan. Use a small steel spatula or your fingers to spread evenly. Bake for 20 minutes.

While the crust is baking, use the same bowl to beat the eggs with the brown sugar. Add pecans, 3 tablespoons flour, salt, and vanilla. Spread over the warm baked crust and bake for 20 minutes.

Cool on a rack. Turn out onto a board and cut into 20 to 24 pieces.

Lace Cookies
Makes 4 dozen.

Lace Cookies have become one of the signature pieces at our daughter's restaurant. A few years ago, I suggested that we form them into baskets. Betty serves her ice cream in a Lace Cookie basket, topping the ice cream with fresh berries and whipped cream. Plan on doing the same thing, but practice with the recipe as suggested below.

8 tablespoons (¼ pound) unsalted butter
½ cup light corn syrup
⅔ cup light brown sugar
1 cup unbleached all-purpose flour
1 cup chopped walnuts
4 ounces dark sweet chocolate

Preheat oven to 325°F. Prepare two or three cookie sheets.

Combine butter, syrup, and brown sugar in a saucepan. Bring to a boil. Immediately remove from the heat. Stir flour and nuts into the mixture.

Using two teaspoons, drop batter 3 inches apart onto a cookie sheet. Bake for 8 to 10 minutes. Cool for 1 minute before transferring to a rack.

To Decorate: Melt dark sweet chocolate in a bowl set over warm water. Use a fork or decorating bag to drizzle the melted chocolate over cookies. Refrigerate until the chocolate hardens. These cookies freeze well.

✳ *Suggestions*

Curled Cookie

Folded in 4 for "fortune cookie"

Small or large dessert basket

- Lace Cookies can be curled into shapes. While they are hot, place a cookie over a rolling pin. It will curl around the pin. Slip it off when it hardens. It will retain the shape.
- Place a hot cookie over the back of a tea cup. When it hardens, it will have taken the shape of a small basket.
- To prepare larger baskets, drop 2 tablespoonfuls of the mixture, spread well apart, on a cookie sheet. Bake two on each sheet. Mold each hot cookie over the outside of an overturned round cereal bowl. The recipe will make six to eight 6-inch baskets.
- Use Lace Cookie baskets on a dessert table filled with mints, dried fruits, or assorted nuts.
- When I entertain guests with a Chinese dinner, my husband types short, humorous quotations. I put one on a Lace Cookie while it is still warm and fold it in four, making a fortune cookie.

Cookie Crescents (Rogelach)
Makes 6 dozen.

I always store a box of these crescent-shaped cookies in my freezer. They make wonderful gifts for friends who live far away. Pack them in layers, separated with foil or wax paper for shipping. They always arrive in good shape for thankful recipients.

    2 sticks (½ pound) unsalted butter, at room temperature
    ½ pound cream cheese
    2 cups flour
    ½ cup jam (apricot, raspberry, or currant)
    ½ cup sugar mixed with 1 teaspoon cinnamon
    1 cup each chopped nuts and raisins

Mix butter, cream cheese, and flour into a ball of dough. Use your hand or an electric mixer with a flat paddle. Divide the dough into six pieces. Form small, compact rounds. Wrap in wax paper and refrigerate for a minimum of 6 hours to overnight.

When you are ready to bake the cookies, preheat oven to 375°F.

If the dough is very hard, bang it with a rolling pin to flatten it. Roll each piece into an 8- or 9-inch round. Spread 1 tablespoon jam around the outer edge of the round. Sprinkle the sugar mixture, nuts, and raisins on top. Use a pizza cutter to cut into 12 even wedges. Starting at the outside end, roll each wedge toward the center point. Turn the shape into a crescent by bending both ends inward. Place on cookie sheets ½ inch apart.

Bake for 25 minutes. Immediately transfer cookies to a cooling rack. Dust with confectioners' sugar before serving (optional).

✳ Suggestion
This is such a simple dough to make! Use it as a basic for a savory or hors d'oeuvre. Fill small rounds with seafood, pâté, or sharp cheese.

Faith's Cranberry Cookies
Makes 3 dozen.

Faith Drobbin grew up with my daughter Betty, and they are close friends to this day. Faith and her husband Lance Tarhan own a successful bakeshop in Brooklyn, New York. They tell me that these cranberry cookies are among their best-sellers, and you will soon discover why.

    3 cups unbleached all-purpose flour
    1 teaspoon baking powder

¼ teaspoon baking soda
¼ teaspoon salt
1 teaspoon cinnamon
¼ pound unsalted butter
1 cup sugar
¾ cup light brown sugar
1 egg
¼ cup milk
2 tablespoons orange juice
12 ounces cranberries
1 cup chopped walnuts

Preheat oven to 350°F. Sift together flour, baking powder, baking soda, salt, and cinnamon.

Cream butter, then add sugar and brown sugar. Use an electric mixer. Add egg and milk. Beat in flour mixture and orange juice. Fold cranberries and walnuts in by hand, using a rubber spatula.

Drop dough, by spoonfuls, onto a cookie sheet, 2 inches apart. Bake for 35 to 40 minutes.

Meringue Cookies
Makes 6 dozen.

The recipe for Meringue Cookies can be used in many different ways. Bake it as a topping for berry, fruit, and lemon pies. Drop it from spoons for small, plain cookies or make fancy ones with a decorating bag.

½ cup egg whites (3 to 4 eggs)
⅛ teaspoon salt
⅛ teaspoon cream of tartar
1 cup sugar
1 teaspoon vanilla extract

Preheat oven to 250°F. Bring egg whites to room temperature in the bowl of an electric mixer.

Place a dot of oil or butter in the corners of two cookie sheets to keep parchment paper from moving. Line the bottom of the cookie sheets with parchment paper.

Add salt and cream of tartar to the egg whites. Beat until the whites become frothy and turn white in color. Add sugar, 1 tablespoon at a time, then add vanilla. Continue beating for 3 to 4 minutes. The mixture will look like marshmallow.

Use two teaspoons to drop meringue in small mounds, 1 inch apart, or use a decorating bag with a large star tube. Pipe out rosettes or 2-inch, finger-sized cookies.

Bake for 1 hour. Turn off oven. Allow cookies to cool in the oven, after which they can easily be removed from the paper. Cookies may be stored in a tin for up to one month in a cupboard, or they may be frozen for up to three months.

✳ *Suggestions*

- Serve with frozen desserts or fresh fruits or layer them with mousse.
- For Chocolate-Nut Meringue Cookies, fold in 2 tablespoons cocoa mixed with 1 tablespoon cornstarch and ½ cup ground filberts or almonds after beating in sugar.

Lady Fingers
Makes 3 to 4 dozen.

Lady Fingers seem to be a thing of the past. Actually, they are individual sponge cookies, the perfect complement for fruit and cream desserts. Since they are truly difficult to find in a shop, why not bake them at home?

> 5 eggs, at room temperature
> ⅔ cup sugar, plus 2 tablespoons sugar
> ¾ cup unbleached all-purpose flour
> ¼ cup cake flour
> Confectioners' sugar (about ¼ cup)

Separate eggs into two bowls of an electric mixer. Preheat oven to 350°F. Prepare a decorating bag with a ½-inch plain tube.

Measure parchment paper to fit two or three cookie sheets. Draw two sets of parallel lines, 4 inches apart, down the length of the paper. This will determine that the Lady Fingers will be 4 inches long.

Dot the cookie sheets with oil or butter to keep the paper flat. Place the paper on the cookie sheet, drawn-side down.

Beat the egg yolks for 1 minute, then add ⅔ cup sugar, 1 tablespoon at a time, until the mixture is light lemon in color and very thick. Use a rubber spatula to mix the flours into the egg yolks by hand.

Beat egg whites until foamy and white. Add the remaining 2 tablespoons sugar, and beat until the whites form stiff peaks and adhere to the sides of the bowl.

Transfer the egg yolk-sugar mixture into the stiffly beaten whites. Fold together gently but quickly. Immediately fill the decorating bag with the mixture. Pipe 1-inch shapes between the parallel lines, leaving ¼ inch between each. The Lady Fingers will spread and come together. Shake confectioners' sugar copiously over all and set them aside for 10 minutes before baking.

Sprinkle more confectioners' sugar on top. Bake for 15 minutes until just golden. Remove them from the paper when just out of the oven. Sandwich in pairs and store in an airtight container for up to two weeks. They may be frozen for up to one month.

After baking, cut apart two at a time and fold in a sandwich for storage.

Mandelbrot
Makes 30 to 35 slices.

Recently there have been numerous recipes published for Biscotti, a ½-inch Italian biscuit. Mandelbrot is the same kind of biscuit. We have been baking Mandelbrot in our home for as long as I can remember. Both Biscotti and Mandelbrot are plain, crunchy, and satisfying, especially when dipped in wine, tea, or hot chocolate.

The following recipe is unique. It is made with matzo meal, which I usually purchase in the spring when the supply is fresh. Selma Bassuck, who contributed this recipe, suggested that I bake this in aluminum freezer trays. Look for these trays at flea markets. They make excellent baking pans for Mandelbrot and Biscotti.

> 3 eggs
> 1 cup sugar
> 1 cup oil
> 1 cup chopped walnuts or almonds
> 1 cup matzo cake meal
> ½ teaspoon cinnamon
> Pinch salt
> ¼ cup raisins, chocolate bits, or candied fruit (optional)
> ½ cup sugar mixed with 1 teaspoon cinnamon

Prepare two aluminum freezer (ice cube) trays. Dot the bottoms with oil or butter and line with wax paper. Extend the wax paper over the two short ends. Preheat oven to 350°F.

Beat eggs with sugar. Add oil, nuts, cake meal, cinnamon, and salt. Add any one or two of the optional ingredients.

Transfer the mixture into the trays. If you do not have the trays, let the mixture rest 20 minutes to thicken, then bake in two long mounds (about 8 inches) on a greased cookie sheet. Use a little more matzo meal if the mixture is too soft to shape. Bake for 40 minutes.

Remove from oven and cool. Cut each loaf into ½-inch slices. Place on cookie sheets. Sprinkle tops with additional sugar and cinnamon. Place back in oven for 10 or 15 minutes until dry and toasted.

Biscotti
Makes 35 to 40.

2½ cups unbleached all-purpose flour
¾ cup sugar
½ teaspoon baking powder
½ teaspoon baking soda
¼ teaspoon salt
3 eggs, slightly beaten
¼ cup corn oil
½ cup freshly ground unblanched almonds
½ cup whole unblanched almonds
1 teaspoon vanilla extract
1 egg white, slightly beaten

Preheat oven to 350°F. Grease one cookie sheet.

Mix flour, sugar, baking powder, baking soda, and salt in a bowl. Add eggs and oil. Beat well by hand or in an electric mixer. Add both ground and whole almonds, then vanilla. The dough will come away from the sides of the bowl.

Transfer to a floured surface. Divide into two logs about 9 inches long. Place them on the greased cookie sheet. Pat down each log to flatten it just a bit.

Bake for 25 to 30 minutes. Cool for 5 minutes. Slice diagonally into ½-inch pieces. Place on cookie sheets. Brush the tops with egg white and bake until dry and toasted—about 15 minutes.

✹ *Suggestion*
If you have the aluminum freezer trays, bake the Biscotti as directed for Mandelbrot.

12

Desserts, Plain and Fancy

These are my selected desserts from the simplest of puddings to elegant hot soufflés. There is a time and place for each one.

Recipes for Family Desserts

Aunt Beatrice's Chocolate Pudding
Serves 6.

I often wonder why people do not make chocolate pudding anymore! As children, that was our special dessert, cooked from a box of My-T-Fine. Years later, my aunt

321

(through marriage) showed me how to cook chocolate pudding from scratch. She made it almost every other day. Quite different from mousse, it is a real taste treat, and there are no eggs in it.

4 tablespoons unsweetened cocoa
6 tablespoons sugar
3 tablespoons cornstarch
2 cups milk

Mix cocoa, sugar, and cornstarch in a heavy saucepan. Gradually stir in milk with a wooden spoon. Cook over low heat, stirring constantly until the pudding thickens. Use a whisk to prevent lumps. Cool in individual bowls or in one large bowl, covered with wax paper to prevent skinning. Of course, a spoonful of whipped cream adds perfection!

Danish Red Fruit Pudding with Cream
Serves 6 to 8.

This is the fruit counterpart to Aunt Beatrice's Chocolate Pudding. The Scandinavians are partial to this one, and for good reason!

1 quart fresh raspberries or strawberries, or a combination (or substitute two 10-ounce packages of frozen berries)
¼ cup sugar
2 tablespoons arrowroot flour or cornstarch
¼ cup cold water
1 tablespoon fresh lemon juice
Sliced toasted almonds
½ cup cream or whipped cream

Hull the berries if they are fresh. Defrost them if they are frozen. Purée the berries in a food processor.

Heat the purée (approximately 2 cups or more) with sugar. Do not use sugar if the frozen berries have been sweetened. Bring to a simmer.

Mix arrowroot or cornstarch with water and lemon juice to make a smooth mixture. Add it to the purée. Allow the mixture to come to a simmer again, then remove from the heat immediately.

Pour into individual stemmed dessert glasses and chill. Serve with sliced almonds and a dollop of whipped cream.

Berry Bavarian Fancy
Serves 6.

There are times when a light dessert other than fresh fruit salad is needed for a pretty finish. Serve this recipe in your best crystal or imported china. It will look good and go down smoothly.

1 quart fresh raspberries or strawberries, or a combination
¾ cup sugar
1 tablespoon fresh lemon juice
2 or 3 thin strips orange rind
1 package unflavored gelatin (1 tablespoon)
¼ cup cold water
3 egg whites

Prepare a 6-cup china or glass bowl, or six wine glasses. Reserve 12 berries for a garnish. Set aside.

In a food processor, pulse berries with ½ cup sugar, lemon juice, and orange rind. Run machine until the mixture is thoroughly blended, pulsing on and off for 30 seconds. Reserve ½ cup of the mixture to be used later as a sauce.

Mix gelatin with water in a Pyrex cup. Place the cup in a pot of simmering water over low heat. When the gelatin is a clear liquid remove it to the side.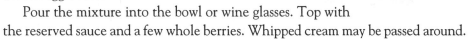

Beat egg whites until frothy and white. Add remaining ¼ cup sugar gradually. Beat until stiff. Blend warm gelatin liquid into the berry purée, then fold gently into the stiffly beaten egg whites.

Pour the mixture into the bowl or wine glasses. Top with the reserved sauce and a few whole berries. Whipped cream may be passed around.

Essie's Plum Cobbler
Serves 8.

Essie Davis was my student and a longtime friend. She shared this recipe with us in the 1950s. I guess there must be hundreds of people baking Essie's Plum Cobbler every September, when these delicious plums are available.

5 cups Italian plums
¼ cup light brown sugar
1 cup unbleached all-purpose flour

1 cup sugar
½ teaspoon cinnamon
1 egg lightly beaten
8 tablespoons (¼ pound) unsalted butter, melted

Cut each plum in half; discard pits. Preheat oven to 375°F. Sprinkle brown sugar on the bottom of a 9-inch round baking dish or a 6" x 10" rectangular dish. Place the plums, cut-side up, on the brown sugar.

Mix flour, sugar, and cinnamon. Add beaten egg to make a thick mixture. Spread it over the plums. Pour melted butter over all. Bake for 40 minutes.

Cut into wedges or squares. Serve warm or at room temperature.

✸ Suggestion

Bake several cobblers in aluminum foil pans when plums are in season. Bake for 25 minutes; cool and cover securely with aluminum foil. Freeze for up to two months. Defrost with covering in a 400°F oven for 1 hour. Uncover and bake for 10 minutes more.

Crustless Peach Tart
Serves 6 to 8.

Bake this recipe only when peaches are in season locally. There is no substitute for that fresh texture and flavor.

Tart

1 tablespoon each flour and light brown sugar
4 medium-sized peaches
2 tablespoons fresh lemon juice
1 cup sour cream (regular or light)
2 eggs
⅓ cup sugar
½ teaspoon vanilla extract

Topping

¼ cup each plain bread crumbs and light brown sugar
1 tablespoon butter

Preheat oven to 375°F. Prepare an 8-inch round ceramic or Pyrex pie pan. Sprinkle flour and sugar over the bottom.

Skin the peaches by immersing them in boiling water and then in cold water. The skin should peel off easily. Discard pits and slice each peach vertically into six slices. Place the slices in one layer in the pan and sprinkle them with lemon juice.

Beat sour cream with eggs, sugar, and vanilla. Pour over the peach slices.

Crumble bread crumbs, brown sugar, and butter into small clumps. Distribute over the top. Bake for 40 minutes.

Melon with Honey and Sesame Seeds
Serves 6.

I am partial to honey as a sweetener for melons, especially when the melons are not perfectly ripe.

> 1 large cantaloupe
> ½ cup honey
> 2 tablespoons fresh lemon juice
> 1 pint fresh berries (raspberries, blueberries, or strawberries)
> ¼ cup toasted sesame seeds

Slice off ⅛ inch from both ends of the melon. Turn melon on a flat side. Skin the melon completely. Cut the melon into 1-inch slices to form rings. Discard all the seeds. Place the melon rings in a shallow glass or ceramic dish. Dribble honey and lemon juice on the melon. Set aside to marinate for several hours at room temperature.

Place one ring of melon on an 8-inch dessert plate. Fill the cavity with berries. Sprinkle sesame seeds over all. Repeat with other rings as needed for servings.

✸ *Suggestions*

- Substitute sliced oranges and grapefruit when fresh berries are not available.
- Two Lady Fingers (page 318) or cookies could be placed on either side of the melon.
- Pass whipped cream or ice cream for topping.

Unbaked Swedish Applesauce Cake
Serves 6.

Imagine, an unbaked cake! There is a catch. It will only be as good as the applesauce, which I hope you will make yourself. Quick and easy, it's a great dessert for sudden company, if you have the applesauce on hand.

> 1½ cups plain bread crumbs
> 1 tablespoon sugar

1 teaspoon cinnamon
3 cups applesauce
½ cup each fresh raspberries and raspberry jam

Use individual wine glasses. Combine bread crumbs, sugar, and cinnamon. Place 1 or 2 tablespoons of the mixture into each wine glass, then layer applesauce, berries, jam, and bread-crumb mixture in that order.

Serve at room temperature, preferably with a whipped cream topping.

Recipes for Party Desserts

Poached Pears
Serves 8.

We have only one Bosc pear tree and one Seckel tree, and yet there are some seasons when they bear more fruit than we can handle. Peeling takes much of the time. Our good friend Sylvia Samuels travels from New York City each year to help us with that tedious job. In Italy, they served us poached, unpeeled pears at a breakfast buffet table. Take your choice.

8 Bosc pears (very firm)
Juice of 1 lemon
Pinch salt
2 cups water
2 cups dry wine (white or red)
1½ cups sugar
1 cinnamon stick

Use pears with stems intact. Peel them if you wish without removing the stems. As you peel each one, place it in cold water, mixed with the juice of one lemon and a pinch of salt, to cover.

Combine 2 cups water, wine, sugar, and cinnamon stick in a saucepan large enough to hold the pears. You have a choice of red or white wine, depending on how you will be using the pears.

Bring the liquid to a boil, stirring at the beginning to melt the sugar. Immerse the pears. Cover the saucepan and cook for 20 to 25 minutes or until the pears are just soft in the center when pierced with a fork. Do not overcook. Transfer the pears to a bowl. Reduce the liquid in the saucepan by boiling for 5 to 7 minutes to thicken the syrup.

For a red-wine glaze, boil the syrup for 10 or 15 minutes or until the liquid reduces by half. It will become dark and shiny. Pears in red wine should be served on 8-inch dessert plates with a garnish of whipped cream decoratively piped around the edge.

Pears cooked in white wine can be drained of their syrup. Serve each pear on a warm chocolate sauce.

In either case, cook pears ahead. Refrigerate in their syrup for up to 1 week. Freeze for up to 2 months.

Charlotte aux Poires (Pears in a Mold of Custard)
Serves 12 to 14.

In 1983 my daughter Betty and I attended two weeks of classes at Le Notre, the renowned cooking school near Paris. The following was one of the recipes taught. We continue to make this fancy pear dessert to this day. Delightful in appearance and in taste, it makes a memorable dessert for a large party and for small ones, too, since it freezes well for up to two weeks.

18 to 24 Lady Fingers (page 318)
2 packages unflavored gelatin
¼ cup each pear syrup and water
6 egg yolks
⅔ cup sugar
2 cups hot milk
1 teaspoon vanilla extract
12 halves Poached Pears (page 326) or good-quality canned pears
1 cup medium (whipping) cream, whipped to soft peak
¼ cup Apricot Glaze (page 338)

Springform pan

Prepare a 9- or 10-inch springform pan. Dot the bottom with butter and grease the inside rim. Place the Lady Fingers around the rim, flat-side facing in, to form a border. Dissolve gelatin in pear syrup and water. Set aside.

Beat egg yolks with sugar in an electric mixer until light in color and thick. Pour hot milk into the mixture, a little at a time, and beat at low speed.

Transfer to a saucepan and cook until the mixture coats a spoon. Add dissolved gelatin and vanilla; keep stirring for 1 minute. Transfer to a bowl and fold in four halves of pears, cut into chunks. Set bowl in ice water so it cools. When the mixture is on the verge of jelling, fold in the whipped cream. Pour this mixture into the prepared springform pan and refrigerate for at least 2 hours, until firm.

Cut remaining halves of pears into lengthwise slices. Keep the pear shape intact. Place pear slices on the jellied cream to cover the top. Brush with Apricot Glaze. Refrigerate until ready to serve. It freezes well for up to two weeks.

Floating Island with Peaches
Serves 8 to 12.

When I think of making a "fancy" dessert, I always think of meringue. Above all, I enjoy the delicate sweet taste of this confection and, furthermore, I can change the fruit and presentations as I wish. Most of us know the Floating Island as small, egg-sized meringues, but Claire Wagner, who taught French cooking with me, bakes it in a mold shape. Then she floats it in a custard with fruits. What an exquisite look and deliciously sweet taste! I generally omit the custard for calorie counters and surround it with fresh fruit and the fruit sauce.

Floating Island

½ cup sugar
¼ cup water
6 egg whites
Pinch salt
12 ounces peach preserves (or apricot or seedless raspberry preserves)

Crème Anglaise (Custard)

1¼ cups milk or medium (whipping) cream
1 vanilla bean
3 egg yolks
⅓ cup sugar
1 teaspoon vanilla extract
2 tablespoons kirsch, cognac, rum, or orange liqueur

Peach Sauce

2 cups skinned sliced peaches
½ cup sugar
2 tablespoons fresh lemon juice
2 tablespoons Grand Marnier

Set out a 2-quart charlotte mold or soufflé dish. Preheat oven to 325°F. Add hot water to a pan large enough to hold the mold or dish.

Melt ½ cup sugar in a metal skillet. When the sugar starts turning caramel color, add ¼ cup water. Boil for 2 minutes until syrupy. Pour caramel into mold. Coat the insides and bottom by rotating the mold. Set aside to cool.

Beat the egg whites with a pinch of salt in a bowl until stiff but not dry. Blend in peach preserves by hand.

Fill the charlotte mold; smooth the top. Place a strip of aluminum foil around the mold extending 2 inches above to protect the meringue from scorching. Put mold into the pan with simmering water. The water should reach half the height of the mold. Bake for 40 minutes. Insert cake tester, which should come out clean when the dessert is finished. Cool on a rack and then refrigerate until cold or overnight.

To make the Crème Anglaise, heat the milk or cream with vanilla bean in a saucepan until hot, not boiling.

In the meantime, beat egg yolks and ⅓ cup sugar together in an electric mixer until creamy.

Add a small amount of hot milk to the egg mixture and beat in well. Beat in another small amount of milk. Add all to the saucepan with the remaining milk. Stir over moderate heat until the custard coats the spoon, about 3 to 5 minutes. Discard the vanilla bean. Do not let the custard simmer. Remove from heat and blend in vanilla and desired liqueur. Cool over ice water or in the refrigerator. Cover with buttered wax paper to prevent skinning, or whisk occasionally.

Blend all Peach Sauce ingredients in a saucepan. Cook over moderately high heat for sugar to melt. Add more liqueur if desired.

Unmold the Floating Island onto a shallow serving dish. Pour the Crème Anglaise around the dessert. Pour the remaining custard in a sauce dish to be served at the table. Top each serving with custard and Peach Sauce.

Baked Caramel Custard
Serves 8 to 12.

Baked Custard is one of the most delicate of desserts, sweet but light. These have always been baked in individual ramekins for family use. Here again, I use the caramelized mold as I did for Floating Island (previous recipe). The finish is a beautiful dessert for a party dinner.

½ cup sugar
¼ cup water
1 quart milk (half-and-half is better)
⅔ cup sugar
One 1-inch vanilla bean
8 eggs
2 tablespoons vanilla extract

Preheat oven to 325°F. Set out a 2-quart charlotte mold or soufflé dish.

Fill a baking pan half full with hot water. It should be large enough to hold the mold. Place the pan in the oven.

Melt ½ cup sugar in an 8-inch skillet. When it starts turning brown, add water. It will sizzle. Boil for 3 to 4 minutes until syrupy, then pour into the charlotte mold. Coat the insides and bottom by rotating the dish. Do not touch the sugar!

Heat milk, ⅔ cup sugar, and vanilla bean in a saucepan over very low heat. In the meantime, use a whisk to beat eggs in a large bowl. Gradually add hot milk mixture and vanilla, a little at a time. Discard vanilla bean.

Pour the mixture into the caramel-lined mold. Place in the pan of hot water in the oven and bake for 50 to 60 minutes. Insert a cake tester. It should come out clean. Chill the mold.

Unmold on a round platter at least 2 inches larger than the mold to catch the caramel syrup. Slice in wedges to serve.

Crème Brûlée
Serves 8.

Crème Brûlée is very similar to the Baked Caramel Custard (page 329).

    1 quart heavy cream
    ⅔ cup sugar
    One 1-inch vanilla bean
    8 eggs
    2 tablespoons vanilla extract
    1 cup brown sugar

Preheat oven to 300°F. Use eight ¾-cup ramekins.

Place the ramekins in a baking pan large enough to allow space in between each ramekin. Fill the baking pan with enough hot water to reach halfway up the sides of the ramekins.

Heat cream, sugar, and vanilla bean in a saucepan over very low heat. In the meantime, use a whisk to beat eggs in a large bowl. Gradually add hot cream mixture and vanilla, a little at a time. Discard vanilla bean.

Pour into the ramekins. Place the filled ramekins in the pan of hot water. The water in the pan should just simmer, *never boil*. Cover the pan loosely with aluminum foil and bake for 1¼ hours. Refrigerate the ramekins for a minimum of 6 hours or for up to 3 days.

Before serving, preheat broiler. Spread a thin layer of brown sugar (about 2 tablespoons) on top of each custard. Broil until sugar caramelizes. Stay close by. It burns rapidly!

Frozen Nut Tart
Serves 10 to 12.

½ cup egg whites (3 to 4 eggs), at room temperature
⅛ teaspoon salt
⅛ teaspoon cream of tartar
1 cup sugar
1 tablespoon unsweetened cocoa
1 tablespoon cornstarch
½ cup ground filberts (or almonds)
1 teaspoon vanilla extract
½ gallon ice cream or frozen yogurt

You will need two cookie sheets to bake the meringue layers and a 9-inch springform pan for this recipe. Cut two lengths of parchment paper to cover each cookie sheet. Trace a circle 8 inches in diameter in the middle of each parchment paper. The meringue usually spreads on baking. Dot the bottom of the cookie sheets with oil or butter and cover each with the paper. Preheat oven to 325°F.

Beat egg whites with salt and cream of tartar in an electric mixer. When the whites become frothy and opaque white in color, add sugar, 1 tablespoon at a time.

Mix cocoa, cornstarch, and ground nuts together. Fold into the egg white meringue by hand along with vanilla. Spread the meringue to cover the traced circles, or use a decorating bag with a ½-inch plain tube. If using a decorating bag, start at the center and pipe a snail-like shape to the edge of each circle.

Bake for 25 to 30 minutes. Cool on a rack, then remove from the paper.

Prepare enough ice cream or frozen yogurt to fill the springform pan almost to the top. Soften the ice cream before the next step.

Place one meringue disk in the bottom of the springform pan. Spoon ice cream on top to cover completely to the edge and up at least 2 inches. Cover with the second meringue disk. Wrap well and freeze.

When ready to serve, cut the tart into wedges. Pass whipped cream around.

✳ Suggestions

- Before serving, decorate the top and sides with Rich Chocolate Coating (page 311) and whipped cream for a celebration cake.

- If you have leftover batter, spoon small amounts onto cookie sheets for meringue cookies.

Frozen Pineapple Torte
Serves 6 to 8.

In Italy they would call this a Semifreddo. Home-frozen combinations have become very popular there. I like this one because a can of crushed pineapple is usually sitting on my shelf ready for use. Make this torte in a loaf pan or an 8-inch pie dish.

1 cup cookie crumbs
3 egg yolks
½ cup sugar
Pinch salt
One 9-ounce can crushed pineapple, drained; reserve juice and set aside
2 tablespoons fresh lemon juice
3 egg whites
2 tablespoons sugar
1 cup heavy cream, whipped

Oil the bottom of a 1-quart loaf pan. Press the cookie crumbs into the bottom and sides.

Mix egg yolks, ½ cup sugar, and salt in a saucepan. Add pineapple juice and lemon juice. Cook over low heat, stirring constantly until the mixture coats the spoon. Transfer to a bowl and add crushed pineapple. Set aside to cool.

Beat egg whites until frothy. Gradually add 2 tablespoons sugar and beat well until stiff. Fold stiffly beaten egg whites into the cooled pineapple custard, then fold in whipped cream. Spoon mixture into the prepared loaf pan or pie dish.

Freeze, well covered, for at least 6 hours or for up to 1 week. Before serving, unmold the torte from the loaf pan. Cut into slices.

✳ *Suggestion*
Bake two disks of meringue without cocoa. Layer them with pineapple mixture and freeze.

Lillian's Cheesecake
Serves 8 to 10.

Lillian Zilliacus baked this cheesecake for the restaurant menu when she and her husband, Peter, owned the Hermitage near Mount Snow in Vermont. Although Peter is a very fine chef, Lillian's mentor for this recipe was Fenno Jacobs, a well-known restaurateur at that time. This cheesecake differs from so many other cheesecakes in that egg yolks are omitted; only whites are used. It is very light and creamy.

2 tablespoons unsalted butter
1 cup zwieback crumbs or plain cookie crumbs
5 egg whites
1 cup sugar
Three 8-ounce packages cream cheese, softened
1 tablespoon vanilla extract
1 pint sour cream
2 tablespoons sugar
1½ teaspoons vanilla extract
¼ cup sliced almonds

Preheat oven to 350°F. Butter a 9-inch springform pan with 2 tablespoons butter. Pat crumbs onto the bottom and sides.

Beat egg whites until frothy in an electric mixer. Gradually add 1 cup sugar until the egg whites are stiff. Blend softened cream cheese, egg whites and vanilla together by hand. Pour into prepared springform pan.

Bake for 25 minutes, then set oven to 450°F.

Mix sour cream, 2 tablespoons sugar, and 1½ teaspoons vanilla. Spread over the hot cake. Sprinkle with sliced almonds. Bake for 5 minutes at the higher temperature. Refrigerate for at least 3 hours. Serve at room temperature.

✳ Suggestions

- Flavor the cream cheese with 1 teaspoon grated orange rind and 1 tablespoon fresh lemon juice.
- Add 2 ounces melted dark sweet chocolate to the sour cream.
- When the cake is cooled, dribble 1 ounce dark sweet chocolate on top of the cake in abstract designs.

Recipes for Soufflés

Soufflés are specially announced in restaurants with advanced ordering. I have always admired this very highly touted dessert. Dessert soufflés are sensational for dinner company and wonderful, delicious fun for the family. They are best prepared for six to eight portions. Of course, it did not take long, when I dissected the technique, to discover that above all, the soufflé is a mountain of egg white combined with flavor.

✳ *Suggestions*

- Think smart: You can concoct your own recipe, using the following as a guide.
  1. Begin with 1 cup of a favorite custard (vanilla or chocolate), or even Aunt Beatrice's Chocolate Pudding (page 321). Add 3 or 4 egg yolks, 6 egg whites, and your flavoring. Follow directions for Soufflé.
  2. Use 1 pint fresh crushed berries mixed with 2 or 3 tablespoons sugar. Omit egg yolks, but use 4 to 5 egg whites.
- Sometimes the center of a large soufflé will be runny when you cut into it. Do not be embarrassed. Spoon some of the runny mixture over each portion as a sauce.
- To achieve a moist soufflé, bake it in a pan of simmering water. As a matter of fact, start it cooking by placing the pan of simmering water, with the filled soufflé dish, on a burner. The soufflé will heat and start to rise. I particularly like this method for individual soufflés. It cuts down the baking time by a few minutes.
- Bake individual soufflés at 400°F for 10 to 12 minutes. It helps to have a glass door on the oven so you can look into the oven without opening the door.
- Individual soufflés can be unmolded onto dessert plates. Do this in front of your guests if you like to perform. Have warm dessert plates ready at the table. As soon as the soufflés are finished, transfer them to a tray and bring them to the table. Use a napkin to hold the hot dish. Loosen the sides of the soufflé with a small knife and turn it over on a dessert plate. Spoon fruit sauce over the soufflé or place a dollop of whipped cream on top.

Chocolate Soufflé

Serves 6 to 8.

Prepare ingredients in advance!

Most of this soufflé can be prepared in advance. If all ingredients are neatly set out, last-minute egg white beating accounts for 3 minutes. Your guests will not miss you for that short time. They will be anticipating something special, and they will love it.

2 tablespoons butter for greasing dish
2 tablespoons sugar for dish
3 tablespoons sugar
3 tablespoons unbleached all-purpose flour
⅛ teaspoon salt
1 cup milk
4 egg yolks
4 ounces dark sweet chocolate melted with 1 ounce
    unsweetened baking chocolate
1 teaspoon vanilla extract
6 egg whites

Butter a 6-cup soufflé dish or deep casserole. Sprinkle enough sugar to adhere to the sides and bottom. Refrigerate dish until ready to bake.

Combine the 3 tablespoons sugar, flour, and salt in a saucepan. Gradually add milk to make a smooth mixture. Cook over low heat, stirring constantly. When the sauce thickens, remove from the heat and whisk in the egg yolks. Then add the melted chocolate and vanilla. This process can be completed early in the day. Cover with wax paper and set aside at room temperature. Egg whites should be set aside in a mixing bowl at room temperature as well.

Forty minutes before serving time (perhaps when you are just finishing your main course or having salad), preheat the oven to 375°F. Warm the chocolate custard over very low heat for 2 minutes (it works best when it is slightly warm).

Beat egg whites until stiff and clinging to the sides of the bowl (do not overbeat). Fold half the whites into the warm custard. Return this mixture to the remainder of the whites. Fold in thoroughly but quickly. Pour mixture into the cold soufflé dish. Run your index finger around the circumference of the dish to form a well around the edge of the soufflé.

Bake for 25 minutes to achieve a moist soufflé, 35 minutes for a dry one. Bring to the table immediately. Cut into the soufflé at the center with a serving spoon and fork, held back to back. Serve with whipped cream or the following Rum Sauce.

Rum Sauce
Makes 1½ cups.

2 egg yolks
½ cup confectioners' sugar
1 teaspoon vanilla extract
2 tablespoons rum (or cognac)
½ cup cream, whipped

Beat egg yolks until light in color. Add confectioners' sugar gradually. Blend in flavorings and whipped cream.

✳ Suggestion
Omit the custard and use 6 ounces melted dark sweet chocolate, 4 egg yolks, and 7 egg whites for basic ingredients.

Soufflé Meringué au Grand Marnier
Serves 4.

Aside from vanilla, Grand Marnier is the supreme flavoring for desserts. These days I use it one tablespoon at a time, mostly for fruit desserts, soufflés, cakes, and cookies. Although the inn at Amboise in France is no longer in operation, my husband and I remember their very special soufflé. What a perfect example of a soufflé composed mostly of egg whites, with no base of custard.

1 tablespoon each butter and sugar for platter
2 egg yolks
1 teaspoon grated orange rind
1 teaspoon flour
7 egg whites
Pinch salt
4 tablespoons sugar
1 teaspoon Grand Marnier
8 thin slices pineapple
1 cup fresh strawberries marinated in ¼ cup Grand Marnier

Preheat oven to 450°F. Prepare a shallow, oval, ovenproof platter. Butter it and sprinkle it with 1 tablespoon sugar.

Beat egg yolks until light in color. Add orange rind and flour. Set aside.

Beat egg whites with salt until frothy. Gradually add sugar until whites are stiff. Pour egg yolks into beaten egg whites and fold in gently with Grand Marnier.

Heap mixture onto the platter in a large mound. Bake for 7 minutes.

Remove from the oven. Surround soufflé with fruits and serve at once.

✳ *Suggestion*

For a dramatic effect, set ¼ cup cognac aflame and pour it over fruit.

Recipes for Dessert Sauces

Dessert Sauces add the finish, the perfect framework to beautiful desserts. They are so easy to prepare! Since they are usually sweet they refrigerate well up to 2 weeks. Dress a ring of cantaloupe, a thin slice of cake or a scoop of frozen yogurt with a spoon of Berry or Mango Sauce for pure enjoyment.

Fresh Berry Sauce
Makes 2 cups.

> 4 cups fresh strawberries, raspberries, or blackberries
> ⅔ cup sugar
> 1 tablespoon fresh lemon juice
> 2 tablespoons liqueur (Grand Marnier, Crème de Cassis, or other)

Purée berries with sugar and lemon juice in a food processor. Strain berries that have seeds. Add liqueur, if you wish. If you prefer a thinner sauce, add a small amount of water. Heat the sauce if you are serving it warm. It may be refrigerated in a covered jar for up to one week.

Red Berry Glaze
Makes 1 ¼ cups.

There are times when a shiny coating enhances a fruit with color and flavor.

> ½ cup currant jelly
> 1 cup Fresh Berry Sauce (this page)

Add jelly to Fresh Berry Sauce in a saucepan. Simmer for 3 to 5 minutes to reduce. Use as a glaze over fruits and cakes.

Apricot Glaze
Makes 1¼ cups.

1 cup apricot jam
1 tablespoon fresh lemon juice
½ cup water

Mix jam with lemon juice and water in a saucepan. Simmer 3 to 5 minutes to reduce. Strain if chunky.

Mango Sauce
Makes 1 cup.

1 ripe mango, peeled and pitted
1 tablespoon sugar or honey
1 tablespoon fresh lemon juice
2 tablespoons water

Purée the peeled mango with sugar or honey, lemon juice, and water in a food processor.

✳ *Suggestions*

- Spoon mango sauce on top of ice cream, frozen yogurt, Basic Sponge Cake (page 301) or Angel Cake (page 305).
- Garnish the Floating Island (page 328) with Mango Sauce and sliced mango.

All-Purpose Chocolate Sauce
Makes 1½ cups.

6 ounces dark sweet chocolate
1 cup light sour cream or light, sweet cream
2 tablespoons strong brewed coffee (optional)

Combine all ingredients in a saucepan and simmer until chocolate is melted and smooth. Refrigerate in a covered jar for up to two weeks. Serve hot or cold.

Hot Chocolate Sauce for Ice Cream
Serves 10 to 12.

We always enjoy ice cream with this chocolate sauce at The Inn at Saw Mill Farm. Many years ago, Ione Williams shared her special secret with me. The magic of the sauce is that it hardens and coats the ice cream.

    12 ounces dark sweet chocolate, chopped
    2 sticks (½ pound) salted butter
    1 cup walnuts, coarsely chopped

Melt chocolate with butter, stirring constantly, over low heat. Add walnuts. Keep warm, not hot. Place a scoop of ice cream in a long-stemmed wine glass. The ice cream should be very hard. Spoon chocolate sauce on top. It will harden at once.

Menus

As a general rule, I market once or twice a week. I purchase at random the freshest and best in the marketplace. Combinations work into simple menus. If my purchases include fish, then fish it will be that evening. There are times when my planned menus for the week have been changed completely. A sale on lobsters or roasting chickens forces immediate choices, and those are wonderfully easy decisions to make.

I have chosen six daily meals and changed them to dinners for company. These special dinners have their bonus. If you cook extra amounts you will enjoy a festive leftover the next day.

Menu 1

Daily Meal
Sliced Tomato and Cucumber Salad
Baked Halibut
Crisp Potato
Zucchini
Orange Slices with Berries

Dinner for Company
Caesar Salad
Baked Halibut on Leek Purée
Potatoes Anna
Green Beans
Berry Bavarian Fancy

Menu 2

Daily Meal
Chicken Breast Sautéed
Ratatouille
Tossed Green Salad
Biscotti

Dinner for Company
Pan-Fried Oysters
Chicken Breast Sautéed
Ratatouille
Orzo, Wheat Berry, and Bulghur Salad
Poached Pears on Chocolate Sauce
Assorted Cookies

Menu 3

Daily Meal

New England Clam Chowder
Spaghetti with Vegetables
Croutons
Aunt Beatrice's Chocolate Pudding

Dinner for Company

Spaghetti with Vegetables
Braised Fish with Clams and Crusty
    Bread
Green and Red Cabbage Salad
Floating Island with Peaches

Menu 4

Daily Meal

Baked Garlic with French Bread
Broiled Veal Chop with Mustard
Steamed Rice
Brussels Sprouts
Melon with Toasted Sesame Seeds

Dinner for Company

Artichokes with Piquant Dressing
Baked Garlic with French Bread
Broiled Veal Chop with Mustard
Bomba di Riso
Shiitake Mushrooms
Salad of Ruby Greens
Rena Gold's Apple Cake with Sorbet

Menu 5

Daily Meal

Chicken Broth
Stir-Fry Vegetables with Chicken
    or Pork
Rice, Chinese Style
Cookies, Fruit

Dinner for Company

Wonton Soup
Grace Chu's Millionaire Chicken
Country-Style Pork Ribs
Stir-Fry Vegetables
Rice Chinese Style
Sliced Fresh Pineapple
Lace Cookies (Insert a fortune and fold
    while still warm)

Menu 6

Daily Meal

Quinoa and Cucumber Salad
One-Bowl Fish and Vegetables
Frozen Yogurt and Maple Syrup

Dinner for Company

Mozzarella in Carozza
One-Bowl Fish and Vegetables
Quinoa and Cucumber Salad
Crunchy Meringue Pie with Frozen
    Yogurt and Maple Syrup

It would be impossible to print all of the menu celebrations we have enjoyed at our home as well as in other homes and restaurants. My husband and I had one especially outstanding idea! Just a few years ago we were faced with our oncoming 50th anniversary. Before our children could present their ideas, we planned our own. We sent family members (15 close relatives) a questionnaire and asked them to insert their favorite food and drink.

When the answers arrived, I planned a menu, dividing the different requests into courses. We served one course at a time, buffet style, so the dinner had intermission times for music, photographs, and fun.

Index

345